We are Sinking, Send Help!

Also by David D. Bruhn

Ready to Answer All Bells

Wooden Ships and Iron Men: The U.S. Navy's Ocean Minesweepers, 1953–1994

Wooden Ships and Iron Men: The U.S. Navy's Coastal and Motor Minesweepers, 1941–1953

Wooden Ships and Iron Men: The U.S. Navy's Coastal and Inshore Minesweepers, and the Minecraft That Served in Vietnam, 1953–1976

MacArthur and Halsey's "Pacific Island Hoppers"

Battle Stars for the "Cactus Navy": America's Fishing Vessels and Yachts in World War II

We Are Sinking, Send Help!

The U.S. Navy's Tugs and Salvage
Ships in the African, European,
and Mediterranean Theaters
in World War II

Cdr. David D. Bruhn, USN (Retired)

HERITAGE BOOKS
2015

HERITAGE BOOKS
AN IMPRINT OF HERITAGE BOOKS, INC.

Books, CDs, and more—Worldwide

For our listing of thousands of titles see our website
at
www.HeritageBooks.com

Published 2015 by
HERITAGE BOOKS, INC.
Publishing Division
5810 Ruatan Street
Berwyn Heights, Md. 20740

Copyright © 2015 Cdr. David D. Bruhn, USN (Retired)

Heritage Books by the author:

Battle Stars for the "Cactus Navy": America's Fishing Vessels and Yachts in World War II

MacArthur and Halsey's "Pacific Island Hoppers:" The Forgotten Fleet of World War II

We Are Sinking, Send Help!: The U.S. Navy's Tugs and Salvage Ships in the African, European, and Mediterranean Theaters in World War II

Wooden Ships and Iron Men: The U.S. Navy's Ocean Minesweepers, 1953–1994

Wooden Ships and Iron Men: The U.S. Navy's Coastal and Motor Minesweepers, 1941–1953

Wooden Ships and Iron Men: The U.S. Navy's Coastal and Inshore Minesweepers, and the Minecraft that Served in Vietnam, 1953–1976

All rights reserved. No part of this book may be reproduced or transmitted in any form or by any means, electronic or mechanical, including photocopying, recording or by any information storage and retrieval system without written permission from the author, except for the inclusion of brief quotations in a review.

International Standard Book Numbers
Paperbound: 978-1-888265-48-4
Clothbound: 978-0-7884-6120-0

To the United States and Royal Navy officers and men
who served aboard tugs, salvage ships, and minesweepers,
and the divers who performed salvage and mine clearance
in the African, European, and Mediterranean Theaters
in World War II

Contents

Foreword by William I. Milwee Jr.	xiii
Foreword by Rob Hoole	xv
Acknowledgements	xvii
Preface	xix
1. French Morocco – Operation TORCH	1
2. The Navy's Tugs and Salvage Ships	19
3. Wolf Pack Attack on Convoy SC-107	33
4. Salvage and Rescue Tug Services	43
5. Invasion of Sicily – Operation HUSKY	53
6. Salerno – Operation AVALANCHE	85
7. Disaster at Anzio – Operation SHINGLE	115
8. Normandy – Operation OVERLORD	149
9. "Human Torpedoes" and Explosive Boats	181
10. Opening the port of Cherbourg	191
11. Southern France – Operation DRAGOON	211
12. Fairbanks and Bulkeley in Combat	227
13. Opening the Southern French Ports	237
14. War Ends in Europe	251
15. Post-War Occupation Duty	259
Postscript	267
Appendices	
A. Fleet Tugs	273
B. Rescue Tugs and Auxiliary Tugs	279
C. Old Fleet Tugs and Yard Tugs	287
D. Anzio Naval Order of Battle	291
E. U.S. Tugs at Normandy	295
F. Terms of Surrender for German Forces	299
G. Tug and Salvage Ship Unit Awards	301
Bibliography	305
Notes	307
Index	337
About the Author	359

Photos

1-1: *Cherokee* under way	5
2-1: *ATR-7* under way	23

Contents

2-2: *ATR-97* under way	24
2-3: *Weight* under way	31
3-1: *Uncas* under way with a barge alongside	39
4-1: *Lafayette* on fire alongside Pier 88 in New York	50
4-2: Commodore William A. Sullivan, USN	51
5-1: *Redwing* sinking off Bizerte, Tunisia	60
5-2: *YT-197* under way near Bizerte, Tunisia	62
5-3: *Hopi* under way	68
5-4: *Brant* as fleet tug before conversion to salvage ship	79
6-1: Large infantry landing craft *LCI(L)-349* under way	98
6-2: *Rowan* under way	101
6-3: *Savannah* after she was hit by a glider-bomb	103
7-1: Rear Adm. Frank J. Lowry, USN	116
7-2: *ATR-1* testing her firefighting monitors	124
7-3: *Spartan* sinking off Anzio (Richard DeRosset)	136
8-1: U.S. forces landing on Omaha beach on D-Day	152
8-2: Tug towing a caisson across the English Channel	158
8-3: Mulberry B pierhead in action	159
8-4: Rhino tug towing Rhino ferry off Normandy	166
8-5: *Susan B. Anthony* anchored at Oran, Algeria	171
8-6: Wrecked landing craft on Omaha beach	174
9-1: "Human torpedo" washed up on a beach at Anzio	185
9-2: *Centurion* sunk as block ship to help form breakwater	186
10-1: Aerial view of Cherbourg Harbor	195
10-2: *BYMS-72* (painting by Richard DeRosset)	197
10-3: *Owl* entering Cherbourg Harbor	208
11-1: Soldiers of the 1st Special Service Force	216
11-2: *LCT-31* being carried aboard *LST-383*	221
11-3: *LST-282* after being hit by a glider-bomb	224
12-1: Lt. Comdr. Douglas Elton Fairbanks Jr., USNR	228
12-2: *Aphis* under way	229
12-3: Fairbanks, Johnson, and Bulkeley	233
13-1: *Barricade* at anchor	243
13-2: *Stanley Dollar* pierside	247
14-1: *Eagle* under way	254
14-2: *DD-925* under way	255
14-3: Former German U-boats at New London	257
15-1: Kaiserhafen dock in Bremerhaven	262
15-2: *Europa* in the turning basin at Bremerhaven	264
15-3: Former *ATR-4* beached on l'Isle-aux-Grues	265
Postscript: *Resolute* under way	268

Maps

1-1: North Africa	3
1-2: Port Lyautey	10
3-1: North Atlantic	34
3-2: Iceland	41
5-1: Sicily	54
6-1: Salerno assault beaches	88
7-1: Amphibious landing at Anzio, Italy	117
7-2: Mers-el-Kebir anchorage near Oran, Algeria	126
11-1: French Riviera in southeast France	213
13-1: Golfe du Lion area of southern France	240

Diagrams

8-1: V4-M-A1-class tug	154
10-1: Royal Navy mine clearance divers	205

Salvor's Poem
Capt. Stephen W. Delaplane, USN

The Navy's Junkmen, or so we're called
A hearty lot are we
Tenacity, skill and resourcefulness,
Our allies … They number three.

Who are these hearty Sailors,
These junkmen of the Fleet
Who are these men and women
With flippers on their feet?

Shoot the guns? … No, nay not we
Nor make the missiles roar.
That glory, fame and glamour
Are not our daily score.

What do you do, they often ask,
You junkmen of the Fleet.
How do anchors, wire, and diving suits
Spell the enemy's defeat?

But on a cold and stormy night
While the Captain's vigil he doth keep
Embracing a cup of coffee
Stamping warm his cold feet.

Calamity befalls his ship
As oft happens in the Fleet
And a mighty greyhound of the sea
Runs smack upon a reef.

"Who do we call?", the cry goes out
How can we save our Queen?
And through the dark and spray of night
The Navy's junkmen can be seen.

Their captains know their business
And their crews do much the same
As they rig those wires and anchors
To prepare for this deadly game.

The days are long
And the nights are tough…
And people and equipment
Just don't seem enough.

Old Murphy has his way sometimes
And Mother Nature vexes pain
But they snatched the ship off the
deadly rock
To go and fight again.

So worry not ye warriors
Ye Trojans of the Blue
The salty Salvors of the Fleet
Will be there to see you through.

And rest assured ye hearty lads
And brethren of the sea
That when the Fleet is sinking
Or the ships have run aground,
U.S. Navy Salvors
Will be there to heave around.

Foreword

During the generation between the two World Wars, American military capabilities diminished as the policies of isolationism endured. When the U.S. began its support of Britain, the Merchant Navy became a primary asset in the shipment of goods into that struggling country, vulnerable to the U-Boats that saw the freighters as choice targets. The American Navy was limited to escorting the convoys and could not take aggressive action.

The entry of the United States into WWII was a game changer. Now American military leaders had to strengthen and expand a military response that required hugely diverse skills and equipment in all areas of war. The United States Navy, including Reserve Units, found itself not only operating the deep water fleets but also keeping ports open through dredging and salvage of damaged or wrecked ships. Old ships continued to serve, others were refitted for new duties and new tugs were built, some that were particularly well suited for operations in shallow waters.

Ports of the Mediterranean were proving grounds for the rapidly expanding tug and salvage navy. Commodore William A. Sullivan was the significant leader of the expansion and function of the salvage navy that was assembled largely of sailors who had little or no previous experience in this field. The men earned their stripes quickly with the amount of work that existed. By the time the war was over, thousands of men had stories to tell and skills that were important not only to the Navy but transferred to the commercial world of tug operations, salvage and diving. Such experiences and pride were not left behind when servicemen rejoined civilian life, as evidenced by the hundreds of ships that hold reunions and organizations specific to types of service.

When I entered the world of Navy salvage in 1967 with Harbor Clearance Unit One in Vietnam, I quickly developed respect for the men and enthusiasm for salvage work that has remained my primary interest throughout my life, both in the Navy and later in the commercial world. Commander Bruhn's account of the operations in Africa, the Mediterranean and Europe is not only the feature of the WWII era but is also the prologue to my career.

These lively accounts of tug and salvage operations reveal the spirit of the jobs as well as the logistics. Operations Torch, Husky, Avalanche, Shingle, Overlord and Dragoon are brought to life as no official reports can, and these are integrated into the greater context of the Allied war efforts. This comprehensive book provides an understanding of how the Allies succeeded as seen from the specific vantage point of tug and salvage operations. It is also a testimony to the many dedicated sailors who rose to the demands of the jobs and thus contributed to that success. It is important that this history be preserved and made available to upcoming generations. Good stories never get old and good men live on in memories.

Commander William I. Milwee Jr., USN (Ret.)

Foreword

Much has been written about the destroyers, corvettes and other escorts that protected convoys, task groups and invasion forces from attack by aircraft, surface ships and U-boats. However, where would such forces have been without the ships and men that fought flood and fire aboard stricken vessels, patched them up and then towed them, together with their valuable cargoes, to safe havens or, more importantly, saved thousands of naval and merchant marine sailors and civilians from a watery death or from being burnt alive?

Once again, David Bruhn has researched his subject meticulously before producing this highly readable and often vivid description of Second World War marine salvage and rescue operations, mostly in the European and Mediterranean theatres, and the events that made them necessary. Although his book deals chiefly with the actions of American ships, particularly tugs, salvage vessels and rescue ships, it also looks at units from other Allied nations, especially the British, because so many of them were involved in tasks achieving operational success or, in some cases, excruciating failure. In the pervading spirit of the time, British tugs were built in U.S. shipyards and U.S. tugs were built to British designs.

With his characteristic flair and painstaking attention to detail, David has documented and described hugely dramatic events ranging from operations involving hundreds of ships and aircraft to the fight for survival by individual ships and their men against a ferocious enemy and the unyielding forces of nature. In most cases, he has taken particular pains to identify and list the names, units and honours ascribed to such activities.

Shipwrecks are not the only detritus of war. As a former Minewarfare & Clearance Diving Officer in the Royal Navy with command experience of mine countermeasures vessels and diving teams, I was particularly pleased to see the comprehensive manner in which David has treated the clearance of beach obstructions, mines, demolition charges and booby-trapped obstacles off the beaches of Normandy and in the port of Cherbourg. I was also interested to read that the first U.S. Navy School for salvage divers was established as the direct result of inadequacies discovered after the troop transport USS *Lafayette*, the former French transatlantic liner *Normandie*, capsized in the Hudson River in 1942.

David's book is a welcome testimony to the valiant but untold efforts of thousands of service personnel and civilians and the awesome work of so many ships and men from various navies and other organizations in fighting for survival, saving lives and generally clearing up after the carnage of war. I have found nothing else approaching its quality.

Rob Hoole
Vice Chairman & Webmaster
Minewarfare & Clearance Diving Officers' Association
www.mcdoa.org.uk

Acknowledgements

I am grateful to renowned maritime artist Richard DeRosset for producing a dramatic and truly stunning painting for the cover art, titled *Spartan Death Throes off Anzio*. The art work captures the efforts of Allied ships, including the U.S. Navy rescue tug *ATR-1*, to save the British light cruiser HMS *Spartan*. Hit by a glider-bomb launched from a German plane, which passed down through her decks, blasted a hole in her hull and set her aflame, *Spartan* sank off Anzio, Italy.

I am greatly indebted to William I. Milwee Jr., an expert on naval salvage and co-author of the definitive work on the subject, *Mud, Muscle, And Miracles: Marine Salvage in the United States Navy* for penning a foreword for the book. A graduate of the U.S. Naval Academy, Webb Institute of Naval Architecture, and the Navy Deep Sea Diving School, Milwee has considerable knowledge of and hands-on experience in marine salvage. During his lengthy career he took part in salvage operation on all seven continents and numerous Pacific islands.

Rob Hoole, a former Royal Navy mine clearance diving officer and commanding officer of HMS *Berkeley* (M40)—a *Hunt*-class countermeasure vessel—provided me with much information about the role of British minesweepers and 'P' Parties (port clearance divers) in opening ports in Europe during World War II. Hoole is a long-standing member of the Ton Class Association and a regular contributor to its publications. He is also founding Vice Chairman and Webmaster of the Royal Naval Minewarfare & Clearance Diving Officers' Association, and holds key positions in related organizations. An acknowledged expert on mine warfare, Hoole is also a keen naval historian and author.

David Hughes, a professor in New Zealand whose father was a survivor of HMS *Spartan*, provided much information and perspective about the loss of the cruiser. These details enriched the account in the book, and enabled DeRosset to produce a magnificent painting that accurately depicts the tragic event.

In the appendices, the tables devoted to tugs and salvage ships are derived largely from shipbuilders' records compiled by Tim Colton, a naval architect, as well as from official U.S. Navy information.

Many other individuals also contributed to or influenced the book. For the sake of brevity, I have omitted the use, where appropriate, of military rank: Charles A. Bartholomew, Rob Burn, George W. Butenschoen, Tom Butterworth, Robert M. Citino, Arnold Hague, Ferdinand Hoffmann, Steve Johnson, Steve Karoly, Tom Linclau, J. D. Lock, Edward H. Lundquist, Patrick Masell, B. G. Marshall, Chip Marshall, Zane Orr, Henry Redder, Stephen S. Roberts, William H. Stoneman, Alwyn Thomas, Bob Umbdenstock, and Hans van der Ster.

George Duddy, a retired civil engineer with a deep interest in and knowledge of the history of shipping along Canada's British Columbia and western arctic coasts, edited portions of the book. More importantly, he served as a critical reader, making many suggestions regarding the organization of material, and providing details about the contributions of Canada's military to the war in Europe. Canada had only a population of about 11 million at the start of the war, but between 1939 and 1945 more than one million of her men and women served full-time in the armed services, most on a volunteer basis. More than 42,000 were killed during the war.

I am particularly grateful to Lynn Marie Tosello for her work as the final editor of this text. Her discerning eye and thorough work contributed both eloquence and substance to the work.

Preface

Salvage work was adventurous and gratifying. But the work never ended until the job was done. You could be expected to get under way on a moment's notice on jobs such as search and rescue. Duty on a battleship was more of a rigid routine. You lived by the book. You would speak to an officer only when spoken to, or by request. Not so in smaller ships.

—Lt. Comdr. Floyd Mathews, USN, on his duty aboard Navy tugs and salvage ships which he found to be comparatively relaxed and informal, but the work long and hard. Over the course of his 30-year career, which began when he enlisted in the Navy in 1919 at age 16, he served aboard a battleship and seven submarines as well as the old fleet tugs *Bobolink* and *Kalima*, the salvage ship *Deliver*, and finally the fleet tug *Chickasaw*, which he commanded.[1]

Although the book's title suggests it is devoted solely to Navy tugs and salvage ships, there are many interrelated themes. They include the activities of the U.S. Eighth Fleet from 1943-1945, the close association of the American and Royal navies, and the mutual support of tugs, salvage ships, minesweepers, and mine clearance divers. During amphibious assaults on enemy shores, stalwart tugs brought ships and craft damaged beyond the repair capabilities of their embarked "salvors" to salvage ships staged in safer but nearby rear areas.

Once Allied troops were ashore, they required sea-supplied logistics to sustain combat operations in progress and forthcoming. Well aware of this stark fact, retreating enemy forces purposely laid mines, and sank vessels, munitions and sundry debris in harbors to prevent their use by ships carrying beans, bullets, and black oil. Following the capture of a critically needed port, minesweepers swept the approaches and harbor to allow salvage ships and tugs to enter it. Within a port, mine clearance divers normally carried out their dangerous work prior to that of the salvage divers. However, urgent requirements to open a port might necessitate concurrent mine clearance and salvage operations in the same waters.

U.S. TROOPS LAND IN FRENCH MOROCCO

America's involvement in the African, European, and Mediterranean Theaters began on 7 November 1942 when American forces landed at Mehdia, Fedala, and Safi on the Atlantic coast of French Morocco, as joint British/American forces struck at the French Algerian cities of Oran and Algiers on the Mediterranean. The Vichy French government—which had been installed by the Nazis after they conquered France in 1940—was in control of French Morocco, Algeria, and Tunisia. The Allies were hopeful that the Vichy French forces would not fight, but they did with support from the German Luftwaffe (Air Force).

Chapter 1 highlights a special operation involving a group of seventeen officers and men detailed from the fleet tug *Cherokee* and the salvage ship *Brant*. Their mission was to breach a barrier spanning the entrance to the Sebou, which prevented ship passage up the narrow, shallow, and winding river. The waters and shoreline adjacent to the obstacle were protected by the guns of Fort Kasbah on the heights above. The successful execution of this dangerous undertaking, in which eight of the men were wounded by gunfire, enabled the destroyer *Dallas* to carry raiders upriver and capture a French airfield. The field was required so that Army planes staged aboard the carrier *Chenango* could use it to launch an attack on Casablanca. All seventeen members of the demolition team received the Navy Cross—the second highest award for heroism behind the Congressional Medal of Honor—as did four men aboard the *Dallas*, including her commanding officer and a Free French river pilot.

OVERVIEW OF THE TUGS AND SALVAGE SHIPS

Chapter 2 provides information about the design and armament of the U.S. Navy's tugs and salvage ships, and some of those of the Royal Navy. American and British tugs and salvage ships worked closely together in the Mediterranean and European Theaters during the war. The two countries' ship design and construction programs were also linked; the U.S. Navy adopted a British design for a new class of tug, and it transferred tugs built in America to the Royal Navy via the Lend-Lease Program.

Details about formation of the associated U.S. Navy's Rescue Tug Service and Salvage Service are provided in Chapter 4. Captain William A. Sullivan, U.S. Navy—a graduate of the Massachusetts Institute of Technology and the Navy's top salvage officer—oversaw this effort. The most prominent U.S. Navy salvage officer, he was promoted to the rank of commodore, and became known as the "commodore of sunken ships." With the Navy woefully short of tugs, and a majority of its newest ones assigned overseas, it was forced to use World War I vintage tugs as well as a few coal or oil-burning ones of the late 1800s—some from before the Spanish America War—along America's coasts. The Rescue Tug Service was established to ensure the optimum use of these vessels to save ships damaged by German U-boat attacks or, for the hundreds sunk, to rescue seamen from frigid waters before they succumbed to the cold.

Casual readers may choose to initially skip Chapters 2 and 4 and return to them as needed for additional background information about the tugs and salvage ships and their supporting organizations.

RESCUE TUGS NEEDED DUE TO U-BOAT ATTACKS

Navy ships and merchant vessels making Atlantic crossings were at grave risk from U-boats well before they ever reached their destinations. Following Germany's declaration of war against the United States on 11 December 1941, U-boats began a submarine offensive off North America and in the North Atlantic against Allied shipping.

Chapter 3 describes the ordeals of Convoy SC-107, sailing from New Jersey on America's east coast to the United Kingdom, attacked by a German U-boat "Wolf Pack." During a series of terrifying nighttime attacks, seamen from sinking ships found themselves in lifeboats, if they were lucky, or the cold Atlantic. Some crewmen perished aboard ship or slipped beneath the ocean's surface and were lost. *Pessacus* and *Uncas*, two newly built yard tugs bound for Naval Operating Base, Iceland, retrieved 197 survivors; they would be the only two tugs to earn a battle star in the American Theater during the war.

EARLY SUCCESS IN THE ITALIAN CAMPAIGN

The book next turns in Chapter 5 to the invasion of Sicily which launched the Allies' Italian Campaign. Admiral Henry Kent Hewitt commanded the Western Naval Task Force, the American naval component during the invasion of French Morocco. Following this operation, he established U.S. Naval Forces, Northwest African Waters, in March 1943 at Algiers, Algeria. This command received the concurrent designation U.S. Eighth Fleet two months later. Hewitt would command the fleet from inception through March 1945 when, near the war's end, it was dissolved as part of the overall reduction of the American presence in Africa and Europe.

Hewitt was the American naval commander for all operations described herein, except for the Normandy invasion in which he did not participate. He had three titles: commander U.S. Naval Forces, Northwest African Waters; commander U.S. Eighth Fleet; and commander Western Naval Task Force. The latter denoted the American naval component during Allied operations, built around the Eighth Fleet.

The invasion of Sicily was a great success; one that helped topple Italian dictator Benito Mussolini from power and opened sea lanes in the Mediterranean for use by the Allies. General George Patton and his Seventh Army moved rapidly across the island and took Palermo before swinging east to Messina, arriving ahead of British general Bernard Montgomery who had first pushed his Eighth Army (which included the 1st Canadian Infantry Division) north to Syracuse and Catania.

Prior to the operation, the salvage force lost its first ship when *Redwing* was sunk by a mine off Bizerte, Tunisia, the site of an Eighth Fleet landing craft base. During the landings at Sicily, *Hopi*—one of the new fleet tugs—shot down a German bomber coming in low and slow to deliver an attack on shipping. In a tragic incident, salvage ship *Brant* suffered men killed and injured due to "friendly fire" from an American destroyer. At the conclusion of HUSKY, British Prime Minister Winston Churchill praised the operation, observing, "The capture of Sicily was an undertaking of the first magnitude." Patton proudly stated that his army had "out-blitzed the inventors of Blitzkrieg."

ENEMY OPPOSITION INCREASES AT SALERNO

After Sicily, the Italian Campaign got much harder for the Allies. As detailed in Chapter 6, crossing the Strait of Messina was easy, though securing a beachhead at Salerno proved to be difficult with much loss of life on both sides. Italy had declared an armistice before the invasion, but the absence of its forces did not impede German commitment to stop the Allies at the shoreline. In addition to artillery, armor, infantry, and air forces opposing American and British assault troops, the enemy also utilized glider-bombs—a new type of weapon—against shipping offshore. The bombardier aboard the parent aircraft launching the bomb directed the flight of the rocket-propelled ordnance via radio wave guidance to the target—normally a carrier, battleship, cruiser, or large merchant vessel.

High altitude and dive bombers continued to use conventional bombs as well. The fleet tug *Nauset* was sunk by bomb blasts and damage wrought by a mine. Higher value targets—the British battleship *Warspite* and ammunition ship *Lyminge*, and American cruiser *Savannah* and freighter *James W. Marshall*—were hit by glider-bombs. In a despicable act that infuriated Allied servicemen, the Luftwaffe bombed the British hospital ship *Newfoundland*—which was easily identifiable due to her white paint, giant red crosses and illumination at night—killing six nurses and all the medical officers aboard. Other dangers were present as well; a German E-boat torpedoed the destroyer *Rowan* and several vessels were victims of mines.

DISASTER AT ANZIO

When opposing German forces stalled the advance of the American Fifth Army and British Eighth Army in their drive towards the strategic objective of Rome, Prime Minister Winston Churchill convinced the Combined Chiefs of Staff (the supreme military staff for the western Allies) to authorize a plan to land one American and one British division at Anzio. Such action behind enemy lines would bypass the German forces in central Italy. The anticipated and actual results following the landings were aptly characterized by Churchill in two different statements. The first held great promise: "Whoever holds Rome holds the title deeds of Italy." The second expressed his displeasure: "I had hoped we were hurling a wildcat into the shore, but all we got was a stranded whale."

Chapter 7 illustrates how this good plan went wrong. In testament to the courage of the soldiers, sailors, and airmen who fought at Anzio, twenty-two Americans were awarded the Congressional Medal of Honor, the most of any single battle of World War II.

NORMANDY

Chapter 8 gives a first-hand look into the successful Allied invasion at Normandy that decisively turned the tide of war in Europe. The results are well known: thousands of Allied soldiers stormed ashore on five adjacent beaches in the face of well-fortified German defenses and despite great losses, began moving forward through France toward Germany. Less known are the contributions made by large numbers of Navy, Army, and civilian tugs sent from America. Roland H. "Rollie" Webb, Former President and Chief Operating Officer of Todd Pacific Shipyards Corporation, summed up the importance of the small vessels to the landings:

When you look at a photograph of the Normandy invasion all you see is little ships. All those ships, thousands of little landing craft, minesweepers and tugs started in the small shipyards of America and Canada. It was little ships that came out of little towns like Bellingham that did it.

Even before the Normandy invasion, German losses were mounting amidst increased requirements to fight Allied forces on ever-expanding fronts. Chapter 9 focuses on one desperate measure taken by the German navy, somewhat analogous to Japan's use of Kamikaze aircraft, in which volunteers, mostly young, inexperienced enlisted sailors, became "Solo Fighters." These men were otherwise known as "human torpedoes."

The book turns in Chapter 10 to the opening of Cherbourg Harbor. The German defense of the coastline of Western Europe was based on an understanding that the Allies would need a port in order to build up sufficient ammunition, armor, food, fuel, and other supplies to support a large invasion force. Both sides well knew that an amphibious assault was a race; the assaulting forces had to establish sufficient men and materials to stay ashore, while defending forces had to be reinforced with enough men and materials to push the enemy back into the sea.

The capture of Cherbourg became of great urgency after a violent storm off Normandy destroyed "Mulberry A"—one of the two artificial harbors the Allies had fabricated to provide support from the sea to the more than 100,000 soldiers marching across Europe to defeat Hitler. German defense forces recognized the strategic importance of the port and accordingly held out despite naval bombardment from a combined force of American and British ships. The U.S. 79th Infantry Division captured Fort de Roule, which dominated the city and its defenses on 26 June. The port fell three days later with the surrender of the remaining outlying forts sited along the breakwaters and jetties to guard the sea approaches. Then began "the greatest minesweeping operation in history," as Winston Churchill described it, a preamble to the clearance of Cherbourg Harbor.

In addition to a variety of mines previously encountered during the war, a new and deadly type—termed Katy—was discovered at Cherbourg, and is detailed in the account. Due to the great quantity of mines present, large numbers of British minesweepers, with assistance from American *YMS*-class minesweepers, were necessary to clear the approaches and harbor. Royal Navy clearance divers worked in the same shallow waters denied minesweepers as did U.S. Navy salvage divers. Commodore Sullivan paid tribute to the mine clearance effort:

> The Salvage operations necessary to clear the port of Cherbourg were complicated by the minesweeping problems encountered in this port, and by the arrangement of the harbor. Almost all of the salvage operations necessary required the use of lifting craft and pontoons, or of large floating cranes. These could not be employed until the approaches to the locations of the various operations were cleared of mines. The mines laid by the Germans were not only numerous, but were of a various sort. The minesweeping problem was undoubtedly the most complicated yet encountered in any harbor clearance work.

INVASION OF SOUTHERN FRANCE

The Allies landed in southern France on the heels of the Normandy invasion. The objectives of the assault were to secure the beachheads, capture neighboring French ports, and strike north up the Rhône valley to link up with Patton's Third Army, to form the right wing of the Allied force invading Germany, and to cut off German forces in the west of France. Chapters 11-13 describe the amphibious assault and the opening of southern French ports to support the advancing Allied armies.

The situation in the Western Mediterranean was favorable in summer 1944. The U-boat menace was rapidly waning, and following losses, the Luftwaffe was no longer able to operate in strength in "the Med." A British sailor later described the relative ease of the operation:

> It was called the Champagne landing this one, I think, there was very little opposition because the Germans had pulled back and when we were on the beach some of the lads, some of the sailors went up and picked grapes out of the vineyards, and it was one of the easier or better operations that we had.

Of course there was German resistance. Lt. Comdr. Douglas E. Fairbanks Jr., USNR, and Lt. Comdr. John Bulkeley, USN, received medals for heroic actions during the operation. Fairbanks was a famous actor turned naval officer, and recognized worldwide. Bulkeley was much less prominent, except perhaps within naval circles. He had received the Congressional Medal of Honor earlier in the war for taking Gen. Douglas MacArthur, his family and staff off the

Philippine Islands. Chapter 12 provides an account of Fairbanks and Bulkeley prevailing in a sea battle with German ships.

POST-WAR OCCUPATION OF GERMANY

Following the end of the fighting in Europe, America's war-weary servicemen wanted to return home as soon as possible. Vice Adm. Daniel E. Barbey, USN (Ret.) described in *MacArthur's Navy* the same perspective among Sailors and Marines in the Pacific following World War II:

> On 15 August [1945] President Truman was able to announce the unconditional surrender by the Japanese Imperial Government. Orders were sent out for the occupation of Japan and Korea.... Overnight [there was] a change in the attitude of the men in the combat zone from one of war to one of peace. Suddenly everybody wanted to go home. No one was interested in becoming a member of the occupational forces.

The U.S. Army did the heavy lifting in post-war Western Europe. On V-E Day, there were sixty-one U.S. Army divisions—1,622,000 soldiers—in Germany. The divisions in the field became occupation troops responsible for maintaining law and order and establishing the Allies military presence in the defeated nation. The Navy's role, carried out by the Twelfth Fleet under Admiral Hewitt, was to support the Army. Operations on the Weser River and in the ports of Bremen and Bremerhaven are discussed in Chapter 15.

Perhaps of greatest interest to former sailors is an account of spoils of war brought back to the United States. These included five Schnellboot (E-boats), which the U.S. Navy desired in connection with the redesign of PT boats for use in the Pacific. Other acquisitions were the sail training ship *Horst Wessel*, which today still serves as the Coast Guard Academy's *Eagle*, and the destroyer *Z-39* and torpedo boat *T-35*. The biggest coup, however, was obtainment of two of Germany's most sophisticated submarines, *U-2513* and *U-3008*, via subterfuge.

A clandestine task group, titled Submarine Mission Europe—comprised of officer and enlisted submariners dispatched from New London, Connecticut—arrived at Lisahally, Ireland (near Londonderry) where the U-boats were in British custody. Talks between representatives of the United States, United Kingdom, and Soviet Union were scheduled to determine the division of German ships that were to be retained and not sunk between the three countries. Before these talks had even begun, the task group—aided by the salvage ship *Brant* and with support from the Royal Navy—spirited the boats away without informing the Russians. More on this operation is found in Chapter 14.

A SALUTE TO SMALL SHIPS AND THEIR CREWS

There are few published works about the thousands of U.S. Navy small ships and craft that served in World War II. Exceptions include the famous PT boats and to a lesser degree, sub-chasers and minesweepers. There are several reasons for this. The war correspondents and historians with the Fleet generally did not ride small ships. They were aboard admirals' flagships such as carriers, battleships, cruisers, or large amphibious ships. They wrote stories about what they witnessed, the large battles, and about what they believed would be of most interest to Americans. Hollywood movie producers followed suit on the silver screen.

At war's end, the Navy rapidly disposed of the bulk of its small ships and sent their crews—mostly reservists—home. These men resumed their civilian lives and likely many years passed before they became nostalgic about their former Navy duty. Those interested in learning more about the ships they had served aboard often found little information. Some junior officers commanding small vessels and landing craft maintained war diaries. Many did not, and details about these type ships and craft must often be gleaned from references to them in reports and war diary entries made by larger Navy ships and shore commands. Readers interested in learning more about a particular tug or salvage ship will find information in the appendices. Summaries of ship characteristics and names of commanding officers, if known, appear throughout the book.

Unfortunately, little information exists about the exploits of the yard tugs, which were commanded by Boatswains (warrant officers), ably assisted by their very small enlisted crews. Yard (harbor) tugs assigned to shallow water salvage forces were in the thick of the action as they assisted vessels damaged during amphibious operations. Aside from their own work, they brought the tow cables of deeper draft ATFs operating further seaward to grounded tank landing ships and craft in order that they might be pulled clear by these powerful ships.

Former sailors reading a book such as this one are usually interested in whether or not their ships are mentioned. In acknowledgement of this fact, an extensive index is included. To reduce its size, multiple ships listed on the same page or pages in the text are combined into a single entry. Entries for American ships are located under their associated ship type headings. For example, the aircraft carriers *Ranger*, *Santee*, and *Suwannee* are consolidated into a single entry under Ships and Craft, and the sub-categories, U.S. Navy, combatants, and aircraft carriers. A reader searching for a particular foreign ship should review all entries under the heading for that country.

Finally, it may be helpful to some readers to have definitions for a few nautical or navy terms and phrases used in the book:

- BHP: Brake horsepower; the actual or useful horsepower of an engine.
- Broach: To turn the ship broadside to heavy seas, or lose control of steering in following seas so that the ship is turned broadside to the waves. An extremely dangerous situation in steep seas since the ship may roll over and capsize.
- Dan buoy/Danlayer: Temporary buoys. A type of vessel assigned to minesweeping flotillas and fitted to lay Dan Buoys.
- Dead in the water: Not moving (used only when a vessel is afloat and neither tied up nor anchored).
- Fathom: A unit of measurement equal to six feet, used to measure water depth.
- General quarters: Battle Stations.
- Guns opened: To begin firing a gun or guns.
- Hawser: A very large rope or chain used for towing barges and ships.
- Land: To put ashore. Disembark.
- Lay to: To bring a ship to a stop in open water.
- Lighter: Flat-bottomed barge.
- Master: The commander of a non-military ship.
- Ratings: A British naval enlisted man.
- Stand (past tense stood): Of a ship or its captain, to steer, sail, or steam, usually used in conjunction with a specified direction or destination, e.g., "stand into port."
- Vessel: Any craft (from largest ship to smallest boat) that is capable of floating and moving on the water.
- Warp: Move (a ship) along by hauling on a rope attached to a stationary object on shore.
- Wherry: A long light rowboat.

1

French Morocco – Operation TORCH

In order to forestall an invasion of Africa by Germany and Italy, which, if successful, would constitute a direct threat to America across the comparatively narrow sea from western Africa, a powerful American force equipped with adequate weapons of modern warfare and under American command is today landing on the Mediterranean and Atlantic coasts of the French colonies in Africa.

The landing of this American army is being assisted by the British Navy and Air Force, and it will in the immediate future be reinforced by a considerable number of divisions of the British Army.

This combined Allied force, under American command, in conjunction with the British campaign in Egypt, is designed to prevent an occupation by the Axis armies of any part of northern or western Africa and to deny to the aggressor nations a starting point from which to launch an attack against the Atlantic coast of the Americas.

In addition, it provides an effective second front assistance to our heroic allies in Russia.

—With these words,
President Franklin D. Roosevelt announced the
landing of American troops on African soil on
Sunday, 8 November 1942[1]

Following a meeting between the Russian Minister of Foreign Affairs and Franklin D. Roosevelt in Washington, D.C. in June 1942, a press release was issued stating that the American president agreed on the "urgent task of creating a second front" that year. Inaction by the Allies in Europe had enabled Germany to concentrate her army on the eastern front, and it was questionable whether Russia could hold out unless something was done, and quickly, to divert German forces elsewhere, via an operation in Europe or Africa. On the heels of this announcement came news of the fall of Tobruk—a port city on Libya's eastern Mediterranean coast, near the border with Egypt—and the advance of German general Erwin Rommel's panzer division into Egypt. The Desert Fox was poised to take Alexandria, gain control of the Suez Canal, and push the British out of Egypt. The Allies were thus threatened with both the defeat of Russia and the cutting of the Suez Canal lifeline. Discussions by the British about opening a front in Africa, which had preceded the entry of the United States into the war, had envisioned a landing of about 55,000 men in the vicinity of Casablanca, a large port city in western French Morocco on the Atlantic. After America's entry, the plan was enlarged to include landings not only near Casablanca but also in the Mehdia-Port Lyautey area—a beach village and port on the Sebou River (known today as Kenitra) to the north of Casablanca—and the port city of Safi to the south. Planners thereafter expanded the operation to include occupation of the entire North African coast as far east as Tripolitania, the coastal region of what is today Libya. Occupation by Allied forces of Morocco, Algeria, and Tunisia would help safeguard Mediterranean convoys, thus dramatically shortening the route to the Middle East around the Cape of Good Hope.[2]

The United States was to have responsibility for the military and naval operations on the Atlantic coast of Morocco. Oran and Algiers, cities on the Mediterranean on the northern coast of Algeria, were to be captured by two joint British and American forces. The British were to supply all the naval service except for a few transports and the landing forces were to be partly American and partly British. Allied occupation of French North Africa was to be achieved through simultaneous assaults by three attacking forces on Casablanca, Oran, and Algiers. Lt. Gen. Dwight D. Eisenhower would exercise command over the forces, with the exception of the British naval units permanently assigned to the Mediterranean, which would remain under the control of the British Admiralty.[3]

Map 1-1

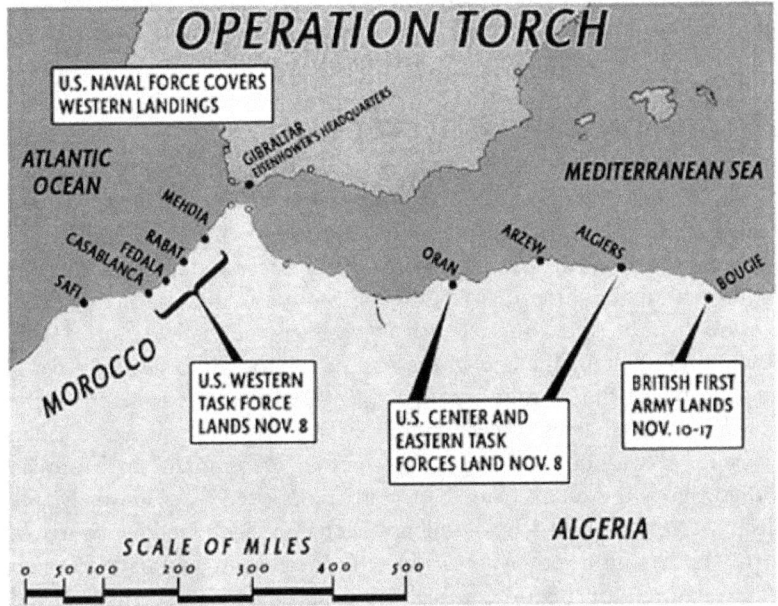

As part of Operation TORCH, assault troops of the U.S. Western Task Force landed on the west coast of French Morocco on 8 November 1942.

THE MOROCCAN EXPEDITION

The naval component of the Moroccan expedition was designated the Western Naval Task Force and was under the command of Rear Adm. Henry K. Hewitt, U.S. Navy. The Army component under Maj. Gen. George S. Patton, U.S. Army, was titled the Western Task Force. The mission assigned to the Naval Task Force was:

> To establish the Western Task Force on beachheads near Mehdia, Fedala and Safi, and support the subsequent coastal military operations in order to capture Casablanca as a base for further military and naval operations.

The objective of the landings at Fedala and Safi was to enable the capture of Casablanca from the land side. Mehdia was to be occupied as a prelude to taking the adjoining airfield at Port Lyautey. At a conference of about 150 naval and army officers convened by Admiral Hewitt at Norfolk, Virginia on 23 October 1942, the day before the task force sailed, General Patton predicted that all the elaborate landing plans would break down in five minutes, after which the Army would take over and win through. He stated in part:

Never in history has the Navy landed an army at the planned time and place. If you land us anywhere within fifty miles of Fedala and within one week of D-day, I'll go ahead and win.... We shall attack for sixty days, and then, if we have to, for sixty more.[4]

ATTACK ON MEHDIA-PORT LYAUTEY

Within the task force was Sub-Task Force Goalpost, under the command of Maj. Gen. Lucian K. Truscott Jr., which was charged with securing Port Lyautey through the capture of the beach village of Mehdia, the Kasbah fortress at the Sebou River mouth, and the airfield. Although Truscott's overall mission was to attack Port Lyautey, the main purpose of his force was to seize the airfield outside the town, preferably by the end of the first day ashore, in order for aircraft staged aboard the carrier *Chenango* (ACV-28) to use it to support the attack on Casablanca. The operation was expected to be a tough slough. It was unlikely the Vichy French government in Morocco would allow the allied troops to land unopposed. Additionally, the destroyer *Dallas* (DD-199)—which was charged with landing a party of Army raiders up the river to capture the airfield—would have to overcome natural and man-made barriers proceeding up the shallow and winding Sebou River to reach its objective.[5]

To carry out her mission, *Dallas* had to pass through jetties extending into the Atlantic and negotiate the narrow river mouth on an ebb tide before encountering a steel cable anti-ship boom stretched across the Sebou. Protected by shore guns at Fort Kasbah on the heights above, this boom, unless breached, would prevent further movement upriver to the airfield adjacent to Port Lyautey which was itself guarded by a number of anti-aircraft guns. In order for the *Dallas* to land the raiders upriver, the boom had to be cut. This chore would fall to a demolition party formed from one officer and ten men from the fleet tug *Cherokee* (AT-66) and a second officer and five men from the salvage ship *Brant* (ARS-32). In preparation, the group had attended a one-week concentrated course on demolitions, explosive cable cutting, and commando raiding techniques at Amphibious Training Base, Little Creek, Virginia prior to *Cherokee*'s departure from Norfolk. The seventeen men detailed from *Cherokee* and *Brant* would make the Atlantic crossing aboard the transport *George Clymer* (AP-57), depart her for the special operation, and return to her immediately following its completion before their eventual return to their own ships. While these men were thus engaged, *Cherokee* would support the landings at Safi. *Brant* did not sail with the Western Task Force to take part in the assault phase of Operation TORCH. She and another salvage ship, *Redwing* (ARS-4), arrived later at French Morocco on 25 November 1942 for harbor clearance duties.⁶

FLEET TUG *CHEROKEE* AND DESTROYER *DALLAS*

The 205-foot *Cherokee*, a *Navajo*-class fleet tug built by Bethlehem Shipbuilding, Staten Island, New York, had been commissioned less than eighteen months earlier on 26 April 1940.

Photo 1-1

Fleet tug *Cherokee* under way in March 1942.
U.S. Navy Bureau of Ships photo # 19-N-29463, now in the collections of the U.S. National Archives

The *Cherokee*'s complement was eight officers and eighty enlisted men. To enable optimal ship control, naval architects had specified diesel-electric propulsion for the *Navajo*-class fleet tugs. Four General Motors 12-278A diesels driving four General Electric generators coupled to a single propeller via a Fairbanks Morse main reduction gear produced 3,600 shaft horsepower, sufficient for a top speed of 16.5 knots. The ship's armament was one single 3-inch/.50-caliber dual-purpose gun mount, two twin 40mm anti-aircraft gun mounts, and two single 20mm AA gun mounts.⁷

Preparations by the *Cherokee*, under the command of Lt. Jacob F. Lawson, USN, for Operation TORCH had included her loading aboard four tons of TNT at Naval Operating Base, Norfolk, Virginia on 8 October. While moored at the base, crewmembers attended firefighting school, gunnery school, and amphibious training camp. The fleet tug put to sea on 19 October to participate in local operations, anchoring that night in the upper Chesapeake Bay off Cove Point, Maryland. The *Cherokee* transferred one officer and ten men to the *George Clymer* on 21 October for temporary duty. These men had received special training and, with the officer and five men from *Brant*, would be charged with breaching the boom.[8]

Cherokee left Cove Point at 0340 on 23 October and took station astern of the transport and aircraft ferry *Lakehurst* (APV-3) as part of a convoy being formed by Task Group 34.3. The task group—comprised of units assigned the landings at Mehdia and at Safi—initially steered a southeasterly course as if headed for the West Indies. Task Group 34.14, made up primarily of the ships assigned the landing at Fedala, put to sea from Hampton Roads the following day and set a northeasterly course as if bound for England. The entire task force was too large to depart from any one port without attracting undesired attention. It assembled well out to sea after a series of departures at various times and places for seemingly different destinations. The Cover Group—a battleship, two cruisers, four destroyers, and an oiler—sailed from Casco Bay, Maine, while the aircraft carriers of the Air Group and three old destroyers sortied from Bermuda. Task Force 34, once formed of these task groups, followed a route that passed south of Newfoundland to give the impression of a regular troop convoy to the United Kingdom, before changing course for North Africa.[9]

On 28 October, five days after the group of which *Cherokee* was a part had sailed from Cove Point, Task Group 34.2—carriers *Ranger* (CV-4), *Santee* (ACV-29), *Suwannee* (AVG-27) and *Sangamon* (ACV-26), light cruiser *Cleveland* (CL-55), destroyers *Bernadou* (DD-153), *Cole* (DD-155), and *Dallas* (DD-199), and oiler *Housatonic* (AO-35)—rendezvoused with the North Africa-bound Task Force 34 and took their stations in the formation. The carriers and destroyers had departed Murray's anchorage off Fort St. Catherine, Bermuda, three days earlier. *Dallas*, an old "four-piper" commissioned on 29 October 1920, and the slightly more elderly *Bernadou* and *Cole*, had entered HMD (His Majesty's Dockyard) Bermuda for modifications and to "strip ship" in preparation for particularly dangerous tasks they were to perform during the invasion of North Africa. The dockyard at Grassy Bay, Bermuda, was the Royal Navy's principal base in the Western Atlantic. Aboard the *Dallas*:

All inflammables and non-essentials were landed. Both boats and boat skids were removed. The loading machine [a tool used to train sailors how to quickly and safely feed ammunition and fire the guns], water cooler, spare depth charges and arbors, as well as 3" illuminating ammunition, were also landed. All confidential publications…except those required for the forthcoming operation were sent to NOB [Naval Operating Base] Bermuda for storage. Splinter mats were installed around all gun and fire control stations and portions of the main deck. Additional splinter protection consisting of steel plates about 3/16" were installed around the wings of the bridge. All hands were issued the U.S. Army fighting suit which is the khaki coverall. New Type steel [battle] helmets had previously been obtained in Norfolk.[10]

The above measures were designed to minimize crew casualties aboard *Dallas* during anticipated combat with enemy forces. To augment the arms she carried aboard, she received from the destroyer *Bernadou* at Murray's anchorage:

- Fifty Springfield rifles
- Fifty Browning automatic rifles
- Fifty .45-caliber pistols
- Eighty Thompson Submachine guns
- 24,000 rounds of .30-caliber ammunition, and
- 36,000 rounds of .45-caliber ammunition

Web belts and canteens sufficient for all hands were also obtained.[11]

ASSAULT ON PORT LYAUTEY

> *We are about to embark on a difficult and historical task—the opening of a second front. In America our people back home and the entire United Nations will watch us with consuming interest. Don't let them down. To successfully carry out our task we must live up to the glorious traditions of the Navy which will require the utmost from all and duty beyond the usual call. This call is your opportunity to strike a blow for America and her allies. Let us be ready to give the enemy hell when and where he shows himself. Make every shot count.*
>
> —Rear Adm. Monroe Kelly, commander Battleships, Atlantic Fleet and commander Task Group 34.8—the Northern Assault Group— embarked in the battleship *Texas* (BB-35)[12]

The Western Task Force was to land troops on the Atlantic coast of French Morocco: at Safi just south of Casablanca; at Fedala, just north of Casablanca; and at Port Lyautey, further to the north of Casablanca. To support these operations—code named BLACKSTONE, BRUSH-WOOD, and GOALPOST—the Western Task Force was divided into three task groups. The troops of the Northern Assault Group (Sub-Task Force Goalpost embarked in Task Group 34.8) were under General Truscott. Nearing French Moroccan waters at the end of the Atlantic crossing, the Northern Assault Group parted company with the Western Assault Force in mid-afternoon on 7 November and proceeded for the assault of Port Lyautey.[13]

Embarked aboard the attack transport *George Clymer* (AP-57) were the 2nd Battalion (reinforced) of the Ninth Infantry Division, U.S. Army, and a 17-man detail comprised of one officer and ten men from *Cherokee* and one officer and five men from *Brant*. The latter ship was a former *Bird*-class minesweeper (AM-24) commissioned in 1918, which in 1942 had first been reclassified a fleet tug and subsequently a salvage ship. *Brant*'s commanding officer, Lt. Harvey Melvin Andersen, USN, had received orders on 10 October 1942 to detail five men and one officer for special instruction under the Army Chief Scout. The salvage officer and men completed the special training duty six days later and prior to boarding *George Clymer*, obtained from *Brant* a ten-man rubber boat, six extra Tommy guns, and a Velocity Power cable cutter for the "special job."[14]

Off North Africa, on the eve of the assault scheduled for 8 November, the final day in transit was spent in making last minute preparations. All hands and the troops aboard *George Clymer* bathed and put on clean clothes—a standard practice followed to minimize infection if wounded in battle. Crewmen checked the boats for proper equipment, ran their engines, tested lowering booms and winches, and then swung the boats out ready for lowering.[15]

Condition 1A (Man Stations for Troop Landing) was set at 2300, and troop combat teams positioned themselves at their boarding nets ready to disembark when ordered. Shortly thereafter two boats were lowered to the waterline in preparation for embarkation by the scout party, and a river-boom cutting detail under Lt. Col. Hanney, USA, and Lt. Mark Starkweather, USNR. Additional boats were lowered as *George Clymer* proceeded on to the transport area (area seaward of the landing beaches for debarking troops and equipment) in preparation for her part in the assault landings.[16]

The 9,000 troops of the 9th Infantry Division carried aboard Northern Assault Group transports were to simultaneously land on five beaches on either side of the village of Mehdia—where the Sebou River emptied into the Atlantic—in order to capture Port Lyautey and its airfield, which lay ten miles up the river, for the use of Army and Navy aircraft. A follow-on objective after gaining control of the Sebou was to seize Rabat-Sale Airfield, southwest of Port Lyautey on the coast. Allied air power for the assault group was to be supplied primarily by fighter and bomber squadrons aboard the auxiliary carrier *Sangamon* (ACV-26), a converted oil tanker. A second former oiler, *Chenango* (ACV-28), was ferrying Army P-40 Warhawk planes readied to fly off and land at Port Lyautey Airfield as soon as it was captured. The field was of great value because it boasted the only all concrete, all-weather strip in Northwest Africa.[17]

On 8 November, the first wave of landing craft beached at 0515 as dawn broke. Vichy French shore batteries opened fire at 0600—and were answered six minutes later by counterbattery fire from gunfire support vessels. However, a new threat soon developed as Vichy fighters and two-engine bombers from the airfield at Rabat-Sale began to strafe and bomb landing craft. Moreover, assault troops making the beach were met ashore with bullets, bayonets, and 75mm fire from the 1st and 7th Regiments Moroccan Tirailleurs (French Army designation for infantry recruited in colonial territories), the Foreign Legion, and naval ground units.[18]

NAVAL DEMOLITION UNIT CUTS ANTI-SHIP BOOM

The obstruction across the mouth of the Sebou was not breached as planned before dawn on 8 November due to heavy gun fire from the shore. When *Dallas* later tried to approach the river, she too was driven off by shore batteries. In the early evening on 9 November, a message was received from Lt. Col. Hanney conveying that he would be at the Fish Cannery about three-quarters of a mile up the Sebou and wait for the demolition party to join him and his engineers. It was an exceptionally dark night and raining, and a heavy surf was breaking over the jetties. Lieutenants Starkweather and Darroch, in charge of the demolition party, were doubtful at first that they could navigate through the dirty sea. (Earlier that day, surf on the beaches had been from 15 to 20 feet high, resulting in swamped or stranded landing craft and discontinuation of operations for a lengthy period.) Preparations were made, however, and by 2130 they were en route in a ship's landing boat. After much difficulty, the boat passed through the jetties about 0100 and entered the river.[19]

Map 1-2

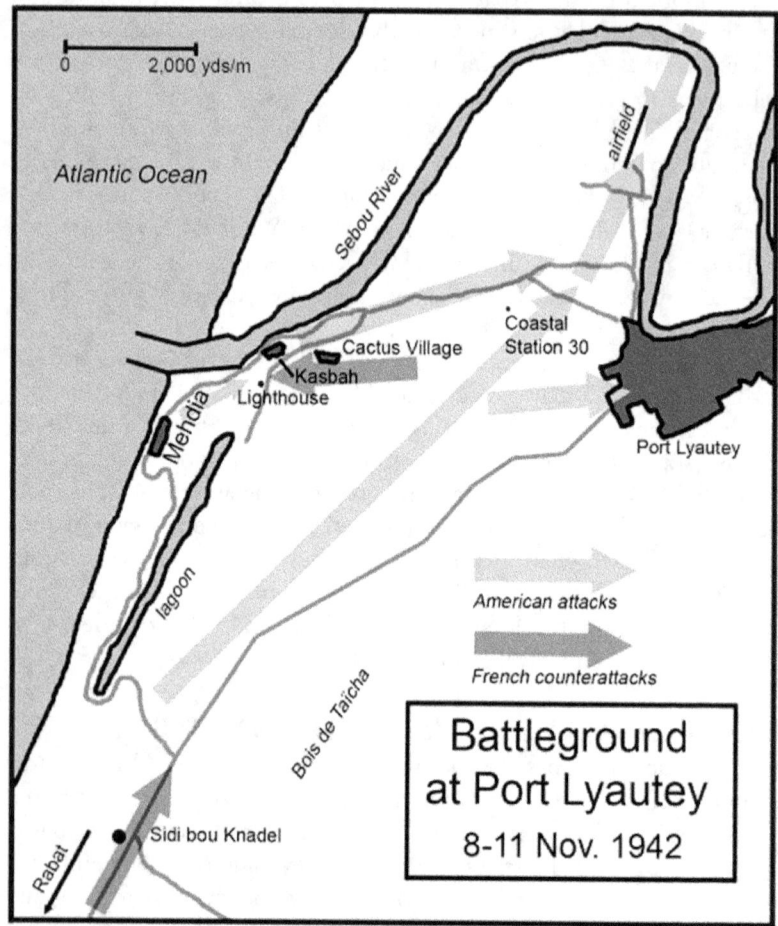

The breaching of a formidable steel cable boom guarding the mouth of the Sebou River was necessary for the destroyer *Dallas* to make a perilous passage up the river and land Army raiders to take the Port Lyautey Airfield.

    Upon arriving at the Canning Factory, the Navy crew was unable to locate Hanney and his party. Undaunted, the boat continued alone up the river and found a net above water supported by a 1 ½-inch metal cable between buoys, two large barges, and two French Navy whaleboats strung across the river. (Hereafter the term buoy refers to one or all of the above.) Running parallel to the cable was a half-inch wire with an electric warning wire attached. The team cut the stout cable with a velocity power cable cutter, and it gave away upon parting. A member then entered the water to be sure there were no problems below. Following the diver's return aboard and before the boat could get clear, enemy on the south bank opened fire with rifles and machine guns. The boat was hit and withdrew downriver under heavy fire until reaching the jetties, firing all the way at gun flashes. The team returned to *George Clymer* about 0430, seven hours after departing her side, with eight wounded members.[20]

DESTROYER *DALLAS* LANDS RAIDING PARTY

Dallas was informed at 0130 on 10 November that the obstruction across the river had been cut, and received orders to proceed upriver three hours thereafter. She headed toward the river mouth at 0400 but, due to the extremely low visibility was not able to locate the jetties off the entrance until 0600. Rene Malavergne then immediately took the wheel. A former river pilot on the Sebou, he had embarked two days earlier along with a 75-man Raider Detachment, 3rd Battalion, U.S. Army, from the transport *Susan B. Anthony* (AP-72). The Free Frenchman had been imprisoned for De Gaullist sympathies, but was later helped by the OSS to escape to England for just such an occasion as this enterprise. The Office of Strategic Services (OSS) was a United States intelligence agency formed during the war and a predecessor of the Central Intelligence Agency. Elimination of the time delay, associated with the helmsman hearing and executing rapidly changing rudder commands, was critical. Malavergne brought the destroyer safely through the narrow jetty passage despite seas breaking astern and ship yawing, with shallow water off the north bank of the channel and the remaining narrow safe portion of the channel very near the south jetty. The *Dallas*'s commanding officer described the Frenchman's superlative ship handling in the face of both adverse weather conditions and enemy fire:

> As the seas were breaking astern the ship yawed violently, heading alternately for the south jetty and the patch of shoal water between the jetties. The channel was narrow and immediately adjacent to the south jetty. The pilot handled the ship masterfully, however, and kept to the channel. Shortly after entering between the jetties a shell splash was noted dead ahead of the ship and about 30 yards from us. It was estimated to be about 37 millimeter. Another was heard to pass by close aboard to starboard but the splash was not observed.... There was much small arms fire heard from the direction of the Kasbah [the fortress that guarded the river mouth], both rifle and machine gun, and the occasional report of a larger caliber gun was also heard.[21]

As the destroyer crossed the bar at the river entrance, she touched bottom and—as her propellers churned the mud and heavy vibrations ensued—her speed dropped appreciably. The commanding officer ordered flank speed, and the engine room, after opening the guarding valve wide to send as much steam as possible to the turbine, proudly announced "answering turns for twenty-five knots." *Dallas* was in fact proceeding at less than five knots, but continued making way and slowly ploughed free of the bottom silt.[22]

A report had been received that the boom had been cut at the northern side of the second buoy near the middle of the river, but as the destroyer approached the obstruction three buoys supporting the steel cable came into view. The pilot informed the commanding officer that there was a shoal beneath the point where the cable had been cut, which the ship could not possibly get past. The buoys supporting the cable were apparently each anchored individually as they maintained their positions despite a strong ebb tide. The only alternative appeared to be to break through at the deepest part of the channel, midway between the first and second buoys from the south bank. Picking up speed, the destroyer struck the cable which, still affixed to the south bank but severed mid-river and no longer under tension, was easily swept aside and *Dallas* continued onward toward the airfield.[23]

Twenty minutes' journey farther upriver from the breached boom, a machine gun on the ridges behind the airport opened fire at 0650, which the *Dallas* answered with 3-inch and 20mm fire. After several bursts the machine gun fell silent without having scored any hits. Two rounds believed fired from enemy 3-inch or 75mm guns produced large splashes in a swamp about 150 yards distant on the ship's beam. The river was becoming even more perilous and the destroyer was touching bottom from time to time, but there appeared to be no danger of becoming stuck hard and fast. Two steamers that had been scuttled in an attempt to block the river came into view as the *Dallas* made a turn around the bend just north of the airport. Malavergne brought the ship neatly between the vessels without touching either, despite one being on its side and almost completely submerged. After rounding the next bend, *Dallas* struck bottom, but her commanding officer Lieutenant Commander Brodie pushed forward anyway until the destroyer reached the seaplane base ramp on the eastern border of the airfield two miles away. During this stretch the engines were making turns for twenty knots, while the destroyer actually made good about ten knots over or through the ground.[24]

Upon arrival alongside the ramp at 0737, the ship anchored and the raider detachment disembarked during which an enemy battery of 75mm guns opened rapid fire. The rounds were hitting very close aboard, some within ten yards of the *Dallas*, and she immediately began counterbattery with 3-inch gunfire. As the gunners aboard the destroyer directed their fire over low-lying buildings near a railroad bridge beyond which they believed the battery was located, a plane from the cruiser *Savannah* bombed the enemy position—permanently silencing the guns. Upon reaching the riverbank the raiders encountered machine gun fire, but were able to occupy the airport immediately, and by the late morning the Army P-40s from the *Chenango* were using the airport. *Dallas* remained at anchor until the mid-afternoon on 12 November when she stood downriver, passed through the jetties, and anchored off Mehdia Beach.[25]

TWENTY-ONE NAVY CROSS MEDALS

The commanding officer, executive officer/engineer officer, and another engineering officer of the *Dallas* all received the Navy Cross for heroism, as did the Free Frenchman who so adroitly took the destroyer up the Sebou River. (The medal, the second highest American decoration for valor, is awarded for extraordinary heroism not justifying the Medal of Honor.) The citation for the ship's captain reads:

> The President of the United States of America takes pleasure in presenting the Navy Cross to Lieutenant Commander Robert J. Brodie Jr., United States Navy, for extraordinary heroism and distinguished service in the line of his profession as Commanding Officer of the Destroyer U.S.S. *DALLAS* (DD-199), in action against hostile forces during the occupation of Port Lyautey, French Morocco, on 10 November 1942. Before daylight on 10 November 1942, Lieutenant Commander Brodie in the *DALLAS* with a detachment of raider troops embarked entered the mouth of the Sebou River leading to Port Lyautey. With gallantry and intrepidity in the face of determined artillery and machine gun fire and the fire of snipers, at the risk of his own life, the lives of his crew and the embarked troops, he broke the steel cable boom with the bow of his ship and forced his way ten miles up the Sebou River. Upon arrival at the Port Lyautey Airfield he landed the raider troops, who successfully captured the airfield. This exceptional feat, which was accomplished without material damage or personnel loss, is a testimonial to the valor, intelligence and seamanship of this gallant officer, and reflects great credit upon

himself and upholds the highest traditions of the United States Naval Service.²⁶

Seizure of the Port Lyautey Airfield was critical to the capture of French Morocco, and the intrepid *Dallas* could not have carried out her mission but for the demolition team. The efforts of its members to breach the otherwise impassable boom enabled the destroyer to sweep aside the steel cable remnant then supported only at one end. There was no realistic way to take the field except by passage up the Sebou River, which was protected by a seemingly impregnable barrier and machine guns and artillery sited to sweep the river waters adjacent to the boom. On the heights above the Sebou, the walled Kasbah dominated the channel. A ship attempting to proceed past these defenses in daylight would be at too severe a disadvantage, while in the darkness of night its chances of running aground were greater.²⁷

Captain Arthur T. Moen, USN, the commanding officer of *George Clymer*, recommended in his After Battle Report that Lieutenants Starkweather and Darroch receive the Navy Cross Medal and that the fifteen enlisted members of the demolition team be advanced in rank. In consideration of the heroic actions of the entire team, higher authority awarded all seventeen members the Navy Cross. It was their actions in the face of very adverse weather and enemy opposition which made the landing of Army raiders possible.

Cherokee (AT-66) Personnel

- Lieutenant Mark Warren Starkweather, USNR
- Boatswain's Mate First Class Roy Benjamin Dowling, USNR
- Gunner's Mate Second Class William Reynolds Freeman, USNR
- Machinist's Mate First Class Ernest John Gentile, USNR
- Shipfitter Third Class Raymond Edward Johnson, USNR
- Shipfitter First Class Richard Wood Joyce, USNR
- Electrician's Mate Third Class William A. Music Jr., USN
- Boatswain's Mate Second Class Edwin Sperry, USNR
- Chief Boatswain's Mate Arthur Wagner, USNR
- Seaman First Class Edward Leo Wisniewski, USNR
- Machinist's Mate Second Class Czeslaw Zymroz, USN

Brant (ARS-32) Personnel

- Lieutenant James W. Darroch, USNR

- Shipfitter Second Class Frederick Lawrence Arsenault, USNR
- Machinist's Mate First Class Joseph Greely, USNR
- Coxswain Andrew Jackson House, USN
- Gunner's Mate Second Class Lucas John Perry, USN
- Boatswain's Mate Second Class Richard Graham Shelley, USNR

The medal citation for Lieutenant Starkweather is representative of those of the other men with some variation in the wording:

> The President of the United States of America takes pleasure in presenting the Navy Cross to Lieutenant Mark Warren Starkweather, United States Naval Reserve, for extraordinary heroism and distinguished service in the line of his profession as commander of a demolition party attached to the Fleet Tug U.S.S. *CHEROKEE* (AT-66), during the assault on and occupation of French Morocco from 8 to 11 November 1942. Assigned the extremely dangerous task of cutting through an enemy obstruction in order that the U.S.S. *DALLAS* could navigate up the Sebou River in order to land raiders near a strategic airport, Lieutenant Starkweather and his crew, on the night of 9 November, proceeded with grim determination toward their objective. Despite the treacherous surf, he and his shipmates skillfully and courageously accomplished their hazardous mission of cutting the cables at the mouth of the river, as guns from the French fort opened fire. Countering the enemy's attack, Lieutenant Starkweather dauntlessly started back and, in spite of enormous breakers which battered his boat, brought her and her courageous crew back to safety. His conduct throughout this action reflects great credit upon himself, and was in keeping with the highest traditions of the United States Naval Service.[28]

FLEET TUG *CHEROKEE*

Cherokee earned a battle star for the period 8-11 November 1942 of the Algeria-Morocco landings, the first and only American tug to so in the African Theater during the war—qualifying her crewmen to affix a star to the European-African-Middle Eastern campaign ribbon on their uniform blouses. This accolade combined with the award of eleven Navy Cross Medals for heroism to one officer and ten men detailed from her for a special operation ensures *Cherokee* a unique place in the annals of Navy tug history. While the demolition detail was engaged with the Northern Assault Group in the Mehdia-Port Lyautey area, the fleet tug was with the Southern Assault Group. She had left the main body of the convoy with the other units of the group on Saturday, 7 November, bound for Safi about 150 miles south of Casablanca. As *Cherokee*—steaming on the flank of the now single-column formation—drew nearer the Moroccan coast, she sighted lights on shore at Safi. The group arrived at the transport area, eight miles off the beach a little before midnight and began lowering boats. While preparations aboard the assault ships continued, the tug's crew readied her towing equipment should it be required.[29]

The destroyers *Bernadou* and *Cole*, which each had aboard 197 raider-trained soldiers in addition to their crews, had the unenviable task of landing the troops inside the harbor. The only factors in their favor were, hopefully, surprise and low ship silhouettes that might help them in darkness avoid being seen by the enemy. In preparation for the mission, the masts had been removed and stacks cut down on both destroyers. As *Bernadou* entered the narrow harbor mouth at 0428, the 75mm battery at the Front de Mer (sea front), machine gun nests around the harbor, and even a 155mm battery two miles to the southward opened up on her. Unfazed, the destroyer swept the jetty on her starboard side and the dock and phosphate pier with 20mm and 3-inch fire, and with her remaining 3-inch guns took the Old Portuguese fort and Front de Mer under fire. These prompt actions prevented manning of any guns in the fort and silenced the 75mm battery as a raider-operated grenade launcher on board the ship took out a machine gun nest on the jetty. The *Bernadou* landed the raiders near the harbor head, who after climbing down a landing net onto the rocks at water's edge, were minutes later pursuing the famous French Foreign Legion as they retired. *Cole* entered the harbor at 0517, having been temporarily lost in the gloom.[30]

Upon observing guns firing on the beach at 0430, the tug *Cherokee* had gone to general quarters. Thereafter, from daylight on, the sailors and troops in the harbor area were shot at from the hill slopes to the east. When the Army asked for naval gunfire on the headquarters of the snipers at the Front de Mer, the *Cole* shot away one corner of the top story with one gun salvo forcing the surrender of those within the building. (For their actions on 8 November, *Bernadou* and *Cole* would receive the Presidential Unit Citation—the highest award for heroism that a military unit may earn, and the equivalent of the Navy Cross for an individual. *Dallas* was similarly lionized for her deeds on 10 November. They would be the only American destroyers that served in the African, European, or Mediterranean Theaters thus honored during the war.)[31]

In the early afternoon, *Cherokee* escorted the transport and aircraft ferry *Lakehurst* and attack cargo ship *Titania* (AK-55) into harbor, and then anchored outside the breakwater at Safi. Following an air warning at dawn on 9 November, the tug maneuvered in the harbor during the ensuing attack before being dispatched to salvage tank landing craft south of Safi. At completion of this chore, she anchored once again off the Safi breakwater. Crew rest was scant that night. In the early morning darkness on 10 November, she got under way at 0258 for Fedala.[32]

Cherokee arrived at her destination fifteen miles north of Casablanca later that day. The following morning she began unloading amphibious-tracked vehicles from a ship alongside and placing them in the water. She broke off from this work to haul a 50-foot Higgins boat off the beach, and then resumed her earlier work. That evening, men aboard the tug witnessed the explosion of the transport *Joseph Hewes* (AP-50) which, lying at anchor in Fedala Roads, was torpedoed by the German submarine *U-173*. The ship sank at 2032, taking the commanding officer and over one hundred seamen and soldiers to the bottom. *Cherokee* stood out to sea and retrieved twenty-three of the survivors, anchoring at 2334 in the outer harbor at Fedala. Early the following day, 12 November, she observed an explosion at 0550. The fleet tug quickly transferred the *Hewes* survivors to *Leonard Wood* (APA-12), and then made her way to the destroyer *Hambleton* (DD-455) hit amidships on her port side with a torpedo fired by the same submarine. She was still afloat with a 12-degree list to starboard. *Cherokee* embarked 200 officers and men from the destroyer, and took her in tow for Casablanca. Following the delivery of her charge, *Cherokee* returned to Fedala Harbor.[33]

That evening she observed torpedo explosions in the transport area off the harbor—the *U-173* damaging the oiler *Winooski* (AO-38)—and picked up survivors before joining ships in convoy clearing the harbor to avoid further attack.[34]

CONCLUSION OF OPERATION TORCH

By mid-November, General Patton's Western Task Force had taken French Morocco, and Oran and Algiers had fallen to the joint British and American Center and Eastern Task Forces, giving the Allies control of French Algeria as well. Patton expressed his appreciation of the assistance provided by the Navy in a dispatch to Hewitt, which the admiral in turn transmitted on Sunday, 15 November 1942, to every ship of Task Force 34 remaining in African waters:

It is my firm conviction that the great success attending the hazardous operations carried out on sea and on land by the Western Task Force could only have been possible through the intervention of Divine Providence manifested in many ways. Therefore, I shall be pleased if in so far as circumstances and conditions permit, our grateful thanks be expressed today in appropriate religious services.[35]

FLEET TUG DUTY

Cherokee remained in North African waters to care for the many ships concentrating there with men and supplies until 3 May 1943, when she left Casablanca for Norfolk, Virginia. She served the Navy until 29 June 1946, when she was decommissioned and transferred to the Coast Guard. Other ships of her class continued their naval service well past that date. Some participated in the Korean and/or Vietnam wars. Others were with the Fleet in hotspots around the world, including Lebanon and the Quemoy-Matsu Islands of Taiwan in 1958; the Dominican Republic in 1961 and 1965; and the Cuban Missile Crisis in 1962. The last of the World War II era fleet tugs, *Paiute*, *Papago*, and *Takelma*—which served in the Pacific Theater—did not leave service until 1992, nearly fifty years after they first joined the fleet. A summary of the fleet tugs and associated data, their builders' yards, and the names of commanding officers (if known), and significant awards earned, is provided in Appendix A.[36]

2

The Navy's Tugs and Salvage Ships

> *They were the workhorses of the fleet—small auxiliary ships that helped to save some of the biggest and most powerful warships. They were, and are the towing, diving, salvage and rescue ships of the U.S. Navy. Perhaps the best known among the ocean-going tugs of the World War II era were the 205-foot fleet tugs of the* Navajo *class, also referred to as the Indian class since they were named for tribes of native North Americans. There were 70 of these ships built, originally classified as* ATs, *but redesignated* ATFs *on May 15, 1944.*
>
> —Comdr. Edward H. Lundquist, director of the Navy's Fleet Hometown News Center in Norfolk, Virginia, who served aboard the fleet tug *Tawakoni* (ATF-114)[1]

FLEET TUGS (ATF)

The 205-foot *Navajo*-class fleet tugs were well suited for their missions of open-ocean towing, emergency salvage and firefighting in naval combat areas. They were long-legged ships with superb endurance due to the 96,000 gallons of fuel that they could carry. This, in conjunction with the thrust of their single 13-foot propeller, enabled the movement of large tows—such as dry dock sections and damaged ships—long distances to or from the theater of operations. The diesel-electric ships were fitted with four General Motors 12-278A diesel main engines driving four General Electric generators, and three General Motors 3-268A auxiliary services engines. To provide immediate assistance to ships in the combat zone, the ATFs were equipped with salvage pumps, 8,000-pound Eells drag-embedment anchors (also called burial anchors or drag anchors), and other special equipment for salvage operations. The tugs also had considerable firefighting capabilities. A 1944 publication, *Navy Seagoing Tugs and Related Craft, General Characteristics and Considerations Governing Use of*, described the strengths and limitations of the excellent all purpose, long range, powerful and very seaworthy ships:

> The large Indian [Navajo] Class tugs are well suited for combat towing and for emergency salvage or fire-fighting in combat areas. Therefore they should not be employed in the rear areas if other tugs suitable for this work are available.
> They are well armed and can take considerable punishment. ATFs [fleet tugs] have a maximum draft of about eighteen feet and consequently are not suitable for inshore work in amphibious operations. When used in combat operations, and unless already included in the ship's company, they should carry as additional personnel: one salvage officer, four salvage divers, six general salvage men, one firefighting officer and eight firefighting specialists.[2]

These workhorses were characterized by tall, straight bows, low freeboard (vertical distance from main deck to the water below) amidships and a rounded stern above the single screw and rudder. The first thirty ships of the class—ATFs *66-95*—were built with a large stack. (The first ship in the class, *Cherokee*, is depicted in Photo 1-1) Designers gave the later tugs a smaller stack, which lowered the ships' center of gravity, thereby increasing stability in heavy seas. Exhaust from the main engines was discharged over the side at the waterline instead of through the funnel. At about 1,600 tons displacement, the oceangoing tugs were only slightly smaller than some of the early World War II destroyers and destroyer escorts. Large and powerful, these workhorses would serve the Navy well for many years. Almost seventy *Navajo*-class tugs were built before the end of World War II and saw service in every theater. Some would remain in service until the early 1990s, nearly fifty years after *Navajo* was launched. The only disadvantage of these sturdy tugs was their draft; they drew eighteen feet of water, making them unsuitable for close inshore work.[3]

The fleet tugs were both rugged and well-armed, enabling them to sustain punishment from working with damaged vessels at close quarters, or from combat operations. Their main battery was a 3-inch/.50-caliber slow-fire mount, augmented by smaller anti-aircraft weapons: 20mm guns on both bridge wings and 40mm anti-aircraft batteries in gun tubs aft on both sides. ATFs were also fitted with depth charges, in the event an opportunity presented itself to steam over the top of an enemy submarine and drop explosives on it.[4]

RESCUE TUGS (ATR)

In anticipation of America's entry into the war, the Chief of the Bureau of Ships sent a letter to the CNO (Chief of Naval Operations) on 12 September 1941 addressing the "need of rescue tugs to tow in disabled vessels." He stated that it was imperative in time of war to salvage, as much as possible, every ship which had been placed in peril of sinking through damage resulting from enemy action or from marine casualties. This could be done only if the capability existed to take such vessels in tow as soon as possible after the damage had been inflicted, by stationing suitable rescue tugs at those points along the coast where casualties to shipping could be anticipated. Vessels used in rescue tug services would need good seaworthiness, endurance, sufficient power to tow large vessels at sea, proper towing arrangements (a towing engine or equivalent system), firefighting equipment, and a basic supply of salvage materials and pumps, though far less extensive than that found on dedicated Navy salvage vessels. These type ships (ARS) are discussed later in the chapter.[5]

Following the creation by the Navy of a Rescue Tug Service, it became apparent that the number of tugs that were available was wholly inadequate. Commodore William Sullivan of the Naval Salvage Service later described the belief by officers of the Navy Rescue Tug Service and the Bureau of Ships Salvage Service that:

> The [fleet] tugs already under construction were altogether too elaborate for wartime needs and that we could not hope for any satisfactory solution of the problem by waiting until the completion of the tug program as then laid down, could be accomplished. We accordingly broke out some plans of [a] 165-foot tug that I had brought back from England, which the English thought was the most satisfactory tug for rescue work that could be developed, considering of course, the cost and time of construction.[6]

These officers soon realized the hopelessness of trying to get any appreciable number of steel-hulled rescue tugs built because, following the Japanese attack on Pearl Harbor, the Navy wanted most destroyers, battleships, cruisers, and other higher priority types of ships. Sullivan explained:

> We contacted some naval architects in Boston [Massachusetts] who had been at work on some designs of some British salvage vessels.... This firm of architects agreed to draw up a plan of a wooden tug with reciprocating engines which could be quickly and

cheaply built and which would be as nearly a copy of the British steel tug as was possible to get.... We also found some patterns up in New York State of some reciprocating engines that were suitable for installation in these boats. We also found the Babcock-Wilcox Company had some scotch boilers that could be quickly obtained. Upon the information that we furnished the Auxiliary Vessels Board, forty of these were authorized and a contract was signed with the naval architects in Boston to prepare working plans.[7]

On 19 January 1942, the CNO directed the construction of forty wooden rescue tugs ATR *1-40* (Batch 1) as part of the U.S. Navy's Maximum War Effort (1799 Vessel) Program. Upon completion, four of these ships, ATR *17-20*, were transferred to the United Kingdom under the Lend-Lease Program as HMS *Director*, *Emulous*, *Freedom*, and *Justice*, respectively. Following the war, these tugs were returned to U.S. custody in March and April 1946.[8]

That summer, the Vice CNO directed on 5 August 1942 the construction of an additional forty wooden ships, ATR *50-89* (Batch 2) using tonnage still available in the program. To minimize the impact of the rescue tug program on other Navy ship procurement—America's shipyards producing steel-hulled ships were operating at full capacity—both batches of ships were to be built of wood and equipped with relatively simple triple-expansion steam engines. The hulls could be constructed by small builders not involved in the main Navy shipbuilding effort and the steam engines could similarly be fabricated by small local machine shops. It is believed that the firm of famed yacht designer John G. Alden prepared the drawings for the rescue tug. In any case, the resultant ships were rugged, as indicated by the pounding that *ATR-15* absorbed during a storm off Normandy, France, in June 1944.[9]

The eighty wooden-hulled ATRs averaged 9.4 months between keel laying and launch and 13.6 months between keel laying and commissioning, over three times longer than the time required to produce one of the Navy's subsequent 143-foot steel-hulled auxiliary tugs (ATA). This was partially due to the greater time needed to cut, shape and fit wooden ribs and planking, versus cutting and weld-fabricating large sections of steel plating to transverse and longitudinal frames. However, most of the additional time was due to the fact that the small shipyards the Navy contracted to do the work had limited capabilities and resources. Plus, each contract was for only a few vessels. Thus, these builders did not benefit from economies of scale enjoyed by big yards churning out large quantities of ships.[10]

Photo 2-1

ATR-7 was one of the eighty U.S. Navy 165-foot wooden-hulled rescue tugs that served in World War II.
Courtesy of Donald Taber, National Association of Fleet Tug Sailors, NavSource: http://www.navsource.org/archives/09/40/094000701.jpg

The 165-foot rescue tugs were built expressly for the war to assist ships in distress or in danger of sinking, such as those torpedoed by enemy submarines in coastal waters. Two Babcock-Wilcox "D"-type boilers, supplying steam to one Fulton Iron Works triple-expansion reciprocating engine coupled via the main reduction gear to a single propeller, could propel *ATR-1* (the first vessel of her ship class) at a top speed of 12.2 knots. Standard speed was 10.3 knots. The ATRs did not have the "long legs" (fuel capacity/endurance) of the ATFs and ATAs (discussed later), but did possess considerable firefighting capabilities. Elwood Gould, who served aboard *ATR-31*, recollected that his ship was well built, albeit hot due to the arrangement of her engineering plant:

> She [*ATR-31*] was built with a million board feet of lumber. Our frames were spaced very close together, just 10 inches apart, so she was sturdy. You couldn't sleep in the crew quarters when the ship

was in the tropics. The steam line ran right through the berthing spaces.[11]

George Bretz, who served aboard *ATR-36*, echoed this sentiment, "We always slept on deck because of the heat." He also described the composition of her crew, and armament: the authorized single 3-inch/.50-caliber dual purpose gun mount and two 20mm anti-aircraft gun mounts, and additional weapons obtained by enterprising crewmembers:

> She was crewed by three officers and 50 men. We … stole a 50mm and a 100mm gun from the beach. When the war was over, we dumped the guns and ammo because we weren't supposed to have them.[12]

The Under Secretary of the Navy ordered the construction of the next batch of forty ATRs 101-140 (Batch 3) on 16 April 1943. By then, top Navy brass believed that steel-hulled ATRs would be more suitable for duty in the warm waters of the South and Southwest Pacific, partly because wooden vessels deteriorated rapidly there from attacks by tropical shipworms. The resultant smaller 143-foot ships were the ATA auxiliary tugs.[13]

Photo 2-2

The 143-foot Rescue tug *ATR-97* before her redesignation as Auxiliary tug *ATA-170*. U.S. Navy photo #80-G-222590, now in the collections of the U.S. National Archives

OTHER VESSELS BOLSTER AUXILIARY TUG FLEET

During the war, the "ATA fleet" was bolstered by two former ATOs (old fleet tugs) and five ex-net layers, bringing to fifty-four the total United States Navy auxiliary tugs. The five net layers originally laid down as yard net tenders, were redesignated net laying ships during construction, and were ultimately commissioned as auxiliary tugs. (The expression "laid down" refers to the first step in construction of a ship when the parts of the keel are placed on the slipway or dry dock where the vessel is to be built.)

Ship	Former Name(s)/ Ship Designation	Length (ft.) Displ. (tons)	Year Built
Chetco (ATA-166)	ex-civilian tug *Barryton/Thomas E. Moran*, Navy tug *Chetco* (AT-166)	150/475	1919
Chatot (ATA-167)	ex-civilian tug *Buttercup*, Navy tug *Chatot* (AT-167)	142/234	1919
ATA-214	Navy net laying ship *Palo Blanco* (AN-64)	194/1,550	1944
ATA-215	Navy net laying ship *Palo Verde* (AN-65)	194/1,550	1944
ATA-216	Navy net laying ship *Allthorn* (AN-70)	194/1,550	1945
ATA-217	Navy net laying ship *Tesota* (AN-71)	194/1,550	1945
ATA-218	Navy net laying ship *Yaupon* (AN-72)	194/1,550	1945[15]

The diesel-powered 143-foot ATAs were smaller than the ATRs, with an associated reduced crew size, three officers and 40 men. Like *Navajo*-class ATFs, the auxiliary tugs had considerable fuel endurance allowing a large radius of action, and were able to conduct major towing operations despite possessing only about half the horsepower. The ships did have other limitations. Possessing no appreciable salvage or firefighting abilities, they were best suited for use in areas just outside combat zones where, for example, they were in a position to relieve an ATF that might be engaged in towing a disabled vessel, thereby permitting the fleet tug to return to the front lines while the ATA brought the ship to a safe area for repairs.[16]

The auxiliary tugs had less power than the fleet tugs; two General Motors 12-cylinder engines coupled to a single propeller via a Fairbanks Morse main reduction gear produced 1,200 brake horsepower. They also were not as heavily armed as fleet tugs, having the same armament as rescue tugs, one 3-inch/.50-caliber gun mount and two 20mm anti-aircraft guns. Some ATAs undoubtedly acquired additional weapons—as had the *ATR-31*—during the war, by whatever means possible. The men aboard small, minimally-armed ships well understood that volume of fire power was all important—

particularly during enemy aircraft attacks. The ATAs, with a draft of thirteen feet, had one advantage over fleet tugs. Drawing less water, these ships could operate closer to shore.[17]

Summary information about the rescue and auxiliary tugs is contained in Appendix B.

OLD FLEET TUGS (ATO) AND YARD TUGS (YT)

> *They are largely World War I type tugs or ex-Mine Sweepers (Bird Class). Some are deficient in stability, reserve buoyancy and freeboard or have been fitted with blisters or ballast as a partial remedy. Others have sufficient stability but insufficient freeboard and radius of action. In general they have widely varying characteristics but due to their age and general condition, limitations, etc., should normally be used to fill demands in rear areas where repair facilities are readily available and duty will not be too rigorous.*
>
> *The facilities of the existing harbor tugs vary widely. Some individual tugs are fitted with good firefighting pumps and other facilities—and some are not. Some of these tugs have been very successfully employed for rescue (towing) along beaches in amphibious operations. Their main and almost exclusive purpose is towing. Their assignment and use should be based chiefly on their size, power and endurance.*
>
> —From a Navy Manual, titled *Seagoing Tugs and Related Craft, General Characteristics and Considerations Governing Use of,* published in 1944, regarding the recommended use of a miscellaneous assortment of seagoing tugs not meeting the requirements of the ATF, ATA or ATR groups[18]

Before the *Navajo*-class fleet tugs came into being, the Navy had a variety of oceangoing tugs designated AT (Fleet Tug), some of which dated back to, or before, the Spanish-American War. A majority of these tugs were former civilian vessels acquired from the private-sector, but their ranks also included sixteen ex-*Bird*-class World War I era minesweepers, as well as some one-of-a-kind naval vessels. In the face of ever-increasing wartime requirements for more tugs, the Navy maintained in service many of World War I vintage and even older. With the newest ships in forward areas, the Service retained the use of a handful of coal- or oil-burning tugs of the late 1800s to serve in America's naval ports and along its coasts.

Ship	Length (ft.) Displ. (tons)	Year Built	Disposition
City Point Iron Works, South Boston, Massachusetts			
Iwana (AT-2)/ ex-harbor tug #2	92/192	1891	Later *YT-2*, then *YTM-2*, to the War Shipping Administration (WSA) in 1946 for disposal
Mare Island Naval Shipyard, Vallejo, California			
Unadilla (AT-4)/ ex-harbor tug #4	110/355	1895	Later *YT-4*, then *YTM-4*, placed out of service in September 1945, to WSA in May 1947
Pawtucket (AT-7)/ex-harbor tug #7	92/225	1898	Later *YT-7*, then *YTM-7*, placed out of service on 13 December 1946, scrapped in 1947
Norfolk Naval Shipyard, Portsmouth, Virginia			
Samoset (AT-5)/ ex-harbor tug #5	93/225	1897	Later *YT-5*, then *YTM-5*, placed out of service in 1945, to the Maritime Commission in 1947
New York Naval Shipyard, Brooklyn, New York			
Penacook (AT-6)/ ex-harbor tug #6	92/230	1898	Later *YT-6*, then *YTM-6*, placed out of service in September 1945, sold on 12 August 1947[19]

The oldest of these tugs, *Iwana*, was propelled by one coal-fired boiler, one single-ended triple-expansion reciprocating steam engine, and a single propeller, giving the ship a top speed of 11.6 knots. Initially placed in service as *Iwana* (harbor tug #2), she performed towing operations and miscellaneous services out of Boston for five decades from 1892 until 1946. Her armament consisted of two one-pounder cannons (37mm deck/landing guns), and one machine gun. The ship's complement was originally nine men, but likely increased during wartime. The Navy reclassified *Iwana* a district harbor tug (YT-2) on 17 July 1920. She remained thus until her name was dropped on 5 October 1942. Finally, as a part of a bigger reclassification by the Navy of existing tugs, she was designated the medium district harbor tug (YTM-2) on 15 May 1944.[20]

During that month, the Navy reclassified all ATs that were still in service as either old fleet tugs (ATO) or yard ("harbor") tugs (YT). The YTs were further categorized as big (YTB) or medium (YTM) yard tugs. These classifications and that of little (YTL) yard tugs—which were not former ATs—were based on the power of the vessels:

- YTB - Harbor Tugs, Big: greater than 800 horsepower
- YTM - Harbor Tugs, Medium: 400 to 800 horsepower
- YTL - Harbor Tugs, Little: less than 400 horsepower

A summary of the old fleet tugs and yard tugs, including ships' characteristics, significant unit awards earned, builders' yards, and the names of commanding officers during World War II, if known, is provided in Appendix C.

The U.S. Navy also had large numbers of modern yard tugs, constructed shortly before or during the war for utilization as harbor tugs. The scope of this book does not allow for coverage of their service. However, harbor tugs *Pessacus* (YT-192) and *Uncas* (YT-242) are discussed in the following chapter because they were the only Navy tugs, of any type, to earn a battle star in the American Theater during World War II. They were units of Convoy SC-107 in autumn 1942. Attacked by a U-boat wolf pack, the convoy suffered the loss of fifteen merchant ships and damage to four others, the most losses by the Allies in a single convoy up to that point in the war.

AMERICAN-BUILT ROYAL NAVY RESCUE TUGS

Thirteen *BAT-1*-class ships were ultimately delivered to Great Britain as part of the Lend-Lease Program. (*BAT-2* was intended for Great Britain but was instead retained by the U.S. Navy and served as *ATR-90*.) The Royal Navy also later received ten 143-foot steel rescue tugs to comprise a total of twenty-three British *Favourite*-class rescue tugs. Three ships of this class—*Reserve*, *Sprightly*, and *Tancred*—were subsequently transferred to the Royal Australian Navy; a fourth, HMS *Athlete* (W150), was mined and sank off Leghorn, Italy, on 17 July 1945.

Royal Navy *Favourite*-class Rescue Tugs

Ship	U.S. Navy Designation	Hull Type	Length (ft.) Displ. (tons)	Completed/ Delivered
Advantage (W133)	ATR-41	Steel	143/835	19 Apr 1943
Aimwell (W113)	BAT-7	Steel	143/835	8 Apr 1942
Aspirant (W134)	ATR-42	Steel	143/835	3 May 1943
Athlete (W150)	ATR-92	Steel	143/835	13 Nov 43/ lost 17 Jul 45
Bold (W114)	BAT-8	Steel	143/835	21 May 1942
Cheerly (W153)	ATR-95	Steel	143/835	18 Jan 1943
Destiny (W115)	BAT-9	Steel	143/835	1 Jul 1942
Eminent (W116)	BAT-10	Steel	143/835	12 Aug 1942
Emphatic (W154)	ATR-96	Steel	143/835	27 Jan 1944
Favourite (W119)	BAT-3	Steel	143/835	17 Feb 1942
Flare (W151)	ATR-93	Steel	143/835	7 Dec 1943
Flaunt (W152)	ATR-94	Steel	143/835	21 Dec 1943
Integrity (W14)	BAT-4	Steel	143/835	28 Mar 1942
Lariat (W17)	BAT-5	Steel	143/835	10 Aug 1942
Masterful (W20)	BAT-6	Steel	143/835	5 Jun 1942

Ship	U.S. Navy Designation	Hull Type	Length (ft.) / Displ. (tons)	Delivered
Mindful (W135)	*ATR-48*	Steel	143/835	31 Aug 1943
Oriana (W117)	*BAT-1*	Steel	143/835	15 Aug 1942
Patroclus (W118)	*ATR-91*	Steel	143/835	22 Oct 1943
Reserve (W149)	*BAT-11*	Steel	143/835	18 Jul 1942/ later HMAS
Sprightly (W103)	*BAT-12*	Steel	143/835	7 Aug 1942/ later HMAS
Tancred (W104)	*BAT-13*	Steel	143/835	1 Jan 1943/ later HMAS
Vagrant (W136)	*ATR-49*	Steel	143/835	2 Oct 1943
Weasel (W120)	*BAT-14*	Steel	143/835	21 Feb 1943[21]

The HMAS *Reserve* (W149) would serve off eastern Australia and in the Southwest Pacific during the war and receive the battle honour "NEW GUINEA 1943-44." Such awards, earned for combat in a battle or campaign, were displayed on a solid wooden board (traditionally teak) mounted on the vessel's superstructure, carved with the ship's badge and scrolls naming the ship and the associated honours. The board was either left completely unpainted, or with the lettering painted gold.[22]

The British also acquired four American-built *ATR-1*-class ships which, with the twenty-three *Favourite*-class ships, increased to 141 the total number of Royal Navy rescue tugs. The ship prefix HMRT (His Majesty's Rescue Tug) was used for these vessels. However, some documents and references to the rescue tugs associated the much more prevalent HMS (His Majesty's Ship) with their names. To avoid confusion, I use HMS in this book.

Royal Navy *Director*-class Rescue Tugs

Ship	U.S. Navy Designation	Hull Type	Length (ft.) Displ. (tons)	Delivered to the U.K.
Director (W137)	*ATR-17*	Wood	165/852	28 Dec 1943
Emulous (W138)	*ATR-18*	Wood	165/852	2 Feb 1944
Freedom (W139)	*ATR-19*	Wood	165/852	20 Mar 1944
Justice (W140)	*ATR-20*	Wood	165/852	24 Apr 1944[23]

British rescue tugs were largely manned by Merchant Navy crews serving under Royal Navy orders. The Royal Navy had, since 1941, based rescue vessels at Campbeltown in southwest Scotland, and in 1943 the sea service began to assign a rescue tug to every transatlantic convoy. By war's end, the "Campbeltown Navy" had assisted in saving more than three million tons of Allied merchant shipping, as well as over 250 warships, and hundreds of Allied seamen.[24]

RESCUE AND SALVAGE SHIPS (ARS)

U.S. Navy Rescue and Salvage ships (referred to as salvage ships) render assistance to disabled vessels. They provide towing, salvage, diving, and firefighting, and have heavy-lift capabilities. Forty-two salvage ships served during World War II:

- Seven converted 187-foot *Lapwing*-class minesweepers: *Brant, Crusader, Discoverer, Redwing, Viking, Warbler, Willet*
- Nine 183-foot, wooden-hulled *Anchor*-class ships: *Anchor, Extractor, Extricate, Protector, Restorer, Swivel, Valve, Vent, Weight*
- Sixteen 213-foot *Diver*-class ships: *Cable, Chain, Clamp, Curb, Current, Deliver, Diver, Escape, Gear, Grapple, Grasp, Preserver, Safeguard, Seize, Shackle, Snatch*
- Six slightly wider-beamed and faster 213-foot *Bolster*-class ships: *Bolster, Conserver, Hoist, Opportune, Reclaimer, Recovery*
- Four miscellaneous converted merchant ships: *Accelerate* (ex-S.S. *Toteco*), *Harjurand* (ex-S.S. *Olesa*), *Rescuer* (ex-S.S. *Nushagak*), *Tackle* (ex-S.S. *Stanley Dollar*)[25]

Most of these ships served in the expansive Pacific Theater. All were steel-hulled, except for the nine *Anchor*-class ships. They, like the modest 165-foot ATR Rescue Tugs, were built specifically for war duty, based on British plans and specifications for a wooden salvage vessel that the British Government had requested be constructed in the United States. Ultimately, the British received four of these type ships via Lend-Lease: *American Salvor* (BAR-5), *Boston Salvor* (BAR-6), *Lincoln Salvor* (BAR-9), and *Southampton Salvor* (BAR-10).[26]

Eight U.S. Navy salvage ships served in the African, European, or Mediterranean Theaters during the war. Seven earned one or more battle stars for the Europe-Africa-Middle East Campaign ribbon that graced the ribbon board on their deckhouses. *Extricate* received a second battle star later in the war, for her Asiatic-Pacific Campaign ribbon. Three of these eight ships were elderly steel-hulled vessels. *Brant* and *Redwing* were converted World War I minesweepers. *Tackle*, even older, was a former lumber schooner built in 1912. *Extricate, Restorer, Swivel*, and *Weight* were new wooden-hulled *Anchor*-class salvage ships commissioned in 1943. *Diver* was also commissioned in 1943, the lead ship in a class of larger, more robust steel-hulled vessels specifically designated for salvage work.

One of the *Anchor*-class ships, *Weight* (ARS-35), is shown below. One hundred eighty-three feet long, she had a draft of fourteen feet eight inches, a displacement of 1,615 tons, and was propelled by two

Cooper Bessemer diesel-electric engines coupled to two propellers to a maximum speed of 12 knots. She was minimally armed, fitted with a single 3-inch/.50-caliber gun mount and two 20mm anti-aircraft guns. The ship's complement was six officers and fifty-nine enlisted men.[27]

Photo 2-3

Salvage ship *Weight* under way on 27 April 1945. Her flag is at half-mast in honor of President Franklin D. Roosevelt, who died, 12 April 1945.
U.S. Navy photo, now in the collections of the U.S. National Archives

Giving aid to vessels, as Army medics and Navy corpsmen give aid to wounded warriors, tugs performed combat repairs on ships and craft off assault beaches before conveying them to safer areas behind the front lines. Similarly, salvage ships were like field hospitals for damaged vessels. Such duty was still hazardous. *Tackle* was damaged, and *Redwing* sunk, by enemy mines. Collectively, the eight ships, listed below, earned thirteen battle stars during the war (represented by the symbol * in the following table).

Ship	Commanding Officer	Length (ft.) / Displ. (tons)	Commissioned/ Redesignated
***Brant (ARS 32); ex-Brant (AT-132)/Brant (AM-24)	Lt. Harvey Melvin Andersen, USN; first CO of the salvage ship Brant	187/950	5 Sep 1918; 1 Sep 1942 (salvage ship)
*Diver (ARS-5)	Lt. Alexis T. Terrio	213/1,897	23 Oct 1943
**Extricate (ARS-16)	Lt. Amie J. Roy	183/1,615	27 Jul 1943
Redwing (ARS-4); ex-USCGC Redwing (WAT 48)/Redwing (AM 48)	Lt. (jg) Martin C. (Ski) Sibitsky, USN, first CO of the salvage ship Redwing	187/950	17 Oct 1919; 28 Oct 1941 (salvage ship)
**Restorer (ARS-17)	Lt. C. M. Boyd, USNR	183/1,615	6 Oct 1943
*Swivel (ARS-36)	Lt. (jg) Martin C. Sibitsky, USN	183/1,615	6 Oct 1943
**Tackle (ARS-37); ex-W. R. Chamberlain Jr.	Lt. J. M. Gillespie, USNR	310/6,500	Built in 1912; 5 August 1943 (salvage ship)
**Weight (ARS-35)	Lt. Frederick J. Leamond, USNR	183/1,615	14 Aug 1943

Listings of battle stars received by the much larger numbers of tugs that served in the African, European, and Mediterranean Theaters—as well as other campaign and unit awards—are provided in Appendices A, B, C, and F.

3

Wolf Pack Attack on Convoy SC-107

> *Ship [in position] 82, which had drifted astern, was reported torpedoed again and sank. At about this time the senior escort [ship], a British destroyer, passed very close to starboard apparently en route from the rear [of the convoy] to his usual station ahead. When about fifty yards off he hailed with a public address system and said "if you can hear me, wave." As the hundred odd passengers as well as the crew and including the captain could easily hear we all waved. It was then noted that he had two photographers taking pictures of us waving as if cheering. This was not the case.*
>
> —Excerpt from a report by Comdr. Drayton Harrison, USN, commanding officer of the cargo ship USS *Pleiades* (AK-46), on German submarine attacks on Convoy SC-107

The first two tugs to earn battle stars in the American or European Theaters in World War II were the yard tugs *Pessacus* (YT-192) and *Uncas* (YT-242) commanded by two naval reserve officers—both of the rank of lieutenant (junior grade)—Arthur T. Guja and Charles. W. Smith, respectively. The 105-foot steel-hulled *Uncas*, a product of Levingston Shipbuilding in Orange, Texas, had been delivered to the Navy on 26 April 1941. She had good seagoing qualities, a cruising speed of twelve knots, and was fitted with two .30-caliber machine guns to provide her small complement of one officer and thirteen men a modicum of self-defense. The slightly newer and smaller 101-foot *Pessacus* was built in the Ira S. Bushey Shipyard in Brooklyn, New York, and placed in service on 11 August 1942 at the New York Navy Yard. Like *Uncas*, she was propelled by a single diesel engine and could make twelve knots. *Pessacus* had a complement of ten men, and was likely also equipped with a pair of World War I vintage small-caliber machine guns. Both tugs—units of the Atlantic Fleet's Service

Squadron One—had received orders to report to Naval Operating Base, Iceland, at Reykjavik, for duty as harbor tugs.[1]

The German submarine campaign and the resultant Allied ship casualties on the North Atlantic convoy routes had brought about the establishment of salvage bases in Iceland and in Argentia, Newfoundland, and the development of the 165-foot rescue tug as a distinct ship type. *Uncas* and *Pessacus* were too small to venture far offshore and battle rough seas, particularly in the winter, trying to bring torpedoed ships to safe haven. Instead, they were to perform harbor work.[2]

Map 3-1

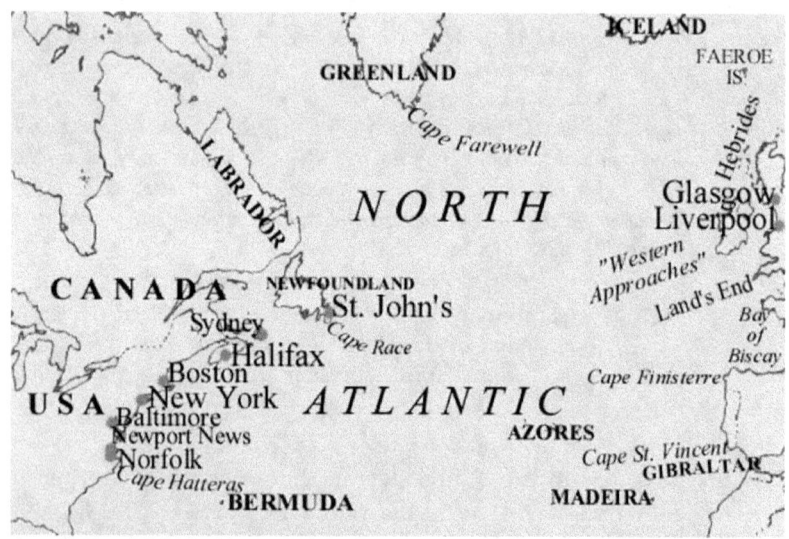

American and British ships and planes operating from Reykjavik, Iceland helped safeguard Allied shipping from German U-boat attacks during Atlantic crossings. Courtesy of http://merchantships.tripod.com

FORMATION OF CONVOY SC-107

Convoy SC-107, with which the tugs would transit to Iceland, formed off Seagirt, New Jersey—a borough touching the Atlantic Ocean in the southeast corner of the state—on 24 October 1942. It was comprised of forty-four Allied merchantmen and five non-combatant U.S. Navy ships: the two yard tugs, yard oiler *Gauger* (YO-55), transport *Gemini* (AP-75), and cargo ship *Pleiades* (AK-46). Once shaped, the convoy proceeded in nine columns with about five ships in each column. The interval between columns was 700 yards, and distance between ships in individual columns 500 yards, but as usual most ships were at a greater distance. This 7-knot convoy was the 107th of the numbered series of "slow convoys" of merchant ships sailing from Sydney or Halifax, Nova Scotia, Canada, or from New York City in the United States, to the United Kingdom.[3]

Four ships of the Royal Canadian Navy Western Local Escort Force—the destroyer HMCS *Buxton* (H96), corvette HMCS *Kamsack* (K171), minesweeper HMCS *Trois Rivieres* (J269), and Royal Navy destroyer HMS *Wanderer* (D74)—screened the convoy between 24 and 28 October 1942. A second group of four combatant ships joined the convoy on 27 October to take over these duties, and remained through 1 November. These were the Canadian destroyer HMCS *Columbia* (I49), corvette HMCS *Fennel* (K194), minesweeper HMCS *Cowichan* (J146), and British destroyer HMS *Walker* (D27). While in Canadian waters, the escort force was augmented on 28-29 October by the minesweeper HMCS *Grandmere* (J258) and the armed yacht HMCS *Elk* (S05). Two additional Canadian corvettes also took up escort duties for short periods, HMCS *Arvida* (K113) from 29 October through 4 November, and HMCS *Regina* (K234) on 30 October for a single day.[4]

Because the U.S. Navy was not then in a position to defend convoys departing America for and returning from Europe, Halifax-based Canadian warships shepherded them between New York and Newfoundland, and brought westbound convoys from Newfoundland to New York. These duties were in addition to the comprehensive network of coastal convoys between Canadian and northern United States ports. Canadian escort vessels also comprised a large quantity of the mid-ocean force that took convoys between Newfoundland and British waters.[5]

SIXTEEN U-BOATS CONVERGE ON THE CONVOY

On 30 October, the German submarine *U-522*, which along with *U-520* and *U-521* was positioned south of Newfoundland, detected Convoy SC-107. Soon these boats and a wolf pack comprised of *U-71*, *U-84*, *U-89*, *U-132*, *U-381*, *U-402*, *U-437*, *U-438*, *U-442*, *U-454*, *U-571*, *U-658*, and *U-704*—sixteen submarines in all—were closing in on the convoy. Following Germany's declaration of war against the United States on 11 December 1941, Adm. Karl Donitz, commander-in-chief U-boats, immediately initiated a submarine campaign off North America, and he continued to send successive groups of submarines. The *Veilchen* ("Violet") Wolf Pack had been stationed in a patrol line eastward of Newfoundland to intercept eastbound convoys. Allied interceptions of radio signals between the submarines left little doubt that the convoy was in imminent danger. The Western Local Escort Force remained with the convoy beyond where it normally broke off, and an air escort was dispatched from the shore. *U-522* attacked the destroyer *Columbia* but was unsuccessful. Two other enemy submarines fell victim to Allied air patrols that day. *U-520* and *U-658* were depth charged by Royal Canadian Air Force Digby and Hudson aircraft, respectively, with the loss of all hands.[6]

The following day, *U-521* and *U-522*—the two submarines nearest the convoy—were driven off by the escort and air patrols as they searched for the convoy, but on 1 November *U-381* sighted the large formation of merchant ships. As the subs converged on his charges, the commander of Canadian Escort Group C4, Lt. Comdr. Desmond W. Piers, grew more and more desperate, as he had only five escort ships—Canadian destroyer HMCS *Restigouche* (H00), which he commanded, corvettes HMCS *Arvida* (K113), HMCS *Algoma* (K127), and HMCS *Amherst* (K148), and Royal Navy corvette HMS *Celandine* (K75)—to battle the wolf pack. His group was a part of the Mid-Ocean Escort Force that provided protection for merchant convoys in transit between Canada and the British Isles, which had assumed the screening duties from the Western Local Escort group. Piers managed to keep the U-boats at bay that night, 1 November. *Restigouche* made large sweeps at the rear of the convoy in an effort to prevent U-boats from closing in on or catching up to the convoy, and the other escorts performed screening duties on the convoy flanks.[7]

WOLF PACK ATTACKS COMMENCE

Beginning after midnight on 2 November, U-boats began to overwhelm the escort ships, and would, over the next three days, sink fifteen merchant vessels and damage another four. The greatest losses occurred on the first day, when:

- *U-402* damaged the British merchant vessel *Empire Sunrise*, and sank the British *Dalcroy*, *Empire Antelope*, and *Empire Leopard*, and the Greek merchantman *Rinos*
- *U-84* sank *Empire Sunrise*
- *U-438* damaged the British merchant vessel *Hartington*
- *U-522* damaged *Hartington*, and sank the British *Maritima* and the Greek *Mount Pelion* and *Parthenon*
- *U-521* sank *Hartington*

These losses occurred despite the arrival that day of the corvette HMCS *Moose Jaw* (K164), and the destroyer HMS *Vanessa* (D29), which had been detached from Convoy HX-212 to reinforce the escort of SC-107.[8]

During the convoy battle, the commanding officer of the *Pleiades* noted in his war diary events detectable from the bridge of his ship, and commented on some of the enemy attacks and defensive measures. He had previously commanded a submarine and a submarine target vessel, and had been in command of the *Pleiades* for over a year with much time spent in convoy in the North Atlantic. Entries made during the early morning darkness of 2 November give hint of the desperate actions of the convoy and escorts during repeated U-boat attacks. Torpedoed merchant ships fired flares signaling their plight. Escorts raced about on the flanks of the convoy, dropping depth charges on sonar contacts. Gun crews aboard some ships indiscriminately opened fire. Both merchant ships and escorts freely fired "snowflakes" in the hopes of illuminating subs on the surface to be engaged with gunfire.[9]

Snowflakes were the products of British signal rockets, which—through the spread of 28 white stars per rocket—created brilliant light to give the gun crews on Navy ships, and Naval Armed Guard gunners aboard merchant vessels, a chance to spot any surfaced U-boats.[10]

In the following entries, particular ships are referred to by their assigned position in the convoy, and not by vessel name:

0013: White flares off port beam [of the *Pleiades*] – radio report No. 12 torpedoed. Many snowflakes observed.
0032: A few depth charges heard to port.
0035: Flares observed to starboard.
0045: Two flares broad on port quarter. General firing of snowflakes.
0058: Radio reported No. 63 and No. 73 torpedoed from starboard [sides of the ships].
0118: Snowflakes observed off starboard quarter and forward of port beam - apparently escorts firing snowflakes freely.
0215: A few depth charges heard off port quarter.
0405: Two flares indicating ship torpedoed on port quarter.
0406: Two more flares on port quarter – may have been only one ship torpedoed. Usual snowflakes.
0410: Flares and snowflakes on starboard quarter – two ships may have been torpedoed.
0413: Ship in 52 position firing 20 MM [naval gun rounds] a few feet over our bridge – personnel took shelter. No enemy beyond this vessel could have been seen by firing ship. Later fire was shifted to a point off starboard bow of this vessel. Much indiscriminate firing by many vessels.

0416: Snowflakes to port and starboard.
0419: Three severe shocks – gauge glasses, etc., in Engine Room broke. Quartermaster striker [a seaman] on Engine Telegraph stopped engines thinking ship was hit. Engines restarted promptly. Ship No. 61 had thought herself torpedoed and turned on one red light to indicate being torpedoed. No escorts had been within several thousand yards. These were not depth charges. No ship hit. No observable geyser of water. These must have been spent torpedoes firing very deep – or might have been magnetically fired torpedoes running at a great depth.
0443: Ship No. 83 and No. 53 (?) torpedoed. Usual snowflakes. There appears to be doubt that No. 53 was torpedoed at this time.
0620: Ship on starboard quarter showed red light.
0656: Sunrise.[11]

Having already sent nine merchant ships to the sea floor on 2 November, the wolf pack continued its grim work the following day as *U-89* sank the British steam merchant *Jeypore* and *U-521* the American tanker *Hahira*. On 4 November, four merchantmen were sunk and one damaged. *U-89* put down the British *Daleby*, and *U-132* damaged the British *Hatimura* and sank the British *Empire Lynx* and the Dutch *Hobbema*. *U-442* then disposed of *Hatimura*. The latter submarine was never heard from again; it apparently fell prey to its victim, and was lost with all hands. It was believed that when ammunition ship *Hatimura* exploded, the U-boat had still been within the lethal radius.[12]

Two days earlier, three escorts were dispatched on 2 November from Hafnarfjörður, a fjord on the southwest coast of Iceland and the site of a naval base used by the British and American navies. United States warships based there supported the Iceland Shuttle, escorting shipping to and from Iceland after taking possession of ships at, or delivering them to a designated mid-ocean convoy meeting point. The cutter UCGC *Ingham* and destroyers *Leary* (DD-158) and *Schenck* (DD-159) arrived in the vicinity of the convoy in the early evening on 4 November, too late to provide any deterrence to the submarine attacks which occurred that day. At 1941, the *Ingham* sighted one of the escorts, HMCS *Algoma*, but not the convoy in the darkness. After spotting snowflakes in the night sky an hour later, she fired three "star shells" (illumination rounds from her No. 3, 4, and 5 guns) in the hope of "catching out" a submarine. The cutter then assumed station five miles astern of the convoy.[13]

TUGS RETRIEVE SURVIVORS OF SUNKEN SHIPS

Following the torpedoing of S.S. *Jeypore*—aboard which Vice Adm. Bertram Chalmers Watson, Royal Navy, the convoy commodore, was embarked—*Pessacus* and *Uncas* retrieved the ship's master, the commodore, six staff members, seventy-four crewmen and eight Naval Armed Guardsmen. Small ships, like yard tugs, with their main deck near the ocean surface, were ideal for plucking survivors from the frigid waters of the North Atlantic but had no medical facilities. Therefore, the men were put aboard *Stockport*, a British rescue ship with a Royal Navy surgeon, a well-staffed sickbay, and accommodations for several hundred survivors. Although rescue ships had expansive freeboard, some employed interesting lifesaving gear to compensate for their height above the sea, including a large dip net for scooping oil-smeared seamen from the briny.[14]

The rescue ship assigned to a convoy was normally stationed at the tail end of the center column to optimize its ability to retrieve, or receive aboard, survivors from ships sunk ahead of it. Small vessels were also usually positioned at the end of a column; thus it was likely that *Uncas* had been on one side of the *Stockport* and *Pessacus* on the other. The tugs also picked up and transferred to *Stockport* seventy-six crewmembers and nine gunners from S.S. *Hatimura*, and retrieved from lifeboats the only sixteen survivors of S.S. *Hobbema*. The nearly six hundred survivors subsequently landed at Reykjavik did not total all the men rescued; some picked up by escorts or merchant ships in the main convoy remained aboard these vessels until put ashore in the United Kingdom.

Photo 3-1

Uncas under way with a barge alongside.
Courtesy of Jim Logan and The National Association of Fleet Tug Sailors

For the considerable contributions made by *Pessacus* and *Uncas* to lifesaving efforts, their commanding officers received Navy and Marine Corps Medals. The medal citation for Lieutenant (junior grade) Guja reads:

> The President of the United States of America takes pleasure in presenting the Navy and Marine Corps Medal to Lieutenant, Junior Grade, Arthur T. Guja, United States Navy, for heroic conduct during World War II. While on a convoy assignment in command of a small, newly commissioned vessel, Lieutenant, Junior Grade, Guja effected the rescue of 113 survivors of a torpedoed ship despite poor visibility and heavy seas. He provided for them aboard his crowded vessel for five days, caring for their needs as adequately as his limited provisions would permit.

The citation for Lt. (jg) Charles W. Smith was similar. It detailed his having rescued eighty-four survivors of a torpedoed ship in spite of poor visibility and rough seas, and providing them the limited facilities of his small ship for five days.[15]

WOLF PACK ATTACKS FINALLY COME TO AN END

The following morning, the three newly arrived escorts took up screening stations in the van and on the flanks of the formation. However, their efforts would not be needed. The 5th of November brought an end to the horrific losses to the enemy submarines of merchant vessels, mariners, and Naval Armed Guardsmen of the convoy. As it neared Iceland, the convoy had closed to within the range of shore-based bombers. Royal Air Force Liberators from Reykjavik damaged *U 89*, and drove off *U-84*, *U-381*, *U-454*, *U-521*, *U-522* and *U-571*.[16]

Under escort by HMS *Celandine* and HMCS *Arvida*, a group of ships—the *Pessacus* and *Uncas*, yard oiler *Gauger*, and British rescue ship S.S. *Stockport*—broke away from the main convoy and proceeded to Reykjavik in the mid-afternoon on 7 November as the convoy continued toward the United Kingdom. These ships arrived at Reykjavik five minutes past midnight on 8 November and landed ashore 539 survivors from eleven merchant vessels. (The below table does not include all the survivors of sunken ships. The crews of some, such as the British S.S. *Empire Lynx* were aboard units of the convoy continuing on to the United Kingdom.)

Convoy SC-107

Nationality and Names of Ships	Number of Survivors	Number of Men Reported Missing
British S.S. *Empire Antelope*	50	0
British S.S. *Dalcroy*	49	0
British S.S. *Empire Leonard*	41	26
British S.S. *Empire Sunrise*	51	0
American S.S. *Hahira*	53	3
British S.S. *Hatimura*	71	19 in boat adrift
Dutch S.S. *Hobbena*	16	28
British S.S. *Jeypore*	91	0
British S.S. *Maritima*	55	0
Greek S.S. *Mount Pelion*	39	0
Greek S.S. *Parthenon*	23	6

Later that day, 8 November, a second group leaving the convoy—the cargo ship *Pleiades*, transport *Gemini*, and two merchantmen, the Icelandic *Bruarfoss* and American *Ann Skakel*—escorted by destroyers *Leary* and *Schenck* arrived at Reykjavik. *Bruarfoss* landed forty-four survivors from the British merchantman S.S. *Daleby*.[17]

Map 3-2

Reykjavik was home to U.S. Naval Operating Base, Iceland and an adjacent airfield from which patrol aircraft operated.

After landing the survivors, *Pessacus* and *Uncas* reported to Naval Operating Base, Iceland for duty as harbor tugs; the 235-foot *Gauger* for duty as district oiler. The officers and men of these three ships, as well as those of the *Gemini* and *Pleiades*, and the Naval Armed Guardsmen aboard merchant vessels *Ann Skakel, Fred W. Weller, Hahira, L. V. Stanford, Olney*, and *Tidewater*, each received a battle star to affix to the American Theater Campaign ribbons on their uniform blouses. The deadly battle between Wolf Pack *Veilchen* and Convoy SC-107 was only a small part of the ongoing Battle of the Atlantic waged "for the protection of shipping, supply and troop transport by United States Atlantic Fleet and Allied Navies against Axis submarines, supporting aircraft, and a few surface ships." The Battle of the Atlantic was the longest campaign of the Second World War and one in which the Royal Canadian Navy played a predominate role. The words "The wholesome sea is at her gates. Her gates both east and west" inscribed over the main doorway to the Parliament Buildings in Ottawa attested to Canada's need for a strong navy. By the last months of the war Canada possessed the third-largest navy in the world after the fleets of the United States and Britain, and approximately 270 ocean escort warships were committed to the Battle of the Atlantic. This account highlights the dangers shipping routinely faced while making Atlantic crossings to Europe or Africa.[18]

4

Salvage and Rescue Tug Services

> *Rescue operations are undertaken to assist persons and ships in distress at sea. The rescue of personnel can be performed by any suitable vessel. The rescue of ships involves a high degree of seamanship, and requires the employment of seagoing vessels, preferably tugs, fitted for towing.*
>
> *Salvage operations are those involved in refloating stranded or sunken vessels and delivering them to repair yards. Salvage operations involve the services of highly specialized technical personnel; the availability of a considerable amount and variety of special salvage gear; and the employment of specially equipped salvage vessels, both self-propelled and non-self-propelled. Salvage may also involve the recovery and lightering of cargo. The assistance of tugs is usually required.*
>
> —U.S. Navy definition of rescue and salvage operations in 1942[1]

The responsibilities and activities of the Navy's Rescue Tug Service and Salvage Service were different, but intertwined. Rescue tugs accompanying assault forces during amphibious landings were somewhat analogous to combat medics ashore, and salvage ships to field hospitals sited in forward areas, but behind the front lines. Upon hearing a shout of "Medic, man down," medical personnel assigned to combat troop units would provide initial first aid and frontline trauma care on the battlefield before evacuation of the soldier to a field hospital. A ship in peril—aground on a hostile shore, on fire, or sinking—might signal "Send a tug," the Navy version of "man down." Tugs were responsible for fighting fire on burning ships and craft, as well as towing disabled vessels into port or, if too badly damaged to allow such action, towing them to a beach and stranding them, or to a sheltered area for anchoring in shallow water. For lesser damage, tugs performed minor repairs to vessels in distress to permit them to continue under their own power, or assisted them in keeping afloat until they could safely make port. Salvage operations were the responsibility of the Shore Establishment under the auspices of the

Bureau of Ships, and—due to their scarcity—salvage vessels were generally not used for rescue operations unless no other suitable ships were available. When salvage vessels were required for rescue service, permission for their use had to first be obtained from the Supervisor of Salvage.²

The Navy had organized a Salvage Service during World War I by obtaining the bulk of its personnel from various salvage companies in the State of New York. After the war, salvage officers of the firm Merritt, Chapman & Scott were carried on the lists of the Naval Reserve for possible future activation at the time of an emergency. However, by World War II, these men were all approaching retirement age and there was no new blood. Acting to remedy this situation, the Navy created a "Salvage Desk" (staff officer billet) within the Bureau of Ships, and established a Salvage Depot at the LaPlaya Fueling Station at Point Loma in San Diego, California.³

Even before World War II, Merritt, Chapman & Scott had a long and illustrious history. The Merritt portion of the firm dated back to the late 1800s. In 1860, the Board of Marine Underwriters of New York began to investigate the causes of mounting losses from shipwrecks along the Atlantic seaboard, and called upon Israel J. Merritt to put marine salvage—an occupation then ad hoc at best and unsavory at worst—on a businesslike basis. Captain Merritt, with a Gloucester mackerel schooner and $8,000 worth of salvage equipment, formed Coast Wrecking. Symbolized by a house flag bearing a black horse on a field of white, the company soon became well-known throughout the shipping world. The steed represented agents in isolated areas that raced on horseback to the nearest telegraph station to notify Coast Wrecking of a ship in distress. Merritt later reorganized the company into Merritt's Wrecking Organization. In a subsequent expansion, Merritt merged with his chief competitor to form the Merritt & Chapman Derrick and Wrecking Company.⁴

The company gained experience in marine investigation and establishing the causes of wrecks and explosions. In 1898, it was employed by the U.S. War Department to determine whether the sinking of the *Maine* (ACR-1) at Havana Harbor, Cuba, on 15 February 1898 was due to an explosion from inside or outside the battleship's hull. The investigation concluded that the explosion was external and attributed it to blast powder—a finding that was a catalyst for the Spanish American War. Company salvage operations expanded during the First World War, and in 1922 a second merger with another competitor resulted in the name Merritt, Chapman, & Scott (MC&S).⁵

The Navy then contracted with Merritt, Chapman & Scott for the use of their salvage vessels as well as associated equipment, personnel, and salvage bases at Kingston, Jamaica; Key West, Florida; and Staten Island, New York. This was the beginning of the World War II Naval Salvage Service which formed one component of the Navy's salvage efforts during the war. The Service—basically an operator of fully equipped and specialized salvage ships—was responsible for offshore salvage operations along America's Atlantic and Pacific coasts, and in the waters of the Caribbean, and off Panama and Alaska. Its vessels did not perform harbor or inshore salvage nor tow disabled ships into port unless other facilities were unavailable or inadequate. The naval districts were responsible for all salvage operations in inshore waters, while those overseas were the responsibility of the fleets.[6]

ACQUISITION OF INITIAL SALVAGE SHIPS

> *A salvage service which hardly exceeds ordinary towage is naturally remunerated on a very different scale from an heroic rescue from imminent destruction.*
>
> —L. J. Lindley, 1884

During its formative years, the Naval Salvage Service received five fully-equipped and civilian-manned salvage vessels from Merritt, Chapman & Scott—*Killerig, Relief, Resolute, Warbler,* and *Willet. Killerig,* built in 1918 by Smith Dock Co., Ltd., Yorkshire, England, operated out of Kingston, Jamaica, while the salvage tugs *Relief* (SP-2170) and *Resolute* (SP-1309) only served the U.S. Navy from 1918 to 1919.

Warbler and *Willet* were two former World War I era *Lapwing*-class minesweepers. Based on satisfactory performance of these two 187-foot steel-hulled ships, the Salvage Service acquired another five of the same type and vintage from other Government owned sources. The *Lapwings* obtained were all still in active service: three were serving as survey ships for the U.S. Coast and Geodetic Survey Service, one was employed as a Coast Guard cutter, and the fifth was an active minesweeper on 1 June 1942, when the Navy reclassified it as a fleet tug. A list of the *Lapwing*-class minesweepers-turned-salvage ships follows:

Salvage Ship	Commissioned	Placed in Service as a Salvage Ship
Viking ARS-1 (ex-*Flamingo* AM-32/USC&GS *Guide*)	12 Feb 1919	3 Jan 1942
Crusader ARS-2 (ex-*Osprey* AM-29/USC&GS *Pioneer*)	7 Jan 1919	17 Sep 1941
Discoverer ARS-3 (ex-*Auk* AM-38/USC&GS *Discoverer*)	31 Jan 1919	26 Aug 1941
Redwing ARS-4 (ex-AM-48/WAT 48)	17 Oct 1919	28 Oct 1941
Warbler ARS-11 (ex-AM-53)	22 Dec 1919	13 Sep 1941
Willet ARS-12 (ex-AM-54)	29 Jan 1920	13 Sep 1941
Brant ARS-32 (ex-AM-24/AT-132)	5 Sep 1918	1 Sep 1942[7]

The vessels acquired were sent to shipyards for modifications similar to those previously made to *Warbler* and *Willet*. Following completion of this work, *Viking* operated from San Diego and San Pedro, California, and *Discoverer* at Port Angeles, Washington. *Crusader* was based in the Canal Zone to support the Fifteenth Naval District headquartered at Balboa, Panama. These salvage ships, along with *Warbler* and *Willet*, were operated by Merritt, Chapman & Scott and manned with civilian personnel. *Brant* and *Redwing*, which operated in the North Atlantic and the Mediterranean, were commissioned ships and had Navy crews. The ships listed in the above table did not constitute the full measure of salvage vessels which Merritt, Chapman & Scott, and Navy crews would operate during the war, only the initial accessions.[8]

By the time of the Japanese attack on Pearl Harbor, Hawaii, on 7 December 1941 the Naval Salvage Service had accumulated a considerable stock of salvage gear in San Diego, and had decided to establish a school for salvage officers and enlisted men. The personnel obtained via the contract with Merritt, Chapman & Scott were all getting old. Some of the officers were seventy years of age and it was apparent they would not be able to continue hard service aboard ship. The Salvage Service was also concerned that the supply of available tugs was inadequate and thus it requested that the Navy Department ease existing specifications on what was desired in a seagoing tug in order to get something that could be built quickly and put in commission. (The resultant ATR rescue tug is discussed in Chapter Two.) Exacerbating this situation, in the view of the Salvage Service, was that existing management and operation of the few tugs that were operating on the East Coast of the United States was very poor because officers assigned to Naval District staffs did not understand the strengths and limitations of the tugs that they were directing.[9]

ESTABLISHMENT OF THE RESCUE TUG SERVICE

> *The impulsive desire to save human life when in peril is one of the most beneficial instincts of humanity, and is nowhere more salutary in its results than in bringing help to those who, exposed to destruction from the fury of winds and waves, would perish if left without assistance.*
>
> —Cockburn, C.J., Scaramanga v. Stamp (1880), L. R. 5 Com. Pl. D. 304.

After some missteps following the collision of the American merchant vessel S.S. *Brazos* and the British aircraft carrier HMS *Archer* off Norfolk, Virginia, on 13 January 1942 the Navy set up a central office for the control of tugs. The new organization was located in New York and placed under Rear Adm. Adolphus Andrews who, as commander Eastern Sea Frontier, was responsible for the coastal waters from Canada to Jacksonville, Florida, extending out to a nominal distance of two hundred miles. Edwin Moran, an executive of the Moran Towing Company based in New York, was selected as the adviser for the admiral on the newly established Rescue Tug Service and, compensatory with his position and duties, he was commissioned a Navy commander.[10]

Both the number and types of station tugs employed in the Navy Rescue Tug Service underwent a significant change in 1943. Before this time, commander Eastern Sea Frontier had maintained oceangoing tugs manned by civilian crews for operation in rescue service at strategic stations along the coast. At the beginning of 1943, six tugs were on station along the Eastern Seaboard of the United States. Over the course of the year, four of them—*Henry W. Card*, *Cumco*, *Thomas E. Moran*, and *Samson*—were withdrawn from Rescue Service duty, and a fifth, *Wellfleet*, sank off Cape Hatteras as a result of a collision with the merchant tanker S.S. *Edward L. Doheny* on 2 March. Three new tugs were acquired but, although substantially better with respect to sea-keeping qualities, they could not fully compensate for the five vessels they replaced. To fill the gap, increased dependence was necessarily placed upon the fleet tugs (ATs) assigned to naval districts. The station tugs and the ATs constituted the basic rescue units, supplemented by other available vessels suitable for rescue operations. A listing of the station tugs and fleet tugs of the Naval Rescue Tug Service in 1943 is shown in the below table:

Civilian Station Tugs

Station Tugs	Location Where Based	Disposition in 1943
Yaquina Head	Cape May, New Jersey	Temporary service 7-15 Nov 1943
Rescue	New York, New York	Acquired 9 April 1943
Samson	New York, New York	Withdrawn 7 September 1943
Cumco	Norfolk, Virginia	Withdrawn 3 February 1943
P. F. Martin	Morehead City, North Carolina	In service at year's end
Trinidad Head	Charleston, South Carolina	Acquired 9 October 1943
Wellfleet	Charleston, South Carolina	Sank off Cape Hatteras
Dry Tortugas	Key West, Florida	In service at year's end
Henry W. Card	Key West, Florida	Withdrawn 17 January 1943
Thomas E. Moran	Key West, Florida	Withdrawn 3 September 1943

Fleet Tugs Assigned to Naval Districts

Tugs	Date Built	Location Where Based	Struck
Ferguson Steel, Buffalo, New York (156-foot, 1,000 ton ships)			
Allegheny (AT-19)	18 May 1918	Cape May, New Jersey	25 Sep 1946
Sagamore (AT-20)	8 Jun 1918	New York, New York	28 Jan 1947
Umpqua (AT-25)	23 Mar 1920	Charleston, South Carolina	3 July 1946
Wandank (AT-26)	23 Mar 1920	Boston, Massachusetts	1946 or 1947
Puget Sound Naval Shipyard, Bremerton, Washington (157-foot, 1,000 ton ship)			
Sciota (AT-30)	13 Nov 1919	Norfolk, Virginia	8 May 1946
Newport News Shipbuilding, Newport News, Virginia (152-foot ship)			
Acushnet (AT-63)	1908	Norfolk, Virginia	8 Jan 1946[11]

During 1943, the Rescue Service—through the operation of the above tugs and spot contracted vessels acquired as a need for them arose—provided assistance to ninety vessels that were stranded along the coast or were in distress at sea by reason of collision, breakdown, enemy action, or stress of weather. The station tugs manned by civilian crews and commercial vessels procured for specific missions did not have any Navy codebooks aboard. Accordingly, communication with these vessels was via plain language. When tugs were accompanied by a Navy escort ship, naval messages were transmitted to her for relay to them by visual signal. In 1944, the Navy reclassified its fleet tugs (AT) as old fleet tugs (ATO) or Yard Tugs (YT).[12]

WARTIME TOWING AND SALVAGE REQUIRMENTS

> *All salvage jobs are unique. This is certain because every casualty is defined by the characteristics of the particular ship and cargo, the location and ambient conditions. Moreover, the type of salvage assets available may determine the type of operation possible and predict its chance of success.*
>
> —Bob Umbdenstock[13]

The Navy "salvors"—seamen and engineers specially trained in marine salvage—worked closely with the men of the civilian station tugs and the Navy fleet, rescue, and auxiliary tugs during World War II. Their often dangerous work included the recovery of cargo or other property from shipwrecks, the refloating of ships stranded or sunk, and the salvage of ships that were damaged but still afloat. There was also a requirement for clearance salvage, which involved the removal or salvage of vessels purposely sunk by enemy forces in harbors or waterways to deny the use of these facilities to the Allies.

LAFAYETTE DISASTER SPURS THE ESTABLISHMENT OF A DIVING SCHOOL

As the Rescue Tug Service was being set-up in 1942, the Salvage Service was frustrated in its plans to organize schools for training personnel. The capsizing of the transport *Lafayette* (AP-53)—the former French liner *Normandie*—and the resultant mammoth effort to raise her, highlighted the deficiency in numbers of Navy salvage personnel. While undergoing conversion alongside Pier 88 in New York City Harbor, the ship caught fire and heeled over on 9 February 1942 due to the vast amount of water poured into her by firefighters, city fireboats, and tugboats.[14]

The well-known and experienced firm Merritt, Chapman & Scott (MC&S) was contracted for the ambitious job of raising the *Lafayette*. At that time it was the world's most-expensive salvage operation and perhaps the most famous one performed by that firm. The Navy placed Capt. William A. Sullivan of the Bureau of Ships in charge. Sullivan, who as Chief of Navy Salvage, Supervisor of Salvage, and manager of the Naval Salvage Service, headed both technical and operational aspects of Navy Salvage. The nineteen-month operation presented an opportunity for establishing a diving school at Pier 88 to train a large number of Navy men in salvage. Through the joint effort of the Salvage Service and MC&S, the school was established. Sullivan explained the criteria for selection of personnel and their subsequent utilization:

> We had ordered to the school Naval Reserve officers who had been graduate engineers. We attempted as far as possible to get men that had one to two years of sea duty. These officers were given a course in diving to qualify them at 75 foot depths. They were given a two-month course in Naval Architecture so that they knew something about ship stability and trim and the stability of damaged vessels. Then I gave them a course of lectures in various types of salvage work and a selected list of case histories of salvage operations to read and study. When not receiving instructions in school we used them as foremen on the work that was in progress on the *LAFAYETTE*.
>
> We also established a school for Naval divers at the Pier. The Bureau of Naval Personnel ordered at first about 150 Naval mechanics, carpenters, ship fitters, shipwrights, etc. to this school for instruction. As these men were trained on the Pier and became proficient in diving we employed them in the various jobs on the *LAFAYETTE*. The major portion of the work on the *LAFAYETTE* was undertaken by civilian divers employed by the Naval Salvage Service through the agency of Merritt, Chapman & Scott.[15]

Photo 4-1

Lafayette rolled over and sank alongside Pier 88 in New York City Harbor due to the quantity of water poured into her to combat a fire on board.
Photo is from the collections of the U.S. National Archives

Photo 4-2

Commodore William A. Sullivan
http://www.pa59ers.com/library/James/images/lj19.jpg

The school would train more than twenty-five hundred officer and enlisted salvors during the war. Most of the graduates were Navy men, but there were also some Army and Coast Guard personnel, and officers and men from Allied navies.[16]

Over the course of the salvage operation, MC&S cut away *Lafayette*'s superstructure, closed up all the openings, and ultimately succeeded in righting the ship on 7 August 1943. The troop transport was reclassified as an aircraft and transport ferry (APV-4) on 15 September 1943 and dry docked the following month. Following a thorough inspection, the ship was declared a total loss due to extensive damage to her hull, deterioration of her machinery, and the necessity to employ the manpower engaged in the ship conversion on other projects deemed more critical to the war effort. *Lafayette* was stricken from the Navy list on 11 October 1945 and a year later was sold for scrap to Lipsett, Inc. of New York City. While the former liner never served as a Navy troop transport as was intended, the salvage work produced scores of highly skilled salvage officers and divers who would be vital to the recovery and emergency repair of vessels damaged during World War II.[17]

SALVAGE FORCE ESTABLISHED IN "THE MED"

Following the Allied invasion of North Africa, Sullivan was ordered to Africa to oversee clearance salvage requirements there, whereupon he terminated his active participation in the Naval Salvage Service. During his tenure as the head of the organization, the Service had successfully salvaged approximately eighty-four vessels. Sullivan selected six salvage officers and six divers from the school and in a specially chartered Pan American clipper left New York in late November 1942. Upon arrival at Casablanca, the group found three vessels there that had been sent to support salvage operations.[18]

Brant and *Redwing* were identical to the former *Lapwing*-class minesweepers that the Naval Salvage Service had been operating so successfully on America's East Coast with Merritt, Chapman & Scott personnel. Up to this point in the war, they had been employed along North Atlantic convoy routes—*Brant* operating out of Argentia, Newfoundland, and *Redwing* from the salvage base in Iceland—provided towing and salvage assistance to the victims of U-boat attacks. Civilian-manned salvage vessels of this type carried a crew of twenty-one and an equal number of salvage men. However, under Navy requirements for *Brant* and *Redwing*, a crew of forty-six officers and men was needed to operate and maintain the salvage ships. This permitted no specialized salvage men to be carried unless additional bunks were fitted aboard, and the only space available for additional berthing was in the holds of the ship which normally carried salvage gear. Thus, *Brant* and *Redwing* carried almost no salvors and the salvage gear they carried was insufficient for the harbor clearance problems that existed at Casablanca. Ultimately, additional salvors were put aboard these ships—and were provided sleeping accommodations on deck or wherever else possible. The third vessel, *Cherokee*, was a modern fleet tug, which carried some pumps and other miscellaneous salvage gear.[19]

After surveying the work required for removing the ships, both large and small, that were sunk or partially sunk in the harbor, Sullivan sent a wire to the Navy Department asking for twelve additional divers to assist the six he'd brought with him. Locally, Rear Adm. John L. Hall Jr., USN, the commander, Moroccan Sea Frontier, drafted about sixty men from various ships in the harbor and from the Naval Operating Base being organized at Casablanca. Only a portion of these men were skilled artificers able to fabricate devices as needed and none were divers.[20]

These limited numbers of support ships and men were the beginning of the Salvage force in the Mediterranean. The Navy sent a considerable amount of salvage gear to the theater, which was, unfortunately, shipped in cargo vessels mixed up with stores for the Army. These vessels were unloaded by the Army, and most of the gear was delivered to Army supply dumps and was lost. After Sullivan took the matter up with General Patton, he arranged for the Army engineers to provide the salvage force similar gear in kind. The Bureau of Ships later sent more gear, and soon the force had a well-stocked storehouse of the necessary equipment.[21]

5

Invasion of Sicily – Operation HUSKY

> *The amphibious assaults were uniformly successful. The only serious threat was an enemy counterattack on D plus one day against the 1st Infantry Division when a German tank force drove across the Gela plain to within one thousand yards of the DIME beaches. The destruction of this armored force by naval gunfire delivered by U.S. cruisers and destroyers, and the recovery of the situation through naval support, was one of the most noteworthy events of the operations.*
>
> —Vice Adm. Henry K. Hewitt, USN,
> commander Western Naval Task Force[1]

On the night of 9-10 July 1943, Allied forces commenced Operation HUSKY—the code word for the invasion of Sicily—which launched the Italian Campaign. This large scale amphibious and airborne operation, followed by six weeks of ground combat that ended on 17 August, drove Axis (Italian and German) air, land, and naval forces from the island. It also opened sea lanes in the Mediterranean for use by the Allies and helped topple Italian dictator Benito Mussolini from power. On 24 July 1943, the Italian Grand Council of Fascism voted a motion of no confidence against Mussolini. That same day, King Victor Emmanuel III replaced him with Marshal Pietro Badoglio and had him arrested.[2]

Mussolini did not remain in captivity for long. Less than seven weeks later, a group of German paratroopers freed him from the Campo Imperatore Hotel where he was being held high in the Apennine Mountains. The commandos landed on the mountain from DFS 230 gliders and overwhelmed Mussolini's captors. Otto Skorzeny, a German Waffen-SS officer whom Hitler had personally selected as the field commander for the mission, greeted Mussolini with "Duce [his nickname meaning "the leader"], the Führer has sent me to set you free!" Mussolini replied, "I knew that my friend would not forsake me!" Mussolini was made leader of the Italian Social Republic (a German puppet state comprising the German-occupied portion of Italy). Near the end of the war in late April 1945, with total defeat looming, he tried to escape north. He was captured and executed near Lake Como by Italian partisans, after which his body was then taken to Milan, where it was hung upside down at a service station for public viewing and to provide confirmation of his demise.[3]

The plan for Operation HUSKY called for the amphibious assault of Sicily by two armies concentrated at the southeastern end of the island, with all landings scheduled for D-day to be at the same H-hour. British forces including the 1st Canadian Infantry Division were to assault the southern Sicilian coast to the east of Pozzalo, and the east coast, south of Syracuse; American forces the south coast in the Gulf of Gela. The landings would be supported by naval gunfire, tactical bombing, and close air support. General Dwight D. Eisenhower, commander-in-chief Allied Forces North Africa, was the overall commander. The British general Sir Harold Alexander was his second in command and the Land Forces/Army Group commander. British admiral Andrew Cunningham, the Allied Naval Force Commander, had under him Vice Adm. Bertram Ramsay, RN, commander Eastern Naval Task Force, and Vice Adm. Henry K. Hewitt, USN, commander Western Naval Task Force formed around the U.S. Eighth Fleet.[4]

Map 5-1

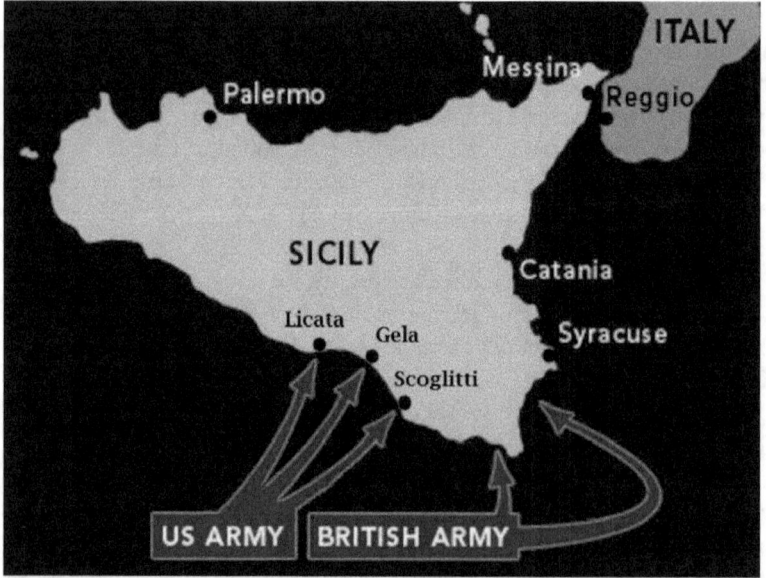

The American Western Naval Task Force assaulted beaches in the Gulf of Gela, and the British Eastern Naval Task Force south of Syracuse.

Invasion of Sicily – Operation HUSKY

This work's central theme is the participation of Allied salvage forces in this and other amphibious assaults. Before proceeding further into details of Operation HUSKY, the next several pages are devoted to an overview of the Eighth Fleet, supporting bases in North Africa, and of William A. Sullivan and Harvey M. Andersen, two key American salvage officers in the Mediterranean.

ESTABLISHMENT OF THE EIGHTH FLEET

The United States Eighth Fleet was titled "U.S. Naval Forces, Northwest African Waters" when Vice Adm. Henry K. Hewitt established it on 16 March 1943 upon his arrival at Algiers, Algeria, the site of his headquarters. The command, which received the dual designation of U.S. Eighth Fleet/U.S. Naval Forces, Northwest African Waters in May, was comprised of six subordinate task forces:

Task Force	Title
81	U.S. Amphibious Force, Northwest African Waters (included Landing Craft and Bases)
82	Moroccan Sea Frontier Forces
83	U.S. Naval Operating Base, Oran
84	U.S. Naval Salvage Force
85	Advanced Base Force
89	Miscellaneous Force[5]

SUPPORTING BASES IN NORTH AFRICA

Landing craft bases were established at Bizerte and Tunis, Tunisia, in May 1943. These cities offered the only deep water ports in Tunisia and lay a mere 120 miles from the ports and airfields of western Sicily. Fleet tug *Nauset* reported to the amphibious force on 4 June. She and *Narragansett*, *Hopi*, and *Moreno* comprised the complement of fleet tugs assigned to the Eighth Fleet. The identity of the harbor tugs also assigned is sketchy; many references do not identify them individually, but instead refer to them in collective terms such as "various 65-ton YTs." Eleven YTs left Arzew, Algeria, on 13 June for duty at Bizerte and Tunis.[6]

Tugs assigned to Landing Craft and Bases (Task Force 81) worked closely with Task Force 84 (the salvage force commanded by Capt. William A. Sullivan) and Navy Salvage Base, Dellys, Algeria, which Sullivan established on 8 June 1943. Dellys—a small coastal town in northern Algeria almost due north of Tizi-Ouzou and just to the east of the Sebou River—dated back to Roman times when it was known as Rusuccuru. The first Navymen to arrive at Dellys were carried there aboard an old Pacific coast lumber schooner, the S.S. *W. R. Chamberlain Jr.*, built in 1912. She would be commissioned salvage ship *Tackle* (ARS-37) on 5 August 1943.[7]

Chamberlain had slipped quietly out of the inner harbor of Algiers in pre-dawn darkness on 8 June 1943 and picked her way through the maze of protective anti-submarine nets before pointing her bow eastward. Two British motor launches escorted her as she trailed a thin black line of smoke from her stack while steering a course toward the rising sun. The day broke with a cloudless sky and the African sun roused men sleeping on cots crowded on the weather deck of the 310-foot ship. Some men tried to extend their sleep by taking shelter under a canvas tarpaulin, but even under cover they were unable to escape the heat of the morning sun.[8]

Even though the journey was only about sixty miles, the roughly two hundred and fifty officers and men aboard were full of expectancy and eagerness to reach their destination. Most of the salvage men new to the Mediterranean, manned the rail to gather in the scenic wonders of the North African coastline. At about 1400 Cape D'Jinet and a few minutes later the breakwater of the small harbor of Dellys came into view. *Chamberlain* crossed the menacing bar just outside the breakwater and turned into the entrance channel to make port. As she steamed into the harbor, her motor launch escorts drew closer to her, waved farewell, and headed back to their base. The harbor was located in a sheltered cove between two points, well protected by a fringe of mountains on the south and eastern side and by a pier and a breakwater on the seaside. Near water's edge was a yacht club and behind it a steep and picturesque hillside with the small town of Dellys located one hundred fifty feet up the slope. Waiting to greet the ship was an American naval officer attired in the tropical uniform of white shorts and white shirt, brandishing a bamboo swagger stick. As soon as the gangway was put over, a steady stream of salvors began to pour ashore.[9]

The following morning, all hands were mustered along the breakwater at 0900, and Lt. Comdr. Harvey M. Andersen, USN, now attired in "blues" with row on row of service ribbons and decorations, read his orders. He then placed the salvage base in commission, and addressed the assembled officers and men. His discourse was brief and to the point. He intended to run a happy and efficient command.[10]

Andersen was a "mustang" (former enlisted man) and recipient of the Navy Cross. He had received the medal for his actions 16 months earlier on 4 February 1942 aboard *Marblehead* (CL-12) as damage control officer, following an attack by Japanese bombers on the cruiser during the Battle of Makassar Strait.

Later that day, 9 June 1943, the harbor tug *Resolute* and LCTs *196* and *200* entered the harbor and tied up alongside the pier. In the ensuing months, the base would provide salvage parties led by one or more of its officers for fleet and harbor tugs. If at all possible, salvors repaired damaged ships and craft in theater. If enemy-inflicted damage to a ship was too great for "battle repairs," a tug brought it to Dellys for repairs. Salvage ship *Tackle* (ARS-37) served as a station ship (mobile base of operations) for harbor clearance units.[11]

IMPORTANCE OF NAVAL SALVAGE

Some salvage requirements resulted from storm damage or navigation error by a ship—not enemy action. Such was the case of S.S. *Lancaster*, an old American freighter built in 1918. The ship ran aground on the rocks off El Hank Light, a lighthouse near Casablanca on 30 December 1942. Sullivan was then still a Navy captain, and Andersen a lieutenant. First Sullivan, and then Andersen, who had taken command of *Brant* after leaving the light cruiser *Marblehead*, noted the condition of the wrecked ship at various stages of the tide. It lay broadside to the reef and inside the breakers except at low water. Salvage did not appear feasible, but the ship's cargo—teletypes, howitzers, motor vehicles, radar equipment, airplanes, food, and ammunition—was too valuable to be abandoned. The officers decided to position three shallow-draft tank landing craft between the ship and the shore at low water and keep them there in the protective lee of the wreck during the full tide. An article published in the *Syracuse Herald-Journal* about the salvage operation described the two principal U.S. Navy salvage officers in the Mediterranean in action:

> Today we had the pleasure of watching a gang of sharp-witted, heavily-muscled Americans…bent on stripping the ship before she broke her back and spilled it all into the sea. The leading "pirate" of the salvage operation was Capt. W. A. Sullivan, U.S. Navy, one of the world's best salvage men…. A native of Lawrence, Mass., Sullivan is a born rover.
>
> In immediate charge of this particular looting expedition was Lt. Harvey M. Anderson, U.S.N., of Chicago. He has been in the Navy 24 years, got the Navy Cross when, as chief damage control officer aboard the U.S.S. *Marblehead*, he patched enough bulkheads to bring the famous cruiser back to port for the [ensuing] Battle of [the] Java [Sea].[12]

The article detailed the efforts of the Navy salvage men, assisted by Army stevedores, to save cargo before pounding waves broke the ship apart. Compressors placed in the LCTs were used to run the ship's steam winches, and stevedores discharged the cargo into the landing craft under Andersen's supervision. Andersen noted and quickly curtailed dangerous activities of a few men presumably unaware of the potential consequences of their actions:

> The ship was a mess. Her fuel oil tanks had been breached and thousands of gallons of sticky stuff had flowed into the holds. When we went aboard, the men were working in rubber suits, laboriously clearing the litter of boxes, beams, tin cans, loose smoke generators and other junk from the principal objects of their attention. These were a collection of trucks, stacks of shells and 500-pound bombs which occupied No. 2 hold, the scene of today's work.
>
> Some of the stuff was dangerous. Box after box of percussion caps were plucked out of the goo and Lieutenant Anderson used language unbecoming to an officer when he found a couple of boys dropping them on the deck. He actually threatened to use physical violence when he discovered some other fellows tossing smoke grenades overboard. But most of the boys were working like beavers and the hold was being cleared fast and efficiently.
>
> Such a job is a race against time. You can work only by daylight and once you start operating on the lower layers of the cargo, can only do it at low tide. The weather is sticky and the ship so low at the beginning of the salvage work caused the loss of one fighter plane which was on deck, and since then had bashed several trucks to pieces.[13]

At the time the article was written, the salvors had retrieved an entire radio station worth one million dollars, a large assortment of 105 and 155mm guns and three fighter planes. Large and small trucks and jeeps had gone ashore and most of the stuff had been cleaned, repaired and sent to the units to which it was consigned. Ultimately, the results of the cargo salvaged justified the effort. The airplanes were salvaged for spare parts, and most of the vehicles, all of the artillery, communications and electronics gear, and much of the food and ammunition also proved usable. Though the ship was lost, the cargo, which was far more valuable, was not.[14]

OPERATION HUSKY FORCES

Over 3,200 ships, craft, and boats made up the Allied naval forces assembled to launch the invasion of Sicily. The Western Naval Task Force—of more than 1,700 vessels—was charged with landing the American invasion troops on the southwest coast of Sicily at Licata, Gela, and Scoglitti. The soldiers carried by the British Eastern Naval Task Force were to land on beaches on the southeastern side of the island. Lt. Gen. George S. Patton and his Seventh Army would push across the island to secure Palermo, and then swing east to Messina, while British general Sir Bernard Montgomery drove his Eighth Army north to Syracuse, Catania, and Messina. The U.S. Army Air Force and British Royal Air Force were tasked to provide air support.[15]

WESTERN NAVAL TASK FORCE

The ships of Admiral Hewitt's Western Task Force sailed from or staged through six different Algerian or Tunisian harbors. The task force was divided into three component attack forces charged with landing the American troops in the Gulf of Gela, with the 3rd Infantry Division coming ashore on the westernmost beaches, the 45th Infantry on the easternmost beaches, and the 1st Infantry on beaches lying between the other two areas.

Attack Force Commander	Task Force	Embarked Troops/Objective
Rear Adm. Richard L. Conolly, USN	JOSS (TF 86)	3rd Infantry Division: capture the town of Licata and its port
Rear Adm. John L. Hall Jr., USN	DIME (TF 81)	1st Infantry Division: capture Ponte Olivo Airfield near the town of Gela
Rear Adm. Alan G. Kirk, USN	CENT (TF 82)	45th Infantry Division: capture the airfields at Comiso and Biscari near the fishing village of Scoglitti[16]

Supporting the attack forces were the Control Force (TF 80)—made up of the Force flagship, (80.1), Escort Group (80.2), Screening Group (80.3), Demonstration Group (80.4), Minelaying Group (80.5), and Reserve Group (80.6)—and the Train (TF 86). The term "Train" was short for Fleet Train (today, known as the Service Force). The fleet train included tenders, oilers, stores ships, and ammunition ships.[17]

Allocated among the attack forces were the salvage ship *Brant* (ARS-32), four fleet tugs: *Hopi* (ATF-71), *Moreno* (ATF-87), *Narragansett* (ATF-88), and *Nauset* (ATF-89); two large harbor tugs: *Intent* (YT-

459) and *Resolute* (YT-458); and four smaller harbor tugs: YTs *161, 165, 186,* and *197*. A primary task of the tugs would be to salvage tank landing ships and craft for their return to service and to keep the beaches clear for subsequent landings. Salvage normally involved firefighting and combat repairs in addition to towing. When large numbers of ships and craft engaged in fiercely opposed amphibious landings, there were increased incidents of damage or groundings.

LOSS OF SALVAGE SHIP *REDWING*

Brant was a substitute for *Redwing*, which had struck a mine off Bizerte, Tunisia, on 29 June 1943 and was lost. At the time of this incident the salvage ship had four harbor tugs—YTs *154, 197, 161,* and *186*—in tow astern. The blast tore a large hole in *Redwing*'s hull plating, port side at frame 30 just below the bridge, and lifted the main deck under and forward of the bridge. The result was a wrecked bridge, both 20mm guns in the circle deck forward of the bridge torn from their fastenings, and five officers and eight men blown overboard. The commanding officer, Lt. (jg) Martin C. Sibitsky, ordered the towline to the YTs tripped and one life raft released for the men in the water. He called the YTs alongside to assist, but before the harbor tugs could make up to *Redwing*, she began to list dangerously, and Sibitzky gave the order to abandon.[18]

Photo 5-1

Salvage ship *Redwing* sinking off Bizerte, Tunisia, due to damage from an enemy mine. Naval Historical Center Photo by Ted Dicecco of Avondale, Pennsylvania

The YTs retrieved from the sea two injured officers and two wounded men, the remaining survivors, and the remains of one man. Two officers and two men were not recovered and were presumed lost. Upon realizing that his ship was still afloat, Sibitzky gave orders to the tugs to take her in tow and try to beach her. Three of the YTs made up to *Redwing* and set course for the swept channel off Bizerte. En route, *Resolute* arrived from Bizerte to lend a hand, with fleet tug *Nauset* standing by to render assistance. At about 1005, as *Redwing* was off the entrance, with decks awash but closing the beach, a British cruiser or large destroyer passed her at high speed, close aboard. The final paragraph of Sibitzky's report on the loss of his ship conveyed her tragic ending:

> It is felt that the wake from the cruiser or destroyer caused the REDWING to roll over and finally sink. The REDWING sank at 1019 in position 37° 19' N. 9° 55' E. in 27 fathoms of water.[19]

PEDIGREE OF TUGS ASSIGNED TO THE LANDINGS

The large harbor tugs *Intent* and *Resolute* had an interesting lineage. They were laid down at Gulfport Boiler and Welding Works Inc., Port Arthur, Texas, as HMS *Intent* and HMS *Resolute* for transfer to Great Britain under the Lend-Lease program. However, the U.S. Navy decided to retain the two ships—which, rated at 1,000 horsepower and diesel-electric powered, could make 11.5 knots—following their completion in 1942. Little is known about their ensuing duty, but the tugs passed from Army to Navy control on 23 April 1943 and the next day reported to commander Landing Craft and Bases, United States Amphibious Force, Northwest African Waters. This command was located at a former French naval base and dockyard at Ferryville on the Lake of Bizerte, near Bizerte, Tunisia, currently in use as a landing craft and general repair base. At some point, the Navy renamed the *Intent* and *Resolute*, *Edenshaw* and *Evea*, respectively. It is unclear when this action occurred. In 1943, war diary entries of a particular ship might refer to *Resolute* by that name, and another as *Evea*. The same lack of convention held true for sister ship *Intent/Edenshaw*.[20]

The much smaller *YT-161* and *165* were built in 1941 by Luders Marine at Stamford, Connecticut, and *YT-186* and *YT-197* a year later. The builder of the latter two craft is unknown. Spanning just 66 feet in length with a 17-foot beam and a 5-foot draft, these small YTs were ideal for operations in shallow, restricted waters, except that they did not possess the power of fleet tugs, or large harbor tugs such as *Evea* and *Edenshaw*. Additionally, while their single 240-shaft-horsepower diesel engine was adequate to propel the 65-ton tugs, there was no redundancy should it fail. During the invasion of Sicily, small YTs assisted *Hopi* by taking her tow wire to vessels stranded on the beach, and separately conducted independent shallow water salvage operations.[21]

Photo 5-2

YT-197 under way in the harbor at Bizerte, Tunisia, in 1944.
Courtesy of Fred Reep Jr. and NavSource

MOVEMENT TO SICILY AND THE BEACH ASSAULT

> *When the enemy uses parachute flares of the quality and intensity employed by the GAF [German Air Force] in the CENT Area, little advantage in attempting to land in darkness remains. Under these flares, our ships, landing craft, boats, etc., are very visible. Above the flare is pitch black; the only gun defense being blind firing, using radar. When such illumination is anticipated, such as off the coasts of France, it is for consideration whether H-Hour should not be about 10-15 minutes after dawn. Precise landing on exact beaches should then be possible; gunfire support on definite targets would be easier; and anti-aircraft defense of the ships offshore would be improved.*
>
> —Rear Adm. Alan G. Kirk, USN,
> commander CENT Attack Force,
> in his report on Operation HUSKY[22]

The fleet tugs *Brant*, *Hopi*, *Narragansett*, and *Nauset*; harbor tug *Intent*; and yard tugs *YT-161*, *165*, *186*, and *197* departed Bizerte on 8 July as part of Convoy TJS-1 (JOSS Slow Convoy). Ordered speed aboard the fleet tug *Hopi*, which was towing two bridge pontoons, was 45-

propeller-shaft RPMs correlating to six knots. During the forenoon of 9 July, the seas, hitherto at all times calm, began to make up. At 1100, the wind was Force 4 and by 1630, Force 6. By the time the formation passed Gozo light in early evening, the LSTs were having difficulty making eight knots, LCIs were taking "seas over solid" (solid waves were crashing down on their decks), and the smaller escort craft were making heavy weather of it. Although these conditions did not impede the troop transport ships, smaller craft fared poorly—particularly the LCI(L)s loaded with soldiers, and the YTs.[23]

In the early evening, various task groups of Task Force 81 rendezvoused at Point Yoke, five miles from Gozo light—sited on a same-named island of the Maltese archipelago that lay south of Sicily—and formed into an approach disposition. An advance group of minesweepers was sent ahead to sweep the approaches, transport area, and as much of the fire support area as possible, and the slower tugs were released to proceed separately to their assigned beaches. As Task Force 81 and the other assault forces of the Western Naval Task Force drew nearer Sicily, surfaced submarines with infra-red blinkers helped guide them to their beaches. In the JOSS area, the destroyer *Bristol* (DD-453) positioned five miles south of a submarine, the sub itself and a sub-chaser to the southward of her, served as lampposts marking the correct route.[24]

TASK FORCE 81 (DIME FORCE)/GELA AREA

As Rear Admiral Hall's DIME Force approached Gela, the entire area was revealed by the light of yellow flares dropped by Allied aircraft, and large fires from associated aerial-bombing to the east and west of Gela, and in the town itself. The additional light aided the amphibious force in finding its way, but also helped illuminate ships and craft to the enemy. The DIME Force would encounter the toughest opposition during the American landings and repel two tank assaults with naval gunfire.[25]

The opposition encountered would have been more formidable, but for a supporting operation, code named MINCEMEAT, which involved purposely allowing a corpse, dressed as a British officer, to wash up on a beach at Punta Umbría in southern Spain on the Atlantic. Attached to the body was a briefcase containing fake top secret documents which revealed the Allies were planning to invade Greece and Sardinia, and had no plans to invade Sicily. German intelligence accepted the documents as genuine, with the result that the

General Staff diverted much of its defensive effort from Sicily to Greece.[26]

The light cruisers *Boise* (CL-47) and *Savannah* (CL-42) and destroyers *Shubrick* (DD-639) and *Jeffers* (DD-621) took up their positions in Fire Support Areas, and other destroyers their screening assignments by 0045 on D-Day, 10 July. A half hour later, tank landing ships arrived in position with their LCVPs—shallow draft, barge-like boats formally designated "Landing Craft Vehicle, Personnel," but commonly known as "Higgins boats." Designed by Andrew Higgins of Louisiana, each boat, typically constructed of plywood, could ferry a platoon-sized unit of thirty-six men to shore at nine knots. Higgins boats normally landed troops and material on invasion beachheads ahead of other types of landing craft, and well in advance of parent tank landing ships.[27]

Large infantry landing craft (LCILs), which at 158 feet in length proceeded under their own power (versus carried aboard ship) arrived at 0125. As other "combat loaders" stood in, they began lowering boats as soon as they were in place in the transport area. Control vessels took charge of individual boat waves as they formed, and escorted them to the line of departure. The first boats hit the beach about 0245. The surf was heavy, about three feet, and these conditions as well as strong winds and currents caused many landing craft to broach. To compound these difficulties, searchlights in the vicinity of Cape Saprano came on, and the enemy directed fire at troops on the beach and in approaching boats. Allied fire support ships' guns opened and the deadly beams were soon extinguished.[28]

Following the initial boat waves, *Shubrick* and *Jeffers* began counterbattery against enemy gun batteries and other searchlights. Gunfire ceased as LCI(L)s were sent in after the LCVPs. Once they had made the shore, *Boise* and *Savannah* began harassment fire on other predetermined targets. Around dawn, the cruisers catapulted their scout planes to assist fire support ships in identifying targets and—by spotting and reporting on the fall of gun rounds—increased the accuracy of shore bombardment. The fire support ships, particularly the cruisers, silenced several batteries and continued to fire intermittently at various targets during the action. At 0830, *Boise*'s scout plane reported tank traffic progressing seaward on the Nisceni Road. The cruiser took the tanks under fire, and continued to engage them as they moved down the road. At about the same time, a lesser tank attack developed on the Gela-Ponte Olivo Road. The *Shubrick* engaged this threat, firing for about thirty minutes with marked effect.[29]

TUGS ARRIVE OFF GELA

> *The situation at dark was pretty bad. Only three LSTs [tank landing ships] had been fully unloaded. Pontoons were strewn on the beach and use of them was impossible due to the exploding ammunition from the burning* LST 313. *To make matters worse* LST 312 *had been damaged and was broached on the beach in showers of exploding ammunition. She was fully loaded. Pontoon crews were scattered and disorganized. The* Hopi *and YTs began salvage operations on the* LST 312 *and were able to pull her clear to anchor at about midnight.*
>
> —Comdr. W. D. Wright, commander LST Group One, regarding the difficulties encountered unloading materials to assault beaches on D-Day in the face of repeated attacks by German ME-109 Messerschmitt fighter bombers[30]

During the initial landings on D-Day, slower forces of Task Force 81, including the tugs, were still crossing the Strait of Sicily bound for the assault beaches. Shortly after *Hopi* sighted Sicily in the gloom, there came a warning at 0445 of an impending air raid. Twenty minutes later, an enemy plane dropped one bomb off the fleet tug's port side. No casualties or damage resulted. Sunrise revealed that one of the four small harbor tugs following *Hopi* had fallen out during the night due to a casualty or navigation error. The fleet tug and her remaining satellite YTs arrived off Gela on the southwest coast of Sicily at 0800, and reported to the task force commander.[31]

Hopi's first chore was to deliver the two pontoon causeways she had in tow to the tank landing ship *LST-338*. Causeways were used to provide a link or bridge between the beach and landing ships and craft grounded off-shore, enabling the rapid discharge of cargo. The pontoons were set up before noon and *Hopi* anchored off Gela Harbor in seven fathoms of water, awaiting further tasking.[32]

That evening, the fleet tug was dispatched to assist the tank landing ship *LST-312*, which was broached on a beach after being subjected to eleven strafing and five bombing attacks from German and Italian planes, and twelve near misses of German 88mm rounds from shore. Enemy bombers had attacked the transport area at 1319 and again at 1621, and in the intervening period planes strafed and bombed landing beaches. *LST-312*'s situation was not as dire as that of *LST-313*, as noted by the group commander of the landing ships:

From 1545 until dark LSTs at beach were subjected to low bombing attacks at about fifteen minute intervals. The planes were fast fighter bombers and came from over the sand dunes to the northwest. There were many close misses. At 1810 I sent in *LST 313* to beach close to *LST 311* in order to unload as soon as *LST 311* had finished. At 1835 a flight of three or four low flying fighters bombed the beached ships, and all bombs fell between them except one, which struck *LST 313* amidships. A large fire and series of explosions occurred immediately on the *LST 313*. This ship had to be abandoned immediately. The pontoon in use by *LST 311* was broken apart by near misses.[33]

The bomb that hit *LST-313* landed on her main deck portside, at frame twenty, passed through her deck and the tank deck below and exploded. The blast propelled soldiers into the overhead (all received very bad flash burns), and set off ammunition and land mines loaded in trucks on the tank deck. Men and equipment on the main deck were thrown in the air as well; witnesses saw some individuals hurled a hundred feet above the ship. Moreover, because the blast had also ruptured the firemain piping, there was no seawater to fight the conflagration.[34]

The commanding officer, Lt. Samuel H. Alexander, USNR, ordered engines stopped and being well aware of the nature of the cargo, he ordered all hands to abandon ship. The men who were able to entered the water from the bow and over the stern. Alexander credited the commanding officer of *LST-311* with rescuing the remaining surviving crewmen and embarked troops:

> The skipper of the *311* brought his ship right up to the stern of the *313* and we were able to transfer all survivors to the *311*. It was due to the skillful ship handling of Lt. [Robert L.] Coleman, skipper of the *311*, that the badly injured were saved. I feel quite certain that if the badly burned men had been put in the water they would never have made the three hundred yards through the surf to the beach.[35]

Upon arrival off the beachhead, *Hopi* anchored a thousand yards from the stranded *LST-312* in three-and-a-half fathoms of water, and one of the two YTs in company took her tow wire to the landing ship aground offshore. A bomb detonation had jammed the LST's rudders hard left, broken her electrical and hand steering apparatus, and made her stern anchor inoperative. The three tugs working in concert for several hours freed the ship after midnight, and brought her to Gela

Harbor. *Hopi* anchored in the harbor at 0332, with one YT made up on her port side and two on the starboard.[36]

Sunrise came two-and-one-half hours later on 11 July beginning a new work day. *YT-186* left *Hopi*'s side at 0625 and *YT-161* thereafter. *Hopi* stood out at 0700 to assist the attack transport *Barnett* (APA-5), gravely damaged only minutes earlier. She had been unloading stores and equipment into waiting tank landing craft, when a flight of six Heinkel He-111 twin-engine bombers in a V-formation attacked the anchorage. A bomb burst at 0652, close aboard *Barnett*'s port bow, ripped through her hull plating, and started a fire in No. 1 hold. Seven members of the hatch crew were killed, and another thirty-five men suffered wounds due to the explosion and fire, all Army. *Hopi* came alongside the transport and, after making fast to her port bow, put a firefighting team aboard with charged hoses to assist in fighting the fire, which they soon extinguished.[37]

Later that morning, *Hopi* towed a large infantry landing craft clear of Red beach. In the mid-afternoon, she was ordered to join the CENT Forces but, following her arrival in the CENT area, she and other tugs were ordered to the DIME area to assist the Liberty ship *Robert Rowan*. A flight of eighteen twin-engine Junkers Ju-88 aircraft— which Germans referred to as *Mädchen für Alles* (maid of all work) because they could be used as bombers, dive-bombers, night fighters, torpedo-bombers, reconnaissance aircraft, or as heavy fighters—had attacked the DIME transport area. The aircraft were driven off by Allied fighter aircraft and anti-aircraft fire, and imposed little damage. But an even larger group then struck; sixteen (give or take) Focke-Wulf Fw-200s and Heinkel He-111 bombers accompanied by six-to-eight fighters. The fighters came in low and strafed beaches, as the bombers dropped ordnance from high-altitude. *Robert Rowan*, loaded with ammunition, was hit and set aflame.[38]

When *Hopi* arrived on the scene, she found the *Rowan*—following an explosion on board at 1702—beyond help. The destroyer *McLanahan* (DD-615) sank the hulk three hours later with gunfire, but the ship's exposed bow continued to smoke throughout the night. While en route to rejoin the CENT assault force, *Hopi* observed heavy anti-aircraft fire from DIME forces at 2156 as enemy aircraft dropped flares and bombs. During a series of attacks that would continue until one hour before midnight, the cruiser *Boise* and all the destroyers, except *Jeffers*, were straddled by bomb strikes, with near misses on other ships, as well.[39]

HOPI SHOOTS DOWN ENEMY BOMBER

During these attacks on 11 July, *Hopi* detected visually at 2240, a flight of bombers less than five miles distant coming in low and slow. As the Ju-88s approached 500 feet off the deck, her No. 1, 3, and 4 twenty-millimeter guns opened and continued to fire until the aircraft were out of range thirty-seconds later. Her gunners shot down one of the planes expending 130 rounds. An incendiary bomb hit close aboard *Hopi*, but caused no damage. Following this action, *Hopi* anchored after midnight off the fishing village of Scoglitti with *YT-161* alongside. The YT cleared her side at 0300, and a few hours later *Hopi* proceeded in mid-morning to Gela Harbor in the DIME area. *YT-161*, with Lt. Comdr. Harvey Andersen aboard, returned to *Hopi*'s side that afternoon to deliver a pontoon; as night fell, *YT-161* and two other harbor tugs made up to the fleet tug's stern.[40]

Photo 5-3

Fleet tug *Hopi* under way.
Courtesy of Bob Roy and The National Association of Fleet Tug Sailors

Early the next morning, 13 July, *Hopi* delivered the pontoon to Licata in the JOSS area. On the return transit, she experienced a heavy explosion at 1026—likely due to a mine—which resulted in head and leg injuries to one crewmember. Lieutenant Owen Huff ordered the main engines stopped, and put the ship's auxiliary motor on line until a determination was made that No. 1 and 3 engines could be used. *Hopi* then limped into Gela. After anchoring in the harbor, her crew set to repairing the vessel, as well as making repairs to three other vessels:

the sub-chaser *SC-649*, a large infantry landing craft, and *LCT-36*, all of which had come alongside her for assistance.[41]

Enemy air attacks on the DIME/Gela area continued until after daylight on 13 July. The heaviest attacks against the Western Naval Task Force were in the DIME area, with some raids overflowing into the CENT area to the southeast. Task Force 81 sustained eight ship casualties:

Ship	Status	Ship	Status
Maddox (DD-622)	sunk by dive-bomber	LST-312	damaged by near bomb miss
LST-313	bombed and burned out	LCI(L)-17	damaged by shell fire
Barnett (APA-5)	damaged by near bomb miss	LCI(L)-188	damaged by shell fire
Dickman (APA-13)	damaged by near bomb miss	LCI(L)-220	damaged by shell fire[42]

Vessel losses would have been much greater save for the actions of Harvey Andersen. He received a Legion of Merit Medal for his performance as Salvage Officer at Gela. The citation reads in part:

> During the assault on Gela, Sicily, many landing craft were stranded on the beaches. Lieutenant Commander Andersen, with great skill, organized salvage parties and with courage and determination, while under constant enemy gunfire from shore batteries and aircraft, directed the salvage of these landing craft. He was responsible for the salvage of 190 landing craft, many of which were expeditiously repaired and returned to service, thereby materially assisting in the support of the Allied armies.[43]

TASK FORCE 82 (CENT FORCE)/SCOGLITTI AREA

Task Force 82 suffered fewer attacks than Task Force 81. However, outlying rocks and heavy surf in their area, which encompassed Scoglitti, presented problems for landing craft. In addition to the surf, a lack of definite landmarks and inexperienced boat crews contributed to high numbers of landing craft casualties. Fortunately, assault forces coming ashore met little enemy resistance. Gunfire from destroyers, the cruiser *Philadelphia* (CL-41), and rocket boats cleared the beaches and silenced gun batteries two or three miles inland. Forced to turn to their air forces, the Germans and Italians initiated a series of attacks on D-Day—Me-109s, Ju-88s and Italian fighter-bombers dropping flares and launching attacks on CENT beaches—that persisted for two days.

During this period, boat crews dismounted their machine guns, dug fox holes, and moved into these defensive positions to assist the shore parties in beach defense.[44]

Undeterred by attacks from the sky, the 45th Infantry Division landed on D-Day with spirit and, advancing rapidly, captured the towns of Ragusa and Vittoria that evening. Comiso Airfield, located nine miles from Ragusa, fell the following day, as Army and Navy forces continued to work in concert. As thirteen enemy tanks advanced toward Gela beaches, naval gunfire beat back the attack, destroying four of the armored fighting vehicles. Three days later, Biscari Airfield capitulated on 14 July.[45]

Although there was no significant damage to ships and landing craft of Task Force 82 due to enemy action, boat losses caused by broaching were quite high, well over two hundred landing craft, including 199 LCVP, 13 LCM(3), and 10 LCS(S). The heavy surf aided boats over sand bars offshore, but continuous pounding by waves while delivering troops and materials ashore prevented many of the craft from beaching properly for retraction. Salvage efforts were carried out but were handicapped; due to shoal water, the *Nauset* and *Narragansett* could not get close enough to the shore to provide assistance to the much less powerful harbor tugs.[46]

CENT FORCE TUGS

Nauset and *Narragansett* had stood out of the Lake of Bizerte with sister ships *Hopi* and *Moreno* on 8 July and joined the Tunisia JOSS Slow Convoy for transit to Sicily. The convoy also included tank landing ships and infantry landing craft, and their escorts. The group made landfall on Sicily at 0502 on 10 July.[47]

After reporting for duty to the task force commander, *Nauset* delivered her pontoon in tow astern to *LST-331* and anchored off Scoglitti. That evening she received orders to retrieve a boat belonging to the attack transport *James O'Hara* (APA-90) and got under way to perform this duty. While *Nauset* was thus engaged, *Narragansett*, also anchored off Scoglitti, experienced her first encounter with enemy forces. At 1832, while making preparations to get under way, the tug set general quarters due to an enemy aircraft sighting and thereafter left anchorage bound for Red beach in the CENT area. Less than an hour after her arrival there, a plane dropped a bomb close at hand. Battle stations at 2321 signaled another air raid, during which *Narragansett*'s number 3 20mm gun expended sixty rounds. It was a draw. She downed no aircraft, but conversely suffered no casualties or damage.[48]

Over the course of 11 July, *Narragansett* repeatedly manned battle stations in response to air raid warnings or for actual attacks:

0835: Sounded General Quarters.
1540: Sounded General Quarters; enemy planes close at hand.
1635: Sounded General Quarters; enemy planes dropping bombs close at hand.
1950: Sounded General Quarters at approach of enemy aircraft [four Messerschmitts].
2200: Sounded General Quarters; enemy air raid [dive-bomber in the area].
2231: Enemy bombs dropped off port bow, distance 100 yards; no apparent damage.

When "all clear" was passed following the final raid that evening, *Narragansett* had expended 1,080 rounds since her arrival in Sicilian waters the previous day.[49]

Nauset, after finding and returning *James O'Hara*'s boat, anchored again off Scoglitti. Around sunset that day, 11 July, she received orders to assist *Hopi* in fighting the fire aboard S.S. *Robert Rowan*. She came alongside the *Hopi* at 1754 to find that only wreckage of the Liberty ship remained, and thereafter returned to Scoglitti. That night, the yard minesweeper *YMS-226* came alongside *Nauset* for repairs. She remained at anchor there as a sort of combination "mooring buoy and floating repair shop" for smaller vessels until the morning of 14 July. She departed at 0803 for Licata, to report for duty to commander Task Force 86 aboard the flagship *Biscayne* (AVP-11). An hour earlier, commander Task Force 85 had ordered all minesweepers, subchasers, tank landing ships, and LCI(L)- and LCT-type landing craft to report to the JOSS area, as well.[50]

TASK FORCE 86 (JOSS FORCE)/LICATA AREA

> *The survivors were in the water for about an hour before they were picked up by the tug* INTENT *which had been about three miles away and had seen the flames on the [destroyer]* MADDOX *and heard the explosions of the [German aircraft dropped] bombs.*
>
> —Commander Landing Craft and Bases, Amphibious Force, Northwest African Waters, War Diary, July 1943

The JOSS Attack Force, which had sailed from Tunisia, was charged with landing the Army 3rd Infantry Division near Licata. The Force consisted of 38 tank landing ships, 54 infantry landing craft, and 80 tank landing craft; units of the Support and Minesweeper Groups; and British landing craft: nine LCG(L), seven LCF(L), and eight LCT. Fleet tug *Moreno* and harbor tugs *Intent* and *Resolute* were assigned as units of the Reserve Group. *Resolute* did not arrive off Sicily until after the initial assault landings. She had been badly holed during an earlier bombing attack on Bizerte on 6 July and was not seaworthy in time to sail.[51]

The attack force, which by the time the tugs arrived had already commenced landings, met little resistance. This surprised Rear Adm. Richard L. Conolly embarked aboard *Biscayne* (AVP-11)—a seaplane tender serving as his amphibious force flagship—because of illumination of his force by enemy searchlights on the beach. He elaborated on this in a report and praised the reference ships guiding the amphibious forces during the approach phase of the landings:

> The navigation phase of the operation could not have been improved upon. The [British submarine] HMS *SAFARI*, the [destroyer] *BRISTOL* [DD-453] and the Patrol Craft assigned this mission deserve the highest praise. It was through their expert navigation and their extreme courage in flashing the required signals in [the] face of searchlight illumination and momentarily expected enemy gunfire that all attack groups were able to obtain their Transport Areas and land at the center of their respective beaches. This was supplemented by the scout boats at Yellow and Green beaches.
>
> At 0250 five shore searchlight batteries illuminated the *BISCAYNE* and remained with their rays crossed on this ship. During the early phases of the landing, the enemy searched Blue and Yellow beaches and their approaches continuously illuminating reference vessels and the *BISCAYNE* in particular. But their gunfire was withheld for some unknown reason. Very little gunfire of any type was noted in Green, Yellow and Blue beaches throughout the landing.[52]

All LCVPs ("Higgins boats") were in the water off Red beach by 0252, and once formed into boat waves, made the beach, followed by large infantry landing craft. Care was exercised by the attack group commanders that the latter landing craft did not overrun the Higgins boats in the assault lanes. This same procedure was used off Yellow, Green, and Blue beaches.[53]

Although the 3rd Infantry Division met little ground resistance while coming ashore on JOSS beaches, the Luftwaffe made repeated attacks against the beaches and shipping offshore. Planes delivered dive-bombing attacks on *Biscayne* and the tank landing ships unloading in the transport areas at 0433, scoring some near misses, but no direct hits. Seven minutes later, fighter-bombers and Ju-88s strafed beaches and landing craft, preceding another dive-bombing attack. At 0450 bomb blasts close aboard the minesweeper *Sentinel* (AM-113) tore a one-foot-by-eight-foot opening in her side. Her crew successfully controlled flooding of the after engine room, but the ship sank later that morning due to additional damage sustained during other attacks. Dive-bombers also attacked the submarine *Safari* and her escort, *PC-543*. Neither suffered any casualties or damage and the submarine-chaser shot down two aircraft.[54]

LOSS OF DESTROYER *MADDOX*

Destroyer *Maddox* (DD-622), which was assigned to the outer screen of the transport area, did not fare as well. She was attacked and gravely damaged by a Junkers Ju-87 "Stuka" dive-bomber. She quickly sank, taking three-quarters of the officers and men aboard with her. Shortly after dawn on D-Day the tug *Intent* rescued the only nine officers and sixty-five enlisted survivors of the destroyer several miles offshore. At the time of the attack, sunrise was less than an hour away and traces of light were beginning to appear on the horizon. However, it was pitch black overhead from where the attack came. The executive officer later described (writing about himself in the third person) in a report on the loss of the ship, what he personally witnessed:

> At about 0458, the executive officer, who was standing on the starboard wing of the bridge, simultaneously heard the roar of an airplane pulling out of a dive, the whistle of bombs, and saw a bomb explode 160° relative distance, about 25 yards from the stern. This was instantly followed by a miss almost under the starboard propeller guard and the terrific shock of the ship being hit.[55]

The blast of the bomb under the destroyer's propeller guard exploded her after magazine and demolished the stern. The explosions collectively ripped open and leveled the deckhouse aft of the after stack, blew the No. 3 five-inch gun mount over the side, and leveled the depth charge racks and projectors aft. Internal damage caused steam and fire to pour from the stack. *Maddox* initially began to settle by the stern, listed five degrees to port and briefly righted herself, and then rolled rapidly over onto her starboard side and sank vertically, stern first.[56]

The survivors *Intent* retrieved from the sea had all been in the forward part of the ship at the time of the explosion, except for four men from the after fire room and two men whose battle station was on the 20mm gun platform just aft of the No. 2 stack. Eight officers including the commanding officer, Lt. Comdr. Eugene S. Sarsfield and two hundred and three men were lost. The captain, last seen on the bridge as the destroyer rolled over and sank, was awarded the Navy Cross posthumously. The medal citation reads in part:

> While his ship was effectively supporting the assault at Gela, Lieutenant Commander Sarsfield, in the face of terrific aerial bombardment, maintained alert and accurate direction of gunfire until the *Maddox* was gravely damaged by one direct hit and two near misses. Grimly standing by to supervise abandonment of the rapidly sinking vessel, he was responsible for saving the lives of nine officers and sixty-five men out of a total of two hundred and eighty-four on board.

Intent delivered the survivors to the attack transport *Harry Lee* (APA-10) in the early afternoon that day.[57]

SALVAGE EFFORTS BY FLEET TUG *MORENO*

The Reserve Group of Task Force 86, which at H-Hour on D-Day was still in passage to Sicily, also came under attack by enemy aircraft. Fleet tug *Moreno*, one of the vessels in convoy, went to general quarters at 0457. She emerged from this action, during which her gunners expended 120 rounds of 20mm ammunition, unscathed. Following the tug's arrival south of Blue beach, embarked Navy "SeaBees" (naval construction battalion personnel) climbed from *Moreno* onto the pontoon causeway she had alongside, for transfer along with it to the tank landing ship *LST-318*. After casting off her ponderous tow, *Moreno* proceeded to Blue beach. There, she received orders to salvage *LCI(L)-88*; holed four feet above the waterline and broached on Yellow beach.[58]

After initial efforts by *Moreno* to remove the LCI(L) from the beach were unsuccessful, a salvage party departed the tug at 1050 to better ascertain the condition of the beach-gripped 158-foot landing craft. Salvage efforts resumed thereafter, interrupted by battle stations being set aboard the tug at 1317 for Me-109s strafing beaches, at 1350 due to an air attack on shipping and beaches, and again at 1515 and 1629 for enemy planes. Following each "all clear" signal, the salvors resumed operations, assisted in late afternoon by the tank landing craft *LCT-19*. All efforts were fruitless and, after *Moreno* parted (broke) her towline in the early evening, commander Task Force 86 ordered her to Red beach for salvage duties. While these air attacks were taking place, American assault troops captured the town of Licata and allied tanks in the JOSS area began moving north.[59]

Upon arrival off Red beach, *Moreno* anchored near the shore in 3-3/4 fathoms of water. That evening, she went to general quarters at 2032 to defend against an aircraft attack during which her gunners expended six hundred rounds of 20mm ammunition and six of 5-inch. No damage to the ship or personnel casualties resulted from the action. The fleet tug ordered battle stations set twice more before getting under way at 2255 and anchoring further offshore in seven fathoms of water. At 0501 the next morning she made all preparations to pull large infantry landing craft, *LCI(L)-1*, off the beach. An enemy aircraft sighting sent her crew to general quarters at 0925. Following "all clear," the salvage efforts began and continued into late afternoon, interrupted periodically by air raids as noted in the ship's deck log:

1203: General quarters [beaches strafed by enemy aircraft].
1214: Secured from general quarters.
1229: General quarters ["hit and run" bombing raid].
1235: Secured from general quarters, expended 170 rounds of 20mm and 2 rounds of 3"50. No casualties or damage.
1327: General quarters [sneak air raids being made on all beaches at periodic intervals], expended 150 rounds of 20mm ammunition. No casualties or damage.
1401: General quarters [Stuka dive-bombers attacking Red beach]. Some bombs dropped close aboard off port and starboard bows, no damage. 190 rounds of 20mm and 3 rounds of 3" 50 ammunition expended. No casualties. Possible hit on one bomber.[60]

An infantry landing craft arrived in the mid-afternoon to assist in the salvage work, which had to cease in late afternoon because of strong winds. After *LCI(L)-10* returned *Moreno*'s towline, the tug anchored once again off Red beach.[61]

While *Moreno* was at anchor, enemy aircraft attacked Blue beach, and in a subsequent attack, both Blue and Yellow beaches. *Moreno* left

Red beach for Blue beach at 2221, having received orders to extinguish a fire on *LST-158*. As she proceeded to her destination with the captain "conning" (personally giving all helm and engine orders), crewmen topside witnessed heavy caliber fire to the southeast, and at 0040 a plane shot down in flames. Arriving off Blue beach, *Moreno* contacted vessels in the area in an effort to locate the tank landing ship. Unsuccessful, she anchored in the early hours of 12 July for the remainder of a fleeting night.[62]

A few hours later, at 0600 on 12 July, her engineers started No. 2 and 3 main engines. Within twenty minutes the ship was under way proceeding to *LST-158*. Upon arrival alongside, *Moreno* put a fire party aboard her. While it carried out its work, *Moreno* stood by to provide assistance. A little past noon, *LCT-210* maneuvered alongside the tug to have her forward ramp replaced. The services of fleet tugs—whether for towing, firefighting, salvage, or repair work—were always in demand. After her fire party returned aboard, *Moreno* proceeded back to the site of *LCI(L)-10* to resume salvage operations. Assisted by *LCT-243* the work continued until mid-afternoon when the tank landing ship *LST-385* moored alongside *Moreno* to unload radar equipment for transfer to the beach. This chore was not completed until 2145 when, with darkness curtailing further operations, the fleet tug anchored off Blue beach for the night.[63]

Operations the next day, 13 July, were similar to those of the preceding one. *Moreno* anchored near *LCI(L)-88*, but preparatory efforts to pull her free from the beach were interrupted by general quarters for an aircraft sighting, followed by the *LCT-210* making up alongside for additional assistance in replacing a ramp. Salvage operations commenced a little past noon. A full day of work by a bulldozer the previous day to undercut the stranded vessel had been successful. *LCI(L)-20* took *Moreno*'s tow wire to *LCI(L)-88* and the landing craft was refloated at 1344, with *LCI(L)-87* assisting *LCI(L)-88* into deeper water. In the late afternoon, *Moreno* set off for Red beach. No tasking awaited her, so she anchored upon arrival. That night, her officers and crew were called to battle stations twice, an hour before midnight and a second time eighteen minutes later, as a result of "Enemy attacking Blue beach."[64]

Moreno commenced salvage operations on *LCI(L)-1* at 0700 the following morning assisted by *LCT-220*. The beach landing craft was refloated in the late afternoon on 14 July and was taken in tow by a sister infantry landing craft the *LCI(L)-87*. The harbor tug *Resolute* came alongside *Moreno*'s starboard side at 1100 the following day, and departed later that afternoon to carry out her own tasking. That same day, *Moreno* loaned her motor launch *19276* with salvage equipment to Lt. Comdr. Walker; enabling salvage work to be carried out in shallow waters the fleet tug could not reach.[65]

STAFF SEVERELY DAMAGED BY MINE

Moreno's repair shop/mooring buoy routine ended abruptly that night, when she got under way to render assistance to the 221-foot minesweeper *Staff* (AM-114). While engaged in sweeping, and exchanging fire with enemy shore batteries, she had cut a moored mine and dodged a second one lying dead ahead through the use of "hard starboard, hard port" rudder orders. She then struck a third one. The mine detonation beneath *Staff*'s forward engine room opened her hull to the sea, killed seven men, and set the ship aflame. Boatswain's Mate First William H. Koch put out the fire and likely saved the ship.[66]

A sister ship, *Skill* (AM-115), took the damaged minesweeper in tow with *Moreno* standing by to provide assistance if needed. The fleet tug assumed responsibility for *Staff* after midnight and arrived with her charge off Licata Harbor two hours later in the early hours of 15 July. As soon as she anchored, *Moreno* began pumping water from *Staff*. As the very long day passed into night, salvage operations continued. Yard minesweeper *YMS-82* came alongside *Moreno* to receive the ammunition aboard *Staff*, and *YMS-84* to take her Dan buoys.[67]

The two YMSs represented a small portion of the largest production run of any World War II warship, which was not, as one might imagine, a particular class of destroyer, frigate, or submarine. Instead, the largest class of warship consisted of 561 scrappy little 136-foot wooden-hulled ships characterized by Arnold Lott in *Most Dangerous Sea* as belligerent-looking yachts wearing grey paint. Minesweepers were generally unsung, but always in great demand during the war.

The salvage ship *Brant* arrived at Licata on 19 July. The following day her salvors began a survey of the damage to the steel-hulled ship in order to quantify and to procure materials to fabricate the large patch required. The repairs involved underwater welding of new metal across badly weakened hull plates and installing additional braces as a prelude to dewatering operations. As this work was accomplished, sea water was pumped from the ship's electrical store room and a ruptured fuel tank. Additional holes exposed as the dewatering continued were patched as well. In order to expedite the work, *Brant* spent much time moored to *Staff*. Fabrication of the patch was finally completed on 2 August and work began to set and tighten it. Sea water intrusion decreased as the patch gradually conformed to the contours of the hull, allowing dewatering of other compartments and the removal of wreckage from *Staff*.⁶⁸

Brant left Licata in late afternoon on 6 August, bound for Gela, Sicily, to inspect beached craft to determine if any were salvageable. Some were, and at the completion of this tasking, she stood out of Gela with two LCMs and two LCVPs in tow to return to Licata. On that same day, 9 August, *Staff* departed Licata under tow by *Hopi*. The latter two ships reached Oran, Algeria, on 16 August 1943 via a stop at Bizerte, Tunisia.⁶⁹

BRANT HIT BY FRIENDLY FIRE

> *Opened fire with guns 2, 3, 4, 5. Target burst into flames. Ceased fire. Total rounds fired: two illuminating projectiles, and seventeen AA common Mk. 18 M.C.B.D. [fuse] projectiles. 0111, was about to resume fire and fire torpedoes when target turned on two red lights in a vertical row. This was proper minor war vessel Fighting Light Identification Signal for that time. This was first indication that vessel was not hostile.*
>
> —USS *Benson* (DD-421) deck log entry for 10 August 1943, describing the destroyer's engagement with gunfire of salvage ship USS *Brant* (ARS-32)

Brant was proceeding on a westerly course in the early morning darkness of 10 August when at 0100, she began taking fire from an undetected contact off her starboard bow. The salvage ship was not equipped with radar, the moon had set early, and visibility was poor. One round hit in the vicinity of the radio room, one struck the boat deck, one hit aft, and one struck the rigging. General quarters was sounded and, as fire broke out, the ship began evasive steering; changing course to a south and then east heading. By 0145 the fire was under control. *Brant* exchanged calls at 0220 with *Benson* (DD-421)—whose gunfire had resulted in five crewmen killed with another five missing and eighteen wounded. One of the destroyer's officers and a pharmacist's mate second arrived alongside the salvage ship by boat at 0247, and her medical officer boarded a short time later. Following the departure of the officers, *Brant* set a course for Licata,

Sicily at 0350, with the pharmacist's mate aboard to help care for the wounded.[70]

Photo 5-4

Brant serving as a fleet tug in 1942, before her conversion to salvage ship. Photo No. 19-N-32383, from the collections of the U.S. National Archives

The tragic "friendly fire" incident was due to a breakdown in standard Navy recognition procedures. The destroyer was escorting the fleet tug *Nauset* (AT-89), with destroyer *Shubrick* (DD-639) in tow, bound for the British Crown Colony of Malta, the previous headquarters of the Royal Navy's Mediterranean Fleet and then current site of a naval base. *Benson* detected at 0044 an unknown surface contact—broad on her port bow, nine miles distant—and noted that it was not transmitting IFF (identify friend or foe) information. Her combat information center began tracking the contact on radar, and thereafter the commanding officer took the conn. At 0051, he ordered general quarters; thirteen minutes later the destroyer was ready for battle. Fifteen minutes later, range to the contact had decreased to 6,000 yards. The destroyer challenged the vessel (requested she identify herself) using the Infra-red blinker tube and, when no reply was forthcoming, challenged with a 12-inch searchlight fitted with red filter and two-inch aperture. There was again no reply.⁷¹

The target continued to close, and at 3,500 yards, *Benson* fired one star shell. The illumination produced revealed a small vessel, but its silhouette was not recognizable. The commanding officer concluded that it was either a large enemy submarine or a small torpedo boat destroyer. *Benson* repeated the challenge with searchlight and as the range to the vessel decreased to 2,300 yards, fired a second star shell. As the challenging continued, the target continued to close and the vessel's hull became visible without illumination. At 0108—after the commanding officer reached "definite conclusion that character of vessel was hostile"—the destroyer opened fire at a range of 1,800 yards to the target. *Benson* ceased fire upon sighting *Brant*'s signal, ordered *Nauset* and *Shubrick* to continue on toward Malta, and stood between these ships and the burning vessel.⁷²

A formal inquest conducted on 24 August 1943 at Bizerte, Tunisia, identified the below Findings of Fact:

- The moon had set and visibility was poor
- *BRANT* was not equipped with radar
- *BRANT* only knew *BENSON* was in area after the first star shell had burst.
- *BRANT* used her Aldis lamp [small hand-held unit] to challenge *BENSON* because her 12-inch lamp was immediately destroyed
- *BENSON* used a blue signal lamp from 4,500 yards (not visible until 2,500 yards)
- *BRANT* was in a regular convoy route
- *BRANT*'s damage was on the main deck
- *BRANT* used the correct challenge under fire
- Neither *BRANT* nor *BENSON*'s challenge lights were strong enough for visibility conditions
- *BRANT* proceeded under her own power to Bizerte in Tunisia
- *BRANT* was tied up to a large repair ship in Bizerte for extensive repairs.⁷³

The blast from the explosion of one of the shells threw Motor Machinist's Mate Second Stephen Evanisko and others from the deck of the salvage ship into the sea. Despite the shock of finding himself plunged into water, Evanisko unhesitatingly removed his own life preserver and placed it near a shipmate who was in danger of drowning, despite the grave risk to himself. By this unselfish, act Evanisko gave his own life. His body was never recovered; the Navy classified him missing in action and awarded the Navy and Marine Corps Medal (posthumously) for heroic conduct in August 1943. On 11 August, the destroyer *Knight* (DD-633) recovered two survivors knocked overboard the previous day.[74]

CONCLUSION OF OPERATION HUSKY

The capture of Sicily was an undertaking of the first magnitude.

—British Prime Minister Winston Churchill

The brilliant achievements of the Allied forces in this conquest, launched on a magnitude which heretofore had never been attempted, were due principally to the singleness of purpose which all forces demonstrated. The appreciation of each other's problems produced an inter-service spirit of co-operation and common endeavor which welded the naval and military forces into a single team possessed with the resolute will to win.

—Vice Adm. Henry K. Hewitt, USN, commander Western Naval Task Force[75]

General Patton and his staff left Admiral Hewitt's fleet flagship *Monrovia* (APA-31) at 1700 on 12 July, and soon thereafter leaped from a landing barge and waded ashore to the beachhead at Gela. His troops advanced across the island to Palermo, then fought their way along the north coast, aided by the Navy. On 27 July, when Palermo Harbor was first opened to Allied shipping, Vice Adm. Henry K. Hewitt organized Motor Torpedo Squadron 15, Destroyer Squadron 8, several minesweepers, and a few other warships left in Sicilian waters, into "General Patton's Navy," to support the Seventh Army. This force was commanded by Rear Adm. Lyal A. Davidson, embarked in the cruiser *Philadelphia* (CL-41). He arrived at Palermo on 30 July—with the cruiser *Savannah* (CL-42) and destroyers *Butler* (DD-636), *Cowie* (DD-632), *Glennon* (DD-620), *Herndon* (DD-638), and *Shubrick* (DD-639)—and after anchoring outside the breakwater, met with Patton to discuss operations along the North coast of Sicily. These would include gunfire support for the Seventh Army as it advanced along the coast, providing craft to Patton for shore-to-shore amphibious operations to "leapfrog" enemy strongholds, and ferrying Army heavy artillery, supplies, and vehicles.[76]

On the night of 16 August 1943, beating the British, the leading elements of the 3rd Infantry Division entered Messina, and the city fell the next day. In just thirty-eight days, the Seventh Army, under Patton's leadership, and the British Eighth Army, under Montgomery, conquered all of Sicily. Thus ended Operation HUSKY, which Patton observed "out-blitzed the inventors of Blitzkrieg."[77]

SALVAGE DIVERS OPEN PALERMO HARBOR

After Patton's army took Palermo on 22 July, harbor clearance units began their work to open the port. The harbor entrance was not blocked, but numerous ships sunk by aircraft lay alongside piers. Raising these vessels would have been a major effort, so deck houses and masts were cut away and the pierdecks extended to cover the wrecks. Opening the port's repair facilities presented a particular challenge. A bomb had split the caisson (closure gate) of the dry dock, and seawater rushing in knocked over the spare caisson and carried it forward, then lifted an Italian destroyer from its wooden keel blocks and capsized it on the installed caisson. Divers could not use torches/explosives to clear the wreckage because of ammunition aboard the destroyer.[78]

Salvage Officer Lt. Comdr. Robert R. Helen, USNR, dove on the wreckage and devised a salvage plan. Working underwater, blocks were cut away so that the caisson could be dragged clear of the destroyer. The undamaged spare caisson was then installed in the sill, and the destroyer, patched and pumped of water, was refloated and removed from the dock. The dock restored to service was ready for further patients.[79]

A small Italian steel-hulled schooner that lay submerged across the slip between Pontile St. Lucia and Pontile Piave, presented another type of problem. Because the wreck was too damaged to be removed intact, it was cut into sections with explosives.[80]

One of the charges produced an enormous explosion that shook the town, dumped a section of pier into the water, tore a Liberty ship loose from its mooring, and caused the cruiser *Philadelphia* to roll violently. The schooner disappeared, leaving a hole about fifty feet deep in the harbor floor. This violent reaction was traced back to three ammunition ships that had exploded in Palermo harbor prior to the American occupation. When the ships blew up, large amounts of munitions had not detonated, but were instead flung about intact, and washed about by bottom currents until they piled up in banks. One of these deposits formed near the schooner and was detonated by the small explosive charge. A more complete survey of the harbor floor showed it to be covered with quantities of unexploded ordnance, which divers methodically disposed of or detonated.[81]

Robert R. Helen received the Legion of Merit Medal for his efforts in supervising the clearance of wreckage at Palermo and, most notably, for salvage work on the destroyer *Mayrant* (DD-402) in a sinking condition during a period of repeated air attacks. A near-miss flooded two main machinery compartments and caused leakage in other spaces. Following pumping and a tow into Palermo harbor, topside weight was removed for a tow to Malta. The damage attracted much attention and brought many distinguished visitors to the ship, including Generals Patton and Montgomery. The attraction may have been the warship's executive officer, Franklin Delano Roosevelt Jr., USN, rather than the damage. Seven salvage divers were awarded Navy and Marine Corps Medals:

- Shipfitter First Class Alonzo J. Bourgeois, United States Naval Reserve
- Shipfitter First Class John J. Burke, United States Naval Reserve
- Boatswain's Mate First Class Earl W. Goodrich, United States Naval Reserve
- Carpenter's Mate First Class Marvin O. Hinch, United States Naval Reserve
- Carpenter's Mate First Class Raymond S. Le Houllier, United States Naval Reserve
- Carpenter's Mate First Class John A. MacDonald, United States Naval Reserve
- Motor Machinist's Mate First Class Murray M. Miller, United States Naval Reserve

The medal citation for Bourgeois, which is representative of those of the others, reads:

> The President of the United States of America takes pleasure in presenting the Navy and Marine Corps Medal to Shipfitter First Class Alonzo J. Bourgeois, United States Naval Reserve, for heroic conduct as a salvage diver during the invasion of Sicily in July 1943. Shipfitter First Class Bourgeois and his comrades carried on the salvage of sunk and damaged ships while the area was under enemy artillery and bombing attack. They dived under extremely

hazardous conditions to conduct underwater surveys which materially contributed to rapid salvage and repair of units required for further operations against the enemy.

AWARDS FOR SALVAGE SHIP *BRANT* AND TUGS

The salvage ship *Brant* and ten fleet, or harbor tugs, earned battle stars for the invasion of Sicily. Associated ships' characteristics, and the identities of commanding officers, if known, follow:

Ship	Award Period	Length (ft.) Displ. (tons)	Commanding Officer
Brant (ARS-32)	9-15 Jul 1943	187/950	Lt. Chester H. Rockbridge, USN
Hopi (AT-71)	9-15 Jul 1943	205/1,240	Lt. Owen W. Huff, USN
Moreno (AT-87)	9-15 Jul 1943	205/1,240	Lt. (jg) Victor H. Kyllberg, USN
Narragansett (AT-88)	9-15 Jul 1943	205/1,240	Lt. Charles J. Wichmann, USN
Nauset (AT-89)	9-15 Jul 1943	205/1,240	Lt. Joseph Orleck, USN
Intent (YT-459)	9-15 Jul 1943	102/310	(Renamed *Edenshaw*) O. W. Norr
Resolute (YT-458)	9-15 Jul 1943	102/310	(Renamed *Evea*) R. L. Self
YT-161	15-21 Jul 1943	66/65	
YT-165	9-21 Jul 1943	66/65	
YT-186	9-15 Jul 1943	66/65	
YT-197	9-15 Jul 1943	66/65[82]	

6

Salerno – Operation AVALANCHE

> *In the early phases of the landings it became apparent that the enterprise was a gamble, and that the narrowest of margins would govern its success. The German artillery, armored force, infantry and air force met the Fifth Army at the shore line. On some beaches the early waves were permitted to land and were then pinned down on the narrow beaches by artillery, mortars and machine guns which also took under barrage fire succeeding waves of landing craft bringing ashore later waves of troops and equipment. The well-placed strong points, which the Germans had established behind the beaches during the fortnight preceding the landing, brought a withering fire against the soldiers debarking from boats and craft, and the numerous formidable "Tiger" tanks, deployed to cover the strong points, greatly increased the scale of opposition thrown against the incoming waves.... The weight of sea power determined the issue.*
>
> —Vice Adm. Henry K. Hewitt, commander Eighth Fleet and Western Naval Task Force, describing how it was "touch and go" whether a foothold would be established on the Italian mainland during Allied landings at Salerno[1]

Only twenty-three days elapsed between the fall of Messina on 17 August 1943—marking the end of the Sicily campaign—and the commencement of Allied attacks against Axis forces in the Gulf of Salerno on 9 September. More than six hundred Allied warships, other type ships, and landing craft participated in the amphibious invasion at Salerno. Many of the ships and most of the landing craft had taken part in the Sicily campaign over the previous two months. Limited port capacities on Sicily made it necessary to disperse these forces over virtually all serviceable Mediterranean ports from Oran, Algeria, to Alexandria, Egypt, during the planning and training phases preceding the landings. This prerequisite presented challenges to command echelons of all services regarding the coordination of a most difficult operation.[2]

After the completion of a short preparatory period, the Western Naval Task Force transported Fifth Army forces to an attack position off Salerno for a pre-dawn assault over beaches against well-established German forces. The Gulf of Salerno was chosen for the landing on the Italian mainland for two important reasons. It was located only about forty miles south of Naples, a major port to the south of Rome, which the Allies wanted to capture for use as a supply base. Additionally, although Salerno lay two hundred miles north of Sicily, it was within range of fighter-plane support operating from Sicilian airfields.[3]

OPERATIONS BAYTOWN AND SLAPSTICK

In support of the planned invasion of the Italian mainland at Salerno, the Allies had launched a supporting operation, BAYTOWN, six days earlier. At 0430 on 3 September 1943, British and Canadian troops of General Montgomery's Eighth Army crossed the Strait of Messina and landed at Calabria on the southwestern tip of Italy. The operation was intended to "tie down" German troops in southern Italy, and perhaps lure German troops away from the Salerno area further north. These objectives were not achieved. Negotiations in progress for Italy's surrender were nearing an end, and the Badoglio government would sign a secret armistice agreement later that day. Accordingly, Italian resistance was virtually non-existent. (A formal announcement of the Italian surrender was made on 8 September.)[4]

Additionally, Field Marshal Albert Kesselring correctly deduced the main Allied target was further north up the coast. He gradually pulled the German LXXVI Panzer Corps back, leaving only a single regiment. Montgomery's force, capitalizing on German withdrawals and Italian capitulation, slowly cleared the toe of the Italian boot and began to advance up the Italian east coast. By 16 September, the British 5th Infantry Division had reached Sapri, approximately sixty-five miles southeast of Salerno. Three days later, British and American troops of U.S. Fifth Army began marching north toward Naples.[5]

The second landing was to be made at Taranto in southeastern Italy by troops of the British 1st Airborne Division. Its intended purpose was to draw German attention away from the main Salerno landings. However, Operation SLAPSTICK was not launched until after the initial D-Day assault at Salerno. The four British cruisers that carried the invasion troops arrived off Taranto in mid-afternoon on 9 September where, as previously arranged, Italians guided them through the defensive minefield offshore. The landing met with no resistance as the German had withdrawn days earlier per Kesselring's orders. Once ashore, the Allied troops carried out their mission of moving north to occupy abandoned airfields and ports on the Adriatic coast.[6]

ORGANIZATION AND GEOGRAPHY

The goal of the British and American Corps, which comprised Fifth Army under American Lt. Gen. Mark W. Clark, USA, was to knock Italy out of the war and shatter the Axis coalition. The overall commanders for the invasion of Salerno, code named Operation AVALANCHE, were Eisenhower, Cunningham, Alexander, and Tedder, the same as in Sicily. Vice Admiral Hewitt, USN, commanded the amphibious force, which was divided into a combined Northern Attack Force—mainly British, under Commodore Geoffrey N. Oliver, RN, and Rear Adm. Richard L. Conolly, USN—and a Southern Attack Force—mainly American, commanded by Rear Adm. John L. Hall Jr., USN. The Gulf of Salerno was split into a Northern attack area on which the Northern Attack Force would land X Corps, British Army; and a Southern attack area on which VI Corps, U.S. Army, would come ashore.[7]

The British Northern attack area was divided into "Uncle," "Sugar" and "Roger" sectors, corresponding to same-named assault forces and, within each of the sectors, the assault beaches. Stretching from furthest north, southward along the coast, were the Red beach and Green beach of Uncle sector, Amber beach and Green beach of Sugar sector, and Amber beach and Green beach of Roger sector. The Uncle and Sugar sectors lay to the south of Salerno Town between the Picentino River (to the north) and the Tusciano River (to the south). Roger Sector was southward of the river Tusciano. The single sector in the American Southern attack area lay in front of the city of Paestum. Renowned for its well-preserved ancient Greek temples, Paestum sat atop the bluffs above the assault beaches. The four beaches below it were designated from north to south, red, green, yellow, and blue.[8]

In supporting actions, U.S. Ranger and British Commando Brigades were to land on the northern shore of the Gulf of Salerno on D-Day; the 1st, 3rd, and 9th Rangers at Maiori beach, and the No. 1 and No. 41 Royal Marine Commandos at Vietri sul Mare beach. The rangers had orders to secure Maiori and destroy nearby coastal defenses before moving inland to capture Chiunzi Pass, near Salerno, to control the road to Naples. The commandos were to seize Salerno.[9]

Map 6-1

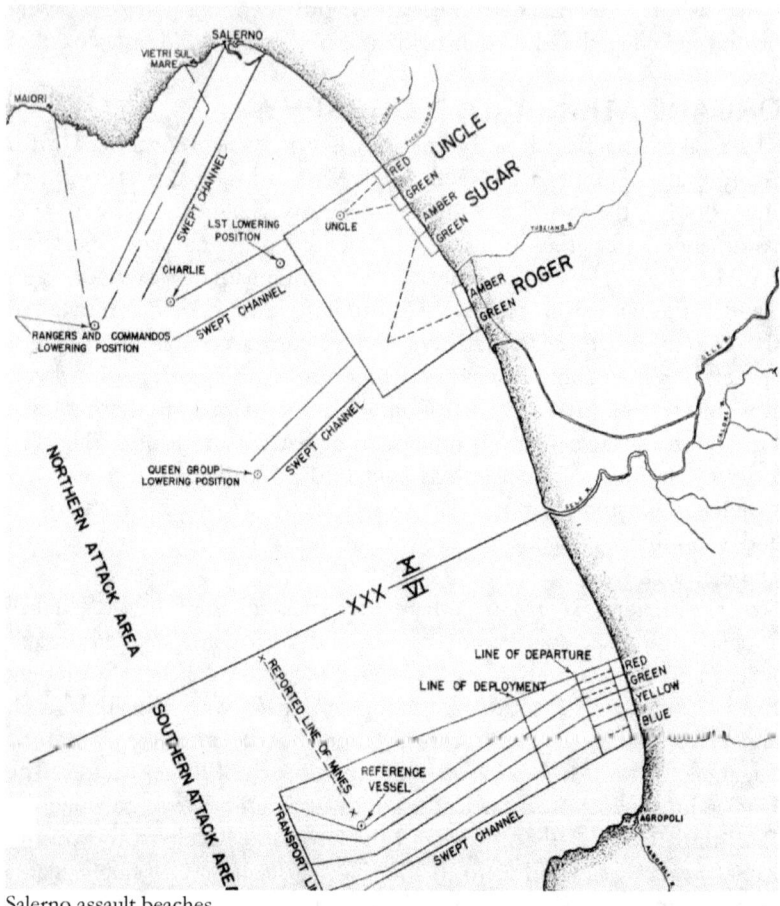

Salerno assault beaches

There were inherent shortcomings to the plan. In order to land two army corps abreast, it was necessary to come ashore between Salerno and Paestum (to the south) because it offered the only beach area broad enough. However, the Sele River bisected the landing area, which would split the two assault corps. Top Army brass were well aware of this weakness. They knew the Germans could exploit it, slice the beachhead into two segments, and mass greater force against one army corps at a time. Lt. Gen. George Patton wrote in his diary, following a brief on the operation, "As sure as God lives, the Germans will attack down that river." Patton was then "in exile" in Sicily, having slapped a soldier whom he believed to be a malingerer. Following this well-publicized episode, wide-spread demands for Patton's removal from command, in Congress and in the press, ensued. General Eisenhower condemned Patton's actions, but asserted that his military qualifications, loyalty, and tenacity made him invaluable in the field.[10]

SALVAGE FORCES

By this time in the war, the U.S. Navy had determined that, ideally, each assault group would have three tugs, either fleet tugs (ATF) or rescue tugs (ATR), assigned to it. These tugs would be equipped with firefighting and salvage gear, and carry in addition to their crews, a combat salvage team of one officer and ten men, and a firefighting team of one officer and eight men. The tugs would accompany an assault group and lay to (come to a stop) or anchor offshore waiting to undertake salvage or firefighting work on stricken ships or landing craft as necessary. Four to six additional seagoing tugs, preferably auxiliary tugs (ATA), would haul vessels damaged by enemy action clear of the area. Two British *King Salvor*-class salvage ships would be stationed nearby in a less hazardous area, but close enough to the action to render assistance to ships brought to them or beached elsewhere for further salvage. Fleet tugs *Nauset* and *Narragansett*, large harbor tugs *Intent* and *Resolute*, and YTs *165*, *186*, *197*, and *210* were assigned to the Northern Attack Force, while fleet tugs *Hopi* and *Moreno*, were a part of the Southern Attack Force. The small unnamed 65-ton YTs were particularly useful for shallow water salvage.

Northern Force (Task Force 85)	Southern Force (Task Force 81)
Nauset (AT-89)	*Hopi* (AT-71)
Narragansett (AT-88)	*Moreno* (AT-87)
Intent (YT-459)	
Resolute (YT-458)	
Green Beach Salvage Unit	
YT-197 and *YT-210*	
LCI(L)-87 and *LCI(L)-324*	
LCT-415	
Red Beach Salvage Unit	
YT-165 and *YT-186*	
LCI(L)-319 and *LCI(L)-349*	
LCT-146	

The British contributed ten vessels to the salvage forces—two salvage ships, one fleet tug, three smaller tugs, and four minesweeping trawlers. Additionally, British tank landing craft *LCT-164* and *169* were fitted out for salvage work and repair of craft on the northern beaches.[11]

William A. Sullivan—whom on 28 May 1943 had been designated Chief of Navy Salvage, with the rank of commodore—and his Royal Navy counterpart, Capt. W. Alec Doust, decided to position the British *King Salvor*-class salvage ships in Sicily. Two additional salvage ships—*Brant* at Palermo on Sicily's north coast, and HMS *Salventure* at Malta—were to be held in reserve. Sullivan and Doust were responsible for directing the salvage operations in their respective areas from Admiral Hewitt's flagship, the *Ancon* (AGC-4), and Commodore Oliver's flagship, HMS *Hilary* (F22). Sullivan and Doust believed that immediate combat salvage work could be done with personnel and gear aboard these ships, aided by the U.S. Navy tugs. British tugs were to take damaged ships, handed off by the fleet tugs, and tow them to the salvage ships while the fleet tugs returned to the fray.[12]

This plan did not come to fruition because the tugs designated to take damaged vessels from the fleet tugs didn't show up. Doust and Sullivan, out of contact for some days following the landings, each thought the other was monopolizing the escort tugs. Neither officer was right; the tugs had been mistakenly held at Bizerte. To compensate for their absence, Doust ordered the salvage ships forward, leaving *Brant* at Palermo to take care of damaged vessels arriving there.[13]

Augmenting the tugs supporting the assault forces were a number of LCIs (infantry landing craft) fitted for inshore firefighting and salvage, as well as some LCTs (tank landing craft) equipped for combat salvage. A special salvage group was set up for harbor clearance. It was to expedite clearing channels and pier space in Salerno and Naples as Allied forces occupied these areas. The initial work was to be undertaken by assault force boat parties followed by U.S. Navy salvage units brought by *Tackle* from Palermo when ordered forward.[14]

NAVAL FORCES SAIL FOR ASSAULT BEACHES

Task Unit 85.1.1 left the outer breakwater at Bizerte, Tunisia, at 0530 on 7 September 1943 to participate in the attack on Salerno Bay, Italy. Designated Convoy FSS-2, the task unit was made up of the flagship

Biscayne (AVP-11), fifteen tank landing ships, and *Narragansett* and *Nauset*. Patrol craft and sub-chasers served as escorts. *Nauset* was positioned 350 yards astern of, and midway between, columns one and two of the three-column formation. She carried one Royal Navy Assault Craft (LCA) cradled on her fantail and secured to the main boom—which increased the quantities of explosives already on board. The LCA was loaded with Hedgerow bombs. Stored below in the tug's hold, were one-quarter ton of TNT and one-quarter ton of dynamite for use in salvage operations. The knowledge that there were sufficient explosives aboard to blow the ship apart must have been a source of disquiet for those aboard: one Royal Navy officer and four "ratings," in addition to twelve ship's officers and 101 crewmembers, salvors and fire fighters.[15]

In mid-afternoon the following day, an enemy plane approached the convoy from out of the sun and dropped a bomb in the vicinity of patrol craft a thousand yards distant off *Nauset*'s starboard bow. Some ships took the plane under fire, but scored no hits. *Nauset*'s guns did not open because she was unable to verify the aircraft was hostile before it had passed out of range. The convoy continued to draw closer to Salerno. In the early evening, the ships set general quarters in compliance with orders received via signal flag hoist from the flagship *Biscayne*. Maximum readiness was observed thereafter.[16]

About 2200 that night, enemy bombers begin dropping clusters of flares to illuminate the convoy followed by ordnance on the silhouetted ships, but luckily made no direct hits. A number of near misses around particular ships seemed to indicate they were specifically targeted. Aboard *Nauset*, located behind the assault ships, it appeared that planes were continuing to attack the convoy intermittently as it moved to the assault beaches, as periodic anti-aircraft fire originating from various ships was observed. *Nauset* sighted the "fifteen-mile station ship"—so called because it was positioned fifteen miles out to sea to help guide the assault force to its destination—at 2330; the "ten-mile ship" at midnight; and the "six-and-one-half-mile ship" at 0045 on D-Day 9 September 1943.[17]

ITALIAN ARMISTICE DECLARED

> *Sailors of the Italian Navy and Mercantile Marines: Your country has terminated Hitler's war against the United Nations. German armed forces have become the open enemies of the Italian people, whom they have so often*

> betrayed.... Take heed; therefore, that you do not scuttle your ships or allow them to be captured....
>
> Ships in the Mediterranean sail to a place safe from the interference of the Germans. Sail, if you can, to North Africa or Gibraltar, to Tripoli or Malta, to Haifa or Algiers, or to Sicily, and await final success. Ships in the Black Sea sail to Russian ports. Ships not able to do this, sail to neutral ports.... Those who are in the Aegean or Black Sea, if you cannot make good your escape from the Germans, who are now your enemies, do not let your ships fall into their hands. As a last resort, scuttle them or sabotage them, rather than let them fall into the hands of the Germans, to be used against Italy....
>
> Ships intending to act in conformity with this message may assure safe conduct by calling Malta, Algiers, or Alexandria on 500 kcs [kilo cycles per second, now referred to as kilo hertz (kHz)].
>
> —Radio message from British Adm. Andrew Cunningham, commander-in-chief Mediterranean Fleet, broadcast on frequency 500 kcs to Italian ships at fifty-three minutes past midnight on 9 September 1943[18]

Vice Admiral Hewitt was informed by the Allied Northwest African Tactical Air Force, while en route to the Salerno landing beaches, that an Italian armistice had been declared and that aircraft encountered bearing Italian markings were not to be attacked, unless they demonstrated hostile intent. Similar reports and guidance from other Allied commanders followed. Following a radio broadcast by Admiral Cunningham, commander-in-chief Mediterranean Fleet, to Italian ships and submarines, providing guidance regarding their surrender, Hewitt instructed Western Naval Force units that operations in progress were vigorously proceeding as ordered, and that:

> Italian armed forces, including aircraft, should be treated as friendly unless they take hostile action or threaten hostile action. Plans for covering fire on beaches are to progress as ordered, but coast defense batteries should not be engaged unless they open fire.[19]

Italian forces on Ventotene Island, one of the Pontine Islands in the Tyrrhenian Sea that lay twenty-five nautical miles off the coast of Gaeta, Italy, had surrendered at 0001 on 9 September without resistance. However, for Allied forces approaching Salerno beaches and landing troops soon thereafter on D-Day, it probably made little difference whether German or Italian forces might be opposing them. At 0215, shore batteries on the beach opened fire.[20]

LOSS OF FLEET TUG *NAUSET*

Nauset commenced lowering the embarked assault craft while lying to near the latter station ship. The LCA left her side at 0230 with the RN officer and his crew aboard. Their mission was to discharge Hedgerow bombs on designated beaches to explode enemy-emplaced land mines intended to prevent or impede the movement of assault troops as they came ashore. The LCA carried only a portion of the cargo of bombs. While awaiting return of the craft for a second load, the tug walked her port anchor out to thirty fathoms, which (with its flukes unset) served as a "sea anchor" and helped retard drifting.[21]

At about 0430, *Nauset* observed anti-aircraft fire approximately one mile distant off her port quarter, but she did not fire her own guns to avoid revealing her position. Shortly after 0500, two or three heavy bomb blasts shattered the quiet of the early morning. The source was either close aboard or in the near vicinity of the fleet tug, it was impossible to tell in the gloom. The aircraft that dropped the bombs was not seen by anyone, but was heard as it pulled up out of its dive. The resultant damage to the tug, and that subsequently wrought by a mine, sank her. Ensign Edwin L. Reel, the senior surviving officer, later described the devastation caused by the blasts:

> The explosions caused fire to envelope the entire boat deck, also extended through passageways and up ladders to the chart room and bridge. Flames leaped in the air just aft of the bridge to a height of fifty feet. The ship immediately took a definite list to port of fifteen degrees.... [There was a] power failure, and all lights, power, and internal communications went out.... All fire plugs were tested for [water] pressure and no pressure was found on any of them. All guns were inoperative due to the explosions and fire being in the vicinity.
>
> Personnel at their gun stations were injured, blown overboard by the explosions, or suffering from extreme shock and burns. The motor launch was suspended over the port side from the boat boom.... Due to lack of power and bent davits, it was impossible to lower either boat. Orders were given to cut lashings on all life rafts immediately. Clusters of flares were dropped, lighting up the entire area. Bombs fell, but no hits were observed. Extensive anti-aircraft fire was in progress from ships in the area. This probably prevented another attack on the ship.[22]

Intent—which was about 800 yards off the port bow of the *Nauset*—closed the burning vessel to provide assistance. When she was within hailing distance, Lt. Joseph Orleck, *Nauset*'s commanding officer, told her to come alongside his ship's starboard side; with the idea *Intent* could use her fire hoses to combat the flames, take off the injured personnel, and tow the ship into shallow water. It was apparent the tug would sink unless put aground because she was taking on water fast and her list to port was increasing rapidly. Reel detailed the efforts made to save her:

> As soon as all tow lines were made fast, the *INTENT* stood in toward the nearest beach and shallow water. One fire hose was streamed from the *INTENT*'s fire main in an attempt to extinguish the flames.... It was difficult to maneuver due to inability to bring rudder from hard left. The injured personnel were transferred aboard the *INTENT* where first aid was rendered to those that were suffering most....
>
> A complete search of all accessible compartments of the ship was made by officers and crew who were not injured for additional survivors. In this search, it was found that the generator room and motor room were flooded with water and burning fuel oil, and it was impossible to enter. It is believed that all missing personnel in these two rooms were killed by the initial explosion....
>
> In the inspection of the ship for the extent of damage it was found that the main deck plates at Frame 57 and in adjoining areas were buckled, and seams had opened from eight to fourteen inches. Plates in the crew's mess hall had also buckled and the seams opened. A bend in the starboard side of the hull was observed above the water line and extended about six feet in toward the keel from its normal position. A definite sag amidships signified that the keel was broken by the explosions.[23]

While *Nauset* was under tow, uninjured crewmen fought the fires, on the boat deck and topside, and were able to get them under control; the fires in the motor and generator rooms still burned. Suddenly, the ship's list to port increased dramatically; her port quarter was awash, and the bow was also down so that the sea was level with the hawse pipe. As the ship settled lower, the captain gave the order to abandon, and those men still aboard transferred to the *Intent*. When all hands were off, seamen aboard *Intent* stood by the tow lines to *Nauset* with axes prepared to cut them if the vessel sank. *Nauset* righted herself to a twenty-degree list, and hopes arose that she might still be beached. Orleck sent a message by flashing light to

Narragansett, which was now on the port quarter of *Nauset*, to make her port side in order to assist *Intent* in beaching the sinking tug. In preparation for this action, Orleck and his first lieutenant and chief boatswain's mate reboarded *Nauset* in order to take lines from the *Narragansett*.[24]

With *Narragansett* still 500 yards distant, there was a violent explosion near the bow of the gravely damaged and sinking vessel. It was later determined that she had ventured into a minefield and the detonation was caused by a mine strike. *Nauset* broke in half, and sank at about 0605 in sixty-five fathoms of water at position 40° 38' north latitude, 14° 38' east longitude. The tug's bow and stern disappeared from view approximately ten seconds after the explosion. The explosion also blew men from the fantail of *Intent* into the water. They were able to grab onto debris coming to the surface and remained afloat until *Narragansett* was able to pick them up.[25]

Following retrieval of all survivors and a thorough search of the area, it was discovered that the *Nauset*'s captain and first lieutenant were still missing. *Narragansett*'s whaleboat was sent back to make another search; it was then daylight, but this effort failed to locate them or anyone else in the water. The two officers were last seen on the fo'c'sle of the tug with the chief boatswain's mate waiting for *Narragansett* to come alongside. It was later learned that *Intent* had picked up the first lieutenant.[26]

Nauset survivors aboard the *Narragansett* and *Intent* were transferred to the tank landing ship *LST-351*. The surviving officers of *Nauset* requested that the few crewmen not severely injured be put aboard a landing ship that had already beached and retracted. This would avoid additional shock resulting from landing operations in the face of enemy gunfire to these men. This request was granted, and three men were transferred to *LST-372*. The remaining ninety-two survivors remained aboard *LST-351*. Most were badly burned and all were suffering from shock. The tank landing ship's crew helped to receive the wounded on board and additional medical aid was summoned from LSTs *157* and *372*. Over the next twenty hours—during which the *351* came under enemy fire and aerial assault—these doctors and pharmacist's mates toiled ceaselessly in aiding the suffering men.[27]

Of *Nauset*'s 113 officers and men: two died of injuries, sixteen were never found and were considered missing in action, and forty-one were injured; fifty-nine total casualties. The ship's captain received the Navy Cross (posthumously) for heroism. The medal citation reads:

The President of the United States of America takes pride in presenting the Navy Cross (Posthumously) to Lieutenant Joseph Orleck, United States Navy, for extraordinary heroism and distinguished service in the line of his profession as Commanding Officer of the Fleet Tug U.S.S. *NAUSET* (AT-89), during the amphibious invasion of Italy on 9 September 1943. During the approach to the assault area in the Gulf of Salerno, the convoy in which the U.S.S. *NAUSET* was proceeding was attacked by enemy aircraft and this ship struck by several aerial bombs which caused extensive damage, numerous casualties, and ignited fires which completely enveloped the boat deck. Lieutenant Orleck coolly and courageously directed the fire-fighting activities, the control of flooding to correct a dangerous list which immediately developed and the transfer of all survivors to the rescue ships. With complete disregard for his own safety, he remained on board the stricken ship to attempt beaching and prevent total loss, but, while engaged in this operation, he lost his life as the ship struck an enemy mine and sank. His persistent and gallant efforts to save his ship were an inspiring example to all and contributed materially to minimizing the loss of life incurred by the initial attack. The conduct of Lieutenant Orleck throughout this action reflects great credit upon himself, and was in keeping with the highest traditions of the United States Naval Service. He gallantly gave his life for his country.[28]

BRITISH NORTHERN ATTACK AREA

> *The decision to delay the pre-assault bombardment in an effort to maintain the element of surprise proved to be a costly one. Personnel on the Uncle Attack beaches were pinned down by enemy 88mm fire, which should have been neutralized or knocked out by adequate naval gunfire prior to the landing. During the final approach to the initial transport area, commencing at 2100/D-1, enemy air attacks indicated that surprise had been lost.*
>
> —Vice Adm. Henry K. Hewitt, commander Western Naval Task Force, commenting on the folly of forsaking shore bombardment to soften German defense positions, and launching the assault on Salerno beaches in darkness—which U.S. Army leadership insisted upon—in the hope of achieving surprise[29]

The mission of the Northern Attack Force—of which *Nauset* had been a part—was to establish the 46th Division of British X Corps ashore over Uncle sector's Red and Green beaches, about five miles south of Salerno at H-Hour on D-Day 0330 on 9 September. The landing plan called for a one brigade front carried in LSTs, LCI(L)s, and LCTs. Six of the tank landing ships in the assault group carried pontoon causeways to ensure unloading of LSTs over beaches expected to be too steep for effective use of ships' bow ramps. Lesser gradients were encountered, and the causeways proved unnecessary—the landing ships and craft beached "dry-shod" to transfer materials ashore.[30]

Enemy fire began with the landing of the first boat wave. Coastal batteries on adjacent hills and mobile batteries located about one mile inland opened fire on the Uncle beaches. British assault troops were forced to abandon Green beach due to heavy enemy shelling. By 1240 on D-Day, the enemy had overrun it and was threatening the right flank of Red beach. Allied reinforcements (one company of the 5th Foresters and one company of the 5th Leicesters) were landed by LCI(L)s on Red beach, and concentrated naval gunfire from ships offshore was brought to bear against enemy targets. Red beach was consolidated (brought under Allied control), about daybreak on D-Day, but quickly became congested due to the arrival of craft diverted from Green beach. Despite limited beach space to unload and ongoing enemy bombardment and aircraft raids, fair progress was being made by noontime on D-Day.[31]

Roger and Sugar sectors received moderate fire from enemy guns during the early hours of the assault, but naval gunfire quickly neutralized enemy defense positions. Tank landing ships were brought in after daylight with smoke employed to cover their approach. Although X Corps was under enemy fire until 26 September, the beaches of British Uncle, Sugar, and Roger sectors were brought to order earlier than the American beaches south of the Sele River.[32]

SALVAGE EFFORTS ON UNCLE SECTOR BEACHES

With a hull length of 158 feet, and eight diesel engines producing a combined 1,600 horsepower and twin variable-pitch propellers providing maneuverability, the LCI(L)s were much more powerful than the 65-foot YTs. They proved to be valuable salvage vessels, and were particularly adept in using their propeller wash to scour beach sand out from alongside and underneath stranded craft. In the early afternoon on D-day, the infantry landing craft *LCI(L)-349*, assisted by YTs *165* and *186*, pulled the tank landing ship *LST-310* off Red beach.

An hour later, the two yard tugs and *LCI(L)-319* freed the *LST-314* from Red beach. There was no salvage activity on Green beach throughout that day.³³

Photo 6-1

Large infantry landing craft *LCI(L)-349*, probably in the English Channel prior to or during the Invasion of Normandy in June 1944.
U.S. Coast Guard photo from the U.S. Coast Guard Historian's collection

Commander Miles H. Imlay, USCG, the salvage officer of Task Force 85 received a report the following morning that *LST-375* was stuck on the beach. After dispatching LCI(L)s *319*, *324*, and *349* to try to tow her off, he boarded the *LCI(L)-324* to direct operations. The tank landing ship refused to come off, despite the combined efforts of three LCI(L)s and three YTs pulling from various angles. Imlay then ordered *Narragansett* to assist, and a combined pull by the fleet tug and *LCI(L)-349* brought the tank landing ship off the beach.³⁴

In the late afternoon, commander Red Beach ordered all pontoons (save one) removed from the beach and delivered to the transport area for turnover to empty tank landing ships returning to their bases. *Resolute* and four YTs set to work and completed this tasking before dark. The YTs *165* and *197* then received orders to tow the remaining pontoon to the Port of Salerno for delivery to the British *LST-368*. After arriving there late that night 10 September, they received a request from the tank landing ship to remain overnight and site the pontoon at daylight. While moving it the next day, enemy shore batteries began shelling the outer harbor. The tugs with the pontoon proceeded to the inner harbor out of range, while larger vessels in the harbor stood out to sea to clear the area.[35]

Commander Imlay later praised the efforts of the infantry landing craft and yard tugs in his report on salvage operations conducted during Operation AVALANCHE:

> The Commander Salvage Unit would like to commend the crews attached to the LCIs *319* and *349*, and the YTs *165*, *186*, *197*, and *210*, who carried out their work of assisting vessels on the beaches at times while being strafed by enemy aircraft and exposed to enemy shell fire from beaches.[36]

AMERICAN SOUTHERN ATTACK AREA

Rear Adm. John L. Hall Jr., commander Eighth Amphibious Force, was in charge of the Southern Attack Force (Task Force 81). This force was responsible for establishing the U.S. Army 36th Infantry Division, and attached troops of the VI Corps, ashore over beaches south of the Sele River. The various elements of the force sailed from Oran and Algiers, Algeria; Bizerte, Tunisia; and Palermo, Sicily, in three convoys and rendezvoused off Salerno around sunset on 8 September. After forming an approach disposition, the force proceeded to the assault area.[37]

Hopi and *Moreno*—Task Force 81's salvage group (TG 81.9)—had made their way to the rendezvous with a group of ships they joined off Bizerte in the early evening of the previous day. During the approach phase, heavy anti-aircraft fire was visible to the north; the Northern Attack Force convoy was then under attack by enemy planes. Aircraft dropped illumination flares near the Southern Attack force convoy, but the ships laid a smoke screen and withheld naval gunfire to prevent disclosing their positions, and luckily no attack developed.[38]

The Force arrived in the transport area on schedule and the work of lowering of boats and debarking personnel was conducted expeditiously. As boat waves formed, patrol craft led them in toward the beaches behind Sweep Unit No. 2—comprised of the minesweeper *Strive* (AM-117) and YMSs *37*, *55*, *62*, *64*, *69*, *82*, *207*, *208*, *226*, and *227*—working to clear a safe channel ahead. The sweepers exploded or cut adrift seventeen contact mines during their first pass, and by noon had accounted for fifty-two potential "ship killers." (British and American minesweeepers had similarly swept the waters off the Northern Assault Force beaches.) On all beaches the first wave of troops was met with machine gun, artillery, and mortar fire.

Despite enemy resistance, the landings continued and by 0600 the two assault regiments (141st and 142nd) were ashore.[39]

Landing craft—LCV(P)s and LCMs—then began landing artillery, tanks, motorized equipment, ammunition, and other equipment. Unloading of craft and ships progressed rapidly and all were empty, except one cargo ship, by the following night, 10 September. Throughout the first two days, considerable enemy resistance was encountered. All beaches came under fire at intervals from artillery, machine guns, and mortars. Enemy tanks penetrated to the vicinity of Blue beach—at the southern extremity of the landing beaches—and the Allied forces ashore abandoned it.[40]

The cruisers and destroyers of the Fire Support Group were late in taking station because of the mines. However, in the afternoon of D-Day, effective fire destroyed enemy machine gun emplacements, knocked out or silenced enemy batteries, and destroyed or scattered enemy tanks. During this period, Allied fighters provided air coverage over the assault area. On the evening of D-Day and early the following morning, a few bombs were dropped on the Transport Area and several attacks by small groups of German fighter-bombers were made on the beaches. That night, as the transports and freighters prepared for departure following unloading, the transport area was attacked for thirty minutes with heavy low-level bombing. The ships suffered no damage and they stood out and formed into a convoy for return to Oran.[41]

LOSS OF DESTROYER *ROWAN*

Shortly after the convoy left Salerno in late night on 10 September, the destroyer *Rowan* (DD-405)—positioned on the starboard beam of the disposition of emptied ships as part of a protective screen—fired approximately eight rounds at a target, which proved to be two German E-boats. The Allied term "E-boat" referred to a fast attack craft of the Kriegsmarine (German navy). The German name for the craft was Schnellboot, meaning "fast boat," or S-Boot. There were different variants of the E-boat. All were more heavily armed, better in rough seas—due to their construction of wood on alloy frames and round-bilged hull design—and had much longer ranges than the American PT boat and the British Motor Torpedo Boat (MTB). The *S-100*-class variant E-boat, produced from 1943-on, boasted two torpedo tubes, a 20mm gun in the bow and two amidships, one 37mm gun aft, and for good measure, depth charge racks to provide an anti-submarine capability. The 114-foot boat's low profile made it difficult to detect visually. Being stealthy, these craft were also used to lay mines and to reseed existing minefields.[42]

Photo 6-2

Destroyer *Rowan* under way, circa 1939-1940.
Official U.S. Navy Photograph #NH 103502, from the collections of the Naval History and Heritage Command

Having apparently driven off the E-boats, *Rowan* was returning to her position in the screen when two shattering explosions were heard at 0133. A ship nearby could see a towering column of smoke. This proved to be the destroyer blowing up. Although the *Rowan* had broken up the impending E-boat attack on the convoy, one of them had succeeded in torpedoing her and she plunged to the bottom taking 202 of her 273 officers and men with her. The destroyer *Bristol* (DD-453) retrieved eleven officers, including the captain, and sixty men from life rafts, one of whom later died on board. *Bristol* remained in the vicinity until after daylight searching for additional survivors; finding none, she rejoined the convoy.[43]

SALVAGE OPERATIONS

After arriving in the Gulf of Salerno on D-Day with Task Force 81, *Hopi* and *Moreno* lay to offshore during landing operations waiting to provide assistance as required. From twelve miles out, aboard the *Moreno*, it was possible to observe intermittent gunfire on the shore. At 0510 the commanding officer ordered "general quarters" due to a sighting of flares and anti-aircraft fire to the northeast, and again at

0738 for the sighting of an enemy plane. In the early evening, *Moreno* proceeded at 1704 to assist the monitor HMS *Abercrombie* (F109) which had struck a mine. The detonation opened a twelve-by-twenty-foot hole in her hull, and sea water rushed in causing a 10-degree list to starboard. Newly commissioned on 5 May 1943, she was fitted with a 15-inch gun turret originally built as a spare for the battlecruiser HMS *Furious* (47). Not surprisingly, her mission was shore bombardment. Following a conference aboard *Abercrombie* attended by *Moreno*'s salvage officer Ens. Frank W. Laessle, the tug transferred sand, gravel and cement to her for repair purposes. After coming back to *Moreno* to pick up other salvors, Laessle left at 2155 to return to *Abercrombie* with two men to begin emergency salvage work on the monitor.[44]

The tug lay to near the British warship about six miles offshore, standing by to render any assistance required. In late morning the following day, *Moreno* moored with her port bow to the starboard quarter of the *Abercrombie*, and put a salvage party on board to affect repairs. At 2037 on 10 September, *Moreno* left her side bound for an anchorage in the Gulf of Salerno. En route the tug sighted anti-aircraft fire and flares to seaward. Falling AA shrapnel caused two small lacerations on the back of one crewmember. *Moreno* was darkened, Material Condition Able was set (watertight doors, hatches, and fittings closed to prevent the spread of fire or flooding in the event of battle damage), and No. 1 and No. 2 20mm guns manned and ready for immediate action.[45]

Moreno got under way the next morning to aid the Royal Dutch Navy sloop HNMS *Flores* (F66). On D-Day, the sloop had assisted Allied ground troops near Paestum by taking under fire an enemy artillery battery and a forest where German tanks were hiding. The following day, *Moreno* escorted *Abercrombie* to Malta. After returning to Salerno, *Flores* was damaged by a German bomber during a heavy air raid. One bomb splashed harmlessly into the water off her starboard quarter. A second one detonated close aboard off her port bow, lifting and twisting the ship with resultant damage to her engine room and equipment.[46]

Upon arrival off *Flores* at 0825, *Moreno* moored starboard side to the sloop with one manila and five wire lines, and made up thus, towed her alongside to anchorage in the Gulf of Salerno. For her next task, the tug was dispatched to provide assistance to the light cruiser *Savannah* (CL-42), which had been hit by a radio-controlled glider bomb launched from a German aircraft.[47]

Savannah was the first American ship to fire against German shore defenses in Salerno Bay. On 9 September she had silenced a railway battery—a large artillery piece transported by and fired from a specially designed railway wagon—forced the retirement of enemy tanks, and carried out eight other fire support missions. The cruiser continued her support of troops ashore until the morning of 11 September, when she was knocked out of action.[48]

Photo 6-3

Savannah just after she was hit by a glider-bomb off Salerno, Italy on 11 September 1943.
Photo #SC 243636 from the U.S. Army Signal Corps Collection, now held by the U.S. National Archives

Sighting a Dornier Do-217 bomber approaching from out of the sun, *Savannah* increased speed to twenty knots as Allied P-38 fighters and her gunners tried unsuccessfully to shoot down a smoke-trailing glider-bomb released by the plane. This type of bomb was manually steered to its target by a radio signal from the bombardier aboard the aircraft. The one fired at *Savannah* hit the armored body of her No. 3 Gun Turret and passed down through the cruiser into the lower handling room before it detonated. The explosion created a gaping hole in the ship's bottom and opened a hull seam on the port side, killing 197 men and wounding fifteen. (Structural damage sealed four men in a compartment for sixty hours, until finally rescued after the cruiser arrived at Malta on 12 September.) Working quickly, *Savannah* crewmen isolated flooded and burned compartments, and ballasted to correct the ship's list.[49]

Moreno moored alongside *Savannah* at 1054 with one manila and five wire lines, and began transferring salvage equipment to her. She assisted in salvage operations aboard for several hours before leaving the cruiser's side at 1730 to anchor in the Gulf of Salerno. Three hours past midnight, the fleet tug went to general quarters for an air attack. She sustained no casualties or damage but her crew was afforded little rest that night. "Secure from general quarters" was passed at 0330, and two hours later *Moreno* was en route to a merchant ship, the British S.S. *Lyminge*.[50]

She moored alongside *Lyminge* at 0644 on 12 September and sent over a firefighting party to assist one from the flagship *Biscayne* (AGC-18), and one from *Hopi*, which had arrived about the same time as *Moreno*. A near miss by a rocket bomb had started fires aboard the ship and the crew had abandoned due to her extremely dangerous cargo—gasoline, ammunition, land mines and chlorine gas. *Moreno*'s salvors got started welding over shrapnel holes in the ship's starboard quarter above the waterline. An air attack at 1102 interrupted the work; two bombs hit about a hundred feet off the starboard quarter of *Moreno*, then made up portside to *Lyminge*, but no casualties or damage ensued. Work resumed, broken by two subsequent raids at 1225 and 1400. During the first of these two attacks, *Moreno*'s gunners shot down a plane. Upon completion of the patching job in mid-afternoon, *Moreno* cleared *Lyminge*'s side to return to anchorage. Later the steamship departed under her own power bound for the Royal Navy Dockyard at Valletta, Malta.[51]

Two *Hopi* crewmembers, Shipfitter First Class John T. Ashcraft and Fireman First Class Frances W. Bush, each received a Navy and Marine Corps Medal for heroic actions aboard *Lyminge*. The medal citation for Ashcraft, which is similar to Bush's, reads:

> The President of the United States of America takes pleasure in presenting the Navy and Marine Corps Medal to Shipfitter First Class John T. Ashcraft, United States Navy, for heroism while serving as a member of the Fire Fighting Party assigned to the U.S.S. HOPI during the amphibious invasion of Italy at Salerno on 12 September 1943. When a fire caused by a plane crash broke out on board H.M.S. LYMINGE, a partially loaded ammunition ship, Shipfitter First Class Ashcraft courageously assisted in laying hose lines to the burning ship and in taking prompt measures to bring

the spreading flames under control. Despite the hazards from the highly sensitive cargo, consisting of gasoline, projectiles, land mines and chlorine gas, he unhesitatingly boarded the imperiled ship and skillfully participated in firefighting operations which led to the ultimate extinguishment of the fire, thereby saving this valuable ammunition ship for future operations against the enemy. The extraordinary heroism, prompt and courageous action and outstanding devotion to duty displayed by Shipfitter First Class Ashcraft were in keeping with the highest traditions of the United States Naval Service.

A fire and rescue party from *Biscayne*, which was anchored nearby, had boarded *Lyminge* (a British merchant ship, and not Royal Navy as indicated by the HMS designation in the citation) at 0458 well before the tugs arrived alongside. Damage to the ship was actually from a glider-bomb, and not a plane crash. Because glider-bombs in flight resembled aircraft, observers sometimes mistook them for planes, and due to their smaller size believed them to be farther away than they appeared. Three *Biscayne* crewmen earned Navy and Marine Corps Medals as well.[52]

CONTINUED EFFORTS

The following day, *Moreno* got under way at 0831 to assist the British HMHS *Newfoundland*, located about forty miles out to sea off Salerno. She was the hospital ship of the Eighth Army and was one of two hospital ships sent to deliver 103 American nurses to the Salerno beaches. Although *Newfoundland* had been painted white, bore giant red crosses, and was brightly illuminated at night, the Luftwaffe repeatedly bombed her, killing six nurses and all medical officers aboard. A U.S. Army nurse, who survived, wrote about the attack and its aftermath in a letter home, excerpts of which follow:

> When we got on the deck we all had to get on one side because the bomb had torn away the other side of the ship. I'll never forget seeing this one British nurse trying to get through the porthole but was too large to make it. She was screaming terribly because her room was all in flames. One British fellow saw that she could never get out so he knocked her in the head with his fist and shoved her back in [her] room—she died but it was much easier than if she had burned to death.
> We loaded in a life boat—70 of us in one boat that had a capacity of 30. [We] were taken on another hospital ship and given tea and hot coffee. I felt a darn good cry coming on so some

British fellow took the four of we girls to his room and we drank a bottle of Scotch. I got "stinko" drunk—cried and when I snapped out of it, I felt fine. All the bruises I got out of it was a scratch on my knee, a cut on my left foot and marks and scratches on my chest where debris fell from the roof.[53]

Moreno steered various courses while proceeding out the channel and once clear increased speed to flank (maximum speed), 16.4 knots. At 1040 she sighted the ship but had to lay to until the destroyer *Plunkett* (DD-433), then engaged fighting fires aboard *Newfoundland*, cleared her side. At 1134 the fleet tug moored with her port side to the port side of the hospital ship. Such an arrangement, with the bows of two ships alongside one another pointing in opposite directions, is termed a "Chinese moor." Her firefighting and salvage repair parties began trying to extinguish fires aboard the ponderous vessel, which was listing to starboard.[54]

Commodore Sullivan boarded the fleet tug a few minutes later. In the early afternoon as firefighting efforts continued, nineteen officer and enlisted survivors came aboard the tug. Twenty-four hours later, after all the fires were finally extinguished, *Moreno*'s salvage repair party began trying to correct the list of the 406-foot former Royal Mail Ship through use of the tug's salvage pumps. As salvage efforts were not succeeding they were ceased in the early evening following receipt of orders to stop work and await instructions regarding the disposal of the hospital ship. These were that *Newfoundland* would be abandoned[55]

At 2115 *Plunkett* on orders fired on and sank the hulk. *Moreno* then proceeded for the Gulf of Salerno. The tug anchored four miles offshore ten minutes past midnight and Commodore Sullivan departed her a half hour later. He had felt that *Newfoundland* could have been saved and, when the order came to sink her, sent a message recommending she be left alone until a salvage tug could take her under tow for a repair facility or at least move her into shallow water. After two hours as no answer was forthcoming, the destroyer sank the hospital ship. It was later learned that both Admirals Hewitt and Cunningham had approved the request, but neither message was received.[56]

A few hours later on 15 September, the freighter S.S. *James W. Marshall* was damaged by a glider-bomb at 0744 and set aflame, and a tank landing craft alongside her, *LCT-19*, also caught fire. As *Moreno* prepared to render aid, three bombs hit the water close aboard off her starboard side, but caused no casualties or damage. Approaching the freighter, the fleet tug maneuvered with difficulty, because the water around her was full of survivors and many small landing craft. By

0814 she was moored portside to *Marshall*'s portside with all five of her fire hoses working. Commodore Sullivan boarded *Moreno* at 0942 and directed the transfer of the surviving officers and men of *Newfoundland* to LST-337. The fires aboard the freighter were extinguished at 1030, and *Moreno* departed her side for Yellow beach.[57]

In early afternoon, *Moreno* witnessed an enemy aircraft being shot down while she was en route to the British freighting-tanker RFA *Derwentdale* which had been hit by a bomb. The damaged ship was part of the Royal Fleet Auxiliary, civilian-manned vessels that supplied Royal Navy ships with fuel, water, ammunition and supplies. *Moreno* came alongside the *Derwentdale* with one fire monitor already spraying a water stream. Upon discovering there was no fire on board she took the tanker in tow; once clear of the combat area, she handed her over to the British tug HMS *Hengist* (W110) for further movement to Malta. Enemy air attacks continued that afternoon and evening, and *Moreno* witnessed three additional enemy planes shot down in flames at 1808.[58]

BATTLESHIP *WARSPITE* DAMAGED

Force H—a group of Gibraltar-based British naval units that had been the cover force for the Northern Assault Area—had departed Salerno 14 September to proceed to the United Kingdom to prepare for the invasion of France. Two of its members, the sister battleships *Warspite* and *Valiant*, remained off the assault beaches to provide support for American forces near Battipaglia. As General Patton had predicted, German troops had launched a counter-offensive in the area between the Sele and Tusciano Rivers, pushed the Americans back toward the Amber and Green beaches of Roger sector, and recaptured Altavilla to the northeast of Paestum.[59]

On the morning of 16 September from a half mile or so offshore, the battleships began bombarding German positions. In the early afternoon, they opened fire on vehicle concentrations and ammunition dumps of the enemy counterattack. The salvos by the vintage *Queen Elizabeth*-class battleships, commissioned in 1916, and U.S. Navy cruisers *Boise* and *Philadelphia* were effective. With its ground force offensive stalled, German aerial-bombing attacks intensified. In the early afternoon, a group of twelve Focke-Wulf Fw-190 fighter-bombers attacked straight out of the sun, but were driven off by *Warspite*'s anti-aircraft guns. In addition to eight 15-inch guns and four twin 6-inch guns for shore bombardment and surface action, the battleships were fitted with smaller caliber guns—which could be trained and elevated more rapidly against fast moving planes. This armament included four twin 4-inch guns, four quad 0.5-inch guns, and four eight-barreled two-pounder guns. The latter guns—which used ammunition left over from World War I, and which were universally known as "pom-poms," because of the sound they made when in action—could pour out rounds for seventy-three seconds without reloading.[60]

Shortly after the fighter-bombers disappeared, lookouts aboard *Warspite* sighted a group of high-level bombers from which three Friz-X glider-bombs were launched. To ensure a high-order detonation (a designed explosive yield) on impact, the bombs utilized Amatrol explosives, a mixture of TNT and ammonium nitrate. The heart of the deadly missile was an ordinary 1,400 kilogram bomb with an armor piercing warhead equipped with four fins to provide sufficient lift for radio-controlled flight control surfaces in the tail unit to guide the munition to its target. *Warspite*, in her third decade of naval service, and a veteran of the Battle of Jutland in World War I, was hit by one of the bombs.[61]

As tracer rounds and anti-aircraft bursts raced up from the battleship toward the glider-bomb, it dove sharply and a few moments later a cloud of smoke erupted from *Warspite*. A mere seven-to-ten seconds passed between the sighting of the enemy planes and the impact of the stubby bomb. This ordnance was designed to trail a streamer of blue smoke, enabling the bombardier controlling it to visually guide it to the target. The 3,000-pound bomb plunged down through six decks of the battleship to the bilge of the No. 4 boiler room before exploding on her double-bottom. Two other such bombs were near misses; one hit amidships off her starboard side and burst underwater, and the other landed aft off the same side. Casualties among the ship's complement of 1,124 men were limited to nine men killed and fourteen injured.[62]

The battleship's situation was grim. One boiler-room was demolished and four of the remaining five soon flooded. Propulsion and steering were lost, and the ship's draft was down by about five feet due to the approximately 5,000 tons of water that had entered her hull. Lying "dead in the water" she was susceptible to attack at any time including from submarines known to be in the area, and in addition to being immobile, she was blind save her lookouts, as her radar was also out of action. Her commanding officer, Capt. Herbert A. Packer, Royal Navy, signaled the cruiser HMS *Delhi* (D47) to provide anti-aircraft protection.[63]

Pursuant to orders from Rear Adm. Richard L. Conolly, USN, commander Task Force 89, *Hopi* proceeded toward the Straits of Messina at 1600 with *Warspite* in tow. Thirty-five minutes later *Moreno* arrived to assist. The assignment of these two tugs to the damaged battleship would denude the American sector of fleet tugs. However, *Warspite* was a capital ship and, as such, deserved special consideration. The three-hundred-mile transit to Malta commenced with *Moreno* and *Hopi* made up together in a double-tow, with 50 fathoms of cable between the two tugs and 257 fathoms of cable between *Hopi* and the battleship.[64]

Hopi had been anchored in Salerno Bay and men topside had witnessed the attack on *Warspite*. They initially believed that the glider-bomb which hit the battleship was an enemy aircraft that had been shot down, due to the smoke trailing from it. Visual misidentification of these bombs as planes in trouble would be common until ships operating in the Mediterranean became more familiar with the new weapon employed by the Luftwaffe. Lieutenant Owen W. Huff, USN, the commanding officer of *Hopi* described the event in an action report:

> At 1405 September 16, 1943, while anchored in Salerno Bay, the red air raid warning was sounded. At 1425 five enemy planes, German fighter bombers, were sighted off our port beam going inland. No. 2 20mm gun opened fire and later number 1, each expending ten rounds.
> At the same time two large two-motored planes at great altitude were observed directly ahead of us and flying west. They were particularly noticeable because of the thin white streak of smoke they left behind. At a point between the HOPI and H.M.S. WARSPITE it appeared as though one plane had been shot down, for a dark object leaving behind it a trail of black smoke glided downward. This was the bomb that struck the H.M.S. WAR-SPITE amidships.[65]

The cruiser HMS *Euryalus* (D42) was en route to Bizerte, Tunisia, when she intercepted the signal that *Warspite* was damaged. She immediately reversed her course in order to provide escort for the battleship and, after joining an hour before midnight, served as formation guide for the tugs following in her wake. *Hopi* and *Moreno*, towing in tandem, were able to make 9 knots dragging their behemoth charge astern.[66]

In the late afternoon on 16 September the British rescue tugs HMS *Oriana* (W117) and HMS *Nimble* (W123) arrived to provide assistance in helping *Warspite* transit the Straits of Messina. The passage, between the eastern tip of Sicily and the southern tip of Calabria in the south of Italy, is characterized by strong tidal currents and at its narrowest point measures slightly less than two miles in width. Not long after entering the strait in darkness one of the British tugs fell off course, crossed *Hopi*'s tow wire, and parted it. *Narragansett*, which earlier had taken the damaged British cruiser HMS *Uganda* (66) to Malta, took *Hopi*'s place towing ahead. *Hopi* then made up alongside *Warspite*.[67]

After initially joining the group, *Narragansett* received orders to tow the battleship from her portside, forward. British sailors hauled the tug's two-and-one-half-inch towing cable aboard and secured it to the fo'c'sle of the battleship, after which *Moreno* passed a tow wire to *Narragansett*, in order that the two tugs could tow *Warspite* in tandem. The 143-foot *Oriana* then came alongside *Narragansett* to add her pulling power as well. Despite the efforts of the five tugs, the battleship which tended to take charge and yawl, swung broadside to the strong currents in the straits producing anxiety aboard both the *Warspite* and tugs. However, with some work, she was again pointed fair. After exiting the straits at 0650, the tugs increased their speed to six knots.[68]

Nearing Valletta, the capital city of Malta, the morning of 19 September, *Narragansett* slowed to Ahead 1/3 and heaved in on her tow wire which *Warspite* had cast off. *Narragansett* then cast off the tow wire from *Moreno* and stood into Bighi Bay, Grand Harbor, Valletta. She moored alongside the minesweeping trawler HMS *Product* (T188) and *Moreno* made up to her portside.[69]

Following the receipt of a Secret Cypher ordering them to Salerno the American tugs stood out in the early evening. In preparation for putting to sea, Material Condition Baker was set aboard *Narragansett* prior to leaving port (watertight hatches, doors, and fittings closed to the maximum extent while still allowing living conditions). After passing St. Elmo light abeam to port, the commanding officer ordered the special sea detail for leaving port secured and Condition Mike Able, normal cruising watches, set. Because of the U-boat threat, Lt. Charles J. Wichmann, USN, ordered "sound gear cut in" (sonar energized and manned) and depth charges armed for immediate use. The two tugs arrived in the Gulf of Salerno late the following day and anchored for the night, concluding another day in the theater of war.[70]

SALVAGE SHIPS/TUGS AWARDED BATTLE STARS

Two salvage ships and nine tugs received a battle star for the period 9-21 September 1943 for participation in Operation AVALANCHE. Reports citing damage to *Intent* identified her with that name; however, the battle star awarded the harbor tug was credited to *Edenshaw*, the name she later received. Similarly, the star for *Resolute* was credited to *Evea*. The date on which these harbor tugs were renamed is unknown.

Ship	Commanding Officer	Lost or Damaged
Brant (ARS-32)	Lt. Chester H. Rooklidge, USNR/ Lt. John N. Tornberg, USNR	
Tackle (ARS-37)	Lt. J. M. Gillespie, USNR	
Hopi (ATF-71)	Lt. Owen W. Huff, USN	
Moreno (ATF-87)	Lt. Victor H. Kyllberg, USNR	
Narragansett (ATF-88)	Lt. Charles J. Wichmann, USN	
Nauset (ATF-89)	Lt. Joseph Orleck, USN	Sunk by enemy bombs and mines
Intent (YTB-459) renamed *Edenshaw*		Bombed; damaged while fighting fire aboard the *Nauset*; repaired
Resolute (YTB-458) renamed *Evea*		
YT-154		
YT-157		
YT-197	Chief Bos'n Fred Reep in 1944 and perhaps earlier	

PORT OF NAPLES OPENED

> Hundreds of vessels and craft such as floating sheerlegs, cranes, lighters, barges, tugs, small tankers, trawlers, corvettes, sloops, sailing ships, landing craft and destroyers were available to him [retreating German commander] for employment with merchant ships in systematically blocking the major and minor ports.
>
> The wreckage of these vessels obviously had been supervised by an expert with a knowledge of salvage, for each vessel had been methodically destroyed internally in the way of bulkheads, and then so badly "blown" as to preclude use of either pumping or compressed air.
>
> —Commander Eighth Fleet, Vice Adm. Henry K. Hewitt, USN, describing the devastation wrought by German forces to the port and harbor facilities at Naples, Italy, prior to their withdrawal from the city[71]

The U.S. Army's 82nd Airborne Division, reinforced by the Ranger Brigade, captured the city of Naples on 1 October following which efforts immediately began to open the port. The approach channels and harbor were swept and the work necessary to make the port operational was begun. The Germans had thoroughly demolished the harbor craft, cranes, and port operation equipment, and sunk quantities of vessels to prevent Allied use of the port. Making matters worse, over each sunken vessel, retreating forces had:

> Invariably sunk a few lighters, a dock crane, an occasional locomotive or a string of trucks, upon which wagon-loads of ammunition, oxygen bottles, and small arms had been dumped in a haphazard manner. This super-tangle of obstructions imposed extensive diving operations even after the main objective had been reached, and many wrecks had been sunk in such a manner as to be invisible from the air.[72]

These conditions notwithstanding, the combined British-American Salvage Party had learned much about the enemy's unwelcome demolition practices while rehabilitating the ports of Bizerte and Palermo. Moreover, unlike previous efforts, the work could be performed by men held in reserve in Sicily rather than by men worn down by salvage work during beach assaults. To increase the number of men available, *Tackle* was sent to Algiers to load salvage material and bring more salvors forward. As a first priority, dry-docks were rapidly restored to use; and as at Palermo, where wrecks could not be quickly moved to clear berths, they were bridged-over and converted to piers. Eight ship berths were cleared in fourteen days with much of the early work accomplished by British boom vessels specially rigged to lift over their bows.[73]

Later these ships were supplemented by British wreck dispersal vessels, the U.S. Navy salvage ships *Tackle* and *Brant*, and two newly constructed salvage ships *Extricate* (ARS-16) and sister ship *Weight* (ARS-35). The latter 183-foot diesel-electric ships were commanded by Lt. Comdr. Paul M. Runyon and Lt. Frederick J. Leamond, respectively. Constructed of wood, they were considered superior to the steel-hulled tugs for firefighting because they could remain alongside a burning ship without their interiors becoming too hot for crewmembers on watch to carry out their duties. A hose continuously discharging water on their decks and hull protected the salvage ships from catching fire. Within three weeks, twelve berths were available.

In one month, the port was adequately restored to accept sufficient deep-draft ships to support Allied armies supplied through Naples.[74]

PROGRESS MADE, BUT...

> *[It was] the most daring amphibious operation we have yet launched or which I think has ever been launched on a similar scale. We must...consider this episode—the landing on the beaches of Salerno—as an important and pregnant victory, one deserving a definite place in the records....*
>
> —Excerpts from British Prime Minister Winston Churchill's summarization of Operation AVALANCHE on 21 September 1943, in which he also highlighted that intervention of strong naval gunfire support forces and air forces had played a large role in the recovery of an unfortunate military situation.[75]

As Allied forces occupied the city of Naples, the Germans were withdrawing to the Volturno River and trying to establish a defensive line across the Italian peninsula. With enemy forces retiring northward, and the Allies having established two armies on the Italian mainland—the U.S. Fifth and British Eighth—the prospects for advancing rapidly to Rome appeared to be good. The Allies did not yet appreciate the extent to which the Germans could use the Italian winter weather, the Italian terrain, and the mettle of their own outnumbered troops to deny the Allies and the Italians quick entry into the capital city.[76]

Crossing the Strait of Messina had been easy, but securing a beachhead at Salerno proved to be more difficult. Though much loss of life was suffered by both sides, neither achieved its objectives. The Germans had wanted to drive the Allies off the beaches and had failed. The Allies were ashore and their position in Italy would never again be seriously threatened. But their hopes of using the surrender of Italy to make quick gains advancing northward up the peninsula toward Rome had not been realized. These setbacks would be miniscule, though, in comparison to what lay ahead. No one could foresee the bitter ground-fighting that would take place at the Volturno and Sangro Rivers, at the small Adriatic Sea town of Ortona, on the approaches to the Liri valley, along the Rapido and Garigliano Rivers, in the shadow of Cassino, and on the Anzio beachhead. No one could anticipate the expenditure of men and material that would be necessary for the Allies to take Rome, least of all the Italians, who on 13 October 1943 would declare war on Germany.[77]

7

Disaster at Anzio – Operation SHINGLE

Whoever holds Rome holds the title deeds of Italy.

—Comment by British Prime Minister Winston Churchill in support of his plan for American and British troops to make an amphibious landing at Anzio to turn the tide of the Italian campaign, which had begun with a combined British-Canadian-American invasion of Sicily on 10 July 1943 and would last until 2 May 1945[1]

I had hoped we were hurling a wildcat into the shore, but all we got was a stranded whale.

—Winston Churchill expressing his displeasure that Maj. Gen. John P. Lucas, USA, who, after coming ashore behind the exposed rear of the German defenses on the Gustav Line, had focused on entrenching his tiny bridgehead against an expected counterattack instead of launching some type of offensive action.

On 22 January 1944 British and American troops, embarked in ships of Rear Adm. Frank J. Lowry's Task Force 81, arrived off beaches about thirty miles below Rome near the twin resort towns of Anzio and Nettuno. They were a delight to the eye, particularly Anzio. It offered bright sandy beaches flanked by gaily colored stucco villas, and above them, the Alban Hills were covered with Roman pines. Anzio had been a popular seaside bathing resort since the days of Nero. The purpose of the impending Allied amphibious assault, code named SHINGLE, was to land Allied troops behind German forces along the Gustav Line that were impeding the advance of the U.S. Fifth and

British Eighth Armies northward to Rome. Anzio offered the best landing site within striking distance of Rome, and it was within range of supporting Allied aircraft operating from Naples.[2]

Comprising Task Force 81 were two task forces: Force X-Ray, directly under Lowry carrying VI Corps of Lt. Gen. Mark W. Clark's Fifth Army and Force Peter, commanded by Rear Adm. Thomas Hope Troubridge, RN, in which Maj. Gen. Ronald Penney and the British 1st Infantry Division were embarked. The American (X-Ray) and British (Peter) led task forces included the following military units:

- U.S. 3rd Infantry Division
- U.S. 751st Tank Battalion
- U.S. 504th Parachute Infantry Regiment of the 82nd Airborne Division
- 509th Parachute Infantry Battalion
- Three battalions of U.S. Army Rangers
- British 1st Infantry Division
- British 46th Royal Tank Regiment
- Two British Commando battalions

The U.S. 45th Infantry Division and Combat Command A (CCA), a regimental-size unit of the U.S. 1st Armored Division, were to land as reinforcements once the beachhead was established.[3]

Photo 7-1

Rear Adm. Frank J. Lowry, USN.
Source:
http://www.johnbakerswarbook.org

At 0200 on 22 January (an hour before a third-quarter waning moon rose), Allied troops began storming ashore at Anzio. The American 6615th Ranger Force (1st, 3d, and 4th Rangers) landed at Yellow beach, a one-mile long strand between Anzio harbor and the Villa Borghese hill. The British 1st Infantry drew the worst landing area, Peter beach, adjacent to and northwest of Yellow beach. The discovery of land mines beneath the sand delayed movement ashore. A British officer remarking on this threat to life and limb succinctly

Disaster at Anzio – Operation SHINGLE   117

observed: "It must be realized that no amount of shouting through loud hailers will induce troops to advance through a minefield." The remaining assault beaches (Red and Green)—which began at the southern boundary of Yellow beach at Nettuno and extended to the southeast—were allocated to the American 3rd Infantry. Major Gen. John P. Lucas, U.S. Army, was the overall commander of the American and British troops comprising VI Corps.[4]

Map 7-1

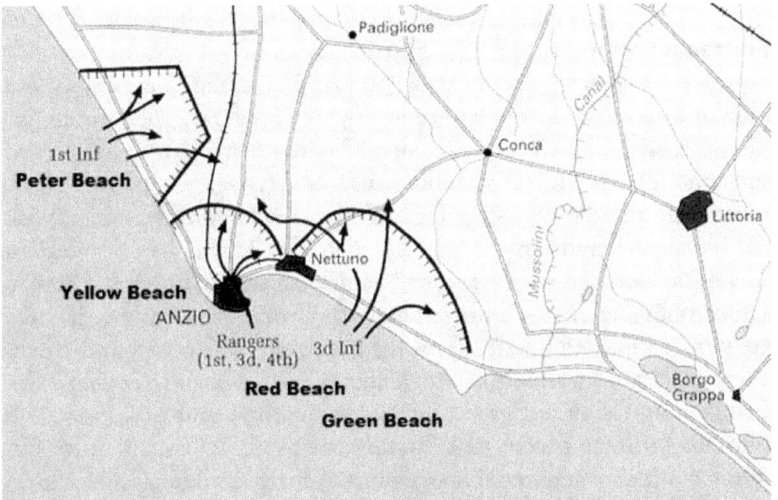

The purpose of the amphibious landing at Anzio was to insert Allied forces behind the Gustav Line, where German defense forces had stalled the advance of American and British armies in their drive to Rome.
Source: http://www.history.army.mil/brochures/anzio/map1.JPG

The landings, which were synchronized with the inland offense of the Fifth Army along the Gustav Line, were comparatively unopposed. The ease of the landings in darkness, and swift advance of British and American troops against slight German ground resistance, were noted by one paratrooper of the 504th Parachute Infantry Regiment, 82nd Airborne Division, who later recalled that it had been sunny and warm on D-Day, making it very hard to believe that a war was going on and that he was in the middle of it. British assault forces made the shore in Peter sector unchallenged, but found the beach heavily mined and, later faced shelling from 88mm guns positioned on the heights above the beaches. The same was true for American forces landing in X-Ray sector; there was no initial ground opposition but shelling started after the troops were ashore. The Ranger landing at Anzio went according to plan with some later fighting.⁵

A diversionary operation was staged at Civitavecchia, a sea port on the Tyrrhenian Sea west-northwest of Rome, concurrent with the landings. Shore bombardment was undertaken by the British light cruiser HMS *Dido* (37), destroyers HMS *Inglefield* (D02) and HMS *Kempenfelt* (R03), and Free French destroyer *Le Fantasque*. At the same time offshore, coastal forces staged a mock invasion by carrying out dummy landings. Following the operation, the cruiser and destroyers took up positions southeast of Anzio to keep the coastal road between Formis and Terracina under fire to check the north-bound flow of German forces to the SHINGLE area.⁶

Overall, apart from the loss of two ships, the landings were a complete success. In the late morning on 22 January the steel-hulled minesweeper *Portent* (AM-106) struck a mine off Green beach and sank, and the large infantry landing craft *LCI(L)-20* took a direct bomb hit during an attack on shipping off Red beach by eight Focke-Wulf Fw-190 aircraft and was destroyed. Enemy air activity had been minor on D-Day and Allied aircraft had largely thwarted the few German fighter-bombers in the area. There was some trepidation that the situation could deteriorate if strong enemy air and/or ground forces were able to react rapidly to the landings. Of particular concern was the slow rate of discharge of vehicles, munitions, and other materials ashore. At Peter beach, tank landing craft *LCT-217* spent forty-five minutes striking and retracting from sandbars until finally beaching. On these beaches, tank landing ships and smaller tank landing craft required pontoons to offload cargo as a result of soft sand and the offshore bars, and their use lengthened the landing procress⁷

THE GUSTAV LINE

> *The landing at Nettuno is the beginning of the invasion of Europe planned for 1944....* [All German armed forces] *must be filled with the fanatical will to emerge from the fight victorious, and not to rest until the last enemy has been destroyed or thrown back into the sea. The battle must be waged with holy hatred towards a foe who is fighting a merciless war of extermination against the German people.*
>
> —Excerpt from an Order of the Day issued by Adolf Hitler on 28 January 1944⁸

As compared to Anzio at the time of the landings, things were much different on the Fifth Army front. There the enemy appeared to have committed the bulk of the general reserves, leaving only weak forces in the Rome area. The latest reports on this front indicated the probability of a strong German counterattack. The amphibious assault at Anzio was mounted to insert Allied forces behind the German winter or Gustav Line at which the northward advancing main Fifth Army and British Eighth Army had stalled in their drive to Rome. After the Allied landings in southern Italy, German forces had fought a delaying action while preparing defensive lines to their rear. The Gustav Line, which ran from Minturno to Ortona, bisecting the Italian peninsula, guarded the approaches to Rome. To make the natural mountain defenses along which it was orientated even more formidable, enemy engineers had set up an elaborate network of pillboxes (dug-in concrete guard posts), bunkers, and minefields.[9]

The German high command had also committed Field Marshal Albert Kesselring, the overall German commander in the Mediterranean Theater, to the defense of Rome. Kesselring had personally taken over command of the entire Italian Theater, and his Tenth Army now positioned at the southern front (Gustav Line) held the Rome area, while the Fourteenth Army guarded central and northern Italy. Opposing the German forces were the Fifth Army on the western, and the Eighth Army on the eastern sector of the front.[10]

At Anzio, the initial landings of the Allied flanking movement were successful, but increased German opposition ashore prevented the breakout that would have led to an early capture of Rome. In addition to the enemy air attacks on D-Day, German shore guns delivered fire, and tanks shelled the breakwater at Anzio. In the days that followed, an increasing number of enemy troops arrived in the area and determined German land, air, and naval forces opposed the landings. The Allied Task Force lost a significant number of ships and craft during the lengthy siege in which American and British troops were pinned on the beach. Much of the salvage work that ensued resulted from the failure to make the breakout.

Readers interested in the total complement of ships and craft assigned to Operation SHINGLE may consult the Naval Order of Battle in Appendix D. The ships of Task Force 81, listed in the tables, were compiled from commander Task Force 81's Operational Plan, war diaries of subordinate task group commanders and ships, and Admiralty war diaries. Details about landing craft that were sent to

Anzio after the initial landings are scarce, thus the "Other Follow-on Ships" section of the table is incomplete.[11]

ALLIED SALVAGE FORCES

> *It is a matter of record that during the first twelve weeks after the landing, the beachhead was raided by enemy aircraft 277 times. The vast majority of these raids occurred during the first two months. Although many of the raids were on the beachhead itself, the shipping in the area came in for its share. The raids occurred at all hours of the day and night, being made by the light of flares and even by moonlight. All types of attacks were made, including low level bombing, dive bombing, glider bombs, and torpedo attacks.*
>
> *In addition to these raids, a German railroad gun approximating an eleven inch gun would drop shells into the area for about a half hour daily. This gun was never located until captured when the army finally broke through at Cassino and moved up through Italy.*
>
> —Excerpt from the history of USS *Herbert C. Jones* (DE-137) compiled on 1 December 1945. At Anzio, the destroyer escort provided anti-submarine and glider bomb protection to the cruisers and destroyers bombarding the shore, and to the ships in the transport area.

The salvage forces initially assigned to Anzio proved to be insufficient in size. There were only a few tugs and salvage ships and, despite the relatively large numbers of landing craft assigned to salvage work, operations were difficult because of shallow water, storm-produced high winds, and heavy seas. The necessary work included freeing grounded landing craft; aiding ships damaged by sea mines, gunfire and aerial attack; firefighting; and rescue of sailors/troops trapped aboard ship or in the water after abandoning. The jobs were numerous and persistent, resulting in a few additional tugs and salvage ships being dispatched to the assault beaches. The siege-like combat that developed at Anzio kept Allied troops contained on the beachhead for a long time.[12]

The associated requirement for sea forces to support these troops, for weeks after the initial landings, resulted in many ship casualties over this lengthy period; most to mine strikes and aircraft attacks as shown in the following table:

Royal Navy/British Ships Sunk at Anzio, Italy

Date	Ship or Craft	Cause	Location
January 1944	Four assault landing craft: *LCA-323, 394, 428, 697*		Anzio landings
January 1944	Seven mechanized landing craft: *LCM-204, 623, 910, 930, 1022, 1064, 1173*		Anzio landings
January 1944	Three large personnel landing craft: *LCP(L)-66, 356, 373*		Anzio landings
January 1944	Medium support landing craft *LCS(M)-46*		Anzio landings
23 Jan 1944	Destroyer *Janus* (F53)	Glider-bomb	Off Anzio
24 Jan 1944	Hospital Ship *St. David*	Glider-bomb	South of Anzio
26 Jan 1944	Tank landing ship *LST-422*	Mine	Anzio landings
29 Jan 1944	Light cruiser *Spartan* (95)	Glider-bomb	Off Anzio
16 Feb 1944	Tank landing ship *LST-418*	Two underwater explosions	Anzio landings
18 Feb 1944	Light cruiser *Penelope* (97)	U-boat torpedo	Anzio area
20 Feb 1944	Tank landing ship *LST-305*	U-boat torpedo	Anzio landings
25 Feb 1944	Destroyer *Inglefield* (D02)	Glider-bomb	Off Anzio
17 Mar 1944	Large infantry landing craft *LCI(L)-273*[13]	Aircraft attack	Anzio

U.S. Navy/Merchant Ships Sunk at Anzio

Date	Ship or Craft	Cause	Location
22 Jan 1944	Minesweeper *Portent* (AM-106)	Mine	Off Green beach at Anzio
22 Jan 1944	Large infantry landing craft *LCI(L)-20*	Aircraft bomb	Off Red beach south of Anzio
25 Jan 1944	Minesweeper *YMS-30*	Mine	Off Anzio
26 Jan 1944	*LCI(L)-32*	Mine	Off Anzio
29 Jan 1944	S.S. *Samuel Huntington*	Glider-bomb	Off Anzio
13 Feb 1944	Tank landing craft *LCT-220*	Heavy weather	At Anzio
15 Feb 1944	*LCT-35*	Bomb hit on S.S. *Elihu Yale*, to which the *LCT-35* was moored	Off Anzio
20 Feb 1944	Tank landing ship *LST-348*	*U-410* torpedo	Off Anzio[14]

British tugs HMS *Prosperous* (W96) and HMS *Weasel* (W120), the rescue tug *ATR-1*, harbor tug *Edenshaw*, and nine landing craft—LCI(L)s and LCTs—comprised the salvage forces that accompanied the invasion fleet. The salvage ships *Restorer* and *Weight*, and fleet tug *Hopi*, joined after the assault.

Having proven their worth in salvage work, four large infantry landing craft—LCI(L)s *10*, *15*, *219*, and *232*—were fitted out with salvage gear to perform shallow-water operations at Anzio. The *10* and *15* were assigned to Red and Green beaches, respectively, and *219* and *232* to Peter beach. *LCI(L)-10* was also the headquarters salvage ship. Lt. Comdr. Gordon Raymond (the Red beach salvage officer) and six enlisted salvors embarked in her for transit to the assault beaches. Once off Red beach, the salvage men transferred to *LCT-198*. Additional landing craft were assigned salvage duties before the assault, and as necessary some reallocations of salvage vessels occurred between beaches during the operation. The salvage group off Green beach on D-Day consisted of the British tug HMS *Prosperous*, large infantry landing craft *LCI(L)-10*, *15* and *16*, and tank landing craft *LCT-198*, *209*, and *221*. The tug HMS *Weasel* later reported for duty and *LCI(L)-48* was added to the salvage forces as well.[15]

During the opening days of the operation the performance of the officer in charge of the salvage forces was less than satisfactory, resulting in his replacement. Commander Task Force 81 noted this deficiency in his report on the operation: "When no ports are open, the unloading of ships over beaches is essential to the success of an operation. This requires a salvage party which is organized and trained, with a competent officer at its lead." Despite a requirement to work in the face of enemy fire, initial poor leadership, and a storm hitting the area, units of the salvage forces performed heroically. Among them the wooden-hulled rescue tug *ATR-1*—whose efforts to save the British cruiser *Spartan* are depicted in the book's cover art.[16]

RESCUE TUG *ATR-1*

Although the rescue tug *ATR-1* was not the only U.S. salvage vessel engaged in the Anzio landings, she played a prominent part in the operation until she too became a salvage candidate. The detailed account of her actions that follows is illustrative of the actions of the entire U.S. and Royal Navy salvage force and the conditions they had to face while being pinned down in the stalled landings at Anzio. *ATR-1* was the first ship in a class of eighty 165-foot unnamed wooden rescue tugs built for war service, and the first to earn a battle star. The next few pages are devoted to describing the very short period between her departure from the builder's yard and participation in combat duty off Anzio. Her crossing of the Atlantic and into the Mediterranean as part of a ship convoy is also detailed, as it is representative of the experiences of other tugs and salvage ships and because this subject is not covered elsewhere in the book.

The Navy described the strengths and limitations of these small, stalwart vessels in a pamphlet published in 1944:

> ATRs are new wooden tugs originally designed to render emergency assistance to vessels disabled on the high seas in enemy submarine infested coastal waters of the United States. They are extremely well fitted for firefighting and have moderate salvage facilities. ATRs have excellent seagoing qualities and good towing power but are sharply limited in endurance and radius of action. These vessels are excellent for towing operations of a large magnitude but of a limited distance. ATRs are well suited to supplement the services of ATFs [large steel-hulled, all-purpose, long-range, powerful, and very seaworthy fleet ocean tugs] in combat areas, where cruising endurance is not an important factor and particularly where fire may be one of the great potential hazards. When a sufficient number of these tugs are available, one should be assigned to each major base for standby duty.[17]

ATR-1, commanded by Lt. (jg) H. L. MacGill, USN, was a mere four months old at the start of her support of Operation SHINGLE. Following construction by Wheeler Ship Building Corp., Whitestone, New York, and being placed in commission at the yard on 24 September 1943, she underwent a series of shipboard operations, tests, and trials. These included "deperming"—in which copper cables were temporarily wrapped around her hull and superstructure and very high electrical current was passed through them to decrease the ship's magnetic signature—due to its metal components and its associated vulnerability to magnetic mines—and "swinging ship" for calibration of RDF (radio direction finding) equipment and the magnetic compass. Standardization runs were made over a measured mile to obtain data needed in conjunction with fuel economy, and vibration test runs to groom *ATR-1*'s propulsion plant.[18]

In preparation for combat duty, Lieutenant MacGill exercised the crew at "fire quarters" (manning firefighting stations and energizing associated equipment) and "battle stations" (general quarters). During the latter training, gun crews fired the single 3-inch/.50-caliber dual-purpose gun mount, and two 20mm anti-aircraft mounts, fitted in the ship to provide a modicum of self-defense. The *ATR-1*'s authorized manning was five officers and forty-seven enlisted men.[19]

Photo 7-2

Rescue Tug *ATR-1* on builder's trials in September 1943
U.S. Navy photo, now in the collections of the U.S. National Archives

EUROPE BOUND

ATR-1 left anchorage in Lynnhaven Roads, a tidal estuary near Virginia Beach, the morning of 14 November bound for Europe. She passed the Cape Henry light abeam to starboard at 0750 and thereafter steered various eastward courses to conform to track, until abeam buoy "x-s" in mid-afternoon when she came right to an east-southeast course. As the hours ticked by, the tug continued steaming under power from boilers No. 1 and 2, making occasional course and speed changes, the highest speed being 12.1 knots. A short time after first light the following day, she maneuvered to join newly formed Convoy UGS-24.[20]

The "slow eastbound convoys" sailing from Hampton Roads, Virginia, for Gibraltar along the southern trans-Atlantic route, to carry food, ammunition, and other war materials to the Army in North Africa and southern Europe, were designated UGS and numbered consecutively. These convoys of merchant vessels, under escort by Navy ships, assembled in Hampton Roads near the mouth of Chesapeake Bay, and terminated at various North African locations. Convoy UGS-24 was comprised of 103 merchantmen and 24 escorts.[21]

Eight days into the Atlantic crossing, the task force commander reported the position of the convoy to commander Tenth Fleet, whose mission was protection of coastal shipping—via destruction of enemy submarines—and centralization of control and routing of convoys. On 28 November the task force received a message from commander Moroccan Sea Frontier providing estimated positions of two submarines close to the track of the convoy, but no threat materialized. Two days later, F.O.C. GIB—the British flag officer commanding Gibraltar who, from "the Rock," controlled virtually all naval traffic passing in and out of the Mediterranean Sea—ordered a delay in arrival from the early evening on 1 December until the following morning. This resulted in the convoy dramatically changing course to lose distance.[22]

The convoy began reducing its front at 0130 on 2 December, forming into four columns to enter the swept channel—a safe lane for the passage of Allied shipping through a minefield intended to deter movements of U-boats in and out of "the Med"—leading into the Straits of Gibraltar. At 0915 a British Escort Unit relieved Destroyer Division 26 of its escort duties off Europa Point. After various ships detached to enter Gibraltar Harbor, the convoy formed into twelve columns to continue passage across the Mediterranean to Oran, a major port city on the coast of Algeria in North Africa. On 3 December *ATR-1* and some merchant vessels left the convoy and formed into a single column to pass through the anti-submarine torpedo nets at the entrance to Mers-el-Kebir ("the Great Harbor") near Oran. Following her arrival in port, *ATR-1* reported to commander Naval Operating Base, Oran, for duty. The convoy continued on to its ultimate destination, Port Said, Egypt.[23]

INITIAL RESCUE WORK

Rescue tug *ATR-1* remained berthed at Oran, waiting to dash out into the shipping lanes to assist merchantmen in distress, until mid-afternoon on 16 December when she got under way to assist the Liberty ship S.S. *John S. Copley*. The merchant vessel had been torpedoed by the German submarine *U-73* while joining Convoy GUS-24 (Gibraltar to United States) about fifteen miles north-northwest of the Mers-el-Kebir harbor entrance, the meeting point for members of "slow westbound convoys" returning to the United States along the southern trans-Atlantic route.24

Map 7-2

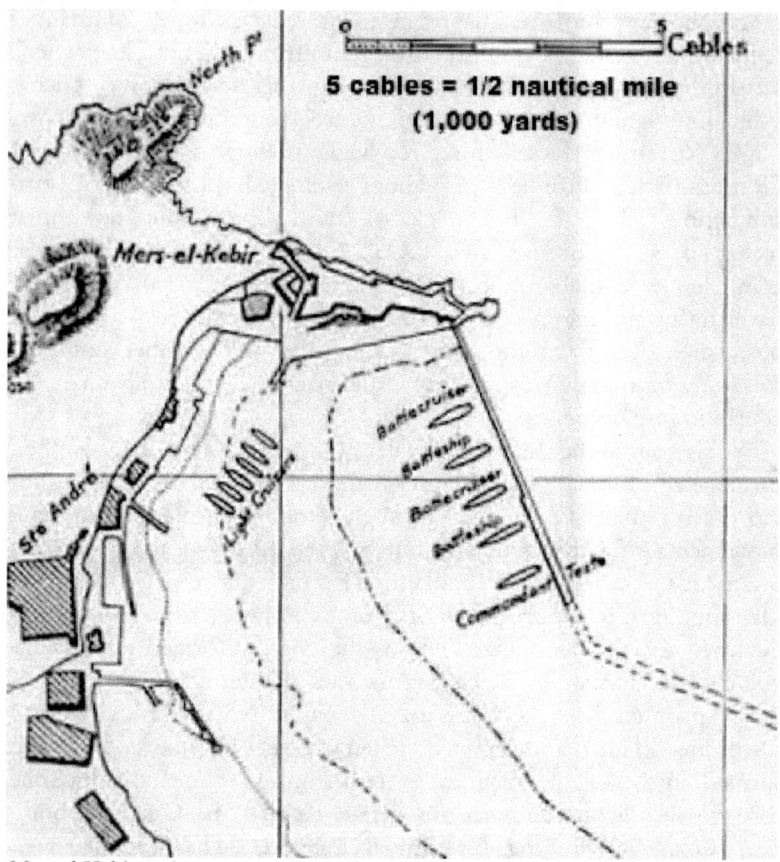

Mers-el-Kebir anchorage near Oran, Algeria

The torpedo that struck *Copley* blasted a hole eighteen feet long on her starboard side, flooding No. 2 hold and causing an eight-degree list. The crew of *ATR-47*, which had arrived at Oran on 22 November a little ahead of *ATR-1*, had already accumulated some experience in maritime rescue work. She and *ATR-1* were dispatched from Oran. As *ATR-47* neared the stricken vessel, her commanding officer, Lt. (jg) Harry L. Lane, USNR, spotted the Liberty ship lying with about a ten-degree port list and two feet down by the bow. *ATR-47* took *John S. Copley* in tow while *ATR-1* stood by to assist. Upon arrival at the Oran

Harbor entrance, the rescue tugs handed off the merchantman to two French harbor tugs, and then moored at Mers-el-Kebir.[25]

For the balance of December, *ATR-1* remained in port, except for getting under way on two occasions; to "swing ship" for compass compensation, and test fire her two 20mm guns. This routine changed with receipt of orders dispatching her to Algiers, Algeria, for convoy protection duties. She set out from the convoy assembly area off Oran, at 0636 on 3 January 1944, and slid into the "Oran Joiners Section" of Convoy UGS-26. *ATR-1* arrived at Algiers the next day and moored at the Mole de Passageurs. Routine duties followed; towing the British rescue tug HMS *Restive* (W39) to the Port of Algiers and Dutch troopship M.V. *Indrapoera* to the Algiers harbor entrance. After several ensuing idle days, *ATR-1* received orders sending her to Naples, Italy, as a prelude to participation in the landings at Anzio.[26]

NAPLES BOUND

The tug left the port in early morning darkness at 0255 on 17 January 1944 to join the Algiers section of a special convoy bound for Naples. After forming in two columns, the ships steered a northerly course until joining the main body a little past daylight. Later that day, as the convoy occasionally executed turns and zigzagged to lessen the possibility of attack by submarines, *ATR-1* exercised at general quarters. On 19 January there was a sighting of a floating object thought to be a mine. Her port 20mm blasted away at it for two minutes, expending eighty rounds, but failed to sink it. Such sightings were not unique. It was learned after the war, that Germany had employed fake rubber mines, as well as real ones, to create perceptions of the presence of mines in particular areas of coastal waters to induce Allied ships to move farther offshore into deeper waters where they would be more susceptible to attack by U-boats.[27]

The following morning 20 January, the convoy formed into a single column to enter the Naples approach channel, with *ATR-1* the last ship in line. At 0905, with Cape Chebrio light to port, she followed the wake of the ship ahead into the Gulf of Naples, departed the convoy and proceeded to anchorage. Lieutenant MacGill then reported to commander Eighth Amphibious Force, Rear Adm. Frank J. Lowry, USN, for duty.[28]

ATR-1 PARTICIPATION IN OPERATION SHINGLE

> *In many ways, Anzio was much like the Pacific war. There was no rear area that was safe from attack. If you were at Anzio at all, you were in the front lines. No bunker, no ship, was safe. One sailor aboard the [destroyer] U.S.S. Trippe [DD-403] described it as a "vision of hell. For four hours we were under continuous attack. The bombers were merciless and the sky was ablaze with shellfire...."*
>
> —Irwin J. Kappes in the article "Anzio - The Allies' Greatest Blunder of World War II," *MilitaryHistoryOnline.com*

Less than twenty-four hours after arriving in southern Italy, the rescue tug *ATR-1* got under way from the Naples anchorage en route to Anzio. In late afternoon, she maneuvered into position 500 yards to starboard of the No. 2 Liberty ship in a special convoy designated NAM-2 bound for Anzio. Arriving south of Cape d'Anzio the morning of 22 January, the convoy broke up and the tug proceeded toward the transport area.²⁹

In the transport area at 0844 on 22 January, *ATR-1* sighted anti-aircraft fire eight miles distant, aimed at six Messerschmitts that had broken through the Allied fighter cover overhead to dive bomb Red beach. A few hours later, at a little past noon, signal flag hoists aboard neighboring ships gave warning of an imminent air attack. In response to this warning and subsequent receipt of a "red alert" via radio communications, MacGill ordered all hands aboard the tug to battle stations. During one raid, Focke-Wulf fighter-bombers dropped ordnance on tank landing ships and infantry landing craft clustered around two pontoon causeways at Red beach. A direct hit by a 500-pound bomb on *LCI(L)-20* destroyed the craft. After each "all clear" signal, the officers and men aboard *ATR-1* transitioned to "watch condition two," a lesser state of readiness than battle stations. At 1747 the rescue tug steamed from the transport area and anchored off the beach. In recognition of the continuing threat, boilers remained "cut in" on the main steam supply line, in order that she could get under way rapidly.³³

LUFTWAFFE GLIDER-BOMBS

The following morning, 23 January, the light cruiser *Brooklyn* (CL-40) began shelling Littoria (renamed Latina in 1947)—a town well-inland that German troops in the area were using as an assembly point—thereby breaking up a counterattack. *ATR-1* got under way at 1018 in preparation for providing assistance to ships requiring firefighting or towing services in the face of continuing air raids by the German Air Force. In mid-afternoon she anchored in twenty feet of water off the invasion beach and attempted to tow British *LST-428* free of the sand. The towing hawser parted in the stern chock of the tank landing ship during this effort. Unable to provide further assistance to this vessel, the tug moved farther off shore and anchored in deeper water. As the early evening twilight deepened a fifty-five plane raid arrived overhead. Thirty-five were driven off by Allied fighters but the aircraft that got through concentrated on attacking the Royal Navy destroyers HMS *Janus* (F53) and HMS *Jervis* (F00). *Janus* was hit by one Hs 293 glider-bomb from a Dornier Do-217 bomber and sank in about twenty minutes, with heavy loss of life. The destroyers HMS *Laforey* (G99) and *Jervis*, and some smaller craft, were able to rescue more than eighty survivors. *Jervis* was also struck by a similar radio-controlled bomb and was damaged but suffered no casualties.[34]

At Salerno, the U.S. Navy had learned to respect the deadly effects of this weapon, and had therefore stationed Army fighter-director teams aboard the U.S. destroyer escorts *Frederick C. Davis* (DE-136) and *Herbert C. Jones* (DE-137) and HMS *Ulster Queen*, an improvised fighter director ship. By monitoring Luftwaffe radio frequencies, these teams could discern when the bombers were warming up at Rome airfields, and from what direction a particular air raid was approaching to make a strike. Fashioned in the shape of a glider, and carried beneath a parent bomber, Henschel Hs 293 glider-bombs were designed for use against capital shipping. Remotely controlled with a joystick, the projectile was steered to its target by the plane's bombardier who visually tracked it with the aid of a guidance flare in the tail. The actual flight path of the missile resembled a series of arcs as it received and followed corrections.[35]

Prevailing fair weather ended on 24 January. After that 20-knot westerly winds and high seas caused some pontoon causeways to broach or be set adrift. *ATR-1* was occupied for a time during the day recovering one. At 1630, she went to general quarters on the receipt of a red alert, the first of several associated with a series of attacks made against shipping in the transport area. The Germans initially sent fifteen fighter-bombers, followed by forty-three at dusk, and another fifty-two after dusk. The destroyer *Plunkett* (DD-431) was hit by a bomb with damage and loss of life, and the minesweeper *Prevail*

(AM-107) was put out of action by the blast from a near miss. Appallingly, British hospital ship HMHS *St. David* was sunk with loss of life. The despicable decision by German pilots to attack her as well as HMHS *St. Andrew* and HMHS *Leinster* while evacuating casualties from the beachhead infuriated the Allied assault forces. These ships were well lighted and clearly marked with the Red Cross.[36]

During the first raid, *ATR-1* opened with 20mm fire as four bombers approaching from the south passed close to her, expending sixty-six rounds. She witnessed at 1840, aircraft flares that drew scattered AA fire. The enemy used flares freely and effectively at night, as attested to by a ditty composed by an officer aboard the destroyer *Frederick C. Davis* (DE-136), which began "The flares at night burn long and bright in the bay at Anzio." There were more flares at 1915 and thereafter a single plane came in low from the north and dropped three bombs, one landed about a thousand yards off *ATR-1*'s port bow but caused no damage to the wooden ship.[37]

January 25th brought more of the same; enemy aircraft arrived overhead at 0530 and 1214 dropping flares and bombs. During the first attack, *ATR-1*'s gunners got off thirty rounds of 20mm. In the late morning between the two attacks, the tug went alongside the British tank landing ship *LST-162* to hoist her spare anchor from deck storage and lower it over the stern for attachment to an anchor chain somehow freed of its original "hook." That evening, a rising west wind with mounting seas induced many ships at anchor to get under way to ride out the storm.[38]

GREAT LOSS OF LIFE ABOARD HMS *LST-422*

In response to a 0520 sighting of fire aboard a ship on the horizon, the rescue tug began heaving in her anchor to get under way to investigate the source of the blaze. She arrived on the scene to find the British tank landing ship *LST-422* aflame. The ship, newly arrived from Naples and waiting to unload cargo at the Anzio docks, had been blown into a minefield offshore by gale force winds. A mine detonation that blasted a huge hole in the underwater hull and starboard side of the ship ignited her deadly cargo. Embarked in the burning vessel were personnel of Companies C, D, and Headquarters of the American 83rd Chemical Battalion, Motorized, as well as their armament—4.2-inch mortar batteries that fired white phosphorous, smoke, gas, and high-explosive shells—and trucks, Jeeps, M3 halftracks, ambulances, and other vehicles. Many of the trucks were loaded with very volatile white phosphorous mortar shells, and scores of 50-gallon barrels of gasoline were lashed to the deck. With so large a cargo of flammable and explosive materials, the fire had spread rapidly.[39]

ATR-1 arrived to find the entire ship aflame and gutted by fire. Two groups of survivors, one at the bow and one on the stern, were dazed and unable to move due to intense heat radiating from the decks and exploding ammunition. A majority of the mortar battalion had been asleep in the tank deck which had flooded rapidly. This inundation sealed the fate of over four hundred soldiers who had no chance of getting out. The surviving American soldiers and British sailors on the main deck were faced with a grim choice, get off the LST or be consumed by the inferno.[40]

MacGill placed the bow of *ATR-1* alongside the starboard quarter of the burning ship and began cooling its decks with water from the tug's monitor in order to provide a safe pathway for survivors. This and other actions resulted in the rescue of twenty-one officers and men from the LST and adjacent water. Limited working room and rough seas caused *ATR-1* to suffer considerable damage during this operation as noted in a war diary entry:

> Loss of port anchor, hawse pipe and lip, port side of forecastle at deck edge stove in slightly, rail damaged, holes in outer planking, steel guard strip on rubbing strake carried away on port side for approximately 15 feet and possible damage to wooden frame forward.

All survivors were given warm food, clothing and first aid. The tank landing ship was a total loss. As nothing more could be done to save her, the tug returned at 0800 to the transport area. In total 454 Americans and 29 British sailors were lost, and during the transit, Pvt. R. V. Payne, U.S. Army, died on board. Midafternoon that day, *LST-422* broke in two and sank. As the tank landing ship went to the bottom, enemy planes were overhead.[41]

Later that day *ATR-1* went to the assistance of Liberty ship S.S. *John Banvard*. She found upon arrival that it was deserted but apparently not damaged. The master had ordered the crew to abandon following a near miss from a bomb. Some of her naval armed guard later returned aboard and manned a gun against a second bomb attack. *Banvard* survived Anzio, but later ran aground in the Azores on 31 October 1944 and was declared a total loss.[42]

A raid at dusk by Focke-Wulf Fw-190 fighters—which could be fitted with rockets and bombs in addition to machine guns and 20mm cannons—damaged HMS *LST-366*, two merchant vessels, seven patrol craft, and *ATR-1*. Three bombs fell in the water about thirty-five yards off the tug's starboard quarter, and another seventy-five yards off her port quarter. The bomb blasts, and associated violent movements of the ship, caused breaks in her main steam feed discharge and main exhaust lines, and dislocated other propulsion plant lines and piping. These were all repaired.[43]

By the morning of 27 January, the wind and seas had abated and tank landing ships were able to unload their cargos. The day was also characterized by many red alerts preceding the arrival of enemy planes and the dropping of flares and bombs. In late morning *ATR-1* came alongside HMS *LST-383* to transfer survivors from *LST-422* and that afternoon the tug conducted a burial at sea off Anzio for Private Payne. Following this solemn ceremony, MacGill anchored off the beach, which required the chain to be walked out the fractured hawse pipe. The next day brought more air raid warnings. Some of these proved to be false; they resulted from radar detection of friendly planes whose flight plans had not been provided to ships in the area. During four of the alerts enemy planes dropped both flares and bombs. *ATR-1* expended 20mm and .50-caliber ammunition scoring no hits, but also suffering no damage from the attacks. This concluded the actions precipitated by the mine detonation that sank HMS *LST-422*.[44]

LIGHT CRUISER HMS *SPARTAN* SUNK

> *Observed red glow under one plane, followed by streaks of sparks like rocket. This red glow was about [the] size of [a] star and was followed with binoculars until it bore 355 degrees relative, seconds later H.M.S. Cruiser* SPARTAN *received direct hit on after [stack] with terrific explosion. Small boats ordered away for rescue of survivors.*
>
> —Entry from the war diary of tank landing ship *LST*-326 describing a glider-bomb attack made on HMS *Spartan* off Anzio that resulted in the loss of the ship, with five officers and forty-one crewmen killed, or missing presumed killed, and forty-two men wounded.[45]

For navy and merchant vessels lying at anchor or under way off Anzio on 29 January, the day was stamped by multiple air raids and the loss of two Allied ships to German glider-bombs. Commander Task Group 81.4 recorded, "During this day had the fiercest air raids since arrival. There were six red alerts with bombs being dropped on four occasions." The first alert at 0734 gave warning of the approach of several enemy planes out of the northeast and sent the crews of ships to general quarters. Aircraft dropped three bombs along Red beach, which appeared to have caused no damage. Aboard *ATR-1*, "Secure from General Quarters, set Condition Two" was passed at 0757. A red alert around noon sent officers and men to their battle stations once again, but no planes were sighted in the vicinity. This changed in the late afternoon when four enemy aircraft appeared without warning off the tug's starboard quarter. They had apparently followed a flight of friendly Curtiss P-40 fighter and ground-attack aircraft coming in from the south. Two Me-109 Messerschmitt fighters dive-bombed tank landing ship *LST-326*, which was at anchor off Port Anzio. Her decks were strafed with machine gun fire and sprayed with shrapnel from bomb blasts. (Some Me-109 variants were fitted with bombs as well as guns.) Multiple bombs were also dropped along Green beach leaving craters in the sand.[46]

ATR-1 went to general quarters at 1735 upon receipt of another red alert. Five minutes later the sounds of aircraft—Dornier Do-217 bombers coming in from the north—were heard passing over the transport area, as well as bomb explosions and anti-aircraft fire.[47]

The sun had set only a few minutes earlier. Visibility was poor as a result of the fading light and purposely generated smoke from ships assigned to "Smoke Patrol." Five sub-chasers—SCs *497*, *506*, *532*, *533*, and *692*—and four minesweepers—YMSs *13*, *36*, *78*, and *82*—had been fitted with Besseler smoke generators. They were responsible for blanketing the eight-square-mile anchorage areas during nighttime red alerts or under special orders, and in the event of favorable winds to cover shore operations.[48]

Proper execution of smoke-screening duties proved challenging. The ships were normally engaged in conducting anti-submarine searches to seaward of the eastern and western anchorage areas. Thus, it often took several minutes for SCs and YMSs to proceed from their patrol stations to the anchorages. Moreover, it was not always possible, due to shoal water, to lay smoke windward of anchored ships, leaving such vessels exposed to the view of enemy planes.[49]

In anticipation of a need for her services (hearing planes approaching), *ATR-1* made preparations to get under way and was dispatched thereafter to aid a British cruiser. As the tug neared HMS

Spartan (95), she found the 512-foot warship aflame from after stack to stern and listing heavily to port. The "droning" heard earlier had been units of the Luftwaffe delivering glider-bomb attacks on ships in Anzio Bay. Before these attacks, individual ships had received orders to make smoke, and *Spartan*, at anchor off the port of Anzio to provide anti-aircraft protection for ships in the vicinity of the beachhead, was doing so. However, strong winds had carried the smoke away, leaving her exposed. As the group of approximately eighteen aircraft approached, the planes first circled over land and then attacked ships silhouetted by the setting sun on the horizon.[50]

By the time ships opened fire in the general direction of the flight of aircraft, six glider-bombs were speeding downward toward the anchorage; most impacted the water. One hit *Spartan* on her starboard side abaft the after stack and started an extensive fire in that area. The momentum of the glider-bomb (average speed of the rocket-propelled ordnance was 325 knots) drove it downward through the cruiser before exploding on the port side of the after boiler room, blasting a hole in the hull. As seawater rushed in, the cruiser developed a port list. The explosion of the 500Kg warhead also destroyed the port torpedo tubes located on the main deck, igniting warheads which exploding air flasks propelled aft. These, in turn, created a large fire between the main mast and "X" turret directly astern. The mast collapsed and ammunition caught fire in "Y" turret, the gun mount farthest aft.[51]

Sadly, gun crews trying desperately to defend *Spartan* apparently assisted in her demise. The minesweeper *Strive* (AM-117) was about six miles to seaward and witnessed the attack. The executive officer described the flight of the bomb that struck the light cruiser, which was steered by the plane's bombardier to its target using tracer fire originating from *Spartan* as his aim point:

> One of these bombs was followed by eye and binoculars just after the release point until it disappeared, a hundred or so feet above the water, into the smoke-screened transport area. A few seconds after the flare in the bomb made it visible to both ships and the parent aircraft, anti-aircraft fire opened up on it. The bomb appeared to maintain constant altitude for a time and then headed straight down into the funnel of fire from one ship accelerated by what appeared to be rocket propulsion bursts.
>
> Tracer for tracer, the bomb was directed into and along the trajectory of that line of fire to its origin, later confirmed to be the H.M.S. *SPARTAN*.[52]

When *ATR-1* arrived on scene, *Spartan* was "dead in the water." With the loss of both steam and electrical power, she had no propulsion available and was unable to fight the fires aboard her. Rescue craft had already taken some sailors trapped by fire, off the aft portion of the cruiser, and the British rescue tug HMS *Prosperous* (W96) was made up to her starboard quarter fighting the fires. MacGill placed his tug alongside the cruiser's port quarter and fought fires until she heeled far over giving warning of impending loss. War diary entries describe efforts by the U.S. Navy rescue tug to save the beleaguered warship:

1830: Proceeded to pour water upon fire at request of British officer on bridge of cruiser. Four monitors and three 2 ½ inch hoses, two with fog nozzles were used.
1838: Fire appeared to be abating.
1847: Ceased pouring water and prepared to back off with intent of placing hose aboard on starboard side of cruiser, to use only fog spray and decrease the amount of water put on board.
1909: Cruiser started listing more to port, unable to go alongside starboard side of cruiser as a tug thought to be the HMS *Prosperous* [W96] was moored there.
1910: Cruiser started turning over to port. HMS *Prosperous* cast off from cruiser....[53]

ATR-1 cleared the side of the burning cruiser two minutes later and lay to off the beach. By 1900 the cruiser's list had increased to 30 degrees and, soon thereafter, her captain gave the order to abandon ship. When the list increased to 35 degrees, all magazine crews and crewmen below decks, not engaged in damage control, were ordered topside. By 1905, HMS *Spartan* had rolled onto her beam and she sank ten minutes later in thirty feet of water.[54]

While *ATR-1* and HMS *Prosperous* were made up to the cruiser, two net tenders placed their bows against the cruiser's starboard side and removed many survivors. (These were likely the British *Bar*-class boom defense vessels *Barndale* and *Barmond*.) Other crewmembers went over the side, and adjacent waters were covered with craft retrieving them from the sea. When the order was passed to abandon, the instructions were to swim as far as possible from *Spartan* because she was in danger of exploding. The vessels engaged in the rescue operations included five landing craft—*LCI(L)-4, LCI(L)-219, LCI(L)-236,* and *LCT-198*—and sub-chasers *SC-522, 697,* and *1029*. The survivors, many of them wounded, were transferred to the light cruiser HMS *Delhi* (D74).⁵⁵

Photo 7-3

Rescue tug USS *ATR-1* alongside HMS *Spartan*; hit by a glider-bomb that passed down through the British light cruiser, set her aflame and blasted a hole in her hull. She sank shortly thereafter off Anzio, Italy.
Painting by Richard DeRosset

A majority of these officers and men were later landed in the Bay of Naples and transferred to the troop ship M.V. *Winchester Castle*. Some of them believed they would be going back to the United Kingdom aboard her. Instead, they were transferred to the French passenger ship S.S. *Champollion*, taken to Algiers, and lodged at HMS Hannibal, a British naval barracks. They were later taken to Malta and spent time there ashore in a rest camp, Camp 12. From there, French destroyers took the *Spartan* survivors to Taranto in southern Italy, where they boarded the light cruiser HMS *Aurora*.⁵⁶

Of course, there were some exceptions of the fates of survivors from *Spartan*. The battle station of one crewman—who had joined the Navy as a boy and was a member of the Royal Marines band embarked on board—was on the lowest deck in the forward TS. In Royal Navy parlance, a TS or Transmitting Station is a compartment deep within a ship where calculations pertaining to gunnery are worked and from which orders, ranges and deflections are transmitted to the guns. He later related that he had never moved so fast in scrambling to the upper deck and that he went over the opposite side of *Spartan* than most did. He ended up on a Liberty ship and was taken straight to Malta, where he boarded the HMS *Aurora* well ahead of the group of other survivors who would later join her at Taranto via a much more circuitous route.[57]

LIBERTY SHIP S.S. *SAMUEL HUNTINGTON* SUNK

A few minutes after *Spartan* was hit, one of the radio-controlled bombs slammed into S.S. *Samuel Huntington*. It passed downward to the boiler room and exploded, killing four men and setting the ship ablaze. Her crew fought the fires for nearly an hour and a half until 1930 when the master ordered abandonment. The crew lowered lifeboats—most likely with some urgency, wanting to be off her before fire found the ammunition, gasoline, and TNT that comprised a large portion of her cargo—and headed clear of the ship.[58]

Following her work trying to save *Spartan*, *ATR-1* was dispatched to *Huntington* to provide assistance, and in preparation started fire pumps and manned fire stations while en route. Upon laying the tug alongside the 441-foot merchant ship, MacGill found her apparently abandoned. The actions of the tug were similar to those used for *Spartan*, except that her fire party boarded *Samuel Huntington*:

> 2138: Commenced pouring water on fire with four monitors and two 2 ½ inch hoses. Liberty ship was aflame in entire midships section, apparently from engine room up to the bridge.
> 2142: Turned off all water to allow coming closer to ship.
> 2145: Passed bow line to Liberty ship which was taken by a member of this vessel's crew as Liberty ship was apparently deserted.[59]

The tug's party of firefighters went aboard *Huntington* at 2148. As two hose teams poured water on the starboard side of the first superstructure deck, the two remaining teams attacked fires on the superstructure from the port side. During this activity, a red alert was received at 2155 and anti-aircraft guns opened on enemy planes over the bay.[60]

ATR-1 SEVERELY DAMAGED WHILE ATTENDING BURNING MERCHANT SHIP, WHICH LATER SANK

> *We are sinking, send help.*
>
> —Report made by the rescue tug *ATR-1* fifty minutes short of midnight on 29 January 1944, followed by information that she was alongside *Samuel Huntington* fighting fires aboard the ammunition and gasoline-laden ship, and that damage from the near misses of Hs 293 glider-bombs had flooded her fire room and engine room[61]

Twenty-three minutes after the air raid warning, three bombs fell near *ATR-1* knocking out her propulsion, electrical power, and firefighting water. She was then still alongside the burning ship—which in itself presented plenty of danger to her—and now had no means to fight fire aboard it, or to protect herself should wind spread the flames. Shock waves from the bombs had damaged propulsion machinery, and the tug was taking on water through opened hull seams. MacGill described the situation:

> This vessel was taking considerable water and developing a decided port list. Salvage pumps were in process of being rigged under difficulties. [The] handybillies [portable emergency fire-fighting pumps] would not start as concussion had loosened gasoline lines.[62]

In rapid succession, *ATR-1*'s boarding party returned aboard, while her engineers below deck closed hull fittings to reduce flooding caused by damage, and seamen launched the ship's motor whaleboat and her starboard life raft. By 2310, the motor whaleboat had pulled the tug clear of *Samuel Huntington*. MacGill then ordered the port life raft and motor launch lowered in case it became necessary to abandon ship. Ten minutes prior to midnight, help arrived in the form of *LCI(L)-196*. The infantry landing craft came alongside *ATR-1* to enable the tug to pass a tow line to her. After fastening the end securely on board, she towed *ATR-1* into shallow water off the lower end of Green beach and cast her off. The tug's stern swiveled around and grounded providing reprieve from the very real possibility of sinking.[63]

The S.S. *Samuel Huntington* exploded a little over three hours later, spreading burning fuel oil over a considerable area, and later sank. Because she went down in very shallow water, much of the ship remained above the surface of the sea and fires still burned aboard her. (Accounts differ as to whether she sank after the first or second shipboard explosion.) A subsequent explosion scattered metal shards and fragments over an even larger area. A sailor aboard the tank landing craft *LCT-221* described the event:

> It was 3:15 [a.m.]; I was on guard and saw a Liberty ship blow up about halfway between the bow and bridge. 15 min later the aft [portion of the ship] blew up & it threw shrapnel & steel about 1,000 ft. in the air or more, and some of it hit our boat. About a mile and a half away, it was the prettiest thing I ever saw but anyone that was alive before that went off was dead after that I'm sure. Shells exploded all night from it.[64]

When dawn broke a few hours later, *ATR-1*'s officers and crew were able to survey her condition. Examination revealed significant machinery derangement and structural damage to her decks, bulkheads and superstructure. The damage included: shifted fuel tanks; cracked brick work in boilers; sprung, raised, or loosened decks and bulkheads; toppled foremast; and loss of the top of the mainmast, which had been carried away.[65]

That afternoon the British tank landing ship HMS *LST-409* approached the rescue tug on her port bow and passed a tow line. After attaching the hawser to a towing bridle, *ATR-1* slipped her starboard anchor and thirty fathoms of chain—having no electrical or steam power to retrieve the ground tackle—and proceeded under *LST-409*'s tow to Naples for repairs. *ATR-1* had been very fortunate; a direct hit by a 500Kg glider-bomb would have obliterated the wooden-hulled ship and killed or maimed everyone aboard. Her officers and men earned a well-deserved battle star for the Anzio invasion, and would later receive a second one for the Invasion of Southern France.[66]

A summary of the characteristics of the U.S. Navy salvage vessels and tugs that received battles stars for their actions at Anzio, and the period of the awards and names of commanding officers, if known, are provided in the following table:

U.S. Navy Salvage Forces

Ship	Ship Hull/ Length (ft.)	Award Period	Commanding Officer
Restorer (ARS-17)	Steel/183	28 Feb-1 Mar 44	Lt. C. M. Boyd, USNR
Weight (ARS-35)	Steel/183	28 Jan-5 Feb 44	Lt. Comdr. Frederick J. Leamond, USNR
Hopi (ATF-71)	Steel/205	1-28 Feb 44	Lt. Owen W. Huff, USN
ATR-1	Wood/165	22-30 Jan 44	Lt. (jg) H. L. MacGill, USN
Edenshaw (YTB-459)	Wood/102	22 Jan-1 Mar 44	R. L. Self
LCI(L)-10	Steel/158	22 Jan-4 Feb 44	Lt. (jg) W. A. Drisler Jr., USNR
LCI(L)-15	Steel/158	22-30 Jan 44	Lt. (jg) Calhoun Shorts, USNR
LCI(L)-16	Steel/158	22 Jan-1 Mar 44	Lt. M. J. Morrison, USNR
LCI(L)-209	Steel/158	22 Jan-1 Mar 44	Lt. Kenneth E. Leake, USNR
LCI(L)-219	Steel/158	22 Jan 44	Lt. Albert J. Corsi, USNR
LCI(L)-232	Steel/158	22-27 Jan 44	Ens. Howard J. Stanley, USNR, or Lt. (jg) William R. Watson, USNR
LCT-198	Steel/114	22 Jan-10 Feb 44	Lloyd E. Dutcher
LCT-221	Steel/114	22-31 Jan 44	Ens. Grover W. Crawford, USNR
LCT-288	Steel/114	22 Jan-1 Mar 44	Unknown

HILLARY A. HERBERT SURVIVES ATTACKS

Valor and obstinate commitment to purpose was a hallmark of the crews of both military and merchant vessels engaged in the Anzio landings. Apart from the fact that plans and resources for salvage operations had been made, the defensive actions of the crews saved many ships so that they could be preserved, repaired, and returned to service. An outstanding example of this is related below.

The Liberty ship S.S. *Hillary A. Herbert* absorbed more punishment than most vessels could take. In the period from 22 to 31 January she reported twenty-seven bombing attacks, but she survived to sail another day. On D-Day, enemy shells were falling 50-100 feet away from the ship. Despite this barrage, Percy H. Hauffman anchored his ship near the beachhead, so that vital cargo could be transferred ashore. For this action Hauffman, who before entering the Merchant Marine in 1942 was captain of the Staten Island ferry, received the Silver Star Medal—the only recipient of this award identified in United States Merchant Marine records. The medal citation reads:

The President of the United States of America takes pleasure in presenting the Silver Star to Master Percy H. Hauffman, United States Merchant Marines, for extraordinary heroism and outstanding devotion to duty in the line of his profession as Commanding Officer of the S.S. *HILLARY A. HERBERT* during the landings of Allied Forces at Anzio, Italy, on 22 January 1944. Master Hauffman showed extraordinary ability and courageous action under fire in landing the S.S. *HILLARY A. HERBERT* at the beachhead and discharging her cargo of ammunition, gasoline and other vital supplies during a terrific aerial and shore bombardment.[67]

Senior naval commanders authorized to bestow high ranking military decorations could award them on the spot, and sometimes it was several months before the associated paperwork was completed. The requisite forms and medal citations might be written by staff members with no personal knowledge of the operation or action. Thus, while the citation specified 22 January 1944 only, the award was likely meant to recognize that Hauffman kept his ship in harm's way for many consecutive days up to 31 January, enabling all of her desperately needed cargo to be offloaded ashore.

On 23 January eight shells landed about fifty yards from the stern of *Hillary A. Herbert*. Her Naval Guard shot down a plane the following day and counted a probable downing on 25 January, a day on which three bombs landed about fifty feet from the ship. The next day, bombs also fell close to her and she shot down another plane. In the early evening, two bombs exploded five yards from the ship, resulting in considerable damage, and requiring Hauffman to beach the ship to save her from sinking. During this action her Armed Guards shot down another plane. On 27 January her gunners hit yet one more for a tally of three planes downed and two probably destroyed. On 28 January bombs again fell close and she was strafed by aircraft. Also land based enemy artillery finally "found the range" and put a gun round into her stern. The next day a glider-bomb missed *Hillary A. Herbert* by only fifty feet and, a day later on 30 January shell fire again fell around her. Battered but still afloat, she left Anzio in tow for Naples for repairs on 31 January 1944.[68]

POSTSCRIPT – CONVENTIONAL ANTI-AIRCRAFT MEASURES ARE CHALLENGED

> There is no question at night but that the proper course of action to follow is minimum [ship] speed with little or no maneuvering. The higher the speed, the more obvious the wake, the closer bombs fall.... It is felt that to go ahead at slow speed is probably better than to remain at anchor; although it is believed that the number of ships hit at anchor was not as great as the number hit under way. In daytime the proper defensive course to pursue is somewhat more difficult to determine. Against torpedoes, unquestionably high-speed maneuvers reduce chances of a hit. Against ordinary dive bombing, however, the commanding officer has come to the conclusion that it makes little difference whether or not a ship maneuvers. From repeated observations, it appears that the chances of turning into a bomb are just as great as turning away from one. This vessel suffered near misses both when maneuvering and when not maneuvering and was widely missed under both circumstances.... Those ships which always remained at anchor did not appear to suffer any more damage than those under way.
>
> If the conservation of a given vessel is itself any consideration smoke laying by that vessel is a big mistake. At dusk and after dark smoke from funnel or fantail makes an even bigger avenue of approach than a wake for an attacking bomber. It is firmly believed that at any given anchorage smoke laying should be confined to small vessels which present a difficult target and whose loss would not be as costly as that of a DD [destroyer] or DE [destroyer escort].
>
> —Lt. Comdr. Reginals Chancey Robbins Jr., USNR, commanding officer of the destroyer escort USS *Frederick C. Davis* (DE-136)[69]

There was, during the war, and there remains today, criticism and debate about the losses of so many ships and men at Anzio including the light cruiser *Spartan*, which the rescue tugs *ATR-1* and HMS *Prosperous* gallantly tried to save. Five British officers and forty-one ratings were killed or missing and presumed killed, and forty-two ratings were wounded, caused by the glider-bomb explosion, the resultant shipboard fires and flooding, or being trapped aboard when the *Spartan* rolled over and sank. Assertions that she was lost because she was at anchor versus under way at the time of the attack, or because she did not have a protective screen of smoke to shield her from view of enemy aircraft, may be invalid; at least, based on the experiences of the commanding officer of a destroyer responsible for jamming the radio frequencies that controlled glider-bombs in flight to their targets.[70]

During the three months preceding the Anzio landings, destroyers *Frederick C. Davis* (DE-136) and *Herbert C. Jones* (DE-137) were assigned to investigate and develop countermeasures against radio-controlled bombs. At Anzio—during the period through 29 February—*Frederick C. Davis* endeavored, on eight separate occasions, to jam radio waves that bombardiers aboard German aircraft used to steer bombs of this type to their targets. Because a majority of the attacks took place when it was too dark to see the path of the rocket-propelled ordnance in flight, the destroyer made no claims regarding the success of the jamming. Fortunately air attacks with glider-bombs constituted but a small part of the enemy's total aircraft activity.[71]

While at Anzio, *Davis* survived ninety-eight attacks from aircraft in which bombs fell either in the anchorage or along the waterfront. Whenever an air raid was anticipated, it was her policy to get close to the beach and, if possible, between the attacking aircraft and the waterfront. This action was necessary because Allied shore-based anti-aircraft battery fire could not prevent enemy planes from approaching unchallenged from seaward, or flying low around Cape d'Anzio into the anchorage.[72]

Lieutenant Commander Robbins highlighted challenges associated with making smoke as a defensive measure, and the potential danger to ships that would be the primary targets of enemy aircraft from doing so at all:

> In connection with the defense of the anchorage at Anzio, the question kept arising as to who should make smoke and when and how. This was a continuing problem partly because wind conditions were varying, partly because the number of small craft available for smoke making also varied and partly because the experience of the commanding officers of these vessels was somewhat limited. The turnover was frequent and as soon as one group was properly indoctrinated another group would take its place and we would have to begin all over again.
>
> At dusk and after dark smoke from funnel [stack] or fantail make an even better avenue of approach than a wake for an attacking bomber.[73]

It can be argued that *Spartan* was lost not because she was at anchor—and thus unable to maneuver and engage aircraft with all her guns—but because the enemy was able, in the dark and smoke-obscured sky, to use the anti-aircraft fire of the gunners aboard the light cruiser as the aim point for the glider-bomb that sank her. *Frederick C. Davis* may have survived because she was not considered to be as high a value target as were *Spartan* and *Hillary A. Herbert*. The Liberty ship—loaded with valuable cargo to support the troops ashore—would have been a prime target. The fact that she survived, and *Spartan* did not, can perhaps be attributed to good luck.

LEST WE FORGET

On the 50th anniversary of the Anzio landings, the office of the Chief of Naval Operations released a statement reading, in part:

> A half-century ago American, British, Dutch and Greek naval forces landed soldiers of the American and British armies on the Italian coast. German resistance was unexpectedly powerful and rapidly increased in strength. For four months the invaders battled foul winter weather, heavy bombing and artillery fire to sustain the Anzio beachhead. Throughout this long struggle on the Italian littoral, our troops were strongly supported by naval gunfire, airpower and a shuttle of ships and craft that braved air and submarine attack to deliver reinforcements. Late in May 1944 the main Allied advance linked up with Anzio's defenders, and Rome was liberated a few days later. In what many consider a land battle, there were a total of 17 ships lost: ten British and seven U.S. Navy. In this action, 166 American sailors were wounded and 160 made the ultimate sacrifice in the cause of freedom.

Casualties among ground troops were much greater. Allied forces —sea, air, and land—suffered 700 killed, 36,000 wounded, and another 44,000 hospitalized from various non-battle injuries. Few foresaw the four-month-long bitter struggle that was to ensue, or the battle for the beachhead which found U.S. defenders repulsing fervent attacks by Germans, who had received orders from Hitler to eliminate the threat by completely destroying its defenders. The Germans committed 80,000 additional troops to the Italian campaign in an effort to push the Allies holding the bridgehead back into the sea.[74]

Zane Orr, a former salvor, recounted during an interview in 2014 the conditions Allied land forces faced at Anzio. He was aboard the salvage vessel *Restorer* (ARS-17), which was shelled by the Germans from land upon her arrival on 28 February at the port of Anzio:

The first days of the campaign went well. The enemy was taken by surprise and Allied troops went ashore on January 22, 1944 without any organized resistance by the Germans. The Americans and British successfully implemented a huge operation to land supplies and troops in the harbor and establish a beachhead.

By the time we arrived, the Allies were in a bad situation at Anzio. The terrain was difficult. There was a lot of rain. The battlefield was in an area of reclaimed marshland which the Germans had flooded, so some of our guys were up to their hips in mud and water. The enemy got organized and resistance was fierce; some of the hardest fighting of the war took place as the Allies tried to break out from their beachhead. The casualties on both sides were terrible. The campaign lasted four months with little progress.[75]

While Maj. Gen. John P. Lucas, USA, consolidated the Allied beachhead awaiting the arrival of more men, armor, heavy artillery and supplies before continuing the offensive further inland, Field Marshal Kesselring moved substantial forces into the area. German ground troops surrounded the beachhead, effectively rendering the Allied force incapable of conducting any sort of major offensive action for four months. Lucas had repeatedly stated, before the landing, that the paltry allotments of men and supplies were not commensurate with the high goals sought by British planners. Lucas wrote in his diary on 15 February 1944:

> I am afraid that the top side is not completely satisfied with my work.... They are naturally disappointed that I failed to chase the Hun out of Italy but there was no military reason why I should have been able to do so. In fact there is no military reason for Shingle.[76]

On 22 February, Lt. Gen. Mark Clark, commander Fifth Army, replaced Lucas with Maj. Gen. Lucian K. Truscott Jr., then commanding VI Corps. After the war, Kesselring expressed his belief that the Allies had committed too few forces to Anzio to mount a credible offense: "It would have been the Anglo-American doom to overextend themselves. The landing force was initially weak, only a division or so of infantry, and without armour. It was a half-way measure of an offensive that was your basic error." This view validated the perspective of Lucas.[77]

There was much angst felt by family members and friends of the Allied troops killed at Anzio, and particularly if they felt their loved ones died in vain. One of the men killed was Eric Fletcher Waters a member of an infantry regiment of the British Army, and the father of Roger Waters, a member of the rock band Pink Floyd. Waters's song "When the Tigers Broke Free" mourns the death of his father, and the many other members of the Royal Fusiliers Company Z, who were ordered to hold the Allied bridgehead against a German Tiger I tank assault:

> It was just before dawn
> One miserable morning in black '44
> When the forward commander was told to sit tight
> When he asked that his men be withdrawn
>
> And the Generals gave thanks as the other ranks
> Held back the enemy tanks for a while
> And the Anzio Bridgehead was held for the price
> Of a few hundred ordinary lives
>
> And kind old King George sent Mother a note
> When he heard that father was gone
> It was, I recall in the form of a scroll
> With gold leaf and all
>
> And I found it one day
> In a drawer of old photographs, hidden away
> And my eyes still grow damp to remember
> His Majesty signed with his own rubber stamp
>
> It was dark all around
> There was frost on the ground
> When the tigers broke free
> And no one survived from the Royal Fusiliers Company Z
>
> They were all left behind
> Most of them dead, the rest of them dying
> And that's how the High Command
> Took my daddy from me

Through sheer bravery and heroism the Allies held on and finally, with long-awaited reinforcements, broke out in late May and marched victoriously into Rome in June 1944. In recognition of the courage and sacrifice of the soldiers, sailors, and airmen at Anzio, twenty-two Americans were awarded the Congressional Medal of Honor, the most of any single battle of World War II. These men, all soldiers, were:

Disaster at Anzio – Operation SHINGLE

Name	Award Date	Location	Unit
Sgt. Sylvester Antolak	24 May 44	Cisterna, Italy	3rd Division
T/Sgt. Van T. Barfoot	23 May 44	Carano, Italy	45th Division
Pvt. Herbert F. Christian	2 Jun 44	Valmontone, Italy	3rd Division
T/Sgt. Ernest H. Dervishian	23 May 44	Cisterna, Italy	34th Division
PFC John W. Dutko	23 May 44	Ponte Rotto, Italy	3rd Division
2nd LT. Thomas W. Fowler	23 May 44	Carano, Italy	1st Armor
Capt. William W. Gault	29 May 44	Crocetta, Italy	34th Division
T/5 Eric G. Gibson	28 Jan 44	Isola Bella, Italy	3rd Division
S/Sgt. George J. Hall	23 May 44	Anzio, Italy	34th Division
PFC Lloyd C. Hawks	30 Jan 44	Carano, Italy	3rd Division
Cpl. Paul B. Huff	8 Feb 44	Carano, Italy	509th Para. Inf.
Pvt. Elden H. Johnson	3 Jun 44	Valmontone, Italy	3rd Division
PFC William H. Johnson	17 Feb 44	Padiglione, Italy	45th Division
PFC Patrick L. Kessler	23 May 44	Ponto Rotto, Italy	3rd Division
PFC Alton W. Knappenberger	1 Feb 44	Cisterna, Italy	3rd Division
Pvt. James H. Mills	24 May 44	Cisterna, Italy	3rd Division
1st LT. Jack C. Montgomery	22 Feb 44	Padiglione, Italy	45th Division
1st LT. Beryl R. Newman	25 May 44	Cisterna, Italy	34th Division
Sgt. Truman O. Olson	30 Jan 44	Cisterna, Italy	3rd Division
PFC Henry Schauer	23 May 44	Cisterna, Italy	3rd Division
Pvt. Furman L. Smith	31 May 44	Lanuvio, Italy	34th Division
PFC John C. Squires	23 Apr 44	Padiglione, Italy	3rd Division[78]

Two British soldiers received the Victoria Cross (the British equivalent of the Medal of Honor) for valour "in the face of the enemy." These men were Maurice Rogers, Wiltshire Regiment, and William Sidney, Grenadier Guards.[79]

8

Normandy – Operation OVERLORD

> *When you look at a photograph of the Normandy invasion all you see is little ships. All those ships, thousands of little landing craft, minesweepers and tugs started in the small shipyards of America and Canada. It was little ships that came out of little towns like Bellingham that did it.*
>
> —Roland H. "Rollie" Webb, Former President
> and Chief Operating Officer of
> Todd Pacific Shipyards Corporation

The Allied invasion of mainland Europe, at Normandy on the north coast of France across the English Channel from Britain, commenced on 6 June 1944 with simultaneous landings on five adjacent beaches. In total the Allies landed around 156,000 troops in Normandy on D-Day, which launched OVERLORD, code word for the operation to defeat Germany and free France. The American forces landed numbered 73,000: 23,250 on Utah beach, 34,250 on Omaha beach, and 15,500 airborne troops. In the British and Canadian sector, 83,115 troops were landed: 24,970 on Gold beach (British), 21,400 on Juno beach (Canadian), 28,845 on Sword beach (British), and 7,900 airborne troops. Operation NEPTUNE, the naval component of OVERLORD, involved 6,479 ships and craft: 1,202 naval combat ships, 4,021 landing ships and landing craft, and 1,256 merchant vessels. Some 195,700 personnel were assigned to Operation Neptune: 52,889 U.S., 112,824 British including 10,000 from the Royal Canadian Navy, and 4,988 from other Allied countries.[1]

Both Allied and German forces suffered massive casualties during the battle of Normandy, which lasted until the end of August. Most occurred on the first day of assault landings, 6 June, in which there were 2,499 American D-Day fatalities and 1,914 from the other Allied nations, a total of 4,413 dead. A recent study assessed that the figures for casualties (of all types) for each beach were as follows: Utah 589, Omaha 3,686, Gold 1,023, Juno 1,242, and Sword 1,304. These figures do not include airborne forces. Estimates of losses amongst the British airborne troops are some 600 killed or wounded, and 600 missing; 100 glider pilots also became casualties. Casualties for U.S. airborne personnel were 2,499, of which 238 were deaths. The total German casualties on D-Day are unknown, but are estimated as being between 4,000 and 9,000 men.[2]

Allied ship losses for June 1944 included 24 warships and 35 merchantmen or auxiliaries sunk, and an additional 120 vessels damaged. Following is a summary of the types and total numbers of naval and merchant shipping that participated in OVERLORD:

Allied Naval and Merchant Shipping

Naval Forces (1,202 total)
Heavy Units (139)
  7 Battleships
  25 Cruisers
  105 Destroyers (79 Fleet, 26 Hunts)
  2 Monitors
  2 Gunboats
Escort Vessels (142)
  26 Escort Destroyers
  27 Frigates
  71 Corvettes
  18 Patrol Craft
Coastal Forces (316)
  145 Motor Launches
  54 Harbour Defense Motor Launches
  82 Large Motor Torpedo Boats
  84 Small Motor Torpedo Boats
  6 Steam Gun Boats
  32 Rescue Motor Launches
  18 Submarine Chasers
  15 Motor Torpedo (PT) Boats
  60 Coastguard Cutters
Minesweepers (277)
  12 F.M.S. Flotillas (98 Minesweepers and 35 Danlayers)
  4 B.Y.M.S. Flotillas (40 ships)
  16 L.L. Trawlers
  18 Yard Minesweepers
Tugs (225)
  125 British
  91 American
  9 Rescue[3]

Naval Forces (Continued)
Warship Blockades (4)
  2 Very Old Battleships
  2 Very Old Cruisers
Miscellaneous (99)
  39 Salvage and Wreck Disposal Ships
  60 Smoke making Trawlers

Allied Landing Ships/Craft (4,021)
  311 Landing Ships (LSI, APA, LST)
  1,211 Major Landing Craft
  2,499 Minor Landing Craft and Barges

Merchant Ships/Tugs (1,256)
  18 Personnel Ships (not including LSI)
  224 Ministry of War Transport Ships
  64 Ministry of War Transport Coasters
  122 Store Coasters
  150 Tankers & Colliers
  136 Cased Petrol Carriers
  55 Blockships
  76 Ammunition Carriers
  18 Ammunition Supply Issuing Ships
  78 Liberty Store Ships

  10 Hospital Ships and Carriers
  10 Accommodation Ships
  295 Miscellaneous

COMMAND STRUCTURE AND ENEMY FORCES

British admiral Sir Bertram Ramsay, RN, was the overall commander of the Allied Naval Expeditionary Force responsible for pre-assault bombardment, landing of troops, and close protection of those troops during Operation OVERLORD. The British-led Eastern Naval Task Force, under the command of Rear Adm. Sir Philip Vian, RN, was charged with putting the Second British Army ashore on Juno, Gold, and Sword beaches. The Western Task force of Rear Adm. Alan G. Kirk, USN, was responsible for landing the American First Army on Omaha and Utah beaches. Subordinates Rear Adm. John L. Hall Jr. and Rear Adm. Don P. Moon, commander Assault Force "O" and "U," respectively, were directly in charge of establishing these components of the First Army ashore at Omaha and Utah.[4]

Five German divisions—the 352nd Field Infantry Division, the 243rd, 709th, and 716th Limited Employment Divisions, and the 21st Panzer Division—would initially oppose the American First Army on Omaha and Utah beaches and by 11 June the equivalent of two more divisions would join these forces. The enemy's formidable shore defenses against amphibious attack included:

- A number of well-emplaced coastal and field batteries sited to cover both the approaches and beach areas
- A line of strongpoints along the coast, close enough in good landing areas to provide interlocking fire over beaches and exits (These were supplemented by groups of rocket projectors just inland, which could lay fire on the beach.)
- Quantities of beach obstacles; mines, wire and anti-tank obstructions placed and organized to hold invading troops within areas of fire of the strongpoints

The purpose of these interrelated measures was to hold the invader on the beach itself until the Germans could launch an effective counterattack. There was relatively little prepared "defense-in-depth," except for crisscrossed anti-landing stakes—well known today to anyone who has watched movies about, or viewed photographs of, the Normandy landings—and land mines sown over possible aircraft landing areas.[5]

Photo 8-1

Watercolor by Navy Combat Artist Dwight Shepler, 1944, showing U.S. forces landing on Omaha beach on D-Day of the Normandy invasion.
Official U.S. Navy photo # KN-17825

ORGANIZATION OF AMERICAN NAVAL FORCES

The U.S. Twelfth Fleet was established on 1 October 1943 from the U.S. naval forces assigned to Adm. Harold R. Stark, USN, commander Naval Forces in Europe headquartered in London. In November, the Chief of Naval Operations, Adm. Ernest King, directed that Task Force 122, under Rear Admiral Kirk, be set up within Twelfth Fleet to conduct the planning, training for, and execution of OVERLORD. Admiral Stark was "double-hatted" as commander Naval Forces in Europe and commander Twelfth Fleet, but the operational and administrative components of these commands were divided. Two important subordinate commands of Twelfth Fleet were (1) Eleventh Amphibious Force and (2) Landing Craft and Bases, Europe, which were established in summer 1943 to receive and control the buildup of landing craft for the invasion.[6]

The next few pages are devoted to an overview of the American tugs which, along with their British counterparts, would be critical to delivery and assembly of two artificial harbors at Normandy—termed Mulberry A and Mulberry B—and to the repair and salvage of ships and craft damaged in combat.

TUGS SAIL FROM NEW YORK FOR BRITAIN

In preparation for Operation OVERLORD, Allied naval vessels, some with embarked troops, began to arrive in the United Kingdom in spring 1944. On the night of 25 March 1944, the ships of Task Force 67 stood out of New York Harbor bound for Britain across the Atlantic. Comprising the task force were the destroyers *Marsh* (DE-699), *Moffett* (DD-362), *Runels* (DE-793), and *Tatum* (DD-789); minesweepers *Staff* (AM-114) and *Swift* (AM-122); oiler *Maumee* (AO-2); patrol craft *PC-564, 565, 567, 568, 617, 618, 619, 1232, 1233, 1252, 1262,* and *1263*; and two groups of tugs. The first group consisted of six Navy fleet tugs and two rescue tugs, one Army tug, and four War Shipping Administration (WSA) tugs. All but the Army tug *LT-23* had two barges in tow.

Task Group 67.4

USS *Abnaki* (AT-96)	USS *Kiowa* (AT-72)	USS *ATR-13*	WSA *Farallon*
USS *Alsea* (AT-97)	USS *Pinto* (AT-90)	USA *LT-23*	WSA *Gay Head*
USS *Arikara* (AT-98)	USS *ATR-4*	WSA *Bodie Island*	WSA *Trinidad Head*
USS *Bannock* (AT-81)			

The second group was comprised of four U.S. Navy rescue tugs—*ATR-15, ATR-97, ATR-98,* and *ATR-99*—and the Royal Navy rescue tugs HMS *Cheerly* (W153) and HMS *Emphatic* (W154). These *Favourite*-class Royal Navy vessels are described in Chapter Two.

Task Group 67.5

USS *ATR-15*	USS *ATR-98*	HMS *Cheerly* (W153)
USS *ATR-97*	USS *ATR-99*	HMS *Emphatic* (W154)[7]

The WSA V4-M-A1 tugs were from among a class of forty-nine 186-foot tugs built in different American shipyards for the United States Maritime Commission. Two 8-cylinder National Superior diesels, producing 2,320 bhp and coupled to a single propeller, could propel them to a top speed of 14 knots. All but one were named for lighthouses in the United States; *Great Isaac* honored an island in the Bahamas. *Bodie Island, Black Rock, Farallon, Gay Head, Great Isaac, Hillsboro Inlet, Moose Peak, Sabine Pass, Sankaty Head,* and *Trinidad Head* would all participate in Operation OVERLORD. These tugs, operated by the Moran Towing Company, towed components of the artificial harbors from the Atlantic coast to Britain. Following their arrival in the United Kingdom, they delivered these and other sections fabricated in England to staging areas and later from these marshalling points across the English Channel to Normandy. Following these duties, WSA tugs brought vessels damaged by combat at Normandy to Britain for salvage or repair. The Naval Armed Guard units aboard nine of the civilian tugs (all except *Sabine Pass*) earned a battle star for the invasion.[8]

Diagram 8-1

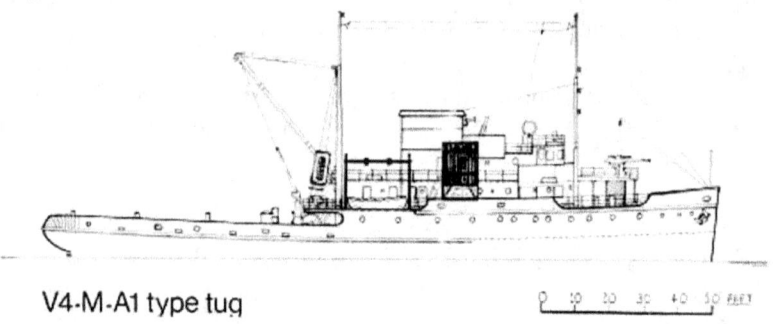

V4-M-A1 type tug

The WSA tugs participating in Operation OVERLORD were fitted with a gun mount and had Naval Armed Guardsmen embarked aboard for ship self-defense.
Courtesy of Hans van der Ster, Marcol Archief Production

The single Army tug in the convoy, the 113-foot *LT-23*, was one of the hundreds of large tugs, small tugs, and harbor tugs built in American shipyards for the Army during World War II. Army large tugs were operated by Coast Guardsmen, Merchant Mariners, or less commonly, by soldiers. Army ships crewed by Coast Guardsmen or which had a Naval Armed Guard assigned to them could receive Navy battle stars, if they met the criteria for them.

SERVICE SQUADRON ONE TUGS

The Navy tugs sailing with Task Force 67 and others that preceded or followed it to the United Kingdom, were units of the Atlantic Fleet's Service Squadron One. A summary of the thirty-six rescue, auxiliary, fleet tugs, and old fleet tugs assigned to the squadron in June 1944 follows, including the eighteen that would receive battle stars for the Normandy invasion. Three salvage ships—*Brant* (ARS-32), *Diver* (ARS-5), and *Swivel* (ARS-36)—would also receive battle stars. Although not members of the squadron, they are included to provide a single list of the Navy tugs and salvage ships that earned these laurels at Normandy.

Operation OVERLORD 155

Ship	Award Period	Commanding Officer
Rescue Tugs		
ATR-1		Lt. (jg) H. L. MacGill, USN
ATR-2	6-25 Jun 1944	Lt. (jg) G. Ulrich, USN
ATR-3	6-25 Jun 1944	Lt. (jg) Stanley J. Lewandowski, USN
ATR-4	6-25 Jun 1944	Lt. (jg) John S. Blank III, USNR
ATR-7		Lt. S. D. Frey, USN
ATR-13	6-25 Jun 1944	Lt. (jg) G. N. Hammond, USN
ATR-15	6-25 Jun 1944	Lt. W. K. Gillett, USNR
ATR-54	6-25 Jun 1944	Lt. (jg) C. G. Sherwood, USN
Auxiliary Tugs		
ATA-121 (ex *ATR-43*)		Lt. (jg) A. C. Schoelpple, USN
ATA-125 (ex *ATR-47*)	6-25 Jun 1944	Lt. Harry L. Lane, USNR
ATA-146 (ex *ATR-90*)		Lt. (jg) W. C. Price, USNR
ATA-170 (ex *ATR-97*)	6-25 Jun 1944	Lt. W. C. Beatie Jr., USNR
ATA-172 (ex *ATR-99*)	6-25 Jun 1944	Lt. (jg) Robert G. Hoffman, USN
ATA-173 (ex *ATR-100*)		Lt. W. H. Moore, USN
Fleet Tugs		
Abnaki (AT-96)		Lt. Dewey Walley, USN
Alsea (AT-97)		Lt. Cecil Cuthbert, USN
Arikara (AT-98)	6-25 Jun 1944	Lt. J. Aitken, USNR
Bannock (AT-81)	6-25 Jun 1944	Lt. Sam Patterson Morgan, USN
Carib (ATF-82)		Lt. Aubrey Hazel Gunn, USN
Cherokee (ATF-66)		Lt. Louis Gerald Johnson, USNR
Chippewa (ATF-69)		Lt. Avery Vernon Swarthout, USN
Choctaw (ATF-70)		Lt. J. D. Garland, USN
Cocopa (ATF-101)		Lt. Justin Cooper Hutchison, USNR
Hopi (ATF-71)		Lt. Oscar W. Huff, USN
Kiowa (AT-72)	6-25 Jun 1944	Lt. William O. Kuykendall, USN
Moreno (ATF-87)		Lt. (jg) Victor H. Kyllberg, USN
Narragansett (ATF-88)		Lt. Charles J. Wichmann, USN
Pinto (AT-90)	6-25 Jun 1944	Lt. Ralph Brown, USN
Seneca (ATF-91)		Lt. Herman B. Conrad, USN
Old Fleet Tugs		
Algorma (ATO-34)	6-25 Jun 1944	Lt. (jg) Robert Marshall Whelpley, USN
Cormorant (ATO-133)	6-25 Jun 1944	Lt. H. V. Randolph, USN
Iuka (ATO-37)		Lt. F. R. Christianson, USNR
Kalmia (ATO-23)		Lt. (jg) J. M. Geortner, USNR
Kewaydin (ATO-24)	6-25 Jun 1944	Lt. W. E. Loebmann, USNR
Owl (ATO-137)	6-25 Jun 1944	Lt. James C. W. White, USNR
Partridge (ATO-138)	6-11 Jun 1944	Lt. Adnah N. Caldin, USN
Salvage Ships		
Brant (ARS-32)	6-25 Jun 1944	Lt. John Norman Tornberg, USNR
Diver (ARS-5)	6-25 Jun 1944	Lt. Daniel D. Hollyer, USNR
Swivel (ARS-36)	6-25 Jun 1944	Lt. Martin Conrad Sibitzky, USN[9]

Service Squadron One was denuded of its tugs to support OVERLORD; fully one-half (sixteen) were sent to Normandy. Six of these tugs were assigned to the Omaha and Utah beaches Assault Forces.

Many of the remaining tugs—and others that arrived in Great Britain, including some from the Eighth Fleet—were initially assigned to the Allied Tug Pool. They and other Allied tugs joined, left, or rejoined based on tasking. The tugs assigned to the Pool operated from English ports carrying out a variety of assignments. Most of these involved towing ships and craft damaged at Normandy back to England for repairs. Some U.S. Navy tugs received orders to support British Assault Forces.

FROM SHIP COMMISSIONING TO NORMANDY

During the war, soldiers and Marines from farms, towns, and cities all across America were sometimes sent directly from boot camp with nominal follow-on specialized training, to amphibious craft landing on hostile beaches under fire. The same held true for many of the officers and men of newly-built Navy ships. One example was the 165-foot, rescue tug *ATR-4*. She was placed in commission at the New York Navy Yard on 27 January 1944 by the commandant of the Third Naval District. Following "shakedown" and accelerated training for combat duty, she stood out of New York Harbor on 28 March, with two barges in tow, and joined Task Group 67.4. Within a relatively short time following her arrival in Europe, she was off Normandy beaches with the British Eastern Naval Task Force. Similar to the experiences of the crew of *ATR-1* at Anzio, the officers and men of *ATR-4* would find themselves off the Normandy beaches less than five months after their ship left the builder's yard.[10]

Atlantic crossings were normally not without incident, and they provided tough on-the-job training, particularly for inexperienced crews. A few days into the Atlantic crossing, *ATR-4* lost boiler feed water, slowed to bare steerage way (the minimum rate of motion required to be maneuvered by the helm), and passed a line to *ATR-15* and was taken in tow. After repairs were completed in early afternoon on 1 April, *ATR-4* rang up "Ahead Full," while still under tow, to make the best possible speed and regain her position in the convoy. Since her top speed was only a little over 12 knots, this catch-up took nearly a day-and-a-half. After *ATR-4* and *ATR-15* and their tows rejoined the convoy, the passage was routine until 13 April, when the task group commander directed by visual signal that all ships transition to an increased condition of battle readiness because of the suspected presence of a large force of enemy submarines ahead. The convoy members maintained this posture for two days until directed to resume normal routine cruising.[11]

On 16 April the first of the two barges *ATR-4* had in tow broke in half. The convoy commander, likely believing it would be unwise to tarry in an area that might contain U-boats, ordered her to pick up only the after barge and to release the forward half of the one still in tow, to be sunk by naval gunfire. Recovering the after barge proved difficult due to heavy swells and the untimely failure of the rescue tug's towing winch, necessitating assistance from the British rescue tug HMS *Cheerly*. The convoy detached the destroyer escort *Tatum* (DE-789) and submarine chaser *PC-1263* to screen the tugs, leaving the four ships in its wake. Within a few hours, *ATR-4* was able to proceed and, after a lengthy day-and-a-half chase, on the morning of 18 April she and the others rejoined the main group. That afternoon, the convoy reformed into three columns, and the next morning into a single column for approach to Falmouth, England, by way of the swept channel (a designated route that minesweepers regularly cleared of enemy-emplaced mines).[12]

Three days after anchoring in Falmouth Harbor, *ATR-4* reported to commander Landing Craft and Bases, Eleventh Amphibious Force for temporary duty as a unit of the tug pool. She left Falmouth for Portsmouth the morning of 24 April for assignment to Task Unit 127.1.3. Upon arrival, *ATR-4* anchored in Stokes Bay—a part of the Solent, the strait separating the Isle of Wight from mainland Britain—off Portsmouth. Her crew experienced their first taste of war two days later, at 0445 on 26 April, when an air raid siren pierced the still, early morning giving warning of approaching enemy aircraft. Five minutes later, flares and bombs fell in the vicinity of the tug, but fortunately she did not suffer any casualties or damage. "All clear" sounded at 0525. Night or early morning attacks continued over the next two days. *ATR-4* shifted to an anchorage in the Solent, off Lee Point, the morning of 28 April, as a prelude to entering South Hampton Dock Yard for voyage repairs before returning to duty.[13]

On 4 June, two days before the Normandy invasion, a Special Salvage and Firefighting group—one officer and nine men—reported aboard *ATR-4*. Repaired and fully manned, the tug left the dockyard the next day per the orders of FOIC (Flag Officer in Charge) South Hampton, a British admiral. A little over four months out of the builder's yard, she refueled from the British tanker S.S. *Teakwood* and then anchored off the small seaside town of Lee-on-the-Solent, five miles west of Portsmouth, to await the commencement of Operation OVERLORD.[14]

"MULBERRY" ARTIFICIAL HARBORS

> *Piers for the use on beaches: They must float up and down with the tide. The anchor problem must be mastered...let me have the best solution worked out. Don't argue the matter. The difficulties will argue for themselves.*
>
> —British Prime Minister Winston Churchill

> *I think it's the biggest waste of manpower and equipment that I have ever seen. I can unload a thousand LSTs at a time over the open beaches. Why give me something that anybody who's ever seen the sea act upon [dislodge] 150-ton concrete blocks at Casablanca knows the first storm will destroy? What's the use of building them just to have them destroyed and litter up the beaches.*
>
> —Rear Adm. John L. Hall Jr., USN

The Allied forces were well aware of the strong German defenses around the ports of Western Europe. Because of this, the Allies did not consider it feasible to seize an existing port in the early stages of an invasion; they had to find another means of facilitating the unloading of supply ships at Normandy. The British solution to this problem was portable ports, code named "Mulberries." The idea for their employment was born of lessons learned from an earlier, failed amphibious raid on the French port of Dieppe in August 1942. Winston Churchill supported the plan; Rear Admiral Hall opposed it.[15]

Photo 8-2

Tug towing across the stormy English Channel one of the 150 concrete caissons which formed the main breakwaters of the Mulberry artificial harbors.
Official British photograph

The Allies' use of these artificial harbors was a unique aspect of the Normandy landings. The Mulberry components were fabricated in Britain and then towed across the English Channel to be assembled off the assault beaches. Each harbor was comprised of roughly six miles of flexible steel roadways (code named

"Whales") that floated on steel or concrete pontoons ("Beetles"). The roadways terminated at pierheads ("Spuds") that could be jacked up and down, supported by legs resting on the seafloor. The harbors were sheltered from the sea by lines of massive sunken caissons ("Phoenixes") and scuttled ships ("Gooseberries"), and a line of floating breakwaters ("Bombardons"). Each port was expected to facilitate the movement of 7,000 tons of vehicles and supplies per day from ship to shore. They were meant to be the primary means for movement of supplies ashore until the Allies were able to capture the port of Cherbourg, France.[16]

Photo 8-3

Mulberry B pierhead in action; wounded being transferred from ambulances to a hospital ship for return to England.
Official British photograph

All operations, including Mulberry installation, began with the 6 June D-Day assault, both on land and sea. Every phase of Mulberry assembly was under combat conditions. Attacks by enemy planes were frequent, and the fire from German 88mm guns was heavy. Mulberry A (for American) was positioned off the town of Saint-Laurent-sur-Mer near Omaha beach in the American sector, and Mulberry B off the town of Arromanches at Gold beach in the British sector.[17]

The British had responsibility for the production of the Phoenixes, the pierheads, the Whale bridge units, and the bombardons, as well as their transportation in tow from the points of manufacture to the marshalling areas from which they were to be dispatched to the Normandy coast. The production of the "rhino" ferries, the sunken causeways, and all other craft to be built of pontoon gear, the manning of those units while in tow across the English Channel, and their installation and operation at the invasion beaches was the responsibility of the U.S. 25th Naval Construction Regiment. In addition, the "Seabees" were assigned the task of manning the Phoenixes, pierheads, and Whale bridge trains (bridge spans and supporting floats) while in tow across the Channel, their installation at Omaha beach, and their operation and maintenance after construction had been completed.[18]

LARGEST OPERATION IN THE HISTORY OF TUGS

> One hundred and thirty-two tugs, including British, American, French and Dutch, were employed in towing the units of this harbour from sheltered anchorages in the United Kingdom to the Normandy coast. Nearly 1,000 tows were made for this purpose in June and July. Tugs were mobilized from far and wide to accomplish this mighty task, made the more daunting by the rough and unseasonable weather in the Channel.
>
> —A statement to the British Parliament in March 1945[19]

The biggest operation in the history of tugs was the towing of components of the artificial harbors across the English Channel and their positioning to form Mulberry A and B. During the Normandy invasion, 132 Allied tugs were employed for this task. An article published in *The Master, Mate and Pilot* in February 1945 cited that of the 132 total tugs, the British Ministry of War Transport provided 42, the Admiralty 30, the U.S. Navy 19, and the U.S. Army 41. Some of the forty-two British Ministry of War Transport tugs flying the Red Ensign were Dutch and French; and of the American tugs, nine were WSA (War Shipping Administration) tugs manned by Merchant mariners. (Of course, the 132 "Mulberry tugs" were only a part of the total 225 Allied tugs cited in the Naval Order of Battle for Operation OVERLORD.) Appendix E identifies the 19 U.S. Navy, 9 WSA, and 61 U.S. Army tugs that were at Normandy. Information about many of the tugs is sketchy. The Army's large tugs were engaged along with Navy and WSA tugs in cross-channel tows of Mulberry components, and its small tugs with positioning these components during installation of the artificial harbors.[20]

The WSA tugs towed Phoenixes across the Channel and turned them over to small tugs operated by the Army Transport Service on 7 June. Construction began off Omaha Beach at 0600 that day under heavy enemy fire. In ensuing days WSA tugs and their crews continued to support logistics operations on "the far shore." The *Farallon*, a representative ship, had a crew of thirty-two merchant mariners plus a detachment of eleven Naval Armed Guardsmen for ship self-defense. The masters of the below nine tugs received the Bronze Star Medal for their heroic action off the Normandy beachheads under conditions of great danger:

Master	WSA Tug	Master	WSA Tug
Walter M. Berg	*Sankaty Head*	Stanley E. Livingston	*Black Rock*
W. H. Halme	*Bodie Island*	R. S. Nowell	*Hillsboro Inlet*
Dan W. Hayman	*Trinidad Head*	C. I. Parkin	*Great Isaac*
F. J. Hughes	*Gay Head*	W. H. Publicover	*Farallon*
Percy A. Jessey	*Moose Peak*[21]		

The citation for the medal awarded by Adm. Harold R. Stark, USN, commander, U.S. Naval Forces in Europe, to Capt. Dan W. Hayman, is representative of those of the other men:

> For meritorious service and courageous devotion to duty during the landing operations in Normandy, France, in June 1944.
> Captain Hayman, Master of the United States War Shipping Administration Tug *Trinidad Head*, was assigned the task of towing vital military and naval equipment to the assault areas on the coast of France. By expert seamanship and navigation skill, and in spite of cross winds and rough seas, he accomplished his difficult task in a most efficient manner. His steadfast courage in the face of enemy artillery fire, heavily mined waters, and sporadic air attack, was an inspiration to his crew.

The courage and devotion to duty of Captain Hayman were in keeping with the best traditions of the United States Merchant Marine.[22]

LOSS OF USS *PARTRIDGE* AND HMS *SESAME*

> From all indications the E-boat fired at extreme range and due to our slow speed with the tow and the fact that we were bucking a strong cross-channel current we were practically a stationary target and therefore they didn't have to allow too much for the speed of the target.
> It seems to me that the E-boats just took advantage of a lull in anti-E-boat patrolling and dashed in and fired at whatever happened to be there. Consequently we were sunk and the ship astern of us [Royal Navy tug HMS *Sesame*], which was even smaller that we were, was also sunk.
>
> —Lt. James C. W. White, USNR, commanding officer of the old fleet tug USS *Partridge* (ATO-130), describing her loss on 11 June 1944 to a torpedo fired by a German E-boat[23]

In early morning on 10 June, the old fleet tug *Partridge* (ATO-138) left Portsmouth, England, en route to the French coast with a "Whale unit," a shallow draft pontoon bridge, in tow. *Partridge* was in company with the British commercial tugs *Empire Folk* and *Queens Cross*, and the Royal Navy rescue tugs HMS *Dexterous* (W111) and HMS *Sesame* (W144). The five tugs, all with tows, were assigned to SNO (Senior Naval Officer) Selsey. This officer, Comdr. John Percy de Winton Kitcat, RN, was the commanding officer of HMS *Queen of Thanet* (a former paddlewheel coastal minesweeping sloop built in 1916, which was stationed at Selsey to serve as the Mulberry Dispatch Control Ship), and the coordinating authority for the movement of all Phoenix and Whale tows across the channel. The tugs assigned to him were part of the larger Mulberry Tug Pool comprised of 132 tugs. Out of this number, 97 tugs were suitable for cross-channel tows. The remaining 35 were small handling tugs, capable only of performing tasks in sheltered waters.[24]

Edmond J. Moran, whose title was Commanding Officer Tugs, was in charge of the entire tug pool. An executive of Moran Towing in New York, he had been overseeing the Navy Rescue Tug Service and was a captain in the Naval Reserve. He was brought to England to organize and manage the towing forces in the Normandy invasion, and did so from Lee-on-Solent. In addition to the requirement for large tugs for cross-channel towing operations, there was a need for smaller tugs to tow Mulberry components to assembly areas off the English coast, and to position the components on the "Far Shore" during installation of Mulberry A and Mulberry B. These duties were carried out by U.S. Army Small Tugs.[25]

There was a moderate sea and swell in the English Channel, produced by a fresh wind from the northwest, but conditions were improving. At 2330, *Queens Cross* sighted in the darkness, flares and tracer fire all around her as the tug drew near Channel Buoy 56A. The seas were then calm, but the tide strong, and she could only make 2 ½ knots against it. E-boats were active in the channel that night, and around midnight E-boat and aircraft attacks, and corresponding counter-fire from other Allied vessels crossing the channel, began developing within visual range of the tugs. At 0130, *Queens Cross* observed the sinking of *Partridge* and *Sesame* and of hits made on other vessels. She sighted two E-boats close to her stern at 0230, but they sheared off without mounting an attack. By 0400, enemy action was tapering off to the east and west, and the remaining three tugs in the group continued their cross-channel transit. *Queens Cross* arrived at Port-en-Bassin, a small Normandy fishing harbor, late that afternoon and handed off her Whale unit to American tugs.[26]

Lieutenant James C. W. White, USNR, the commanding officer of *Partridge*, cited in post action reports that his ship was torpedoed later than the time entered in *Queens Cross*'s deck log. Aboard *Partridge*, the second ship in the column of tugs, 20mm tracer fire was sighted at 0200 well off the starboard quarter of the ship, far enough distant that the point of origin could not be ascertained, nor the intended target, just the arc of firing. The general alarm was sounded, and battle stations manned. White was on the circle deck forward of the bridge where the 3-inch guns were located, because it offered him a commanding view from dead ahead to approximately 160 degrees aft on either side by just taking a few steps to either port or starboard. At about 0215, as he again sighted fire in about the same location, the ship was rocked by a terrific explosion, accompanied by a blinding flash, and sank immediately about ten miles off the French coast.[26]

White initially believed, after finding himself in the water, that *Partridge* had likely struck a mine. Although the ship was transiting a "swept channel" en route to France, they had been in a part that went through a known minefield. Moreover, the Germans were dropping by aircraft and laying by surface craft a great many mines each night. He later learned that the officer in the radar room had detected a fast moving contact on the scope 2 ½ to 3 miles away, but before a report could be made to the bridge the tug had been hit. It appeared that the torpedo had struck portside amidships, in the vicinity of the fire room, exploding the boilers and the magazine and thereby sinking the ship so rapidly.[28]

Partridge suffered 67 casualties: five crewmen killed, thirty-three wounded—including White—and twenty-nine missing. This number would have been higher but for the actions of the Canadian corvette HMCS *Prescott* (K161) and the fact that *Partridge*'s Whale unit remained afloat after she sank, enabling some of the men in the water to climb aboard it. White described the surprise of Navy construction battalion personnel riding the tow, whom had been asleep, to awake to find the tug sailors aboard their temporary home:

> Our tow, I might explain, was a series of bridge spans 50 to 75 feet long connected by pontoons. There were six or seven of these spans connected together, about in the middle there were groups of Seabees, four or five who were riding the tow and who were asleep in a tent. I have heard that when some of the men from our ship, after it had been sunk, when they swam to the tow, they climbed onto the tow expecting these Seabees to give them a hand and didn't see them around. One of the men tells the story of going back to the tent, he pulled back the flap and woke one of them and their first inquiry was, "What the hell are you doing here?"
>
> They were informed that the ship had been torpedoed and sunk and that was the first thing they had heard about it. However they did come up and lend valuable help in getting the men to the tow all through the night and I have heard that some them even swam out and got some of the men in the water and pulled them over to the tow. The tide was such that if a man was very seriously wounded and couldn't maneuver in the water he could be swept within three feet of the tow and just right by it without having a chance to grasp anything.[29]

The remaining surviving officers and men from *Partridge* were in the water from one to two hours before being rescued by *Prescott*. (There was also a small British minesweeper involved in the rescue.) The survivors were afforded excellent care and treatment aboard the Canadian ship. Five deceased men whose bodies were recovered were buried at sea by *Prescott*'s commanding officer, A/Lt. Comdr. Wilfred J. McIsaac, RCNVR. The wounded were landed ashore and taken to British hospitals, and eventually transferred to U.S. Army or U.S. Navy hospitals.[30]

The Royal Navy tug HMS *Sesame*, which had been directly astern of *Partridge*, was torpedoed about the same time, and quickly sank with the loss of most of her officers and ratings. There were few survivors. Five men were rescued by the passage crew aboard her Whale unit. The senior non-commissioned officer in charge aboard the tow reported that at the time of the attack, all of the passage crew were inside the shelter hut. A large flash was seen, but little attention was paid to it because there had been gunfire and flares for a considerable period. About one minute after the flash, one of the men looked out of the shelter to find that *Sesame* had disappeared, with only a puff of smoke marking her former position ahead of the tow.[31]

Lance Corporal Williams of P.F.E. Co., Kite Hill Camp, United Kingdom, entered the water to assist the commanding officer, third officer, first radio officer, and two ratings aboard the Whale unit. An escort destroyer, believed to be HMS *Fernie* (L11), approached and took aboard the five survivors and passage crew, and later delivered them along with four other survivors to the British depot ship S.S. *Aorangi*. A sister tug, HMS *Stormking* (W87), also rescued crewmen from *Sesame*; either the other four men taken aboard *Fernie* or other additional survivors.[32]

The commanding officer of *Sesame* reported that immediately before the explosion, he saw six E-boats approaching, and had given orders to open fire when the ship was hit by what he believed to be a torpedo. Examination of the sunken wreckage by divers years later revealed that the 156-foot *Assurance*-class tug had been struck by a torpedo starboard side amidships, which produced a gaping hole and sent her to the bottom.[33]

STORM-INDUCED DESTRUCTION OF MULBERRY A

In addition to the Mulberries, barges, lighters, docks, cranes, dredges, timber rafts and other equipment had to be towed across the Channel. From D-Day onward all the "Mulberry tugs," except those undergoing maintenance or repairs, were working continuously—and there were never enough tugs. By the end of July, Allied tugs had made 295 cross-channel tows, many of which were of considerable length.[34]

All went well with installation of the Mulberries until 19 June when disaster struck. After twelve days of ceaseless construction, with the harbors operational but not yet completed, a violent storm hit and did not abate for five days. The wind and waves took a tremendous toll on Mulberry A; it broke up and was lost. The American forces then had to revert to the conventional but slower method of beaching landing ships, offloading their cargo, and refloating them on the next high tide. Mulberry B remained in service for British forces over the next ten months delivering to shore two-and-a-half-million men, a half-million vehicles, and four million tons of supplies.[35]

Photo 8-4

"Rhino" tug RHT-3 towing "Rhino" ferry RHF-3 off the Normandy landing beaches. Official U.S. Coast Guard photo #26-G-2335, from the U.S. National Archives

Fortunately for the American forces, Navy Seabees had assembled thirty-six pontoon "rhino ferries" in England that were designed to come alongside supply ships and lighter their cargo ashore, as well as three dozen pontoon "rhino tugs" to provide propulsion for the 42 feet wide by 176 feet long rhino ferries. The Seabees also supplied:
- Twelve causeway tugs to assist tank landing craft in berthing and unberthing at causeways
- Twelve warping tugs, used for assembling, towing, anchoring, and salvaging operations; to pull broached boats off the beach
- Two rhino repair barges, each fitted with two 5-ton cranes, and a toll house
- Two floating dry docks, each able to accommodate a tank landing craft[36]

OMAHA BEACH, NORMANDY

> *I was the first one out. The seventh man was the next one to get across the beach without being hit. All the ones in-between were hit. Two were killed; three were injured. That's how lucky you had to be.*
>
> —Capt. Richard Merrill, USA, 2nd Ranger Battalion

> *The* Pinto, *the* Arikara *and the* ATR 2 *did a magnificent job. For the first three weeks, these ships and their crews hardly stopped for a moment. Often they worked directly exposed to enemy batteries. It was necessary for them to go into the beach time and time again in small boats, taking heavy lines to be secured to wrecks stranded there in order to refloat them. Often they worked aboard landing craft which had been heavily hit by enemy fire, literally wading in blood on the decks in order to complete repairs.*
>
> —Comdr. Byron S. Huie Jr., USNR, commander Task Unit 122.3.1[37]

Many U.S. Navy tugs participated in the Normandy invasion. All of them served valiantly, but for brevity, the contributions of only a few are detailed in this chapter. (Additionally, because a majority of the American ship and personnel casualties occurred at Omaha beach, a description of the action at Utah beach is not included.) Most notable were the actions of fleet tugs *Arikara* and *Pinto* and rescue tug *ATR-2*, which comprised the Combat Salvage and Fire Fighting Unit (Task Unit 122.3.1) assigned off Omaha beach. These three tugs received the Navy Unit Commendation ("NUC") for salvaging many ships and craft, and saving crewmen aboard ships aflame or sinking, or from the water after abandoning. The highlight was their key role in the rescue of 2,200 Navy and Army personnel from the *Susan B. Anthony* after a mine blasted a hole in her hull, set the transport aflame, and ultimately resulted in her loss. (This will be discussed later.)

All other such awards were for service in the Pacific. Only seven other tugs received a "NUC" during the war. These were units of Ship Salvage, Fire Fighting and Rescue Unit, Seventh Fleet Service Force— the fleet tugs *Apache* (ATF-67), *Chickasaw* (ATF-83), *Chowanoc* (ATF-100), *Hidatsa* (ATF-102), and *Quapaw* (ATF-110), and rescue tugs *ATR-6* and *ATR-31*.

Almost immediately after the landings began at Omaha beach on D-Day, *Arikara*, *Pinto*, and *ATR-2* were working furiously to help keep the beach clear of damaged craft that might interfere with ensuing landings, including larger ships and craft damaged offshore that could sink and become obstacles. The salvors aboard the tugs made emergency repairs to damaged craft whenever possible, and sank those which could not be mended and were hazards to navigation.[38]

Proficiency of the salvors and firefighters aboard the tugs did not occur by chance. A Salvage and Firefighting Group (Task Group 122.3) had been organized ahead of D-Day in May 1944 as part of the Western Naval Task Force under the direct command of Commodore William A. Sullivan. Comprising this task group were a number of subordinate units:

- Assault Force "O" (Omaha beach) Combat Salvage and Firefighting Unit (Task Unit 122.3.1): Fleet tugs *Arikara* and *Pinto* and rescue tug *ATR-2* under the command of Comdr. Byron S. Huie Jr., USNR
- Assault Force "U" (Utah beach) Combat Salvage and Firefighting Unit (Task Unit 122.3.2): Fleet tugs *Bannock* and *Kiowa* and rescue tug *ATR-3* under the command of Lt. Comdr. Marshall L. MacClung
- A Reserve Unit (Task Unit 122.3.3): Salvage ships *Brant*, *Diver*, and *Swivel* under Lt. Martin C. Sibitsky, USN
- A Harbor Clearance Salvage Unit (Task Unit 122.3.4) under Comdr. Wiley L. Wroten, USN
- A Harbor Clearance Mine Disposal Unit (Task Unit 122.3.5) under Comdr. Francis Landon DeSpon, RNR
- A Harbor Hydrographic Group (Task Unit 122.3.6) under Lt. Comdr. Charles Peter Warwick Marshall, DSC, RN[39]

The six American tugs assigned to the Omaha and Utah invasion forces each carried, in addition to their own crews, a group of two salvage officers and twelve salvage mechanics, and a second group of one firefighting officer and eight firefighters. These specialists had been chosen from a cadre of experienced personnel: veteran salvage and firefighting personnel from the Mediterranean Theater and graduates of the salvage school at Pier 88 in New York City. They had been training at Base Two (located on the Roseneath peninsula on the Firth of Clyde in Scotland) since December of the preceding year. In preparation for firefighting and salvage work off the assault beaches, additional gear and equipment—firefighting pumps, hoses, foam nozzles, salvage pumps, welding machines, compressors, diving gear, and small amounts of explosives and scuttling charges—were also placed aboard the tugs.[40]

The American salvage ships comprising the Reserve Unit—*Brant* (ARS-32), *Diver* (ARS-5), and *Swivel* (ARS-36)—were assigned to stand by in Falmouth to protect the Channel. The activities of the Harbor Clearance Salvage Unit, Harbor Clearance Mine Disposal Unit, and Harbor Hydrographic Group, are detailed in Chapter 10, titled Opening the Port of Cherbourg.[41]

Assault Force "O" destined for Omaha beach weighed anchor the afternoon of 5 June and put to sea in the direction of Portland Bill—a narrow promontory at the southern end of Isle of Portland, and the southernmost point of Dorset. The amphibious force command ship *Ancon* (AGC-4) Admiral Hall's flagship which Commander Huie was aboard led the force, with troop transports in line astern of her. *Arikara*, *Pinto*, and *ATR-2* were positioned immediately astern of the last transport. To their right and left, ships of the invasion fleet stretched out as far as a person on board the tugs could see. The men aboard them did not yet know whether this sortie was a maneuver designed to confuse the enemy, or the start of the invasion. Aboard *Ancon* it was announced that night after dinner that she was headed for the Normandy coast.[42]

The assault force arrived off northwest France in early morning darkness and anchored around 0330 several miles off Omaha beach to await the completion of pre-landing naval bombardment by American, British, and French gunfire support ships. At 0715 all firing ceased, whereupon LCVPs (Higgins boats) and LCMs (mechanized landing craft) carrying Army infantrymen and Navy combat demolition teams moved forward through the line of ships, formed boat waves, and started for the beach. As the craft neared the shore, the enemy opened fire from very close range. Many craft were lost to gunfire or were wrecked by heavy surf breaking on the beach.[43]

Because the tugs had a draft of about eighteen feet, they could not venture into the shallow water close to the beach to aid stranded craft. This limitation was known, and it was understood that salvage crews, drafted from various transports of the amphibious force, would have sufficient equipment to take care of beach salvage. This equipment consisted mainly of LCM type landing craft fitted with an "A" frame rigged forward and a small winch capable, in calm water, of lifting a LCVP landing craft. These salvage crews headed for the beach shortly after the initial wave, and their landing craft were themselves destroyed by enemy action or by heavy surf. With this salvage capability eliminated, the tugs began to receive urgent appeals for assistance from the hostile beach within fifteen minutes after the first wave landed. To meet this need, they employed boats to take their towing hawsers to damaged or stuck craft.[44]

Priorities for the combat salvage units had been previously established. Of the greatest urgency was undertaking all salvage work necessary to permit operations on the beaches, and to immediately remove any ship or craft in danger of sinking or forming an obstruction while Mulberry A was being built. Large concrete floats had been towed over from England and were to be sunk off shore to form a breakwater for the Mulberry. Big piers were under construction to facilitate discharging cargo from LCTs and LSTs across pontoon causeways to the beach. If necessary, the tugs were to tow sinking ships clear of the all-important Mulberry out to deep water and to scuttle them where they would not form an obstruction. The second priority was to save every ship damaged by enemy action or marine casualty, but not so as to interfere with priority one.[45]

A summary of the salvage and rescue activities of the three tugs on D-Day follows:

Time	Tug	Action
0825	*Pinto*	Repaired battle damage sustained by *LCT(A)-2037* and dispatched her with cargo of material and personnel to the beach
0840	*Pinto*	Similarly repaired and dispatched *LCT-612*, which had also taken shelter alongside battleship *Arkansas* (BB-33)
0928	*Pinto*	Transferred cargo of guns and motor transport from *LCT-294*, which had been mined and was sinking, to *LCT-20*. Dispatched the latter craft to the beach and towed the former craft out to deep water where she was scuttled
1152	*ATR-2*	Performed emergency repairs to keep *LCT-210*, *LCM-9*, and *LCM-11* afloat
1252	*Arikara*	Performed emergency repairs to *LCT-590*
1405	*Arikara*	After attempting to repair and pump water from *LCI-85*, forced to tow her to deep water where she was scuttled
1442	*ATR-2*	Surveyed [inspected] *LST-375* and aided her to anchor to await arrival of a repair ship for major repairs
1442	*Pinto*	Performed emergency repairs to *LCT-200*
1514	*ATR-2*	Pumped and made repairs to LCTs *27* and *197* close off Dog Green beach
1646	*Arikara*	Delivered two damaged LCTs to LST Group 34 for towing to the U.K.
	ATR-2	Likewise delivered two LCTs within same hour
1745	*Arikara*	Repaired the main control lines of *LCT-541* and dispatched her to the beach
2030	*Arikara*	Transferred twenty-eight survivors of *LCI-85* to *LST-134*[46]

LOSS OF TRANSPORT *SUSAN B. ANTHONY*

The second day off Omaha beach (7 June 1944) was even busier; one in which numerous tank landing craft, infantry landing craft, and lesser craft were either hit by enemy shore batteries or struck mines. No effort was made to perform repairs to them of a permanent nature, only patch-ups and movement sufficient to keep them afloat and prevent them from drifting toward shore and sinking. Damaged and immobile craft were taken in tow as rapidly as conditions would permit, and secured to a mooring offshore which had been provided for that purpose. The most important rescue was that of 2,200 Army and Navy personnel from the transport *Susan B. Anthony*, which struck a mine at 0750 that morning in the swept channel off the beach. The mine exploded under her No. 4 hold leaving her without power, her rudder stuck hard left, and water flowing into both No. 4 and No. 5 holds through breeches in her hull. By 0805 the ship had an eight-degree list to starboard. In an effort to save his ship, Comdr. Thomas L. Gray, USNR, ordered embarked soldiers to shift to the port side of the main deck, and this human ballast brought her back to an even keel.[47]

Photo 8-5

Susan B. Anthony anchored at Oran, Algeria.
Official U.S. Navy photo # 80-G-215100, now in the collections of the U.S. National Archives

Pinto was the first ship alongside the sinking transport, a former Grace Steamship Company ocean liner. She moored starboard side to the port quarter of *Susan B. Anthony* at 0820, and prepared to take the stricken transport, whose stern was then awash, in tow. Within eight minutes, *Pinto* had put a salvage crew and a pump aboard, had begun removing water from No. 5 hold, and had signaled British destroyer HMS *Mendip* (L60)—which had a medical officer—to come alongside her. The fleet tug then transferred approximately ten Army and Navy casualties from the transport across her deck to *Mendip*. Despite the pumping in progress, the *Anthony* continued to settle by the stern. Accordingly, *Pinto* transmitted an urgent radio message to commander Task Force 124 requesting that landing craft be sent to take off the troops.[48]

As ships and craft arrived to assist, *Pinto* transferred Army troops as rapidly as possible across her decks to *Mendip*, and directed the destroyer escort *Bates* (DE-69), landing craft *LCT-624*, *LCT-625*, and *LCI-496*, and other American and British vessels, including HMS *Norbo* and *LCI-489*, to come alongside. Loaded with troops, *Mendip* departed, and other vessels in turn came alongside *Pinto*, to continue taking men off the transport. During this activity, fires erupted in *Susan B. Anthony*'s engine and fire rooms, and the transport began to settle more rapidly. *ATR-2* stood in close aboard, and directed streams of water onto her burning superstructure. *Arikara* aided in the search of surrounding waters for survivors.[49]

Following the removal of all Army troops and portable Army equipment, by 0955 all other ships were away from alongside the transport. *Pinto* then began to take aboard naval personnel; the ship's crew and her salvage team. All were off the ship by 0959, with the exception of a few survivors stranded on the forward well deck who could not reach the tug via passage through the transport's blazing superstructure. *Pinto*'s commanding officer, Lt. Ralph Brown, instructed the survivors to get into the water. He then cast off the tug's mooring lines and backed clear of the transport, whose after well deck was now completed submerged. At 1012 *Susan B. Anthony* sank in approximately seventeen fathoms of water, ten miles off the Normandy fishing village of Port-en-Bessin. Remarkably, all the survivors in the water were picked up by American and British ships and craft. No one was killed, and few of the forty-five wounded were seriously hurt.[50]

SALVAGE PRECEDES AND FOLLOWS STORM

By the end of the second day of the invasion, the combat salvage and firefighting unit assigned to Omaha beach had repaired twelve large landing craft—four LCT(A)s, seven LCTs and one LCI, all loaded with personnel and equipment—enabling them to beach. This work was done within easy range of enemy shore batteries, as were diving operations to unfoul propellers of craft that had ensnared line, wire, and other wreckage off the beach. Diving operations in positions vulnerable to enemy fire were only done on a voluntary basis, but to their tremendous credit every diver courageously offered to go down. Fortunately, not one was hurt.[51]

The days that followed were very much like preceding ones, except that, as Army troops moved off the beaches and drove further inland, enemy fire at ships offshore lessened. However, as soon as darkness came each night German planes would arrive overhead. Bombs were dropped and some near misses were sustained, but there were few direct hits on vessels off Omaha beach.[52]

By 18 June the only landing craft remaining on Omaha beach were a few LCIs that had been so badly damaged by gunfire or mines their recovery was impractical. Up to this point the combat salvage and firefighting unit had been busy. Their accomplishments were many and varied as shown in the following summary:

- Made emergency repairs to fifteen craft, and assisted them to the beaches with their cargo
- Repaired another eighty-nine craft, well enough to keep them afloat
- Removed fifty-five craft from the beaches
- Sank twenty-five vessels as menaces to navigation
- Retrieved a total of 2,320 survivors from damaged vessels or from the sea
- Performed thirty-nine miscellaneous jobs—surveys, laying of buoys, etc.[53]

Early on 19 June, a terrible storm—with heavy rain and winds just shy of gale proportions—hit and lasted for five days. Most operations were curtailed, but the three tugs off Omaha beach did their best to provide assistance to the forces offshore. Many ships lost anchors when wind and seas broke their moorings. The tugs found and supplied replacement anchors to some, while other ships and craft were towed out to sea and secured to an offshore mooring. Admiral Hall ordered reinforcements for the overwhelmed salvage unit, and additional salvage and rescue craft began to arrive about the second day of the storm. These included the old fleet tugs *Algorma* (ATO-34) and *Cormorant* (ATO-133), rescue tug *ATR-13*, auxiliary tug *ATA-125*, Army tug *Cayhead*, and British tugs *Empire John* and *Empire Bascobeal*.54

Photo 8-6

Wrecked landing craft on Omaha beach.
Official U.S. Navy Photo #80-G-286424, now in the collections of the U.S. National Archives

As heavy storm surf pounded the beaches, ships offshore dragged anchor and fouled one another, landing craft were driven ashore, and Mulberry A was destroyed. The wind finally abated on 22 June; leaving Omaha beach a shambles of stranded and wrecked craft. Until cleared, this mass of obstructions would cause great difficulty in supplying the Army with ammunition, food, fuel, and reinforcements. There were approximately 200 large landing craft aground, and the collective damage done was more than four-times that caused by earlier enemy action. Prior to the storm, the artificial harbor had been just about completed. Now, large metal floats called "Bombardons," which had formed an outer breakwater, had broken their moorings. Some were adrift, and others upended, hanging on to one or more of their four-legged moorings. The first job of the tugs was to dispose of these bombardons. Those still moored to one or more legs were unshackled, taken out to sea, and sunk by gunfire. Then the work of clearing the beach began.[55]

The first day, a stretch, some 200 yards long, was cleared and tank landing ships waiting offshore began to beach and discharge their cargo. Among the more important vessels stranded on the beach were a number of coasters, a term for shallow-draft merchant ships. They could be refloated only by employing heavy sets of beach gear and powerful tugs. The largest beached ships required assistance from bulldozers, furnished by the Army and Seabee battalions. Dozers scooped out deep channels, running seaward, to assist the tugs to "skid" sand-gripped ships to the sea. The combat salvage and firefighting unit was also augmented by *Bannock* and *ATR-3* from Utah beach, as the storm damage there was not nearly as bad. Finally, three British wreck dispersal vessels—the HMT *Maria*, HMT *Tehana*, and HMT *Admiral Sir John Lawford*—reported for duty. They were laying to off the beach, waiting for Cherbourg to fall to begin port clearance operations. These British ships carried divers and explosives for demolition purposes, and were soon busily engaged in clearing sunken wrecks off the shore.[56]

ATR-4 ASSIGNED TO BRITISH NAVAL FORCES

During the Normandy landings, some of the U.S. Navy tugs were assigned to the British. Early in the month, *ATR-4*'s first tasking had come on 7 June when FOIC (Flag Officer in Charge), Portsmouth sent her to search for the Royal Navy tank landing craft *LCT-2423*, reportedly broken down and adrift. Upon her arrival in the specified area, *ATR-4* searched visually and by radar for the LCT without success and, thereafter, returned to Lee-on-the-Solent. The next day, FOIC, Portsmouth dispatched her to retrieve a rhino ferry reported to be adrift. She returned to Lee-on-the-Solent with it in tow.[57]

On 9 June *ATR-4* received secret orders to proceed across the English Channel to Juno beach, the second beach from the east, among the five assault beaches of the Normandy invasion. Three days earlier, on D-Day, the first wave of the Canadian 3rd Infantry Division had taken heavy casualties assaulting the beach, but by the end of that day, had succeeded in wresting control of the area from German troops and had obtained the farthest penetration into enemy territory of any of the assault forces. Upon arrival that night, *ATR-4* anchored in the Baie de la Seine, off the town of Courseulles, and reported to Rear Adm. Sir Philip Vian, RN, naval commander Eastern Task Force, for duty. The Bay of the Seine River—a rectangular-shaped inlet on the English Channel bounded to the west by the Cotentin Peninsula, to the south by the Normandy coast, and to the east by the estuary of the river Seine and the port city of Le Havre—encompassed the five Allied beaches.[58]

ATR-4 got under way in late morning on 11 June to assist the Royal Navy frigate HMS *Halstead* (K556) and a merchant vessel, but was unable to locate either ship. (*Halstead*, her bow blown off after being torpedoed by a German E-boat in the English Channel, had been assisted into port by another ship.) The tug recovered three bodies from the water, which she transferred to the minesweeper USS *Owl* (AM-2). She later recovered the body of a soldier. The following morning, after anchoring for the night off Courseulles, the rescue tug got under way with Reverend Gamon, RNVR, and the burial for the soldier was performed at sea. At completion, she returned to the anchorage.[59]

That afternoon, a German Focke-Wulf Fw-190 fighter-bomber made an attack on ships in the vicinity of *ATR-4*. The nearest bomb fell a good distance from the tug. However, following this nominal effort, after midnight on 13 June there were a series of enemy air attacks and a corresponding barrage of anti-aircraft fire. Most of the planes were beyond the range of the rescue tug's guns, but she did take a diving aircraft off her starboard quarter under fire with her 20mm.[60]

ATR-4 lay at anchor off Courseulles from 14 to 16 June "on Immediate Notice" to provide assistance to damaged vessels. During this period, she and other ships in the vicinity were subjected to periodic enemy air attacks, as noted in her war diary below. One bomber—a multi-role, twin-engine Junkers Ju-88—came within range of her guns.

Date	Time	War Diary Entries
14 June	0000-0340	Intermittent air raids and heavy AA fire
	2025	Air raid
	2250	Fired 3 rounds 3"50 and 232 rounds 20MM at three high flying aircraft
	2335	3"50 gun opened fire at high flying aircraft on starboard beam, 12 rounds expended, no observed hits during firing
15 June	0258-0243	Air raid, heavy AA fire
	2345	Fired 10 rounds 20MM at [Junkers] Ju-88 in searchlight beam, no hits observed
16 June	0025	Air raid with heavy AA fire
	0320	All clear
	2346	Air raid with heavy AA fire[61]

The rapid firing and easily trained and elevated 20mm anti-aircraft guns were the tug's weapon of choice against aircraft. Her larger caliber and longer range (but much slower) 3-inch gun might be used in the case of high flying planes. However, shooting at distant bombers was almost always futile, analogous to a hunter trying to bring down snow geese high overhead with a rifle. More important, in the case of small-caliber guns, directing fire at enemy aircraft often served no useful purpose and attracted unwanted attention to small ships possessing little means to defend themselves.[62]

RESCUE TUG *ATR-15* AGROUND

While lying at anchor off Courseulles the night of 18 June, a rocket bomb passed the starboard beam of *ATR-4*, signaling yet another air raid but she suffered no harm or damage. The following morning brought heavy seas, rising high winds, and an associated requirement for rescue work. She got under way at 0630 to assist the British tank landing craft *LCT-2441*, whose mooring alongside the landing craft repair ship *LSE-2* had been broken. The rescue tug was able to put a line on the LCT and pull her clear, thereby preventing the possibility of the craft being blown onto the beach. In late afternoon the following day 20 June, *ATR-4* observed *ATR-15* aground, but received no orders to assist her. That evening a rocket bomb flew by *ATR-4*, only two hundred yards off her port beam, reminding everyone aboard that, despite the existing nasty weather, enemy planes still posed a threat.[63]

A short time later, *ATR-4* was dispatched to aid her fellow tug. As she approached the shoal water where *ATR-15* lay at anchor—no longer aground but without power—*ATR-4* took continuous depth soundings. Fortunately, the tide was in or she might have grounded. *ATR-4* let go her port anchor—keeping her head into the wind in the face of heavy seas and a fresh northeast gale—and was able to get close enough to pass a line to the stranded tug. As *ATR-4* heaved around on her anchor, and began to take a strain on the line made up to *ATR-15*, the latter vessel slipped the anchors holding her fast and at 2205 shifted into deeper water. With her work done for the night, *ATR-4* anchored off Courseulles. Just before midnight, her port 20mm gun opened fire on an aircraft approaching her port beam. No hits were observed, but forty rounds expended apparently served to deter the enemy; the plane dropped flares but no bomb runs followed.[64]

ATR-15 BROUGHT TO ENGLAND

Early the next morning, *ATR-4* took *ATR-15* in tow for repairs in England. With rough seas, and the sinking condition of the towed ship, the effort proved difficult. *ATR-4* had to anchor with her charge six miles off Courseulles. The British salvage ship HMS *Sea Salvor* approached *ATR-15* a little past noon to put pumps aboard, but was unable to come alongside her due to the sea conditions. With no other options available, *ATR-4* prepared to resume her salvage efforts. At 1350 she set off with *ATR-15* in tow seeking the sanctuary offered by Mulberry B. After entering the artificial harbor, she anchored, hauled *ATR-15* alongside her to port, put pumps aboard her, and began dewatering the ship. Continuous pumping was necessary while awaiting fair weather to attempt the English Channel crossing.[65]

In early morning darkness on 23 June *ATR-4* set off with *ATR-15* in tow, stern first, because of damage to the forward part of the wooden ship caused by the grounding, for Portsmouth. Conditions were ideal—fair weather and calm seas—but the damaged ship towed badly, shearing from side to side, and the towing bridle parted. *ATR-4* then passed seventy-five fathoms of two-inch main tow wire and a new bridle to *ATR-15*, and once again took her under tow. This effort was successful. Arriving off Lee-on-the-Solent late that night, *ATR-4* brought her charge alongside, and anchored for the night.[66]

The following day, per orders from Lee-on-the-Solent Port Tug Control, she got under way in early afternoon with *ATR-15* alongside her bound for Portsmouth Dock Yard. Upon arrival at Portsmouth, she moored *ATR-15* to the minesweeping trawler HMS *Jacinta* for the night, and then continued pumping water from the tug and furnishing electrical power to her. The following day, *ATR-4* shifted *ATR-15* to the dockyard. After relinquishing her tow, the tug moored for the night at the dockyard's Boat House jetty. In the morning, the mission successfully completed, she departed to return to Lee-on-the-Solvent for additional duties. Apparently, dockyard repairs failed to completely restore *ATR-15*, or she developed additional problems after she left the yard. She arrived at New York City on 7 January 1945, with Task Group 27.4, in tow by WSA tug *Tybee*. Having been found unfit for further service or in excess of the needs of the Navy, *ATR-15* was decommissioned on 28 May 1945.[67]

POSTSCRIPT – OVERLORD/NEPTUNE

Following the completion of Operation NEPTUNE, Rear Adm. Alan G. Kirk, USN, commander Task Force 122, praised the men under his command and also the leaders to whom he reported:

The total number of U.S. personnel in the Western Task Force was approximately 125,000. It is my opinion that the performance of all hands from flag officers to seamen was in the highest traditions of the naval service; to command so fine a force in so large an operation was a great privilege.

Equally, the performance of British and other Allied vessels in the Western Task Force fulfilled my highest expectations, and the close association in combat with these fine sailors of other nations is a source of real satisfaction.

Finally, the skillful coordination of this vast operation by the Supreme Commander, General Eisenhower, and the high professional skill and sympathetic leadership of the Allied Naval Commander, Admiral Ramsay, will be remembered by all who served under them in the Western Naval Task Force.[68]

9

"Human Torpedoes" and Explosive Boats

Inexperienced, ignorant young enlisted men, ranging from eighteen to twenty-three years of age, of the Navy, who have volunteered for a widely advertised new service as "Solo Fighters," in which they hope to gain promotion and honor. All rates, up to petty officer first class, are represented; they know little about what they are getting into.

The group probably was intended for Normandy operations, for it started into France; two weeks ago it was diverted to Italy by railroad.

The group has not been in combat before.

It is not believed any of the coxswains interrogated had ever been in action.

—Observations made by Capt. Walter Ansel in his report on the interrogation of German POWs following a Human Torpedo Attack in the Ventimiglia area in northern Italy on 10 September 1944[1]

Prior to commencement of Operation OVERLORD on 6 June 1944, Allied naval forces had believed that German destroyers, torpedo boats, and E-boats would pose the principal enemy surface ship threat to cross-channel convoy routes. It was also anticipated that E-boats would attack follow-on convoys through the use of torpedoes or mines, and would attempt to infiltrate into the assault areas off Normandy. And, there was concern about possible German use of a new weapon; one-man submarines termed "human torpedoes." However in a night action on 9 June off Ile de Batz, the Royal Navy's 10th Destroyer Flotilla had dealt with a force of four German destroyers attempting to come into the convoy area from Brest. Several days later an armada of large force of Royal Air Force Lancasters attacked E-boat pens at Le Havre and Boulogne with penetration bombs on 14 and 15 June (D-Day+8). The attacks inflicted heavy losses, and greatly diminished the Kriegsmarine light naval forces previously available to oppose Allied forces at Normandy.[2]

Despite the almost complete absence of a German surface ship threat, United States and British naval forces suffered the loss of forty-six ships, torpedo boats, and gunboats at Normandy, mostly due to enemy mines and other types of conventional weapons. Twenty-four vessels were lost to mines, one to a combination of mine damage and shore battery fire, and one to a mine or torpedo. E-boats or other type surface vessels sank seven Allied ships; aircraft accounted for three; and shore battery fire, one.

The German Navy was increasingly desperate by this point in the war, following the attrition of large numbers of its own ships and submarines, and was employing unconventional weapons as well. "Human torpedoes" and explosive motor boats sank nine Royal Navy ships—a cruiser, a destroyer, an escort destroyer, a frigate, a trawler, three minesweepers, and an examination vessel—off the Normandy beaches and damaged other vessels. The cruiser was on loan to Poland.

Damage vested on Allied ships by human torpedoes and explosive motor boats off Normandy and in other coastal areas during the latter part of the war created additional work for Allied salvage forces. The remainder of this short chapter is devoted to these craft and the brave German sailors who carried out predominately suicide missions.

U.S. Navy Ships Sunk by German Forces at Normandy
(Does not include landing craft)

Ship	Date	Cause of Loss
Osprey (AM-56)	5 Jun 44	Mine
Corry (DD-463)	6 Jun 44	Mine
PC-1261	6 Jun 44	Shore batteries
Susan B. Anthony (AP-72)	7 Jun 44	Mine
Tide (AM-125)	7 Jun 44	Mine
Rich (DE-695)	8 Jun 44	Mine
LST-499	8 Jun 44	Mine
Meredith (DD-726)	9 Jun 44	Aircraft attack and mine
LST-314	9 Jun 44	E-boat
LST-376	9 Jun 44	E-boat
Glennon (DD-620)	10 Jun 44	Mine and shore batteries
Partridge (ATO-138)	11 Jun 44	E-boat
LST-496	11 Jun 44	Mine
LST-523	19 Jun 44	Mine
YMS-350	2 Jul 44	Mine
YMS-304	30 Jul 44	Mine
YMS-378	30 Jul 44	Mine[3]

A review of the above table and the ensuing one highlights the devastation wrought by Germany mines at Normandy, and serves as a primer for the next chapter, titled Opening the Port of Cherbourg. This lengthy and dangerous endeavor required the coordinated efforts of American and British tugs and salvage ships, American, British, and Canadian minesweepers, and Royal Navy clearance divers to open the port for sea-supplied logistic support to Allied armies.

Royal Navy Ships Lost to German Forces at Normandy
(Does not include landing craft)

Ship	Date	Cause of Loss
Destroyer HNoMS *Svenner* (G03) (on loan to Royal Norwegian Navy)	6 Jun 44	Surface ship torpedo
destroyer HMS *Wrestler* (D35)	6 Jun 44	Mine (damaged beyond repair)
Frigate HMS *Lawford* (K514)	8 Jun 44	Aircraft bomb
Netlayer HMT *Minster*	8 Jun 44	Mine
Motor gunboat HM *MGB-17*	11 Jun 44	Mine
Tug HMS *Sesame* (W144)	11 Jun 44	E-boat torpedo
Destroyer HMS *Swift* (G46)	12 Jun 44	Mine
Motor minesweeper HMS *MMS-229*	13 Jun 44	Mine
Destroyer HMS *Fury* (H76)	21 Jun 44	Mine (damaged beyond repair)
Trawler HMS *Lord Austin* (FY220)	24 Jun 44	Mine
Motor gunboat HM *MGB-326*	28 Jun 44	Mine
Large infantry landing ship HMS *Empire Broadsword*	2 Jul 44	Mine
Motor torpedo boat HMCS *MTB-460* (on loan to Royal Canadian Navy)	3 Jul 44	Mine
Frigate HMS *Trollope* (K575)	6 Jul 44	Human torpedo (damaged beyond repair)
Minesweeper HMS *Cato* (J16)	6 Jul 44	Human torpedo
Minesweeper HMS *Magic* (J400)	6 Jul 44	Human torpedo
Minesweeper HMS *Pylades* (J401)	8 Jul 44	Human torpedo
Motor torpedo boat HMCS *MTB-463* (on loan to the Royal Canadian Navy)	8 Jul 44	Mine
Cruiser ORP *Dragon* (D46) (on loan to Polish Navy)	8 Jul 44	Human torpedo (damaged beyond repair)
Motor torpedo boat HM *MTB-434*	9 Jul 44	Surface craft
Motor minesweeper HMS *MMS-55*	10 Jul 44	Mine
Destroyer *Isis* (D87)	20 Jul 44	Human torpedo or mine
Motor torpedo boat HM *MTB-430*	27 Jul 44	Rammed by E-boat
Trawler HMS *Lord Wakefield* (FY170)	29 Jul 44	Aircraft
Motor minesweeper HMS *MMS-8*	1 Aug 44	Mine
Trawler HMS *Gairsay* (T290)	3 Aug 44	Explosive boat
Escort destroyer HMS *Quorn* (L66)	3 Aug 44	Human torpedo
Motor gunboat HM *MGB-313*	16 Aug 44	Mine or torpedo
Examination vessel HMS *Fratton*	18 Aug 44	Human torpedo[4]

GERMAN EXPLOSIVE MOTOR BOATS

Explosive motor boats normally operated in groups of three, two explosive boats and one control boat. The former carried an explosive charge, and was operated by a single helmsman until near the target vessel, when the control boat took over by radio control. The operator would then dive overboard to be picked up by the control boat. The *Linsen*-class explosive boats were originally developed by the Abwehr, a German intelligence organization, for use by its Special Forces Unit the Brandenburg Regiment.[5]

The boats were first used in an ineffectual attack on the Anzio bridgehead in April 1944, while still under Army control. Interservice fighting then ensued regarding who should maintain and utilize the boats. Almost immediately the existing thirty boats came under the control of the Kriegsmarine's K-Verband ("small battle unit"). The mission of the newly established naval unit under Rear Adm. Helmuth Heye was to operate mini-submarines and explosive boats.[6]

The 18-foot boats achieved relatively little success during their war service. Small and unarmed, they had almost no chance of surviving an encounter with an Allied ship, patrol vessel, or aircraft. Since such encounters were frequent, many boats were sunk and their operators killed during failed missions. There were a few exceptions, such as the action off Normandy on 3 August, described below, in which the boats sank the trawler HMS *Gairsay*, a motor launch, and a landing craft.[7]

MINI-SUBMARINES ("HUMAN TORPEDOES")

The first German *Neger*-class human torpedoes a former torpedo modified to serve as a delivery craft, operated by a single sailor seated in a cavity beneath a bubble on top, with a torpedo slung below—were employed ineffectively, along with explosive boats, at Anzio. After loaded on trailers and covered with camouflage nets, the mini- or one-man submarines were easily transported on public roads to their launch sites. Their second usage occurred on the night of 5-6 July against Allied ships at Normandy. Twenty-six *Neger*s sortied from Villers-sur-Mer, located to the east of Sword Beach (the easternmost beach of the five Allied landing areas) across the Orne River. Human torpedoes managed to sink the minesweepers HMS *Cato* and HMS *Magic*, but only nine members of their group returned from the mission. Two had suffered mechanical problems and fifteen were lost to Allied gunfire or other causes. A second attack against ships off Normandy on 7-8 July by twenty-one *Neger*s resulted in the British minesweeper *Pylades* being sunk and the Polish cruiser ORP *Dragon* sufficiently damaged that she was towed to Mulberry B, and scuttled to form part of the artificial breakwater near Courseulles. All of the human torpedoes that took part in the mission were sunk by Allied aircraft or surface vessels.[8]

Photo 9-1

American soldiers inspecting a German "human torpedo" washed up on a beach at Anzio, Italy.

The loss of the British destroyer *Isis* twelve days later on 20 July is perhaps also attributable to a human torpedo. She is believed to have been sunk by either a mine or a human torpedo with the loss of 11 officers and 144 men, all but twenty of her crew.[9]

LARGE MASSED ATTACK ON 3 AUGUST

Although commonly referred to as mini- or one-man submarines, the *Neger*-class human torpedoes could not submerge. An upgraded, slightly larger human torpedo equipped with a ballast tank fitted in front of the cockpit solved this problem. The tank, when filled with seawater, allowed the craft to descend to a depth of thirty-three feet. However, the resultant 27-foot, 5.5 ton *Marder*-class mini-submarine was not without flaws. These included limited speed (4.2 knots on the surface) and mobility and the lack of a periscope, which left the coxswain virtually blind underwater and necessitated continuing to make the approaches to, and attacks on, target ships on the surface.

On the positive side, the silhouettes of the manned vehicles operating awash were still difficult to sight at night. Moreover, the canopy (bubble) above the cockpit could be released from the inside allowing the coxswain to escape from a submerged craft that was damaged or had experienced mechanical problems.[10]

Photo 9-2

HMS *Centurion* was one of sixty Allied Navy and merchant ships that were scuttled to form part of the breakwaters for the Mulberry Harbors.
Official U.S. Coast Guard photograph

In the early morning darkness, between 0250 and daybreak on 3 August 1944, German forces launched an attack on shipping in the British assault area off Normandy. The attack was by conventional forces employing low flying aircraft and E-boats, but also included the use of twenty-two *Linsen*-class explosive motorboats and fifty-eight human torpedoes (*Neger*s and *Marder*s of K-Flotilla 361 and 362, respectively). The attacks on ships by explosive boats followed those of the human torpedoes.[11]

The K-Verband forces sank the British escort destroyer HMS *Quorn*, trawler HMS *Gairsay*, landing craft HMS *LCG(L)-764*, and a motor launch. Human torpedoes also damaged other vessels and "block ships." These included two cargo ships chartered to the Ministry of War of Great Britain, S.S. *Samlong* and S.S. *Fort Lac La Ronge*, and two block ships of Mulberry B. "Block ship" was a term for old ships which had crossed the English Channel either under their own power or were towed, and then scuttled to create sheltered water at the landing beaches. The resultant cost to the German seamen who operated the craft was high; 41 of the 58 human torpedoes and 14 of the 22 boats were lost during the mission.[12]

HUMAN TORPEDO FOUND ADRIFT

> *Occupant of the mother torpedo was apparently dead. Was of small stature and build wearing a white canvas helmet and a bright red life saving device. Bottom torpedo (child) was no longer affixed to mother. Rudder assembly – (vertical) appeared to be somewhat damaged.*
>
> —Description of human submarine found adrift off Normandy beaches at 2300 on 4 August 1944 by patrol craft *PC-552*[13]

While patrolling off the Normandy beaches the night of 4 August, the patrol craft *PC-552* found adrift one of the many human torpedoes that would not return from the previous day's mission. A preliminary examination by binoculars of the craft disclosed that it had no "way on" (was motionless) and the coxswain was still inside, visible through the Plexiglas dome. The patrol craft informed the destroyer HMS *Grenville* (R97) of her finding, and then lowered and manned her wherry, and dispatched it to the craft. Following a more thorough examination, a towing line was secured to the rudder assembly of the mother torpedo and the ship's boat took it in tow. At 2045, the craft was made up alongside *PC-552*.[14]

Grenville closed *PC-552* to hailing distance and ordered her to stand by the craft until a salvage tug arrived to take it. The destroyer lowered a boat at 2125, which proceeded to the human torpedo and affixed a mooring line and anchor to same. *Grenville* then dropped a buoy over the side to mark the position of the human torpedo, recovered her boat, and departed. *PC-552* retrieved her line from the craft. Daylight a few hours later revealed that the human torpedo had apparently sunk during the night. Following an unsuccessful search for the craft, *PC-552* returned to her assigned patrol.[15]

ONE OF THE FORTUNATE COXSWAINS

German sailor Ferdinand Hoffmann was the coxswain of the human torpedo that sank HMS *Quorn*. He had volunteered for the human torpedo program in order to escape from court-martial after falsifying his leave pass to spend additional time with a woman. Years later, he told his story to Alfons Steck, who recorded it for posterity. Hoffman who died in 2009 at the age of 86 years recalled his training, travel by railroad to the French coast via Paris, and the attack on Allied ships off Normandy:

> In Surendorf at the Baltic Sea I got my Examination. There we were trained and learned, how to handle the emergency diving-dress. Already in the time of examination one of our comrades died, when he shot his torpedo, but the explosive torpedo did not depart from the human torpedo. After the invasion of France we should have a mission there. By train we came to France close to Paris. We continued only slowly, because the partisans had blown up the railroads nearly everywhere and this firstly had to be repaired. Because I had a toothache, I was able to leave the place of our accommodation to Paris, where I was attended by a French doctor. In this way I could visit the Eiffel Tower, too. The next day we drove to the coast, but we had to interrupt our ride again and again because of the lots of low-level flying aircraft. At last we arrived at the bay at the mouth of the river Seine, from where we had to attack the allied fleet. We were not located in a village, but somewhere outside on the beach.[16]

He and the other human torpedo "coxswains" in his group began their mission around 2200. They had been briefed about the location of the anchorage of Allied ships and told that German aircraft would fly an attack on the ships to help them orient themselves. Hoffmann, who was not aware there was to be an attack by German explosive boats, following their attacks, described sinking the *Quorn*:

> It had been expected, that the ships would fire on the aircraft and that we in this way could find the ships. But there was nothing to be seen of German aircraft and there was nothing to be seen of firing ships, it was rather dark, you could see next to nothing. The sight out of the cupola of a human torpedo is extremely bad. At

last however I found the warships. I saw a destroyer, fired my torpedo and hit the destroyer. The time was about 03.00 a.m. I am sure, that the ship was a destroyer, because I had seen the high upstanding canon, and I am of the opinion, that the destroyer sank at once. An old cruiser, which had been hit in the same night and which was destined by the allies to be sunk as a breakwater ["block ship"] would have given a much higher silhouette and could not have been changed [*sic*] by mistake despite the fact that it had been an old ship.[17]

Following his success, Hoffmann tried to flee to safety, but was attacked by an Allied gunboat on patrol in the area and was wounded. The craft carrying him caught fire, and with it damaged, and himself wounded, he sat it on the bottom in the shallows and tried to wait out his vengeful pursuers:

After my shot I turned at once and tried to reach the saving coast. I was terribly afraid. With my human torpedo I passed the middle of the allied ships and I always thought they truly must have seen me. The ships towered incredible high out of the water, the situation was ghostly, but firstly I got away. Round about 05.00 a.m., when the dawn came, I was hit. An English gun boat took me over, went into the bank and returned. When the bullets of a machine gun tore the cupola of my torpedo into pieces, I made myself as small as possible and I pulled down my head as deep as possible, in order not be hit. In spite of that I was hit in my neck by splinters of the cupola.... When the gun boat approached, I sank down with my torpedo round about 20 m on the ground of the sea, but I kept sitting in it. I still had my emergency diving suit case and so I could breathe for some time. Under water you can hear every noise and I noticed that the gun boat over me turned again and again.... So I stayed waiting down on the bottom of the sea.[18]

When the gunboat searching for him withdrew, Hoffmann escaped to the surface in diving gear, and then tried to reach the beach, but he apparently passed out due to fatigue or his wounds, and awoke to find himself a prisoner. He was taken, initially, to England for confinement and later to the United States:

I dived up and tried to reach the French coast by swimming. I still wore my life-jacket and swam about 1 hour. At some time or other I must have lost consciousness, because I cannot remember, how I got on board of the English gun boat, which saved my life. At once everything was taken away until I only wore my trousers.

Before the beginning of my mission I had sewed a death's head on to my cap. This cap, my clock and my compass were taken at once as a trophy. From this gunboat I was carried to a greater warship. When I climbed up the ladder-rope and arrived at the deck, I saluted smart: Heil Hitler! At that time I still was extremely proud of myself. From this warship I was carried to the French Side of the Channel and separated at once from the other prisoners of war, because I had told the English soldiers before, that I had sunk one of their destroyers. From here I was brought into captivity to England, where I was kept about 4 weeks and I was interrogated by the British Secret Service. Because I had told them already on the destroyer, that I had sunk one of their destroyers, I was kept in solitary confinement.... From England I was carried by ship to the United States into the prison camp of Fort Devens in Massachusetts.... I was carried on my own request to Texas into the navy prison camp of Fort Bowie, where we had to mount Jeeps or could fell trees.[19]

Unlike the Q-boats the Japanese would later introduce, the human torpedoes were not true suicide craft, but they might as well have been. Most of the craft not sunk by enemy fire were lost to accidents. The coxswains could not get a clear shot at a ship, unless they were very close to it and the target was stationary—the sights used were similar to those of a rifle, requiring the pilot to aim and fire. Such an attack was after proceeding on the surface from a beach, at about 4 knots, often without any element of surprise. It was an extremely dangerous undertaking. Despite the challenges associated with the craft they used and the dangerous missions, the German sailors who engaged in this form of warfare were able to achieve a measure of success off Normandy beaches, and other coastal areas later in the war. One source indicated that by the end of 1944, human torpedoes had sunk 50,000 tons of shipping.[20]

10

Opening the Port of Cherbourg

> *Hennecke performed a feat unique in the history of coastal defense; he carried out an exemplary destruction of the harbor of Cherbourg.*
>
> —Remarks made by Adolf Hitler when he presented the Knights Cross of the Iron Cross to Rear Adm. Walter Hennecke, the naval commander at Cherbourg prior to the capture of the French port city by Allied forces[1]

Around the middle of July 1944, Commodore Sullivan dispatched two British ships to augment the Combat Salvage and Firefighting Unit at Omaha beach, which had been working furiously to clear all the craft driven ashore or sunk by the horrendous storm. These were HMSV *Abigail* and HMSV *Help*, two large salvage ships employed for lifting sunken wrecks. *Abigail* was a former Dredging Support Vessel that originally bore the unglamorous moniker *Hopper No. 4*. Some believed her new name was a tribute to Mrs. Abigail Smith, the most prized office-cleaner at the Admiralty. By 20 July the only wreckage remaining at Omaha were a few LCIs sunk by enemy action, and a few large metal bombardons (floating breakwaters), which the storm had driven high and dry on the shore.[2]

The salvage problems at Normandy had been quite different from those in Sicily and Italy because the Allies had almost complete control of the skies. German air attacks during daylight were non-existent, and night attacks were generally limited to bombing raids. Only one ship in the American sector was sunk by a bomb, and the absence of direct or near bomb hits meant an absence of fires aboard vessels. The only serious fires aboard the ships off the Omaha and Utah beaches had been due to mines. Many vessels were hit and suffered significant damage, but only four were lost. As their services were no longer needed off the Normandy beaches, the tugs and salvage ships were dispatched to other areas.[3]

With the loss of Mulberry A to the storm, the Allies' capture of Cherbourg—the nearest major port to the Normandy beaches—became of great urgency. The Allies had gained a foot-hold at Normandy and, although losses were high (more than 9,000 allied soldiers wounded or killed), more than 100,000 soldiers had begun the march across Europe to defeat Hitler and they required logistic support landed from sea. The port was guarded along the sea approaches by a series of outlying forts along breakwaters and jetties. The port finally fell to VII Corps of the U.S. First Army on 29 June. Despite naval bombardment from a combined force of American and British ships, German defense forces inside the forts had held out to the end.[4]

Three days after the U.S. 79th Infantry Division captured Fort du Roule—the fort which dominated the city and its defenses—Commodore Sullivan and Commodore Thomas McKenzie, CB, CBE, RNR, the heads of American and British salvage sections, flew to the French city to survey the port area and develop a plan for its rehabilitation. Because of the immense destruction wrought by the Germans and the substantial numbers of different type mines they had sown in harbor waters, their inspection led to the belief that restoring the port to use, in a reasonable amount of time, would be a truly daunting task. This work was begun as soon as resources could be mobilized. It included minesweeping; employment of Royal Navy volunteer divers trained to render bombs and mines safe; removal of sunken vessels and other obstructions; and hydrographic work, necessary to enable safe maritime navigation within the port.[5]

Although all divers had been thoroughly trained, the tasks they faced remained highly dangerous. Particularly challenging conditions, such as strong currents, murky waters, or encounters with new, previously unknown enemy ordnance, could "tip the scales" for a diver defuzing a mine or bomb, and result in severe injury to them or, more likely, death. Harbor mine clearance was a British responsibility with assistance from American minesweepers, and restoration of the port facilities an American one, carried out by American and British salvage teams under Sullivan.

As will be described in greater detail later, the British 9th and 159th Minesweeping Flotillas and the American Y Flotilla were tasked with minesweeping operations, and when conditions were safe salvage ships would enter the harbor. These included the American salvage ships *Brant* and *Diver* and six British vessels with twelve lifting camels including HMSV *Abigail* and HMSV *Help*. A camel was an external floatation tank, which was sunk using water ballast and installed on a sunken ship. When the water was pumped out, the increased flotation helped to refloat the ship. As minesweepers and divers searched for and cleared mines, explosives, and other dangerous contrivances from the harbor bed; salvors cleared the jetties and landing-stages (platforms used to land goods and passengers from a vessel) and reconstructed the port facilities.[6]

Sullivan's Port Clearance Group was formed from American and British naval forces of his Salvage and Firefighting Group (Task Group 122.3), without task units 122.3.1 and 122.3.2, which had been the Combat Salvage and Firefighting Units at Omaha and Utah beaches.

Port Clearance Group

Task Unit	Title	Commander	Vessels or Personnel
122.3.3	Reserve Unit	Lt. Martin C. Sibitsky, USN	Salvage ships *Brant*, *Diver*, and *Swivel*
122.3.4	Harbor Clearance Salvage Unit	Comdr. Wiley L. Wroten, USN	Coaster S.S. *Whitstable*; Salvage ships HMSV *Abigail* and HMSV *Help*; Wreck dispersal vessels HMT *Maria* (4.67), HMT *Tehana* (FY.525), and HMT *Admiral Sir John Lawford* (4.415)
122.3.5	Harbor Clearance Mine Disposal Unit	Comdr. Francis Landon DeSpon, RNR	Two barges and Royal Navy personnel
122.3.6	Harbor Hydrographic Group	Lt. Comdr. Charles Peter Warwick Marshall, DSC, RN	Royal Navy personnel[7]

MOBILIZATION OF SALVAGE FORCES

Preparations for the salvage operations began on 26 June 1944, even before the Port of Cherbourg had been captured by Allied forces. The salvage ships *Brant* and *Diver*, and tank landing ship *LST-291*, left anchorage in Weymouth Roads, Portland, on that date en route to the Omaha beach area of the French coast. In company were eight vessels of the Royal Navy, which, along with the American ships, formed the Cherbourg Salvage, Wreck Dispersal, Mine Dispersal, and Hydrographic Survey Task Unit. Embarked aboard *Diver* were United States and Royal Navy personnel—four USN officers and thirty-two men, and two British officers and eight ratings—for transport to the Normandy beach, as well as one 28-foot motor launch, one 16-foot motor launch, one 10-foot skiff, and other hydrographic survey equipment. *Brant* had in tow a U.S. Army barge loaded with demolition charges, two 40-foot motor launches, three British power boats, and six pontoon sections.[8]

In company with the task unit were two Royal Navy Port Clearance Parties (Naval Party 1571 and Naval Party 1572) packed tightly into two former British whale-catchers and *LST-291*. These Port Parties—made up of mine clearance divers commanded by Lt. Comdr. James L. Harries, RCNVR, a Canadian, and Lt. Comdr. Henry J. Horan, RNVR, respectively—comprised the Harbor Clearance Mine Disposal Unit. The ships in which they were embarked had sailed from Falmouth Bay on 22 June for the French coast, via Portland, as part of a convoy that included *Brant* and *Diver*. The ships transporting the Port Parties were initially given a protected place in the center of the convoy. However, after the senior naval officer learned that the two U.S. Army barges the vessels had in tow carried nearly 400 tons of explosives for demolition purposes, he immediately ordered their vessels to take up positions well astern of the convoy and thereby keep their dangerous cargo isolated from the other ships.[9]

The men of the "P" Parties had a wretched passage and were battered, bruised, wet, and cold when they arrived off Omaha beach on 27 June. Because of the loss of Mulberry A, there was urgency to take Cherbourg—despite the German's demolition of docks, basins, and harbor installations that might render the port unusable for a significant period of time. The Allies had counted on the availability of both artificial harbors to land reinforcements until the capture of a larger established port. American troops had taken the city of Cherbourg on 26 June, but German-held forts commanded the harbor entrances, making it impossible for "P" Parties to arrive there by sea. While the two groups of divers remained afloat in their uncomfortable ships awaiting orders, Comdr. Francis L. DeSpon, RNR, who commanded the Harbor Clearance Mine Disposal Unit, ordered Harries to travel overland to Cherbourg to investigate the conditions there, and to determine when "P" Parties could move in. The other men remained in the anchored ships—which offered little protection from the abominable weather—and subsisted on a diet of "K" rations that were full of vitamins but empty of interest.[10]

Harries reached Cherbourg, about 28 kilometers away. His was a hazardous business, but he made his way through fighting in progress and sniper fire, to survey the dock area and learn what he could about mines in the harbors. Cherbourg was on a steep hill facing the English Channel with its harbor protected by two breakwaters: the inner one made up of large round pillars, and an outer one that was more solid. The big guns of Fort du Roule that had protected the city from attack by land had been silenced, but German guns looking out to sea were now firing into town. Fighting was taking place there and both sides suffered casualties.[11]

Photo 10-1

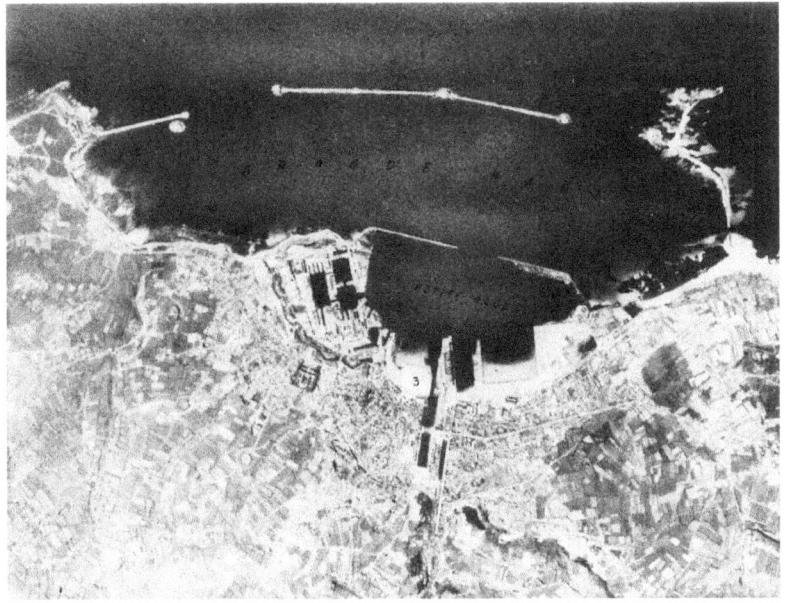

Aerial view of Cherbourg showing the outer (Grande Rade) and inner (Petite Rade) harbors.
Source: http://www.ibiblio.org/hyperwar/USA/USA-E-Logistics1/img/USA-E-Logistics1-p291.jpg

Harries found unbelievable destruction. There were vessels sunk by the jetties and in the entrance to the docks; cranes and railway trucks were piled on top of the wrecks and sticking up out of the water. It was later found that booby-traps and mines were mixed with wreckage all over the harbor. The quays were demolished and grain elevators had been blown into the water. The only failing of the Germans was to block the entrances through the breakwaters with wrecks, but they apparently did not have ships of a suitable size available. Harries returned to Utah beach to report the grim news to DeSpon, and plans were made to move "P" Parties on to Cherbourg as by this time the port had been captured.[12]

As the Port Parties were embarked in ships, it had been hoped that they could enter Cherbourg by water. However, the extensive mining of the approaches, and in the harbor itself, necessitated transporting the clearance divers overland to the port city. The British persuaded the Americans to take over their explosives barges and deliver them to Cherbourg. They also succeeded in getting their gear ashore and loaded into transport vehicles in pouring rain. The "P" Parties then set off for Cherbourg two hours shy of midnight. En route, they passed lines of bewildered-looking German prisoners, who seemed unable to comprehend what was happening to them. The Port Parties reached their destination four hours later in a deluge of rain—more suitable to January than mid-summer. The British ratings were billeted in an American naval camp on a sports field about a mile outside the city, and the officers went to the American officers' mess nearer the center of Cherbourg to get some rest before commencing diving operations.[13]

SALVAGE FORCES ARRIVE AT CHERBOURG

Brant left her anchorage off the Normandy beaches for Cherbourg in the early afternoon on 8 July, with a salvage party aboard and one of the barges in tow loaded with high-explosives. She was part of a small convoy whose other members were two British Admiralty-type motor fishing vessels—*MFV-1024* and *MFV-1027*—and the naval trawlers HMT *Domino* (FY1764 – ex-*Sabra*) and HMT *Sluga* (FY1773), both former whalers acquired by the Admiralty in March 1940. *Sluga* had the other Army barge in tow, also loaded with high-explosives for demolition. The convoy arrived that night in Grande Rade, the outer harbor at Cherbourg, and anchored, after first mooring the barges to buoys at opposite ends of the cleared area of the harbor.[14]

A second American salvage ship, *Diver*, left the Normandy beaches on 20 July in company with HMS *Help*, but was delayed en route while rescuing thirty survivors of a mined and sinking ship, the Norwegian freighter S.S. *Norfalk* (ex-British *Empire Kittiwake*). *Diver* came alongside *Norfalk* at 1258, put a salvage team and pumps aboard, and started pumping water from the ship's engine room. With winds and sea increasing and the freighter sinking by the stern, her master Einar Thoresen, four ship's officers, and twenty-five men abandoned at 1410 and came aboard the salvage ship. *Diver* took the *Norfalk* under tow, and at 1757 anchored her three miles from Marcouf Island off the Normandy coast, where she later sank. *Diver* stood into Cherbourg's outer harbor around noon the following day, and reported to Sullivan for duty. A third American salvage ship, *Swivel*, joined *Brant* and *Diver* to comprise the Reserve Force for Cherbourg, and would remain engaged towing vessels from Utah beach back to England for the next several months. *Swivel* subsequently proceeded to Le Havre, France, on 12 November, and assisted in clearing that harbor before moving to Cherbourg, on 25 December 1944, where she assisted ships until 27 June 1945.[15]

MINESWEEPING

With the surrender of the remaining Cherbourg forts on 29 June, "the greatest minesweeping operation in history," as Winston Churchill called it, began. The first challenge was to sweep approach channels through the two main entrances, and clear areas for anchorages and landing points in the vast outer harbor. The British 9th and Canadian 31st Minesweeping Flotillas—made up of steel-hulled 162-foot *Bangor*-class fleet minesweepers—began this work on 30 June. The first sweep by these ships was followed by multiple passes through the same waters by BYMSs of the British 159th and 206th flotillas. Concurrently, YMSs of the American Y2 Squadron began sweeping off the eastern entrance.[16]

Photo 10-2

Richard DeRosset's painting "Moonlit Assault in the Aegean" depicting a Luftwaffe glider-bomb attack on *BYMS-72* as she neared Leros Island during the 1943 British Aegean Campaign. The British Yard Minesweeper was a sister ship to the BYMSs that conducted mine clearance operations at Cherbourg.

The twenty 136-foot wooden-hulled Yard Minesweepers (YMSs) and the many BYMSs at Cherbourg were of the same type. The

BYMSs had been built in American yards and immediately transferred to the Royal Navy as part of the Lend-Lease Program. The smaller 126-foot "long boat" wooden-hulled MMSs (Motor Minesweepers) of the 206th Flotilla were commonly referred to as "Mickey Mouses" by British sailors. The Royal Navy vessels present also included 112-foot *Fairmile B*-class motor launches (MLs). Built by Fairmile Marine, the versatile coastal craft could perform a variety of roles, but were mostly employed during the war for anti-submarine patrols. The MLs at Cherbourg were fitted with miniaturized gear to sweep ahead of BYMSs and thus, hopefully, provide them safe passage. The MLs could not sweep as wide, or as deep a swath as a BYMS, or a MMS for that matter, but they drew less water (had shallower drafts) and hence were less likely to be blown up. However, their light sweep gear parted (broke) easily, due to strain when streamed astern, and the MLs had difficulty operating in confined waters.[17]

While the larger fleet minesweepers continued operations outside the harbor, the YMS, BYMS, and MMS flotillas began sweeping the Grande Rade (outer harbor), which contained wrecks of every size and shape, as well as moored-contact, acoustic, and magnetic mines. By 13 July one hundred thirty-three mines had been swept, but many more remained. In spite of these conditions, concurrent salvage operations began due to the pressing requirement to open the port. In clearing the Grande Rade, the MLs swept ahead of YMSs and BYMSs, and behind them came the MMSs, although only the MLs could sweep in all the corners. Within the smaller and more confined Petite Rade (inner harbor), landing craft functioning as "snag line sweepers" led the way, followed by MLs and MMSs. In the Petite Rade the MLs found mines believed to be the new Katy type fitted with snag lines. They left these mines alone as sweeping methods to counter them had not yet been developed and they were potentially very lethal.[18]

Katy mines were seven-feet tall, and sat quietly on the sea floor waiting for unsuspecting ships. They could be triggered in two ways: The first was by contact with the single horn on top of the Katy during low tide or while anchoring. The other was by a propeller ensnaring the snag line affixed to the firing mechanism when passing above one of the mines. The propeller would draw the snag line tight, thereby exploding the ordnance. Seventeen ships and craft were sunk or damaged by mines during the Cherbourg harbor clearance, mostly of the Katy variety, in July and August. They are listed below:[19]

Date	Vessel	Location/Cause of Loss or Damage
2 July	YMS-347	Damaged by a mine detonation outside breakwater
2 July	YMS-350	Lost outside breakwater; 11 of 34 crewmen killed and 9 injured
2 July	MMS-1019	Lost outside breakwater
8 July	LCP(L)-267	Sunk inside Petite Rade while clearing snag mines with Senior Royal Marine officer of the flotilla lost.
20 July	Army Small Tug ST-344	Blew up and sank in Grande Rade after striking a mine
20 July	British Hopper barge	Blew up and sank in Grande Rade after striking a mine
20 July	Army barge	Keel broken by a mine in Grande Rade, but towed to shallow water
21 July	British Hopper barge Dredge 36	Sunk in Querqueville Bay by a Katy mine
21 July	ST-253	Holed and sank, presumably due to a Katy mine
30 July	HMT Sir Geraint (T.240)	Damaged by a mine
2 August	LCG-1062	Mined and sank off outer approaches to Cherbourg Harbor; three crewmembers missing
4 August	British Dredger	Mined in vicinity of Fort de l'Quest, probably by a Katy mine; raised on 21 September by a Salvage Force lifting craft.
5 August	MMS-279	Damaged by a near miss from an acoustic mine detonation
12 August	British LBO-68	Sunk near Fort de l'Quest, probably by a Katy mine
13 August	BYMS-2034	Damaged by the explosion of a ground mine, probably a Katy, in Grande Rade
16 August	LST-391	Struck a mine, believed to be a Katy, in east end of Petite Rade
26 August	British Coaster	Struck a mine in channel outside harbor, sank in three minutes with fifteen crewmen missing[20]

Because of the plethora of mines remaining to be cleared, the Royal Navy began dispatching additional minesweepers to Cherbourg. This took the form of either entire flotillas or, in some cases, one or more ships of a flotilla. An exact accounting of the ships that plied the mined waters is difficult to ascertain. The flotillas identified by a single asterisk in the below table were present at Cherbourg, and there were likely other flotillas and/or ships of flotillas as well. Eric David Minett, in *The Coast is Clear the Story of the BYMS*, indicates that a number of BYMSs drawn from south coast flotillas for reserve duty, were standing by in Portland or Portsmouth for minesweeping operations at Cherbourg, if needed. The ships he cited were a part of the flotillas identified with two asterisks in the table. The remaining flotillas listed (without asterisks) are ones that Rear Adm. John Wilkes,

USN, commander U.S. Ports and Bases, France (then headquartered at Cherbourg) identified in war diary entries as either being under his command, or ready to be sent to him when needed. Because Wilkes was responsible for mine clearance in other captured French ports as well as Cherbourg, these flotillas may or may not have swept at Cherbourg.

The table also lists the danlayers assigned to the minesweeping flotillas. These vessels were usually small trawlers, which followed the minesweepers as they worked an area and laid Dan buoys (temporary buoys) to mark the boundaries of safe channels swept clear of mines.

Country	Flotilla	Minesweepers
United States	Y*	Y1 Squadron: Yard Minesweepers *YMS-305, 356, 358, 375, 377, 378, 379, 380, 381, 382, 406*
United States	Y*	Y2 Squadron: *YMS-231, 247, 304, 346, 347* (damaged at Cherbourg), *348, 349, 350* (sunk at Cherbourg), *351, 352*
Canada	31st*	*Bangor*-class Fleet Minesweepers: *Blairmore* (J314), *Caraquet* (J38), *Cowichan* (J146), *Fort William* (J311), *Malpeque* (J148), *Milltown* (J317), *Minas* (J165), *Wasaga* (J162) Danlayers: *Bayfield* (J08), *Green Howard* (FY632), *Gunner* (FY568), *Mulgrave* (J313) Motor Launches: *ML-345, 454, 465, 473*
Britain	9th*	*Bangor*-class Fleet Minesweepers: *Bangor* (J00), *Blackpool* (J27), *Boston* (J14), *Bridlington* (J65), *Bridport* (J50), *Eastbourne* (J127), *Sidmouth* (J47), *Tenby* (J34) Danlayers: *Bryher* (T350), *Dalmatia* (FY844), *Ijuin* (FY612), *Sigma* (FY1709) Four Motor Launches
Britain	15th	*Bangor*-class Fleet Minesweepers: *Ardrossan* (J131), *Bootle* (J143), *Dunbar* (J53), *Fort York* (J119), *Fraserburgh* (J124), *Llandudno* (J67), *Lyme Regis* (J193), *Worthing* (J72) Danlayers: *Calvay* (T383), *Dorothy Lambert* (FY558), *James Lay* (FY667), *Niblick* (FD77)
Britain	102nd	Based at Sheerness: Motor Minesweepers: *MMS-8, 19, 40, 44, 45, 71, 110, 113, 115, 181*
Britain	131st	*MMS-15, 56, 59, 78*
Britain	157th	Based at Great Yarmouth: *BYMS-2034* (damaged at Cherbourg), *2038, 2039, 2076, 2078, 2141, 2213, 2214, 2221, 2230*
Britain	159th*	Based at Grimsby: *BYMS-2032, 2052, 2055, 2070, 2071, 2157, 2173, 2211*
Britain	163rd*	Based at Lowestoft: *BYMS-2079, 2167*
Britain	165th**	Based at Harwich: *BYMS-2035, 2041, 2058, 2202, 2205, 2206, 2233, 2252*
Britain	167th*	Based at Ardrossan and Liverpool: *BYMS-2047, 2051, 2061, 2069, 2155, 2156, 2182, 2210*
Britain	168th**	Based at Portsmouth: *BYMS-2234*
Britain	169th**	Based at Dover: *BYMS-2154, 2255*
Britain	170th**	Based at Swansea: *BYMS-2050, 2188, 2256*

Britain	206th*	*MMS-1002, 1004, 1019* (sunk at Cherbourg), *1020, 1047, 1048, 1077*
Country	**Group**	**Minesweepers**
Britain	139th	Three flotillas of minesweeping "LL" trawlers: HMT *Conway Castle* (FY509), *Courtier* (FY592), *Georgette* (FY804), *Northcoates* (FY548), *Perdrant* (FY1714), *Probe* (T186), *Proctor* (T185), *Prowless* (T196), *Sir Agravaine* (T230), *Sir Gareth* (T227), *Sir Geraint* (T240; damaged at Cherbourg), *Sir Kay* (T241), *Sir Lamorak* (T242), *Sir Tristram* (T229)[21]

The 16 January 1945 edition of the *London Gazette* heralded that twenty-one members of the minesweeping force at Cherbourg had received recognition from the Crown for "gallantry and skill in minesweeping operations off the coast of France." The honors took the form of one Distinguished Service Cross (DSC), four Distinguished Service Medals (DSM), and sixteen lesser Mention in Dispatches (MID). A service member mentioned in dispatches was then, and is today, one whose name appears in an official report written by a superior officer and sent to the high command. These individuals, the ships and flotillas to which they were assigned, and the associated honors they received are listed below:

Ship	Name	Rank or Rate	Date "Gazetted" Type of Award
157th Minesweeping Flotilla			
BYMS-2039	Frank William Strudwick	A/Chief Engineman	16 Jan 1945/MID
BYMS-2078	Ambrose Ernest Fisher	A/T/Skipper RNR	16 Jan 1945/MID
BYMS-2078	William James Gowen	Engineman	16 Jan 1945/MID
159th Minesweeping Flotilla			
BYMS-2032	Alexander Young	Chief Engineman	16 Jan 1945/MID
BYMS-2055	James Simpson Hamilton	Chief Engineman	16 Jan 1945/MID
BYMS-2070	Joseph Gregson	Chief Engineman	16 Jan 1945/MID
BYMS-2070	David Reid Hughes	Second Hand	16 Jan 1945/DSM
BYMS-2071	William MacMurray Dougall	T/Lt., RNVR	16 Jan 1945/DSC
BYMS-2071	John Henry Coram	Petty Officer	16 Jan 1945/DSM
BYMS-2071	Robert Fountain	Leading Seaman	16 Jan 1945/MID

BYMS-2157	Douglas Arthur Coombs	Leading Wireman	16 Jan 1945/MID
BYMS-2157	Desmond McGrath	T/Lt., RNVR	16 Jan 1945/MID
BYMS-2157	Alan Wardley	Signalman	16 Jan 1945/MID
BYMS-2173	Percy James Chilvers	Leading Wireman	16 Jan 1945/DSM
BYMS-2173	Robert Colquhoun	Signalman	16 Jan 1945/MID
BYMS-2173	Arthur Leonard Mulcare	T/Lt., RNVR	16 Jan 1945/MID
BYMS-2211	George Edward Galloway	Chief Engineman	16 Jan 1945/DSM
BYMS-2211	Reginald Alexander Hope	PO Wireman	16 Jan 1945/MID
168th Minesweeping Flotilla			
BYMS-2234	Thomas Henry Spall	A/T/Skipper Lt., RNR	16 Jan 1945/MID
BYMS-2234	Robert George Thompson	Leading Seaman	16 Jan 1945/MID
170th Minesweeping Flotilla			
BYMS-2188	Gerard Christians	Chief Engineman	16 Jan 1945/MID[22]

A: Acting
T: Temporary

The group of awardees included commanding officers, Leading Signalmen and Signalmen, Chief Enginemen, Leading and Petty Officer Wiremen (electricians), and Leading Seamen. The signalmen would have been kept busy making and answering the relentless flag hoists and signal lamp messages used during formation/coordinated minesweeping and keeping the Command advised of orders from the senior officer. Chief Enginemen and Wiremen would have been crucial for the maintenance and repair of mechanical and electrical systems, respectively, so that vessels could remain in service during prolonged operations. The Leading Seamen were responsible for supervising the rigging of sweep gear and would likely have been on deck during all sweep evolutions—which infrequently resulted in an unexploded mine being found entangled in sweep gear during recovery (while being brought back aboard) by the ship. The mention in dispatches likely reflected initiative, perseverance, and success as much as valor. The Distinguished Service Medals, and particularly the Distinguished Service Cross, recognized very significant or heroic actions.[23]

The clearance of mines from the harbors was made possible by the capture of Cherbourg by U.S. forces, following bombardment on 25 June of German fortifications in and near the city by a force of U.S. and Royal Navy battleships and destroyers. Commander Henry Plander, USN, commander Mine Squadron 7, received the Silver Star Medal for gallantry in action while leading his group of minesweepers in sweeping ahead of the bombardment group, while under fire for a period of about one and a half hours from German shore batteries. Two groups were assigned this task, one comprised of twenty-one British minesweepers under Comdr. Roger W. D. Thompson, RN; the other, under Plander, consisted of *Auk* (AM-57), *Broadbill* (AM-58), *Chickadee* (AM-59), *Nuthatch* (AM-60), *Pheasant* (AM-61), *Swift* (AM-122), *Threat* (AM-124), the Canadian HMCS *Thunder* (J156), and British MLs *139, 142, 257,* and *275*.[24]

MINE CLEARANCE BY PORT PARTIES

As minesweepers cleared the profusion of mines from the approaches, channels and anchorages, the "P" Parties searched Bassin Des Flots, the Avant Port de Commerce and the shallows of the Nouvelle Plage, working outwards to meet the sweepers. The clearance divers and minesweepers sometimes worked in the same waters, but not at the same time. To avoid danger to themselves from exploding mines, the divers dove only for three hours either side of low water, the time when the minesweepers were most at risk (and thus not engaged in sweeping) due to the minimum water column between them and the mines. The minesweepers swept three hours either side of high water when they were least vulnerable. Once safe entry to a landing point was assured, clearance was extended to the docks and basins, which had been thoroughly blocked by shallow-water mines, booby-traps, wreckage, and other items the Germans employed for that purpose.[25]

The situation regarding Katy mines improved after Comdr. Francis DeSpon, RNR and Lt. Comdr. James Harries, RCNVR, recovered four of these "ship-killers" from a 2- to 3-fathom area of the eastern section of the Grande Rade. One mine was transported by ship to England for analysis, and the development of countermeasures for use against them. This event is described by J. Grosvenor and L. M. Bates in *Open The Ports - The Story of the Human Minesweepers*:

> It was known that there was a heavy lay of mines in the outer harbour.... Harries got hold of a motor dory. With de Spon steering and Harries looking over the bow, they proceeded gently

round the outer harbour. It was not long before they had a Katy snag-line round their propeller.

De Spon managed to stop their craft before the snag-line had been hauled taut, which would, of course, have fired the mine. Then Harries went straight over the side, just as he was in his working uniform. He cleared the propeller without disturbing the mine and returned on board dripping seawater everywhere. But they were much too relieved at their narrow escape to mind a little discomfort. They found three other snag-lines not far away.

Harries afterwards spent many hours buoying the four mines in readiness for further action. As he came ashore he felt that the first round in the battle with the Katies had gone to him.[26]

Harries had earlier advised H.M.S. Vernon—the Royal Navy's torpedo, mining, and mine countermeasures training school and technical command at Portsmouth—that he was confident of finding a Katy mine for recovery. Following this news, Lt. Comdr. Leon V. Goldsworthy—the Royal Australian Navy's premiere mine disposal expert, and its most highly decorated officer during the war—was ordered to proceed to Cherbourg from the Normandy coast, where he was engaged with a mine recovery Party looking for new types of enemy mines. Goldsworthy dove on, and rendered safe, the first Katy buoyed by Harries and then returned to H.M.S. Vernon. Harries did the same for the remaining three mines, and recovered all four mines—one for delivery back to England.[27]

To bring this mine to the surface, Harries obtained the services of an American tug with suitable lifting gear—a boom. Grosvenor and Bates describe in their book the understandable reluctance of the captain to take his ship into an area containing mines, and the warm reception that Harries and Sub-Lieut. E. D. James, RNVR, later received aboard the tug:

> Harries says that her crew were not very happy at having to proceed in such mine-infested waters. The captain had to rely upon Harries, who, after buoying the mines, had a good idea of the lay, to guide the tug through the channel.
>
> When the mine had been lifted to safety in preparation for its journey to Portsmouth Harries and James were invited to go aboard the U.S. tug. On board Harries in particular was treated as a hero. They were given a wonderful meal consisting of fabulous steaks and all the other things men conjured up in their minds when they were on regulation rations.
>
> [The tug master] could not do enough for them. He pressed them to have several more steaks. But Harries and James were

divers, not camels, so they had to refuse with regret. Memories of those rejected steaks were to haunt them later on when they were hungry!²⁸

Following arrival of the mine in England, experts at H.M.S. Vernon examined it and quickly developed a trawl sweep as a countermeasure, which Royal Navy minesweeping trawlers brought over to Cherbourg from England. As minesweeping in the port continued, the clearance divers rotated home. Apart from the physical strain the men had endured, it was thought that the daily use of an enriched air mixture for diving also presented some danger to them. Accordingly, Port Party 1572 was sent back to England for a short rest and for re-equipment, and Party 1571 soon followed. They were replaced at Cherbourg by a recently formed Party, No. 1573, led by Australian Lt. Francis Frederick Pearse, RNVR. Its members helped clear the area of the port remaining to be searched, which included a wreck containing eight mines.²⁹

Diagram 10-1

This illustration from *Deep Diving and Submarine Operations* by Sir Robert H Davies depicts 'P' Party members performing their various tasks.

The *London Gazette* informed readers, on 16 January 1945, that five clearance divers had been honored for "gallantry and distinguished services in the work of mine-clearance in the face of the enemy." The identities of these men and their most recently acquired awards follow:

- Distinguished Service Cross: Lt. Comdr. Leon Verdi Goldsworthy, GC, GM, RANVR
- Distinguished Service Medal: Leading Seaman George William Jackson
- Mention in Dispatches: Acting Leading Seaman Raymond Harold Smith; Able Seaman Arthur McCourt, GM; and Able Seaman John Henry Martin, DSM, BEM.

Three of these individuals had other medals for rendering safe mines or other ordnance. Goldsworthy had previously been awarded the George Cross (second only to the Victoria Cross in precedence among British awards for valor) and the George Medal; McCourt, the George Medal; and Martin, the Distinguished Service Medal and British Empire Medal.

SALVAGE WORK

> *The Salvage operations necessary to clear the port of Cherbourg were complicated by the minesweeping problems encountered in this port, and by the arrangement of the harbor. Almost all of the salvage operations necessary required the use of lifting craft and pontoons, or of large floating cranes. These could not be employed until the approaches to the locations of the various operations were cleared of mines. The mines laid by the Germans were not only numerous, but were of a various sort. The minesweeping problem was undoubtedly the most complicated yet encountered in any harbor clearance work.*
>
> —Commodore William A. Sullivan, USN[30]

The U.S. Navy Salvage Party was the first active group in the harbor and beginning 6 July it raised several tugs and other miscellaneous boats through pumping and patching at low water. Because minesweeping operations were continuing, and considerable underwater demolition work was in progress, diving and salvage operations were further delayed because diving was not permitted for three hours before and three hours after high water, to preclude the possibility of injury to divers.[31]

The rescue tug *ATR-3* arrived at Cherbourg from Omaha beach on 18 July, anchored in Baie de Saint Ann, and reported for duty to commander Cherbourg Area and commander Salvage Group. She had been previously engaged towing, pumping water from, and providing electricity to, *ATR-13*. Her sister ship had run over a wreck off Utah beach on 6 July breaking her keel, splitting timbers, and opening hull seams. Without Lt. (jg) G. N. Hammond's action (*ATR-13*'s commanding officer) in ordering full speed to make the side of the fleet tug *Kiowa* (ATF-72) as quickly as possible, while crewmembers rigged a collision mat, the ship would have been lost. As this was happening, her engine room was then taking water fast and water was rising in the fire room. Following diving operations to affect makeshift repairs at *Kiowa*'s side, *ATR-3* towed the damaged ship to the Portsmouth Royal Dockyard arriving on 11 July. The transit was "touch and go" as the portable pumps placed aboard the tug could barely keep pace with the inrush of water into the vessel. After entering dry dock No. 10, *ATR-13* rested on keel blocks undergoing repair until 13 August, when she undocked and moored to the yard's North Corner Jetty. She left the dockyard on 26 August to rendezvous with Convoy FTC 79 for transit to Chatham, England.[32]

While lying at anchor at Cherbourg, in late July, *ATR-3* had maintained No. 1 and 2 boilers steam up ready for immediate notice to get under way. Her commanding officer's vigilance was warranted. In late afternoon on 20 July the Army small tug *ST-344*, which lay anchored about 1,000 yards off *ATR-3*'s port quarter, swung over a mine and was sunk. Five minutes later, a British hopper barge struck a mine and sank by the stern in the same area. Within the hour, a U.S. Army barge loaded with vehicles also detonated a mine in that area; the explosion broke her back, but she did not sink, and was towed to shallow water. In mid-afternoon the following day, *ATR-3* transferred her salvage and firefighting officers, and eighteen men to Commodore Sullivan for salvage duty.[33]

Despite all the challenges and setbacks, salvage operations had proceeded rapidly. The U.S. Naval Advanced Base, Cherbourg was placed in commission on 15 July and the following day, four Liberty ships entered the port and berthed. The first men and supplies were landed by lighters (flat-bottomed barges) on 18 July. By month's end, facilities for the handling of twelve to sixteen Liberty ships were available. The first ships using the harbor were limited to an anchorage in its western end, but by 29 July, the eastern end had been opened to traffic as well. In the next few months, Cherbourg would become of critical importance as a port of logistic supply to the U.S. Army in Europe, second only to Marseilles. Mines still remained, though, and minesweeping continued. That autumn, a BYMS or YMS flotilla was usually at Cherbourg, plus a number of MMSs.[34]

Photo 10-3

Old fleet tug *Owl* entered Cherbourg Harbor on 15 July 1944 towing two composite barges loaded with heavy U.S. Army Engineer equipment.
Official U.S. Navy photo SC 193943, now in the collections of the U.S. National Archives

MINESWEEPERS LAUDED

British Prime Minister Winston Churchill visited Cherbourg on 20 July while the minesweeping and salvage efforts were in progress. He later asserted that the mine clearance at the French port was "the greatest minesweeping operation in history." Following Germany's surrender, he sent a message to the officers and the men of the British Minesweeping Flotillas, praising their vitally important and generally unsung efforts throughout the war:

> Now that Nazi Germany has been defeated I wish to send you all on behalf of His Majesty's Government a message of thanks and gratitude.
> The work you do is hard and dangerous. You rarely get and never seek publicity; your only concern is to do your job, and you have done it nobly. You have sailed in many seas and all weathers.... This work could not be done without loss, and we mourn all who have died and over 250 ships lost on duty.
> No work has been more vital than yours; no work has been better done. The Ports were kept open and Britain breathed. The Nation is once again proud of you.[35]

THE ALLIES MOVE FORWARD

On 11 October 1944 Rear Adm. John Wilkes left Cherbourg and the following day reestablished his U.S. Ports and Bases, France headquarters at Le Havre, which lay to the east across the Baie de Seine at the mouth of the River Seine. His challenge remained the same: to run the captured ports and unload materials from vessels so that extended supply lines might be kept operating with sufficient volume.[36]

11

Southern France – Operation DRAGOON

Three months after Normandy...in August 1944, we joined in an amphibious assault force to land in the South of France, on the French Riviera. We left from North Africa, and strangely enough we took French troops that had left France in 1940 when the Germans pushed them out of France, so they were going back to their own homeland. We also took some Americans and we operated from North Africa to the South of France and it was to a place called St. Raphael on the French Riviera. It was called the Champagne landing this one, I think, there was very little opposition because the Germans had pulled back and when we were on the beach some of the lads, some of the sailors went up and picked grapes out of the vineyards, and it was one of the easier or better operations that we had.

—Alwyn Thomas, crewmember of the
tank landing ship HMS *Bruiser* (F127)[1]

In August 1944, two months after the Normandy landings, an amphibious assault was made on the southern coast of France between Hyères and Cannes. The objectives of the operation were to secure the beachheads, capture neighboring ports, and strike north, up the Rhône valley, to link up with Patton's Third Army. This would form the right wing of the Allied force invading Germany, and cut off German forces in the west of France. During its early planning, the code name initially given was Anvil to complement Sledgehammer, code name for the invasion of Normandy. Subsequently, Sledgehammer became Overlord and Anvil, Operation Dragoon. Reportedly Winston Churchill, who opposed the plan and claimed to having been "dragooned" into accepting it by Roosevelt and Eisenhower, chose the latter name. The British prime minister believed that the operation would divert military resources that could be employed supporting ongoing operations in Italy. He preferred, instead, an invasion of the oil-producing regions of the Balkans. Churchill reasoned that by attacking the Balkans, the Allies could deny Germany oil, as well as hinder the advance of the Red Army of the Soviet Union; thus achieving a superior negotiating position in post-war Europe with that nation.[2]

When the invasion of southern France was initially considered, the Allied landing at Anzio had gone badly, and planning was "put on hold." The operation—renamed DRAGOON—was revived, following the successful Normandy invasion. After the capture of Rome on 5 June, it was possible to allocate troops to the invasion of southern France and to obtain the necessary shipping, but it was not possible to do this concurrently with the Normandy invasion. The additional assault shipping needed for DRAGOON became available following the landings at Normandy. There was also increased urgency to bring these ships into the Mediterranean to join the Eighth Fleet and capture additional ports, as the Allies were struggling to resupply their armies in France. Since the Germans had destroyed the port facilities at Cherbourg, and a violent storm had damaged the artificial harbor "Mulberry A," it was important to seize the ports at Marseilles and Toulon. Also, Allied French leaders were pressing for an invasion from the south.[3]

The situation in the Western Mediterranean was favorable for an amphibious landing in southern France in late summer 1944. By this time in the war, the German U-boat menace was rapidly waning because of better and more effective countermeasures by Allied ships and aircraft. Finally, after attrition during the Normandy invasion requiring the redeployment of its squadrons, the German air force was no longer able to operate in strength in the Mediterranean.[4]

The assault beaches of southern France were well protected by German coast defenses. However, enemy fortifications lacked depth and there were few reserves for counterattack. Allied planners chose the Cavalaire Bay–Rade d'Agay area for the assault because it was within range of supporting Allied aircraft operating from fields in Corsica. It offered a favorable sea approach with only a narrow coastal area suitable for enemy mining, and it had the fewest German coastal gun batteries capable of reaching the approach, transport areas, and landing beaches. A bridgehead in this area would provide a suitable base for a landward attack on Toulon and Marseilles, and rapid movement up the Rhône Valley.[5]

Map 11-1

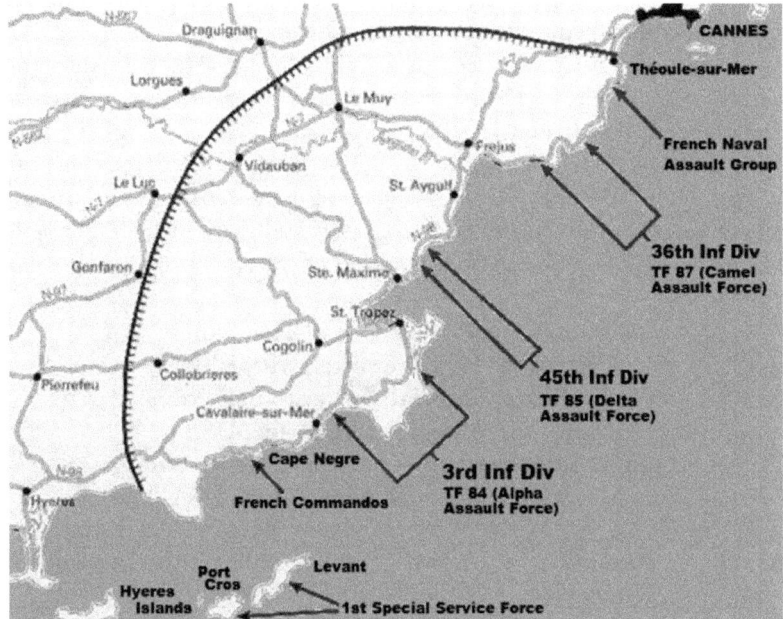

Three divisions of the U.S. Seventh Army and two divisions of French Army B landed on the French Riviera of southeast France as part of Operation DRAGOON.

ALLIED ASSAULT FORCE

On D-Day, 15 August 1944, the Allied naval force arrived off the southern France assault beaches. They found low clouds over the entire coast, with local bands of thick fog in the eastern part of the Golfe du Lion. The winds were light and seas calm, and, in the remainder of the western Mediterranean, the skies were clear with visibility of ten miles. The lower clouds thinned by mid-morning and dissipated by noon.[6]

The naval force under the command of Vice Adm. Henry K. Hewitt, commander Eighth Fleet and commander Western Naval Task Force included 503 U.S. ships and craft, 252 British, 19 French, 6 Greek, and 63 merchant ships of various nations—a total of 843 vessels. Ship-borne on this fleet were 1,267 landing craft.[7]

The Allied Assault Force comprised three divisions of the U.S. Seventh Army—assault force Alpha (U.S. 3rd Infantry), Camel (U.S. 36th Infantry), and Delta (U.S. 45th Infantry) under their respective commanders—and two divisions of French Army B under the command of Gen. Jean de Lattre la Tassigny. In support of the main landing, Rear Adm. Lyal A. Davidson's Support Task Force (TF 86) carried out assaults with commando forces (Operations SITKA and ROMEO), and Capt. Henry C. Johnson's Task Group 80.4 (Special Operations) handled related diversionary operations.[8]

Actor-turned-naval-officer Lt. Comdr. Douglas E. Fairbanks Jr., USNR—an Eighth Fleet Staff Special Operations officer—commanded a task unit of this task group. The sinking of two German corvettes in battle due to actions taken by Fairbanks and Lt. Comdr. John Bulkeley, USN—who won the Medal of Honor for taking Gen. Douglas MacArthur, his family and staff off the Philippine Islands in 1942—are taken up in the next chapter.

Commander Western Naval Task Force:
Vice Adm. Henry Kent Hewitt, USN
Commanding General Western Task Force:
Maj. Gen. Alexander M. Patch, USA
Commanding General VI Corps, Seventh Army:
Maj. Gen. Lucian K. Truscott Jr., USA

Assault Force	Naval Commander	Army Commander	Troops	Assault Areas
Alpha TF 84	Rear Adm. Frank J. Lowry, USN flagship: *Duane*	Maj. Gen. John W. O'Daniel, USA	U.S. Army 3rd Infantry Division (reinforced)	Cavalaire and Pampelonne
Delta TF 85	Rear Adm. Bertram J. Rodgers, USN flagship: *Biscayne*	Maj. Gen. William W. Eagles, USA	U.S. Army 45th Infantry Division (reinforced)	Baie de Bougnon and Golfe St.-Tropez
Camel TF 87	Rear Adm. Spencer S. Lewis, USN flagship: *Bayfield*	Maj. Gen. John E. Dahlquist, USA	U.S. Army 36th Infantry Division (reinforced), French Army units	Frejus, St.-Raphaël, and Calanque d' Actheor
Sitka TG 86.3	Rear Adm. Theodore E. Chandler, USN flagship: HMCS *Prince Henry*	Col. Edwin A. Walker, USA	Joint Canadian-American 1st Special Service Force	Îles d'Hyères
Romeo TG 86.3	Rear Adm. Theodore E. Chandler, USN	Lt. Col. Georges-Régis Bouvet	First Groupe Commandos d'Afrique	Cap Nègre and le Rayol
Special Operations TU 80.4.2	Lt. Comdr. Douglas E. Fairbanks Jr., flagship: HMS *Aphis*	Capitaine de Frégate R. Seriot	French Groupe Navale d' Assaut	Théoule-sur-Mer and Baie de La Ciotat[9]

The Allied plan called for a daylight assault over beaches between Cap Cavalaire and Agay, a seaside resort near St. Raphaël. The night before the main attack, commandos of the 1st Special Service Force were to seize the offshore islands of Levant and Port-Cros. Two French commando groups were also attached to the invasion force. The First Groupe Commandos d'Afrique under Lt. Col. Georges-Régis Bouvet, was to go ashore at Cap Nègre on the left flank to block the coastal road, and the French naval assault group of Capitaine de Frégate R. Seriot, was to carry out a similar mission at Théoule-sur-Mer on the right flank. At the same time, an airborne task force was to be dropped in the vicinity of Le Muy, ten miles behind the landing beaches, to cut off enemy reinforcements and neutralize gun positions. French Army B was to begin landing on the second day, and swing westward to take Toulon and Marseilles, while VI Corps advanced up the Rhône Valley toward Lyons and Vichy.[10]

SUPPORTING OPERATIONS SITKA AND ROMEO

A precursor to the main landings was neutralization of the gun batteries of German garrisons on Levant and Port-Cros—two French islands in the Îles d'Hyères group off the coast of the Riviera, near Toulon—which could threaten transport ships prior to their arrival in Cavalaire Bay en route to the Alpha Assault Force beaches. The Canadian-American 1st Special Service Force commanded by Col. Edwin A. Walker, USA, was assigned this task and designated "Sitka Force." The 1st Special Service Force—a commando-like unit numbering about 1,800 rangers—consisted mainly of men recruited at Army posts with preference given to those who had been lumberjacks, forest rangers, hunters, game wardens, and the like in civilian life. The recruits received rigorous and extensive training in stealth tactics, hand-to-hand combat, the use of explosives for demolition, parachuting, amphibious warfare, rock-climbing, mountain warfare, and winter warfare. Much feared by the enemy after demonstrating its fighting prowess at Anzio, it had been dubbed "The Devil's Brigade" by the Germans. The diary of a dead officer contained the passage, "The black devils (Die schwarzen Teufel) are all around us every time we come into the line." (The commandos smeared their faces with black boot polish prior to covert operations in the dark of the night.)[11]

It was thought that Port-Cros and Port Levant were lightly defended by guns, except at Levant there was believed to be a 164mm gun battery on the eastern end of the island. No initial resistance was met on either of the islands and surprisingly, the large coastal defense guns on Levant proved to be clever dummies. However, a pocket of stubborn enemy resistance was met on the west end of Levant that was not overcome until 2330 on D-day. Capture of Port-Cros was not finally completed until 1300 on D plus two, because of the presence of an old Chateau Fort of heavy masonry that resisted five-inch and 8-inch naval gunfire as well as two bombing runs. Finally, the battleship HMS *Ramillies* (07) was acquired from commander Task Force 84 on 17 August. Twelve well-placed rounds of 15-inch high-explosive did the job, and the white flag went up.[12]

Photo 11-1

Canadian and American soldiers of the 1st Special Service Force receiving bayonet instruction at Fort William Henry Harrison near Helena, Montana.
Source: http://www.ibiblio.org/hyperwar/USA/USA-SS-Canada/img/USA-SS-Canada-p263.jpg

The purpose of Operation ROMEO was to land the First Groupe Commandos d'Afrique at Cap Nègre and at le Rayol on the mainland, to secure the left flank of the main assault forces and to block German reinforcement troops being ushered forward from Hyères. ROMEO was of special significance to the French people as it enabled their troops to finally return to their homeland. The force included a raiding party of 75 men to overcome the defenses of Cap Nègre, and the main body of commandos, about 750 men, landed two-and-a-half miles to the east at Rayol beach.[13]

The two British assault landing craft towing rubber boats with 75 commandos, to whom were assigned the task of neutralizing enemy defenses on Cap Nègre, found themselves west of the cape. Lt. J. F. Brigen, RNVR, in the leading LCA, turned sharply to starboard and was able to make a landing on the eastern side of the cape. As he was making the turn, both LCAs were illuminated and fired upon. The second craft, unable to maneuver, was forced onto the rocks under a hail of bullets. Two members of its crew leapt into the water and with great effort, managed to refloat the craft but as it cleared the area, Acting Leading Seaman Edward Smith was not aboard. Last seen in the water, he was heard to shout "Carry on, I can swim." The freed LCA was able to make a successful landing at Point Layet. The commandos scaled the cliffs, joining the group from the other LCA on Cap Nègre at the opposite end of the crescent-shaped beach that formed the Bay of Bormes and carried out the operation.[14]

Because of a westerly current and low lying haze, the main party also landed westward of their intended beach. They were fortunate in this turn of events, as Rayol beach, one-quarter mile to the east, was under fire of small arms and mortar. Upon realizing their mistake, the commandos took advantage of the lack of enemy opposition on the alternate beach, and promptly worked their way inland.[15]

The naval assault group of Capitaine de Frégate R. Seriot did not fare as well after landing in rubber boats (carried by Fairbanks's task unit) at Pointe de l'Esquillon—a headland near the city of Théoule-sur-Mer in the Gulf of Napoule. The Frenchmen waded ashore to a road at the foot of a steep cliff, but then ran into a minefield. When exploding mines eliminated the element of surprise, the commandos reembarked only to be strafed by Allied aircraft. Forced to abandon their boats, they were captured ashore by the Germans, but later freed by French Forces.[16]

DESTRUCTION OF GERMAN *SG-21* AND *UJ-6081*

At 0435 after transports of the Sitka group had departed unloading areas en route to their rendezvous point, a salvo fired by the destroyer *Somers* (DD-381) broke the stillness of early morning. After spotting two unknown vessels *Somers* had challenged them—subsequently identified as the German escort vessel *SG-21* (ex-French minesweeping sloop *Amiral Sénès*) and the sub-chaser *UJ-6081* (ex-Italian corvette *Comocio*)—with her searchlight. They were approaching from the vicinity of Marseilles. As *Somers* failed to receive a reply to a signal she made to them, she opened fire. Rounds from the destroyer's first salvo directed at *UJ-6081* apparently found their mark; the sub-chaser immediately slowed. *Somers* then closed the second vessel, the larger of the two. *SG-21* was about 5,000 yards distant, making heavy black smoke and maneuvering radically in an attempt to escape. *Somers* fired a broadside at the escort vessel from 2,890 yards away. She was hit and a few seconds later burst into flames, which spread rapidly with detonations from stem to stern.[17]

At 0520 the destroyer returned to *UJ-6081* and opened fire. The first salvo at a range of less than a mile-and-a-half struck the sub-chaser, stopping her dead in the water and killing the crews of the 4.1-inch (100mm) bow guns and the 3.9-inch (99mm) gun. The only return fire was a few bursts of 20mm. After the ship's crew abandoned, a party from the *Somers* boarded the ship removing books and papers including charts of minefields and communication publications. The sub-chaser sank southwest of Port-Cros at 0703, a few minutes after the departure of the boarding party.[18]

Craft from transports and PT boats searched the area for survivors from the two German vessels. Ninety-nine prisoners were retrieved from the sea; twelve were injured, mostly due to burns. These men were put aboard LSI(L) landing craft for transfer to Corsica.[19]

The German Navy (Kriegsmarine) had obtained the *SG-21* following its capture by German troops in November 1942 while under construction as the *Amiral Sénès*. When Germany invaded the Netherlands, France, Norway, and Greece, it acquired ships. Many of the vessels were patrol boats, gunboats, torpedo boats, or destroyers. Several of the torpedo boats and destroyers were put into naval service, while older coastal defense ships were modified for use as floating anti-aircraft batteries. The Germans also took over shipyards with vessels still under construction. A number of the ships, such as the *SG-21*, were completed and put into service. The *UJ-6081* and other naval units based in German-controlled areas of Italy were captured by Allied forces after her surrender in 1943.[20]

DIVERSIONARY OPERATIONS

> *Enemy reaction to these operations was most satisfactory. Most of the coastal battery fire against the Eastern Unit was directed at the decoy screen and passed well over it, and the rest fell short of or burst in the air and over the gunboats. The effect of the gunboats' bombardment could not be determined, though numerous bursts and several flashes of fire were observed. Shelling by the Western Diversion Unit drew no return fire except some AA bursts directly in the area where the white phosphorous shells exploded.*

The repeat diversion produced considerable enemy reaction. Much shore fire was expended against the imaginary gunfire support and transport areas, but no serious hits were sustained. Searchlights, star shells and tracer fire were tried, but the smoke screen laid by the [Allied] ASRC [air-sea rescue craft] in combination with high-speed maneuvers allowed them to evade the barrage that crisscrossed the bay.

—Admiral Hewitt, commander Western Naval Task Force, commenting on the execution of diversionary surface operations employed during the invasion of southern France.[21]

The primary purpose of the diversionary operations executed prior to D-Day was to present multiple threats to enemy defense forces in order to make it harder for them to anticipate when and where the actual assault was to take place. To accomplish this goal, two small diversionary units were formed. The Eastern Unit was to sail along the west coast of Corsica on a northerly course—similar to that of the main attack forces behind it—as though bound for Genoa, before breaking away and turning west toward the Nice-Cannes area to carry out a minor amphibious demonstration there. Meanwhile, the Western Unit was to proceed west-northwest from Corsica toward the Sete-Agde area. When off the Marseilles-Toulon area, but still well out to sea, it was to turn to the northeast and proceed directly into the Bay of Ciotat to stage a mock landing there. A second simulated assault was to be launched in the same location the following night.[22]

During the repeat diversion, Allied gunfire support ships aroused heavy enemy fire, star shells, tracers, and searchlights. Most of the hostile fire was inaccurate and caused no damage to the diversionary operations. During the retirement of the ships and craft assigned, two German ships the *Capriolo* and *Nimet Allah* were met, engaged, and sunk by the destroyer *Endicott*, and two British gunboats HMS *Aphis* and HMS *Scarab*. Only minor damage to Allied ships and craft resulted, and 211 prisoners were captured from the German vessels.[23]

ALLIED TROOPS ADVANCE INLAND

The amphibious landing by the main assault forces was carried out with great success. Delaying H-Hour (the specific hour on D-Day at which time the first assault elements are scheduled to land) until 0800 provided the daylight necessary to supporting forces to exert the full power of naval artillery on weakening German coast and beach defenses prior to the landing, as well as aerial-bombardment immediately prior to the assault. As anticipated, strong residual coast defense was encountered during movement ashore, but the Germans lacked air power and reserve ground forces for an effective counterattack. The Allied troops gained the beach without significant losses, and began to advance against varying degrees of German resistance. Admiral Hewitt summarized these post-landing operations:

> After having cracked the crust of the beach defense all our troops were able to move forward very rapidly towards the Rhône Valley and there was very little resistance. The French troops, however, pulling to the westward towards Toulon encountered very heavy resistance from the Germans and from the German Navy-manned shore defenses in that area. They, however, with the assistance of naval gunfire, made very rapid advances and were able to completely surround Marseilles and Toulon and cut off its defenders from the other German troops to the north.[24]

ALLIED SALVAGE FORCE

> *The activities of [salvage-equipped tank landing craft] LCT 31 are noteworthy. While this craft herself had a fouled propeller, in ten days she salvaged all or parts of 7 LCVP, 1 DUKN, 1 artillery observation aircraft, 1 tank turret; cleared propellers of 15 LCMs and recovered two LCT anchors. These jobs were accomplished by means of sheerlegs [cranes] installed over the bow with a lifting capacity of 30 tons.*
>
> —Rear Adm. Frank J. Lowry, USN, commander Task Force 84[25]

A long period of study had been available to the Eighth Fleet staff to plan DRAGOON, enabling lessons of previous amphibious operations in the theater to be applied, insofar as circumstances permitted. One of these lessons was the need for a more robust salvage force than had been devoted to the invasion at Anzio, and the requisite leadership to guide it. A senior salvage officer and an experienced firefighting officer were assigned to each attack force, and the salvage ships and craft were organized so that shallow water salvage, deep water salvage, and firefighting could be undertaken independently, yet each was prepared to assist the other. The landing craft configured for salvage duty LCI(L)s and LCTs were initially employed to carry assault troops and vehicles and after the initial landing, became available for salvage and firefighting. Alterations made to

LCI(L)s included installation of heavy bitts, stern chocks, heavier stern anchor and anchor wire, and outfitting with the necessary miscellaneous gear required for salvage operations. The landing craft designated for firefighting were provided gasoline-driven fire pumps and related foam, hose, and equipment. Salvage LCTs were equipped with sheer legs which, powered by a gasoline-driven winch mounted on deck forward of the superstructure, had a lifting capacity of 30-tons.[26]

Photo 11-2

Tank Landing Craft *LCT-31* being carried aboard Tank Landing Ship *LST-383*. Courtesy of Steve McKenna, *LST-383* website

Two American salvage ships were staged at Calvi—*Extricate* (ARS-16) and *Restorer* (ARS-17)—and at Ajaccio one American and one British salvage ship—*Weight* (ARS-35) and HMS *Salventure* (A384). Their purpose was intercepting and relieving tugs towing damaged ships from the assault areas. Except for a few minor repair jobs, these salvage ships—which were positioned in Corsican ports out of harm's way but within easy reach of the assault area—had little to do until harbor clearance work at Toulon and Marseilles started. A summary of the tugs, salvage ships, and salvage craft assigned to DRAGOON, with names of commanding officers or officers-in-charge, if known, follows.[27]

Task Force 84 (Alpha Attack Force):
Rear Adm. Frank J. Lowry, USN
Combat Salvage and Firefighting Unit (Task Group 84.9):
Comdr. Harvey M. Andersen, USN (embarked in *Hopi*)
Red Beach Deep Water Salvage: Comdr. H. M. Andersen
Shallow Water Salvage: Lt. Comdr. Greene

Ship	Commanding Officer	Ship	Commanding Officer
Hopi (ATF-71)	Lt. Owen W. Huff, USN	LCI(L)-42	Lt. (jg) L. J. Brooks, USNR
ATA-170	Lt. W. C. Beatie Jr., USNR	LCI(L)-234	Lt. (jg) W. F. Chapman, USNR
HMS *Empire Ann*		LCT-16	
HMS *Empire Spitfire*	Lt. J. Evans, RNR	LSM	
HMS *Barholm* (Z211)		Warping Barge	

Yellow Beach Deep Water Salvage: Lt. McGill
Shallow Water Salvage: Lt. (jg) Hayden

Evea (YTB-458)	O. W. Norr	LCI(L)-235	Lt. (jg) A. B. Mullen
ATR-1	Lt. (jg) H. L. MacGill, USN	LCT-31	Lt. (jg) T. O. Torkelson
YTL-165		LSM	
YTL-186		Warping Barge	

Task Force 85 (Delta Attack Force):
Rear Adm. Bertram J. Rodgers, USN
Combat Salvage and Firefighting Group (Task Group 85.14):
Lt. Comdr. T. N. LePage, RCNVR (embarked in *Narragansett*)

Narragansett (ATF-88)	Lt. Charles J. Wichmann, USN	LCI(L)-37	Lt. (jg) George F. Schneider, USNR
Pinto (ATF-90)	Lt. Ralph Brown, USN	LCI(L)-41	Lt. (jg) Charles F. Henderson, USNR
ATA-125 (ex-ATR-47)	Lt. Harry L. Lane, USNR	LCI(L)-43	Lt. (jg) R. D. Geppert, USNR
YTL-196		LCT	
HMS *Aspirant* (W134)		3 LCMs	
HMS *Athlete* (W150)			
HMS *Charon* (W109)			
HMS *Barford* (Z209)			
HMS *Barmond* (Z232)[29]			

Task Force 87 (Camel Attack Force):
Rear Adm. Spencer S. Lewis, USN
Combat Salvage and Firefighting Group (Task Group 87.9):
Lt. L. R. Brown (embarked in flagship *Bayfield*)

Ship	Commanding Officer	Ship	Commanding Officer
Arikara (ATF-98)	Lt. J. Aitken, USNR	*LCI(L)-76*	Lt. (jg) William M. Walker, USNR
Moreno (ATF-97)	Lt. Victor H. Kyllberg, USN	*LCI(L)-100*	
Edenshaw (YTB-459)	R. L. Self		
ATA-172 (ex-*ATR-99*)	Lt. Robert G. Hoffman, USN		
YTL-210			
HMS *Mindful* (W135)			
HMS *Vagrant* (W136)			
HMS *Bardolf* (Z171)[30]			

Reserve Forces

Positioned at Calvi, Corsica		Positioned at Ajaccio, Corsica	
Extricate (ARS-16)	Lt. Chester H. Rooklidge, USNR	HMS *Salventure*	
Restorer (ARS-17)	Lt. C. M. Boyd, USNR	*Weight* (ARS-35)	Lt. Comdr. Frederick J. Leamond, USNR[28]

LOSS OF TANK LANDING SHIP *LST-282*

The deep water salvage ships—American and British tugs and British boom defense vessels—were stationed to render assistance as necessary during the operation, but no damage requiring salvage occurred. Numerous assignments were given to tow damaged craft out of the area and to tow several Liberty ships blown ashore in a storm off the beach. No major fires occurred aboard any ships, with the exception of the tank landing ship *LST-282*, which was hit by a glider-bomb at 2225 on D-Day in the Camel Assault area and was lost. A nearby tank landing ship observed an enemy plane, assumed to be a Focke-Wulf 200, launch a glider-bomb. The bomb made a direct hit on the *282*, which was immediately enveloped in flames, exploded, and burned all night and the next day.[31]

Following the receipt of a request from *LCI(L)-76* to sink the tank landing ship with gunfire, Lieutenant Brown—the commander of the

Combat Salvage and Firefighting Group assigned to Camel beach—denied the request. He then shifted from *Bayfield* in which he was embarked to the fleet tug *Moreno* and asked her captain to get him as close as possible to the burning LST. *Moreno* took him as near her as the water depth would permit. It was difficult to locate the ship because the fire aboard her blended in with fires on the beach. Brown described the efforts made by the harbor tug to save the amphibious ship:

> I attempted to get hold of the *LCI 76* but could not; however, we did raise the *YTL-210* who came alongside us. The *YTL 210* was working on some causeways at Green Beach at the time the *LST 282* was hit by [a] radio-controlled glider bomb. The Captain of the *YTL-210* says he saw the glider bomb hit the *LST 282* forward of pilot house and [blast] out long sections of ship port side…. The *YTL 210*…manned two fire hoses and went within 25 feet of [the] fire. The fire had now spread to [the] tank deck with great violence and many explosions. [The captain of] the YTL…could see he was doing no good [and was only] endangering his men and ship so he proceeded to pick up seventeen survivors and take them to the [attack cargo ship *Achernar*] AKA 53.[32]

Photo 11-3

LST-282 destroyed by fire after being hit by a glider-bomb.
Photo by Morris Levine, courtesy of Thomas Aubut's *LST 282* website

Offshore Salvage units also assisted in picking up survivors of the minesweeper *YMS-24*, the British motor launch *ML-563*, and the motor torpedo boats *PT-202* and *PT-218* lost the following day to mines. For heroic action on 15 August, Chief Engineman Leslie C. Merrill, aboard the *YT-210*, was awarded the Navy and Marine Corps Medal. This medal, established on 7 August 1942, was normally awarded for sea rescues involving risk to life, which had previously been recognized by awarding the U.S. Coast Guard Silver or Gold Lifesaving Medal. The Navy and Marine Corps Medal was created because "top brass" considered it more prestigious than the Lifesaving Medal.[33]

Apart from the fact that the southern France landings were not prolonged, due to the troops' ability to quickly push inland from the beaches, salvage operations were less hazardous than at Anzio because the Germans no longer had the capability, after the Normandy invasion, to apply the force they had in Italy. Diminished air attacks—none during the day and few at night—and reduced shelling from coastal defenses, produced few ship casualties. The shallow water salvage force was kept busy, however, hauling beached landing craft off the shore, clearing craft from underwater obstacles, raising sunken craft, and making emergency repairs. All damaged craft were cleared from the beaches in the first fifteen days after D-Day.[34]

Twenty-seven American salvage ships received a battle star for the Invasion of Southern France. *Tackle* was assigned to Task Group 89.6 (Salvage Group Eighth Fleet) and YTLs *160* and *161* to U.S. naval detachments Ajaccio and Calvi-Ile Rousse (TG 80.9).

Ship	Award Period	Ship	Award Period
Arikara (ATF-98)	15 Aug-25 Sep 1944	*YTL-165*	19 Aug-25 Sep 1944
ATR-1	15 Aug-25 Sep 1944	*YTL-186*	19 Aug-25 Sep 1944
Edenshaw (YTB-459)	15 Aug-25 Sep 1944	*YTL-196*	19 Aug-25 Sep 1944
Evea (YTB-458)	15 Aug-25 Sep 1944	*YTL-210*	19 Aug-25 Sep 1944
Extricate (ARS-16)	15 Aug-25 Sep 1944	*LCI(L)-37*	15 Aug-12 Sep 1944
Hopi (ATF-71)	15 Aug-25 Sep 1944	*LCI(L)-41*	15 Aug-22 Sep 1944
Moreno (ATF-87)	15 Aug-25 Sep 1944	*LCI(L)-42*	15 Aug-22 Sep 1944
Narragansett (ATF-88)	15 Aug-25 Sep 1944	*LCI(L)-43*	15 Aug-12 Sep 1944
Pinto (ATF-90)	15 Aug-25 Sep 1944	*LCI(L)-76*	15 Aug-25 Sep 1944
Restorer (ARS-17)	15 Aug-25 Sep 1944	*LCI(L)-234*	15 Aug-25 Sep 1944
Tackle (ARS-37)	15 Aug-25 Sep 1944	*LCI(L)-235*	15 Aug-25 Sep 1944
Weight (ARS-35)	15 Aug-25 Sep 1944	*LCT-16*	15 Aug-25 Sep 1944
YTL-160	19 Aug-25 Sep 1944	*LCT-31*	15 Aug-10 Sep 1944
YTL-161	19 Aug-25 Sep 1944		

Four British boom defense vessels—*Bardolf* (Z171), *Barford* (Z209), *Barholm* (Z211), and *Barmond* (Z232)—were awarded battle honours SOUTHERN FRANCE – 1944 by the Royal Navy.[35]

DRAGOON A GREAT SUCCESS

The success of the Allied assault forces in their rapid advance ashore and movement inland during the Invasion of southern France, is evidenced by messages sent by dignitaries present offshore, as paraphrased by Admiral Hewitt in August 1944 war diary entries:

- 1157 on D-Day (15 August): From Winston Churchill aboard HMS *Kimberley* (F50): Best wishes to you all for the great success of your joint enterprise and good luck to all concerned. The Prime Minister sends his compliments to Secretary Forrestal.

- 1616 on 16 August: From Admiral Hewitt to Vice Adm. Alan G. Kirk, commander U.S. Naval Forces, France: Landings carried out 15th at 0800 against light resistance. At the end of the first day all troops landed except on ST RAPHAEL-FREJUS Beaches. These towns occupied the 16th morning. During night and morning 16th, American troops progressed deeply inland and arrived on a line GONFARON-LE MUY where contact was made with paratroops. Ships have operated counterbattery and support fire. Light expense ammunition. No casualties. General Lattre and French divisions arriving today under French escort will land immediately.
- 2243 on 16 August: From Secretary of the Navy James Forrestal, aboard USS *Augusta* (CA-31), to Maj. Gen. Lucian K. Truscott Jr., commanding General VI Corps: To you and your division Commander[s], I send the Navy's 'Well Done' and the Navy's appreciation of good partners and gallant fighters.[36]

12

Fairbanks and Bulkeley in Combat

At 0700 [the German corvette] Capaiulo suffered a direct hit from the gunboats which seriously crippled her and set her afire. She slowed appreciably. [Nimet] Allah [a German sub-chaser] swung back to keep contact with her mate. Three minutes later [Nimet] Allah received a water line hit and began listing to port. With both enemy vessels brought to, fire was continued with [the gunboats HMS] Aphis and Scarab closing from starboard and [the destroyer USS] Endicott steering various courses to complete the enemy destruction.

—Excerpt from a report by commander Task Group 80.4 on Operation DRAGOON. Lt. Comdr. Douglas E. Fairbanks Jr., embarked in HMS *Aphis*, commanded a task unit that included two British gunboats and some motor launches employed as amphibious raiding craft, and American air-sea rescue craft and PT boats. Lt. Comdr. John D. Bulkeley commanded *Endicott*, which administered the coup de grâce to the enemy ships.[1]

Although this short chapter is not directly related to the subject matter of the book, I believe that readers will find its description of a little known sea battle, involving two very well known Americans, interesting. On the night of 16-17 August 1944, a Beach Jumper Unit designated the Eastern Diversionary Force, under the command of Hollywood-actor-turned-naval-officer Lt. Comdr. Douglas E. Fairbanks Jr. and supported by the destroyer *Endicott* (DD-495), carried out a mission involving shore bombardment on the Ciotat area between Marseilles and Toulon. It was designed to convince the Germans the main landing would be in the Marseilles-Toulon area, thereby diverting their attention from the actual landings on the beaches of the French Riviera near Cannes. The Western Diversionary Force—a Beach Jumper unit made up of the above forces minus *Aphis* and *Scarab*—had carried out the first night's operation by simulating a large landing force approaching Marseilles. These units were tasked with tactical cover and deception and the concept for their creation came about as a result of then Lieutenant

Fairbanks, having been assigned to duty with the British Combined Operations Commandos in England.²

Comprising Fairbanks's Eastern Diversionary Force were the British gunboats HMS *Aphis* (T57) and HMS *Scarab* (T59), four British motor launches, four U.S. Army Air Force air-sea rescue craft, and eighteen USN PT boats. Following the assault, with its attendant bombardment from fire support areas, the vessels began withdrawing at about 0430 bound for a rendezvous point to seaward. En route there, the air-sea rescue craft *ASRC-21* detected a contact on radar to the north-northwest. It was initially thought to be the destroyer *Endicott*, which had been supporting the diversionary operation with shore bombardment. As the range closed, the "pip" divided into two representations of ships thought to be two motor launches involved in the operation. As the interval lessened to 1,500 yards, the two hitherto-believed-friendly vessels opened fire with star shell-illumination rounds. It was then possible to discern, in the glare produced over the water, other ASRCs (air-sea rescue craft) retiring to seaward.³

Photo 12-1

Lt. Comdr. Douglas Elton Fairbanks Jr., Source: http://www.history.navy.mil/bios/fairbanks_douge.htm

The only reply to *ASRC-21*'s signal challenge to the ships to identify themselves was increased gunfire from what now appeared to be two fairly large corvettes. As *ASRC-21* was kept under continuous fire by one corvette, the second one attacked other ASRCs in the area. The small craft employed evasive tactics: maximum speed, zigzagging, and generation of smoke. Return fire was withheld to avoid presenting the enemy a definite point of aim in the half light. The courses steered by the air-sea rescue craft and their pursuers were generally southwesterly.⁴

GUNBOATS *APHIS* AND *SCARAB* JOIN THE BATTLE

At 0540 lookouts aboard HMS *Aphis* and HMS *Scarab*—which by then had withdrawn well off the coast—reported star shell and tracer fire off their starboard bow, some miles away. Embarked in HMS *Aphis*— an old Yangtze River gunboat—was Lt. Comdr. Douglas Fairbanks Jr., USNR. He was a special operations officer on the staff of Admiral Hewitt and for this operation he was commander Task Unit 80.4.2. HMS *Aphis* and *Scarab* were 237-foot sister ships with much service between them, having been commissioned in 1915. Each of the ships mounted two 6-inch guns as their principal weapons, and for anti-air defense they had one 3-inch high-angle gun sited immediately before the bridge structure, as well as smaller 20mm Oerlikon and Breda machine guns on both the port and starboard sides. *Aphis*'s main battery had been replaced in 1939 with longer barreled 6-inch Mk XIII .50-caliber guns from the dreadnought battleship HMS *Agincour* (1913).[5]

Photo 12-2

River gunboat HMS *Aphis*.
Courtesy of Gordon Smith, http://www.naval-history.net

On learning of their predicament, Fairbanks dispatched a PT boat, ahead, to provide assistance to the beleaguered ASRCs. As the gunboats increased to their maximum speed of only about 10 knots, and altered course to a westerly direction to intercept, he reported the situation to Hewitt's flagship *Catoctin* (AGC-5)—aboard which Secretary of the Navy James Forrestal was embarked as an observer— and radioed *Endicott* to come to their assistance. At 0610 the gunboats opened fire on the enemy ships. The first, *UJ-6083*, was the ex-Italian corvette *Capriolo* (C22). The second, *UJ-6073*, had formerly been the *Nimet Allah*, yacht of Khedive Abbas II Hilmi Bey, Egyptian ruler of the Ottoman Empire. *UJ-6073* had been purchased by the Germans and converted to a warship with two radar-controlled 88mm guns. (The *Nimet Allah* was misidentified as the *Kemid Allah* in war diaries and reports related to DRAGOON. I have replaced the latter name with the former in all succeeding references to the ship.) The two corvettes, commanded by Lt. Comdr. Hermann Pollenz, had just left Toulon and were proceeding to Marseilles.[6]

Saved from enemy attack, the four 63-foot air-sea rescue boats—ASRCs *14*, *21*, *24*, *37*, commonly called "crash boats"—formed up with the intention of remaining in the area, but the battle moved rapidly away and they set course for their Corsican bases. None of the boats suffered more than near misses, including *ASRC-21*, except for the *ASRC-14*, which sustained several minor shrapnel hits. Dawn had just broken, the seas were calm, and visibility was about six miles.[7]

Because of their limited speed, *Aphis* and *Scarab* planned to take position to landward of the German ships, but *Scarab* fell behind during the approach, resulting in a change in course by the gunboats to the southwest, bringing the enemy on their starboard beam. Their guns opened at a range of 10,500 yards, and by "stair-stepping" in stages toward the west, the *Aphis* and *Scarab* were able to close to less than 5,000 yards. *Aphis*' six-inch guns were temporarily out of action as a result of overheating from shelling the shore in the preceding operation. As efforts were made to bring her 3-inch gun to bear, *Scarab* took over the principal shelling. After quickly deducing that they were outclassed by the enemy, Fairbanks ordered nearby motor launches to screen the gunboats to seaward, while they endeavored to head off the enemy's further westward progress. As the enemy's accurate gunfire straddled them ever closer, *Aphis* and *Scarab* began making smoke in an effort to shield themselves from view. Captain Henry C. Johnson, USN, who commanded Task Group 80.4, of which the task unit was a part, described the action:

> A violent exchange of fire then ensued between the corvettes and gunboats. About 50 "straddles" and "near misses" were noted by *APHIS* while her radar antennae and gunsights on her 3 inch battery were shot away. Ranges now varied 3500 yards to 6000 yards with the Gunboats endeavoring to enfilade the Corvettes [fire at the enemy formation] on northwesterly course. As the enemy fire became more and more accurate and intense, it was decided advisable for the Gunboats to make smoke. This they did and orders were given for them to reverse course and circle widely to port and return through on a course of 030° T. The time was now about 0615 and lookouts reported sighting what appeared to be *ENDICOTT* off the port bow, about 7000 yards. Because of

radar control, enemy fire on the Gunboats persisted with considerable accuracy and evasive tactics were difficult.[8]

"CROSSING THE T"

Although damaged, the two gunboats had not suffered any personnel casualties when, fortuitously, *Aphis*'s gunnery officer reported that her 6-inch guns were cool enough to use again. Emerging through a thin spot in the smoke screen, the gunboats found themselves at right angles across the bows of the oncoming Germans. (This classic naval warfare tactic, termed "Crossing the T," involves obtaining an advantageous situation, in which a line of warships crosses in front of a line of enemy ships, allowing the crossing ships to bring all their guns to bear on the enemy while receiving fire from only the forward guns of their adversary.) Through sheer luck, the gunboats had gained the upper hand and took advantage of it. They concentrated their fire on the leading vessel, the *UJ-6083*. *Aphis* fired a point-blank salvo at the corvette without benefit of a targeting device and scored a direct hit, crippling her and setting her afire, while *Scarab* scored a damaging near-miss. Three minutes later, *UJ-6073* received a water line hit and began listing to port.[9]

DESTROYER *ENDICOTT* ARRIVES ON SCENE

Endicott had completed her shore bombardment mission between the hours of 0300-0430, and had retired to the rendezvous point. At 0545 the destroyer received a transmission from the *ASRC-21* that she was being attacked by two enemy corvettes. At about this time what appeared to be anti-aircraft tracer fire was seen to the northward. Ten minutes later, the *Endicott* set course 325 true and rang up 35 knots, all speed possible, without making smoke and warning the enemy ships of her approach, to close the scene of action. Visibility was then only about two miles because of the early morning haze. At 0620 she sighted the *Aphis* and *Scarab* on her port bow retiring to southward (before the close engagement with the enemy ships described above). The *UJ-6083* and *UJ-6073* were then pursuing the gunboats and firing at them from outside the effective gun range of *Aphis* and *Scarab*, which by then, had expended almost all of their 6-inch ammunition, and also had suffered numerous gun and electrical power casualties. The latter degradation resulted in the loss of all director control to the guns, requiring the use of manual control for the impending "Crossing the T" engagement. The destroyer concurrently came under fire from one or both of the unseen, and more distant corvettes, which (hidden in the haze and smoke produced by the gunboats), were also located off her port bow.¹⁰

At 0646 *Endicott* sighted the enemy ships and opened fire. Lt. Comdr. John Bulkeley described the engagement and difficulties encountered with overheating guns, because of previous shore bombardment, similar to those experienced by the gunboats:

> Sighted two corvettes almost dead ahead. On challenging these vessels by a flashing light this vessel received the same challenge as reply. Commenced firing immediately on the larger of the two ships, the [NIMET] ALLAH. Closed the range to 3000 yards at a speed of 35 knots. At this time 5"/38 Gun #3 was the only main battery gun able to fire due to jammed breech blocks on the other three guns from over-heating due to heavy shore bombardment in a short period of time shortly before the surface engagement. As each 5"/38 gun was able to fire, it was brought into action, although at no time was it possible to fire a full four-gun salvo. Heavy return fire was encountered from the main and machine gun batteries of the two enemy vessels. Numerous straddles were observed but high speed maintained by this vessel and frequent changes of course reduced effectiveness of enemy fire.¹¹

Receiving two hits to her engine room, *Nimet Allah* slowed, and Bulkeley shifted fire to the second ship *Capaiulo*, which by then had been set aflame by HMS *Aphis*. Recognized as an ex-Italian torpedo boat that carried torpedoes and mounted 4.7-inch guns, she was thus the more dangerous of the two vessels. The *Capaiulo* came about, attempting, though damaged, to escape. *Endicott* rounded the enemy vessel to thwart evasive action, and the range between them closed to 3,000 yards. As the combat action continued, Bulkeley alternately engaged the two vessels:

> When the *CAPAIULO* had been hit several times, fire was shifted to the [NIMET] ALLAH. Fire was then shifted back and forth between targets to prevent either from maneuvering radically or making their gunfire effective.
>
> Throughout this engagement which lasted slightly less than one hour, the course of this vessel was changed as necessary to bring the maximum number of guns to bear on the enemy and to maintain an aggressive position relative to the enemy. When one enemy ship was hit severely and her firepower rendered useless temporarily, this vessel took the other ship under fire.¹²

At 0648 the ex-yacht *Nimet Allah* was also set on fire and began to list to port and explode. Her crew abandoned ship in life rafts. The fierce engagement with *Capaiulo* continued; *Nimet Allah* sank at 0709; and, with *Endicott* firing all batteries at the other enemy vessel and making many direct hits, the action completed at 0717. *Capaiulo* then listed to port and began exploding, from stem to stern, following which *Endicott* commenced picking up survivors. The German corvette sank at 0830, after which the three Allied ships proceeded to the Delta Assault area. *Endicott* carried 169 prisoners and, between the two British gunboats, 41 prisoners.[13]

Bulkeley stated in his report on the action, "Since this engagement was the USS *Endicott*'s first real contact with the enemy, it is the opinion of this command that the entire ship's company showed excellent and above-average fighting spirit." Understated but high praise from someone with his combat experience, and associated awards for personal valor including the Congressional Medal of Honor.[14]

Photo 12-3

Lt. Comdr. Douglas Fairbanks Jr., USNR, Capt. Henry C. Johnson, USN, and Lt. Comdr. John D. Bulkeley, USN, aboard the destroyer *Endicott*.
U.S. Naval Historical Center Photo # NH 54383

FAIRBANKS, BULKELEY AND GUNBOATS LAUDED

Lt. Comdr. Douglas E. Fairbanks Jr. received the Legion of Merit Medal with Combat V for his part in planning the diversionary tactics used in DRAGOON, and command of one of the Beach Jumpers detachments during a fierce sea battle with superior enemy surface combatants. The medal citation reads:

> For exceptionally meritorious conduct in the performance of outstanding services to the Government of the United States as Special Operations Planning Officer on the Staff of a Major Naval Task Force Commander and as Commander of a Naval Task Force Unit prior to and during the amphibious invasion of Southern France in August 1944. Working tirelessly and with sound application of superior tactical knowledge, Lieutenant Commander Fairbanks participated in the development and coordination of plans for the execution of special operations in support of the main Allied landings. Subsequently, as Commander of a Task Unit, he expeditiously established special troops on the flank of the major assault area for the purpose of immobilizing enemy reinforcements attempting to resist the landings. On the morning of August 17, when two hostile vessels attacked a group of smaller craft, he courageously led the ships of his unit into action and, aggressively directing the combat operations with expert seamanship against heavy odds, greatly aided in the ultimate sinking of the two vessels. By his brilliant leadership and steadfast devotion to duty throughout this vital period, Lieutenant Commander Fairbanks contributed materially to the successful invasion of a highly strategic area.

Lt. Comdr. John Bulkeley was awarded his second Silver Star of the war for his heroic actions as the commanding officer of *Endicott* during the Eastern Diversionary Force operation. The citation reads:

> The President of the United States of America takes pleasure in presenting a Gold Star in lieu of a Second Award of the Silver Star to Lieutenant Commander John Duncan Bulkeley, United States Navy, for conspicuous gallantry and intrepidity in action as Commanding Officer, U.S.S. *ENDICOTT* (DD-495), during the amphibious invasion of Southern France, on 16-17 August 1944. Lieutenant Commander Bulkeley, exercising fearless determination, first brought his ship within easy range of enemy coastal batteries in the Bai de la Ciotat area and effectively bombarded short targets in support of a special assault mission. After withdrawal of this group on the morning of 17 August, he went to the assistance of several units which were engaging enemy vessels

of superior strength. Despite intermittent main battery gun failures incidental to prior bombardment, he pressed his attack with great skill and courage in delivering accurate and vigorous gunfire against the enemy and exerted unrelenting pressure during the running action which ensued until both ships were sunk by the combined efforts of our forces. The aggressive leadership, cool and intrepid action, and outstanding devotion to duty displayed by Lieutenant Commander Bulkeley throughout this action reflects great credit upon himself, and was in keeping with the highest traditions of the United States Naval Service.

The Royal Navy gunboats HMS *Aphis*—under Lt. Edward Ernest Clifton, RNR—and HMS *Scarab*—T/Lt. Edward Albert Hawkesworth, RNVR—each received Battle Honours for "SOUTH FRANCE – 1944," as did twenty-five motor launches that participated in Operation DRAGOON. It is likely that the four MLs assigned to the Eastern Diversionary Force (Task Unit 80.4.2) were among this group.

13

Opening the Southern French Ports

> *Experience in this theater has shown that beach maintenance after mid-September is inadequate, and that it is essential to have protected ports available to insure adequate facilities to supply advancing armies.*
> *In order to accomplish the above:*
> *Seabee personnel have been placed at Toulon and Port de Bouc;*
> *All personnel and salvage equipment under my command are being brought up;*
> *Such personnel and salvage equipment that can be employed gainfully in Marseilles have been allocated to that port;*
> *That additional equipment that cannot be used in [Marseilles] has been temporarily allocated to Port de Bouc and Toulon....*
>
> —Excerpts from a dispatch sent by Adm. Henry K. Hewitt, naval commander Western Task Force, to Lt. Gen. Alexander M. Patch, commanding general Seventh Army, on 1 September 1944, providing status on efforts in progress to open French ports for logistic support of Allied armies advancing across Europe[1]

After the assault phase of Operation DRAGOON cracked the German beach defenses, American troops began fighting their way from the southern France beaches toward the Rhône Valley and met very little resistance. However, French troops moving to the westward toward Toulon encountered very heavy resistance from German ground forces and from German Navy-manned shore defenses in that area. Despite this enemy opposition, they made rapid advances with the assistance of Allied naval gunfire, and were able to surround the port cities of Marseilles and Toulon, to cut off their defenders from the other German troops to the north.[2]

The port of Marseilles was especially desired by the U.S. Seventh Army because it was near the mouth of the Rhône River and was the terminus of the railroad system up the Rhône Valley. From Marseilles, American troops could advance north in France by rail. The port's harbor was artificial, formed by a breakwater and divided into a number of different basins with rather small deep water entrances. The Allies also wanted to open the port of Toulon—which offered a large sheltered harbor and had been a principal naval base for the French fleet—for use by shipping.³

Until the Allies could gain control of Marseilles, most of the Army supplies had to come over beaches on the Gulf of St. Tropez, the Gulf of Frejus, and Cavalaire Bay. The supplies then had to be hauled by truck, which were in short supply. Existing conditions on the beaches were expected to be much worse when mistrals started up in September. These violent and cold north or northwest winds accelerated when channeled through the valleys of the Rhône and the Durance Rivers into the northern Mediterranean, sometimes reaching 62 miles per hour.⁴

The major obstacles to the Allies gaining control of the ports of Toulon and Marseilles were the coastal gun batteries at these locations. The most formidable was sited on the island of St. Mandrier guarding Toulon. Joined to the mainland only by a very narrow causeway, the steeply slopped island formed the southern border of the Bay of Toulon. Its guns were the center of a very elaborate, permanent defense. Two twin turrets of 13.4-inch guns, taken from French battleships scuttled early in the war, were mounted in low profile to the ground with supporting underground barbettes, passageways, power plants, and quarters for the crew. The island and Toulon were also ringed with very strong anti-aircraft defenses.⁵

The French battleship FR *Lorraine*, British battleship HMS *Ramillies* (07), American battleship *Nevada* (BB-36), and some cruisers with eight-inch guns all took the battery under fire. The Allied bombardment was conducted under the cover of smoke to prevent the defensive guns from clearly sighting the attacking ships. Although return fire from the battery did not hit any of the ships, it came very close. One turret opened fire on the cruiser *Augusta* (CA-31) when she was ten miles distant, and continued to fire as she withdrew beyond its range to about twenty miles out to sea. Allied planes also bombed the island. One of the turrets was knocked out by a bomb and the other by a projectile likely fired by one of the battleships.⁶

Another French port was needed to support the advancing U.S. Seventh and French Armies. On 24 August 1944, with Marseilles and Toulon still in German hands, Admiral Hewitt directed immediate effort to open Port de Bouc, a small port west of Marseilles located at the entrance to a channel leading to Etang de Berre (a lagoon). After the first Allied assaults, forces of the French resistance had taken the port by force, started flying French flags, and finally established communications with American motor torpedo boats letting the Allies know the port was secured. Chosen out of necessity, it would prove to be a poor substitute for Marseilles or Toulon because of its small size and limited facilities. As with Cherbourg, holding and using the port were two different things. British and American minesweeping forces would find in the coming days, Port de Bouc was defended by French mines in the approach channel south of Golfe de Fos, German mines at the entrance to the gulf and in the port itself, and large-caliber shore batteries on Cap Couronne at the entrance to the gulf.[7]

MINESWEEPING IN APPROACHES, GOLFE DE FOS, AND PORT DE BOUC

> *Sweeping by the fleet sweepers was rapid enough but owing to the damage caused to the gear by mines exploding much time was spent in retrieving gear, bending on new sets, and clearing mines from sweeps when fouled therein and in ships having to "underrun" others to clear the mines from them.*
>
> *On seeing the number of mines we were cutting I asked C.T.F. 86 to send mine disposal officers to deal with those which obviously would drift ashore before they could be sunk in deep water....*
>
> *The loss of sweeping gear amongst the fleet sweepers began to assume ominous proportions, and delay was arising through having to transfer spares from one ship to another. This must have been largely caused by the [mine] snag lines as in many cases the float was sunk as well as the otter [referring to shipboard minesweeping gear] – sometimes the float being blown to pieces and the otter remaining.*
>
> —Observations by Comdr. Alister Angus Martin, RNR, Senior Officer 13th Minesweeping Flotilla and Commanding Officer HMS *Rothesay* (J19), in a report on efforts to sweep an approach channel to Port de Bouc through Golfe de Fos[8]

The steel-hulled minesweepers of the British 13th Minesweeping Flotilla under Comdr. Alister A. Martin, RN—HMS *Aries* (J284), *Brixham* (J105), *Bude* (J116), *Polruan* (J97), *Rothesay* (J19), *Stornoway* (J31)—and danlayers *Borealis* and *Nebb* (FY1722) began operations in the approaches to the Golfe de Fos upon their arrival on 24 August

1944. *Borealis* and *Nebb* were former whalers, whose job was to lay Dan buoys to mark the boundaries of the approach channel after the minesweepers swept it clear of mines.⁹

Map 13-1

A large force of British and American minesweepers swept an approach channel through Golfe du Lion, and cleared mines from Golfe de Fos and Port de Bouc itself, to enable salvage forces to open the port for sea-supplied support of Allied armies advancing from southern France invasion beaches toward Germany.

In addition to this flotilla, an unintended armada of other American and British minesweepers had assembled twenty miles to the south of the gulf, as a result of a mix up in communication call signs and orders. These included the British 19th Minesweeping Flotilla: HMS *Antares* (J282), *Arcturus* (J282), *Brave* (J305), *Rinaldo* (J225), *Rosario* (J219), *Spanker* (J226), and *Waterwitch* (J304), supported by danlayers *Satsa* (FY1734) and *Calm*; Mine Division Sixteen: *Dextrous* (AM-341), *Pioneer* (AM-105), *Prevail* (AM-107), and *Seer* (AM-112); minesweepers *Incredible* (AM-249) and *Mainstay* (AM-261); and a number of YMSs. The 13th M/S Flotilla was assisted by ships of all the groups present, but by the end of the first day the senior officer had detached the 19th Flotilla, all of the AMs, and six of the YMSs to return to Cavalaire Bay.¹⁰

After commencing formation sweeping on 24 August, the ships of the 13th M/S Flotilla were shelled by batteries at Cap Croisette (located south of Marseilles opposite the island Maïre), whereupon the ships turned away, recovered their sweep gear, and moved to the southern end of the Golfe de Fos. *Prevail* laid a Dan buoy to mark the southern end of the approach channel, and the minesweepers resumed their effort along a north-south line. They began to cut moored French Sautter-Harle mines which—freed of their tether to the sea floor—bobbed to the surface and were exploded with rifle fire. When the formation started to turn at the northern end of the swept channel, gun salvos from batteries at Cap Méjean (south-southeast of Toulon) and in the Marseilles area began falling among the sweepers. A smoke screen was immediately ordered and the formation carried on in the normal manner. Two destroyers, *Rodman* (DD-456) and *Somers* (DD-381), were assigned to protect the minesweepers, but they did not fire because the shore batteries were out of range of their guns.[11]

During this work, two sub-chasers (SCs), equipped for "skim-minesweeping," led the flotilla flagship HMS *Rothesay* and other British minesweepers performing echelon minesweeping astern of her. The primary duty of the sub-chasers—which were fitted with captured German sweep gear—was to sweep ahead of larger, deeper draft minesweepers to protect the latter from "close-to-the-surface mines." Their secondary duty was to sweep in confined and shallow harbor waters too shallow to allow AMs and YMSs to operate. After *Rothesay* and the rest of the flotilla ships had swept a return lap down the centerline of the channel, Commander Martin altered the pattern of sweeping due to persistent danger from the coastal shore batteries.[12]

The operations described above were supported by the six motor launches of the British 13th Minesweeping Flotilla—MLs *338*, *462*, *554*, *565*, *569*, and *575*. Two of the launches were detailed as standby ships to replace the sub-chasers, should they fall out during sweeping in Golfe de Fos. The remaining MLs followed astern of the 13th M/S Flotilla for mine disposal purposes, exploding French mines, severed from their moors and adrift on the water's surface, with rifle fire.[13]

MOTOR TORPEDO BOAT *PT-555* DAMAGED

During the sweep operations, *PT-555* came up the channel. The commanding officer of the USN motor torpedo boat, Ens. Howard Boyce, told Commander Martin that he had a French officer aboard and was taking him into Port de Bouc. He asked Martin for any information he could give him. Martin warned him of the enemy gunfire and that the gulf was reported to be mined, and that he had no details as to their locations. Boyce replied that he was going in, and departed at high speed.[14]

PT-555 had been sent to ascertain whether or not there were any enemy forces remaining in the port. Capitaine de Frégate Bataille was to determine the situation and go ashore, if possible. The motor torpedo boat proceeded via the channel being swept and under fire of shore batteries in the vicinity of Carry-le-Rouet, she dashed for the port entrance and entered safely. Bataille and an American officer, Lt. Walker, went ashore. At the completion of their inspection, they returned aboard *PT-555* and stood out to sea, bound for the cruiser *Augusta*, the flagship of Rear Adm. Lyal A. Davidson, commander Task Force 86.[15]

While proceeding in early evening along a route believed to be safe by local fishermen, *PT-555* caught the snag line of a mine, near Cap Couronne buoy, at the east side of the entrance to the gulf. The detonation damaged the boat, from the forward bulkhead of the engine room aft to the stern, killing five crewmen and breaking the leg of a sixth. The five men—which included the gun crew of the aft 40mm mount were blown off the boat and the body of only one of the men was found. A French fishing boat picked up surviving officers and men, whereupon it also hit a mine and sank. Fortunately it suffered no personnel casualties. Another boat arrived and *PT-555*—which amazingly, although down by the stern, was still afloat—was towed to Carro, a fishing village located to the southeast of Port de Bouc.[16]

A seaplane from *Philadelphia* arrived with medical supplies and food, and evacuated the man with the broken leg. It, and other planes from the cruiser, had been keeping Port de Bouc and the surrounding land areas under surveillance and had earlier sighted the French colors flying as far eastward as Carry-le-Rouet.[17]

MINESWEEPING OPERATIONS CONTINUE

Earlier, following the departure of *PT-555* for Port de Bouc, the British minesweeper *Rothesay* had detached from the formation to guide the cruiser *Quincy* (CA-71) through the cleared area to enable her to get close enough to shoot at the shore batteries. At Martin's request, Mine Flotilla 19—then cruising to seaward of the southern end of the swept channel—detached three ships to similarly sweep ahead of the cruiser *Philadelphia* (CL-41) so that she might bring the batteries within range of her guns, and lead *Quincy* back out to sea on completion of her shooting. With sundown approaching and *Quincy*'s shore bombardment concluded, *Rothesay* withdrew down the channel and formed up the sweeping force ready for cruising to seaward during the night. The minesweepers had swept thirty-eight mines that day despite shelling from shore batteries prior to their location and silencing by the cruisers.[18]

That evening Capt. W. L. Messmer, USN, commander Escort Sweeper Group, Mediterranean embarked aboard the minesweeper tender *Barricade* (ACM-3), informed Martin that aerial reconnaissance had revealed two lines of mines stretching almost entirely across the Golfe de Fos entrance. Every other one was reported as having a snag line. Messmer recommended an approach through the eastern side.[19]

Photo 13-1

Barricade, ex-U.S. Army mine planter *Colonel John Storey*, served as a minesweeper tender following her transfer to the Navy in 1944.
Naval History and Heritage Command photo #NH 79737

Philadelphia provided protection for the minesweepers for the next two days before departing for Marseilles. Following her arrival there, the commanding officer, Capt. Walter Ansel, USN, went ashore on the island of Ratonneux, supported by a landing party of Marines from *Philadelphia* and *Augusta*, and received the surrender of the French islands of Pomegues, Ratonneux, and the Chateau d'If from Kapitan Leutenant Fullgrabe. These islands—familiar to all readers of *The Count of Monte Cristo*—defended the French city. (The terms of the surrender are provided in Appendix F.)[20]

Following the minesweeping effort to clear a safe channel through waters leading to the entrance of Golfe de Fos, Shallow-draft minesweepers then worked the gulf waters shoreward to the Port de Bouc channel entrance, where a mine disposal party was put ashore. Situated northwest of Marseilles, the Golfe de Fos was neither an estuary nor a pure sea gulf, because it received fresh water from the

Etang de Berre lagoon and was also influenced by the Rhône River delta.[21]

BOAT MINESWEEPERS (BMS) REPORT FOR DUTY

> The work done by these Boat Minesweepers was splendid both during and after the Assault. Their attachment to a major sweeping unit is of considerable value and it is recommended that whenever possible they should be so attached as an integral part of the unit, particularly when opening up new inshore areas and ports suspected of minelaying.
>
> Despite long hours and lack of any physical comforts the crews of these little craft were at all times zealous and undaunted and carried out their duties well.
>
> Whilst operating under my orders Ensign [T. H.] Greene carried out his duties as Officer in Charge, BMS Section 2, with efficiency and diligence and I add my appreciation of the work which he and the Boats under his command did during the time they were attached to my sweeping force.
>
> —Comdr. Alister Angus Martin, RNR[22]

Over the next three days, 25-27 August, Commander Martin had available to him six British *J*-class minesweepers, eight American YMSs, and several British motor launches and American LCVPs. The fleet tug *Hopi* had rendezvoused with the minesweeper tender *Barricade* in Cavalaire Bay, off southeast France, and taken under tow four LCVPs (Higgins boats) for delivery to the sub-chaser *SC-978* in the Golfe de Fos off Marseilles. The 36-foot wooden landing craft were fitted with Size 5 sweep gear and titled BMS (boat minesweepers). This designation was short lived and changed to LCVP minesweepers. Their shallow 3-foot drafts allowed the craft to work constricted port and harbor waters denied larger minesweepers. Other LCVPs were made ready for tow and larger 136-foot wooden minesweepers, *YMS-27*, *199*, and *251*, dispatched to join the sweepers assigned to Martin. As the J-class and YMS minesweepers performed "check sweeps" of the swept channel leading to Port de Bouc, the smaller MLs and LCVP minesweepers worked shallower areas of the gulf and the port inself.[23]

A reconnaissance party of twenty men led by Captain English (a member of Hewitt's staff) went ashore at Port de Bouc in mid-afternoon on 26 August to set up radio communications and to inspect the harbor. They found two barges loaded with contact and influence mines, which an accompanying U.S. Naval mine disposal officer rendered harmless. The survey identified that the entrance to the harbor was partially blocked by two sunken ships, and that the inner harbor was only large enough to berth two Liberty ships.²⁴

SALVAGE FORCES ORDERED TO PORT DE BOUC
On 27 August I French Corps began landing over the beaches in the Gulf of St. Tropez. Also, the French Army B reported that all organized resistance had ceased in Toulon, except for the St. Mandrier Peninsula. That same day Golfe de Fos was swept clear of mines to the 4-fathom line, 55 mines having been detonated. A channel into Port de Bouc was cleared in early afternoon of that day.²⁵

Earlier that morning, the tank landing ship *LST-134* had arrived off the port with four pontoon causeways of the 1040th Construction (Seabee) Battalion. The Seabees aboard her immediately went ashore and commenced clearing debris. By early evening the inner harbor was ready to accept cargo ships with drafts up to twenty-two feet and tankers of 26-foot draft.²⁶

With the port now marginally open, Admiral Hewitt ordered Task Forces 84, 85, and 87 to send designated salvage ships then assigned to Operation DRAGOON to Rear Admiral Davidson, commander Task Force 86 (Support Forces, Western Naval Task Force). Within a few days Naval Salvage Group U.S. Eighth Fleet (Task Group 80.11) was established. Charged with opening the ports of Marseilles, Toulon, and Port de Bouc, it consisted of all salvage forces then available to Hewitt, less those still required at the assault beaches, supported by men and equipment from U.S. Navy Salvage Base Dellys, Algeria.²⁷

As German forces surrendered at Toulon and Marseilles, minesweepers continued expanding their operations to other ports. On 28 August, two channels into Marseilles were swept. On the same day at Port de Bouc, the inner harbor was swept and as no mines were found the area was declared safe. A naval detachment was established that day consisting of two officers and five enlisted men responsible for port operations.²⁸

Twelve American and British salvage vessels, tugs, and boom defense vessels arrived at Port de Bouc the following day, as well as eight Fairmile "B" type motor launches of the British 3rd ML Flotilla:
- Rescue tug *ATR-1*
- Harbor tug *Edenshaw* (YTB-459)
- Salvage ship *Tackle* (ARS-37)
- Boom defense vessels HMS *Bardolf* (Z171) and HMS *Barholm* (Z211)
- Rescue tug HMS *Mindful* (W135)

- Coastwide tugs HMS *Empire Ann* and HMS *Empire Spitfire*
- *LCT-16* and *LCI-950*
- Tank landing ships *LST-16* and *LST-268*
- Motor launches *121, 134, 338, 462, 554, 565, 569,* and *575*

The salvage vessels were under the direction of Lt. Comdr. George R. Whitmyre, USN. Embarked aboard *Tackle*, he was Officer in Charge of the Harbor Clearance Units at Port de Bouc, and Toulon, France.[29]

Shortly after the vessels arrived, the MLs commenced minesweeping in the harbor, and tugs *ATR-1* and *Edenshaw* began pumping water from the sunken French tanker *Le Langangere* while *Tackle* and LSTs *16* and *268* worked on a second tanker, *Le Dauphine*. The Navy Seabees were clearing a demolished bridge from Arles Canal, which connected Port Arles, located inland, to Port de Bouc. *Dauphine* was refloated on 1 September, and moored alongside the unfinished French ocean liner *Marechal Petain*, which the Germans had sunk in Martigues Canal, a waterway linking Martigues, a town on Etang de Berre, to Port de Bouc. (The war interrupted construction of the liner and she was towed to Port de Bouc for the duration of hostilities. Despite being torpedoed by the Germans to serve as a canal obstruction, she would be raised after the war and completed as the M.V. *La Marseillaise*.) The salvors also removed the French tug *Carqueiranne* from the port entrance, swung the bow of tug *Laborieux* clear of the entrance, and removed two barges as the last step in opening the port. On that same day Seabees completed extraction of the railroad bridge from Arles Canal.[30]

To open Toulon and Marseilles as rapidly as possible, Hewitt utilized Navy salvage forces and Seabees and U.S. Army 335th Engineers. There were many challenges to overcome in these operations, and some losses of men and ships as well. *YMS-21* was sunk by a moored mine in Equillette Roads, a part of the inner harbor at Toulon, and a British LCM landing craft detonated a mine at Marseilles off the entrance to Vieux Port. To expedite salvage efforts at Vieux, a British submarine and a French submarine were sent to Marseilles to furnish electrical power for Army engineers in the port. At Port de Bouc, HMS *Empire Ann* struck an underwater obstacle while conducting salvage operations—breaking her propeller and rendering herself inoperable—and a mine detonation sank the French tug *Provencal*, and damaged the salvage ship *Tackle*.[31]

PROVENCAL SUNK AND *TACKLE* DAMAGED

One or more passes by minesweepers through suspect waters did not necessarily ensure complete clearance because some German mines were equipped with ship counters, an anti-minesweeping device designed to allow a designated number of vessels to pass near a mine before it detonated. YMSs *13*, *20*, *27*, *199*, and *251* arrived on 3 September with orders to base at Port de Bouc and conduct maintenance sweeps of Golfe de Fos. The following afternoon, the small French tug *Provencal* was astern of *Tackle*, assisting her to back, stern first, into Bassin Petrolier ("tanker dock") to berth alongside a sunken tanker serving as a pier, when she detonated a mine under her stern. The explosion sank the tug and propelled a geyser of water 100 feet in the air, which crashed down over the entire after portion of *Tackle*. *Edenshaw* was towing ahead but no casualties or damage resulted. *Tackle* suffered split hull seams, as well as damage to her propeller, rudder, and main shaft. Topside, her three-inch gun platform buckled, and deep inside the ship, shock effects caused considerable machinery derangement. *Tackle's* casualties from the blast were: two crewmen killed, one missing and presumed dead, twelve injured—three critically.[32]

Photo 13-2

S.S. *Stanley Dollar*, a West Coast lumber steamer, was renamed *W. R. Chamberlain Jr.* and later became USS *Tackle* in 1943. She retained her two lumber-handling masts with their eight booms during her service as a salvage ship.
U.S. Naval History and Heritage Command photograph

Three crewmen from *Provencal* went missing as well, and were also presumed dead. All ship movements in the area were suspended and a thorough sweep was begun in the harbor. *YMS-27* performed a magnetic acoustic sweep but did not detonate any sea mines. She had previously conducted a magnetic sweep in the harbor on 27 August, assisted by minesweeping boats towing her magnetic cable into various inaccessible areas.[33]

Tackle's berth alongside the tanker dock, in almost constant use for the preceding five days, had been previously swept for acoustic and magnetic mines by YMSs, and had been swept by MLs each day, from 29 August through 3 September. The commanding officer of *YMS-83* described difficulties experienced in sweeping the mouth of Port de Bouc inner harbor in a war diary entry:

> This was extremely tricky because of the "block" ships [sunk by the Germans to prevent the use of the port] and a torpedo net at the entrance and wrecks all though the harbor.[34]

Although booby traps had not been found in the port area, a mine may have been attached to a buoy which *Provencal* scraped. The consensus of opinion among minesweeping officers at Port de Bouc tended toward a magnetic mine of 500 pounds or more, triggered by a proximity device with a "click" (ship counter). After a day of sweeping and no additional mines found, the harbor was reopened the morning of 5 September. The first Liberty ship to enter Port de Bouc berthed alongside Quai de la Caronte. A second berth was also available on this day. At Toulon, salvors had cleared piers and docks for eight merchant vessels, where a Liberty ship had already entered port and was readied for unloading. Marseilles was not yet open. Mine clearance continued at Vieux Port (the Old Port of Marseilles), and in the harbor of Nice eighty-five miles to the east-northeast.[35]

SUMMATION OF EFFORTS

Despite the loss of French tug *Provencal*, and damage to salvage ship *Tackle* from an explosive device, likely a mine, and attendant loss of life in Port de Bouc, the minesweeping effort to open the port in such a short time was considered a great success. A total of 172 mines had been cleared from the approaches, Golfe de Fos, and Port de Bouc, and when the work was completed on 29 August, the 13th M/S Flotilla was ordered to the Marseilles area. A majority of the mines—126 German moored contact mines, many with snag lines—were cut in a dense field laid across the entrance to the gulf. Commander Escort Sweeper Group, Mediterranean attributed the success to Comdr. Alister Angus Martin, RNR:

[The] clearance of Golfe de Fos and Port de Bouc approach channel, anchorage and harbor…was accomplished, and very thoroughly, in an amazing short time, chiefly because of the careful planning of the Senior Officer, 13th Minesweeping Flotilla, and the minesweeping skill of himself and of his forces.[36]

Martin was awarded the Distinguished Service Order (DSO) and Distinguished Service Cross (DSC) with two bars, and mentioned in dispatches three times during the war. He would retire in 1958 with the rank of captain.[37]

In his own report, Martin praised British and American naval officers who had operated under his direction:

> I was particularly fortunate in having as my second-in-command - until the arrival of Commander [Norman Eyre] Morley in H.M.S. "RHYL" - so able and experienced an officer as Lieutenant-Commander C. R. [Charles Robertson] Fraser, R.N.R. of H.M.S. "ARIES". This officer knows the flotilla well and was able to take over his temporary attachment to us in his stride. Lieutenants Morley and Belknap of the Y.M.Ss and S.Cs respectively very soon showed me that they had a sound grasp of all the requirements and at all times had their ships on the top line for any assignment. Lieutenant Jenkins with three of his ships was attached for only a comparatively short period but during that time he gave much and willing help. Lieutenants Duffy and Edmundson and Ensign [T. H.] Greene of the Boat sweeper sections, gave grand service and deserve high praise for their handling of these little craft and their crews. We did what we could for them to make their lot less uncomfortable and although this was not very much I think they knew where they belonged.
>
> The feeling of team work between the ships was complete and I could not wish to have had the honour of commanding a better unit, which I trust has played its part in this vast and brilliantly planned operation.[38]

Following the surrender of Marseilles and Toulon on 28 August, and the opening of these major ports, the need for Port de Bouc lessened and it was thereafter used mainly for petroleum discharge and storage. The port was situated near a large airfield and was, thus, ideal for landing the gasoline necessary to support the shore air operations. It also served admirably as a staging point for small tankers that loaded and delivered fuel to beaches and other French ports.[39]

The Small Boat Mediterranean Minesweeping Unit, of which the LCVP sweepers at Port de Bouc were a part, was awarded a Navy Unit

Commendation for operations from 15 August to 30 September 1944 in southern France waters—the only such award garnered by minesweeping boats during World War II.

14

War Ends in Europe

> *The Allied Armies, through sacrifice and devotion and with God's help, have wrung from Germany a final and unconditional surrender. The western world has been freed of the evil forces which for five years and longer have imprisoned the bodies and broken the lives of millions upon millions of free-born men. They have violated their churches, destroyed their homes, corrupted their children, and murdered their loved ones. Our Armies of Liberation have restored freedom to these suffering peoples, whose spirit and will the oppressors could never enslave.*
>
> *Much remains to be done. The victory won in the West must now be won in the East. The whole world must be cleansed of the evil from which half the world has been freed. United, the peace-loving nations have demonstrated in the West that their arms are stronger by far than the might of dictators or the tyranny of military cliques that once called us soft and weak. The power of our peoples to defend themselves against all enemies will be proved in the Pacific war as it has been proved in Europe.*
>
> —Excerpts of a proclamation read by American President Harry S. Truman during a radio broadcast on 8 May 1945, informing listeners that Germany had surrendered

The Invasion of France in late 1944 enabled men and munitions to pour onto the Continent through Marseilles, Toulon, Cherbourg, Le Havre, and Rouen, France; and Antwerp, Belgium, in support of the Allied armies advancing ever deeper into Germany. During the early months of 1945, with German military strength greatly diminished, the U.S. Navy began to eliminate bases in Africa and Europe that were no longer needed and to disestablish commands. In March, the Eighth Fleet was dissolved. Admiral Hewitt had commanded it since its inception in March 1943 as U.S. Naval Forces, Northwest African Waters. The following month, naval forces and bases in the Mediterranean Theater were placed administratively under commander, U.S. Naval Forces in Europe. (Hewitt succeeded Adm. Harold R. Stark as both commander Twelfth Fleet, and commander U.S. Naval Forces in Europe, on 16 August 1945.)[1]

The final battles between Allied and German forces took place in late April and the first week in May 1945. Adolf Hitler committed suicide on 30 April—as the Battle of Berlin raged above his command bunker below the city—after designating Grossadmiral Karl Donitz as his successor. Donitz initially vowed to fight on, but quickly changed his mind. On 7 May General Alfred Jodl, chief-of-staff of the German Armed Forces High Command, signed surrender documents for all the German military forces at Reims, France, only eight days after Hitler's death. The following day, Field Marshal Wilhelm Keitel (chief of the General Staff of the German Armed Forces, and the representative of the army) signed a similar document in Berlin, surrendering to Soviet forces in the presence of Gen. Georgi Zhukov and other Allied and Axis representatives. The other representatives present at the signing of the second Act of Military Surrender were:

- Air Chief Marshal Arthur William Tedder (deputy Supreme Commander of the Allied Expeditionary Force)
- General-Admiral Hans-Georg von Friedeburg (commander-in-chief of the German Navy)
- Colonel-General Hans-Jürgen Stumpff (representative of the German Air Force)[2]

Following the capitulation of Germany, the U.S. Navy accelerated military downsizing efforts already in progress and began transferring personnel and material no longer required in Europe either home to the United States, or to the Pacific Theater. Nearly all naval advanced bases and supply and repair facilities in Britain and the Mediterranean were also closing at a rapid rate. By July, Naval Operating Base, Oran, in the African Theater, was disestablished and replaced by a naval detachment. That same month, the Moroccan Sea Frontier command was abolished and the naval facilities at Port Lyautey, Casablanca, Dakar, and Agadir were organized as a naval task group. The naval advanced base at Bizerte was turned over to the French Navy, and reductions were effected at Naples and Palermo, Italy. In France, Italy, and North Africa, the operation of most of the liberated ports was returned to the national authorities. U.S. port detachments were maintained at Le Havre and Marseilles, France; and at Naples, Italy, to aid in the Army's redeployment program.[3]

In June 1945 U.S. Naval Forces, Germany was established, with headquarters at Frankfurt. Its commander Vice Adm. Robert L. Ghormley assumed operational control of all naval forces on the Continent assigned to occupational duties, or otherwise in support of U.S. Army forces in the European Theater. Rear Adm. Arthur G.

Robinson (commander, U.S. Ports and Bases Germany under Ghormley) was responsible for the operation of the ports of Bremen and Bremerhaven in the Weser River Enclave. These ports, the only ones under American control in Germany, served as supply and evacuation points for U.S. occupational forces, and their shipyards provided a means to repair German and Allied vessels in the area.[4]

THE SPOILS OF WAR

Allied countries and the Soviet Union were very interested in obtaining particular type ships of the German Navy, because of their technological superiority. On 12 July 1945 the Chief of Naval Operations requested that commander United States Naval Forces in Europe provide a complete list of captured vessels over 900 tons transferred from Germany to the United Kingdom since V-E Day. Nine days later Admiral Stark forwarded to the British Admiralty an urgent request for two ex E-boats (which the Germans called Schnellboot) of the 3,000 horsepower super-charged type, which the U.S. Navy desired in connection with the redesign of PT boats for use in the Pacific War. In response to this query, two Schnellboot (*S-218* and *S-225*) were sent to New York for study and operation.[5]

Ultimately, five S-boats (Schnellboot) were brought to the United States. The first was salvaged in LeHavre harbor and transported by ship to the New York Navy Yard. Because her hull number was never identified, she was designated as captured enemy equipment (*CEE #6527*). Of the other four Schnellboot, the *S-116*, *S-218*, and *S-225* were taken to New York for analysis, while *S-706* ended up at the Philadelphia Navy Yard. *S-218* was determined to be in the best condition and she was destined to be the most active of the four Schnellboot at the New York Navy Yard. The Navy assigned her to commandant, Third Naval District, and placed her in service as small boat *C-105180*. Work in progress, to make *S-116* and *S-225* operational, was suspended due to limited funding on 29 March 1946. By the end of the decade, *CEE #6527* had been destroyed and the remaining boats sold off.[6]

Soon other requests followed the one for the S-boats, attesting to the quality and innovation of German design, engineering, and fabrication. The U.S. Coast Guard expressed interest in the 295-foot sail training ship *Horst Wessel*—a three-masted sailing barque commissioned in 1936—and was informed by commander, U.S. Naval Forces in Europe on 26 July 1945, that the ship was deemed suitable for use at the Coast Guard Academy following dry-docking and an overhaul to make her operational. *Horst Wessel* had been selected by the Soviet Union during the division of German vessels by the principal Allied nations. The four available sailing vessels had been split into three lots, with two large merchant ships grouped together. In a draw to determine the order of selection, the Soviets drew number one, Great Britain number two, and the U.S. number three. Before the results of the draw were officially announced the U.S representative, through quiet diplomacy, convinced the Soviets to trade draws—and thus the Coast Guard acquired its desired vessel. Following completion of the work necessary to make her ready for the Atlantic crossing, the barque was commissioned as USCG *Eagle* on 15 May 1946, and sailed from Bremerhaven to New London, Connecticut, the home of the U.S. Coast Guard Academy. *Eagle* is still in service today, the only active commissioned sailing ship in the U.S. maritime services.[7]

Photo 14-1

USCG barque *Eagle* near New London, Connecticut.
Source: https://www.uscg.mil/datasheet/wixtrain.asp

On the morning of 30 July 1945, the ex-German fleet torpedo boat *T-35* and ex-German destroyer *Z-39* sailed from Plymouth, England, for America. Onboard were nucleus German crews and supplemental personnel from Amphibious Bases, United Kingdom, under two U.S. Navy commanding officers and engineering officers. Commander, Destroyer Mission Europe (Task Group 120.6) was responsible for the operation. Although classified a torpedo boat, *T-35*—which was equipped with anti-surface and anti-air guns, as well as torpedoes and mines—was comparable to a medium-sized destroyer. The two ships arrived at Boston, Massachusetts on 8 August, and reported to commandant, First Naval District for duty. They were commissioned as USS *DD-935* and *DD-939*, respectively, and conducted trials that autumn, but were eventually transferred to France in 1947 for use as spare parts for ships that it had acquired.[8]

Photo 14-2

USS *DD-935*, the ex-German fleet torpedo boat *T-35*, in 1945.
Photo from Die deutschen Flottentorpedoboote von 1942 bis 1945, http://www.navsource.org/archives/05/0593501.jpg

BRANT ESCORTS U-BOATS TO AMERICA

On 5 August 1945 Capt. George A. Sharp, USN, embarked aboard the salvage ship *Brant* at Lisahally, Northern Ireland, to oversee the escort of two German war prizes, submarines *U-2513* and *U-3008*, across the Atlantic to Naval Submarine Base, New London, Connecticut. Sharp was the commander of a clandestine task group titled Submarine Mission Europe (Task Group 120.2) that had been sent to Lisahally in Lough Foyle (near Londonderry) to obtain two of the Kriegsmarine's sophisticated "Elektroboote" U-boats. These electric boats were the first submarines designed to operate primarily submerged, rather than as surface ships that could submerge as a means to escape detection or launch an attack. Sharp's group, comprised of 150-200 officers and men formed in New London, had arrived at Lisahally, in May, to find and sail these high-technology submarines to New London with

American crews. The specific objective was to obtain two of the newly-developed, 1600-ton, high-speed, quiet-running XXI U-Boats.[9]

On 4 May in anticipation of Germany's surrender, the Kriegsmarine ordered all U-boats to cease under way operations and return to their Norwegian ports. Reichspräsident Karl Donitz, the former commander of submarines and commander-in-chief of the Navy, then directed Alfred Jodl to sign the German instruments of surrender in Reims, France, on 7 May. Because the Soviet representative in Reims had no authority to sign the German instrument of surrender, the Soviet leadership considered the Reims surrender as a preliminary act, and thus, it was repeated the following day in Berlin. The Allies then directed all U-boats to surrender; those at sea were to head for one of a number of designated reception ports, the prime one being Loch Eriboll in northwest Scotland. Upon the arrival of submarines in Great Britain, their crews surrendered and the U-boats were moved to Lisahally, or to Loch Ryan in southwest Scotland, which offered a natural harbor and calm waters for shipping plying between Scotland and Northern Ireland.[10]

As a result of discussions between Marshal Stalin, President Truman, and Prime Ministers Churchill and (later) Attlee at Potsdam near Berlin, between 17 July and 2 August, it was decided that only thirty U-boats would be retained and the rest destroyed. Those kept were to be divided equally between Great Britain, America, and the Soviet Union. A Tripartite Naval Commission, set up to recommend the specific allocations to each country, began its work on 15 August 1945. On 10 October it announced that, of the 135 U-boats in the United Kingdom, 8 were to go to Great Britain, one to the United States, and ten to the Soviet Union.[11]

However, well before this decision, Captain Sharp's group, assisted by the *Brant*, had spirited two coveted XXI U-boats to America. None of this type submarine had surrendered from sea in America. Thus, if the U.S. Navy was to acquire the two submarines it desired, they would have to be from among the 12 Type XXI U-Boats that were in Royal Navy custody at Lisahally. Moreover, it was expected that the allocation process would not be completed before the end of 1945. Accordingly, the U.S. Navy, with support from the Royal Navy, took covert action to acquire the boats without informing the Russians.[12]

Brant—which had arrived loaded with Type XXI spare parts to support the submarines at Lisahally from Bremerhaven, Germany, the site of one of the main bases for the Kriegsmarine—departed Northern Ireland on 6 August, bound with the *U-2513* and *U-3008* for

America. That evening, she was forced to enter Lough Foyle, the estuary of the River Foyle in Ulster, to make repairs to the latter submarine. The group resumed its transit on 8 August, with *U-3008* in tow behind the salvage ship. The Atlantic crossing was uneventful. Following an overnight stop at Argentia, Newfoundland, the salvage ship and submarines continued on to New London. Upon their arrival on 25 August, Capt. Sharp disembarked from *Brant* and the salvage ship reported for duty to commander Service Force, Atlantic Fleet.[13]

Photo 14-3

Former German submarines *U-2513*, *U-3008*, and possibly *U-505* at New London, circa 1945.
Courtesy of Scott Koen and ussnewyork.com,
http://www.navsource.org/archives/08/0835800.jpg

15

Post-War Occupation Duty

> *On 15 August [1945] President Truman was able to announce the unconditional surrender by the Japanese Imperial Government. Orders were sent out for the occupation of Japan and Korea.... Overnight [there was] a change in the attitude of the men in the combat zone from one of war to one of peace. Suddenly everybody wanted to go home. No one was interested in becoming a member of the occupational forces.*
>
> —Excerpts from a description by Vice Adm. Daniel E. Barbey, USN (Ret.) in *MacArthur's Navy* about the perspective of Sailors and Marines in the Pacific following the end of World War II, which could also describe the attitude of servicemen in Europe after the cessation of fighting there[1]

The Allied post-war occupation of Germany was a huge and diverse undertaking; one that would last until the mid-1950s. On V-E Day, there were sixty-one U.S. Army divisions—1,622,000 soldiers—in Germany. The divisions in the field became occupation troops responsible for maintaining law and order, and establishing the Allies military presence in the defeated nation. These security troops manned border control stations, maintained checkpoints at road junctions and bridges, conducted roving patrols to apprehend curfew and circulation violators, and served as guards at Displaced Persons' Camps, jails, banks, railroad bridges, telephone exchanges, and factories. The camps were temporary facilities primarily for refugees from Eastern Europe and for the former internees of the German concentration camps.[2]

The role of the U.S. Navy, led by Twelfth Fleet subordinate commands, was to support the Army. As part of the reduction of American presence in Africa and Europe, the Eighth Fleet had been dissolved in March 1945, and Admiral Hewitt had relieved Adm. Harold R. Stark as commander Twelfth Fleet on 16 August 1945.

Twelfth Fleet: Adm. Henry Kent Hewitt, USN

Task Group or Force	Commander
Task Force 124 – U.S. Naval Forces, Germany	Vice Adm. R. L. Ghormley
Task Force 126 – U.S. Ports and Bases, Germany	Rear Adm. A. G. Robinson
Task Group 126.1 – U.S. Naval Advanced Base, Bremerhaven	Capt. H. R. Holcomb
Task Group 126.2 – U.S. Naval Advanced Base, Bremen	Capt. C. R. Jeffs
Task Group 126.3 – Weser River Patrol	
Task Group 126.4 – Inshore Patrol	
Task Group 126.5 – Minesweeping	Lt. Comdr. E. J. T. Payne, RNVR
Task Group 126.6 – Salvage Group	Col. William F. Way, USA
Task Group 126.7 – CBMU 636, Bremen – Bremerhaven	Lt. L. J. Murphy[3]

Vice Adm. Robert L. Ghormley, USN was the overall commander of U.S. Naval Forces, Germany and under him, Rear Adm. Arthur G. Robinson, USN, headed the U.S. Ports and Bases, Germany command. Surprisingly the command structure included an Army colonel as head of the salvage group instead of Commodore Sullivan. Sullivan had been called away to take on an even greater undertaking than that awaiting in Europe. The majority of the U.S. Navy salvors who had performed Eighth Fleet salvage work during the war had either returned to America or were in the Pacific engaged in post-war salvage work. Much of this work involved the clearance of wrecks, munitions, and other debris from Japanese and Korean ports and harbors, so that ships could safely enter to take off former Allied prisoners of war and to land occupation troops.

Sullivan had flown to Australia at the bequest of General MacArthur, about the time of the Anzio landings, to discuss clearance of Manila harbor as a part of the Philippine Islands Campaign. Following this meeting, Sullivan went back to the Mediterranean for a time. When he returned to the Pacific, he brought with him some of the most experienced salvors from the European Theater, and others from the United States. As work progressed at Manila, it became evident that the number of vessels sunk there, greatly exceeded those in any other harbor cleared during the war. Divers kept finding more and more wrecks resting on the bottom until roughly 750 ships, barges, and craft had been removed from Manila Bay.[4]

Rear Adm. Arthur G. Robinson's initial objectives were to establish control of the Weser River and its estuary in the Bremen-Bremerhaven Enclave, to obtain control of German Naval activities,

and to effect primary naval disarmament in the area. Once these missions were accomplished, he began efforts to:
- open, operate, and control the ports of Bremen and Bremerhaven to the extent necessary for the maintenance of the United States occupying forces
- effect the final Naval disarmament, control, and disposal of German war materials, demolition of German defenses, and seizure of Naval Records[5]

MINESWEEPING OPERATIONS

Just as at other captured ports, mine clearance operations were necessary before Bremerhaven and Bremen could be opened. British minesweepers began working the ocean approaches to the port city of Bremerhaven on 2 June, and dredging operations to deepen the channel leading to the port commenced three days later. On 16 June the first German prize ships—the cargo ship S.S. *Eichberg* and merchant vessel *Veservehr*—sailed from Bremerhaven for the United Kingdom. That same day, Konteradmiral Eberhard Godt, former chief-of-staff to commander U-boats, arrived for questioning about the disposal of submarines present in the Weser River before the arrival of Allied forces. The first Allied merchant ships arrived in port on 22 June. Meanwhile, minesweeping operations progressed upriver to other port facilities, amongst them, Brake and Nordenham which opened four days later to receive Liberty ships.[6]

To augment the efforts of the Royal Navy's 163rd Minesweeping Flotilla, British-supervised German minesweepers were used for the thirty-seven mile section of the Weser River, from Bremerhaven on the North Sea upriver to Bremen. On 7 September minesweeping operations in the Weser were completed and all Allied minesweepers sailed for the United Kingdom. Supervised German minesweepers continued working in the Cuxhaven Channel, an inland waterway leading from Bremerhaven to Cuxhaven on the North Sea. British clearance divers who had responsibility for clearing the ports completed their diving operations at Bremen on 20 September. Rear Admiral Robinson commended them for a job well done.[7]

NAVY SHIPS ORDERED TO BREMERHAVEN

Following the arrival of four patrol craft and other vessels to support and protect shipping in late June, river and harbor patrols were established in the Weser River and its estuary. The patrol craft—*PC-565*, *PC-568*, *PC-619*, and *PC-1176*—had sailed from Le Havre, France, on

15 June, in company with salvage ships *Brant* (ARS-32) and *Diver* (ARS-5), and rescue tug *ATR-4*, bound for Bremerhaven. Each of the salvage ships had one Navy fireboat in tow. Leaving there, calls were made at Ostende, Belgium, and Bertghaven and Den Helder, Holland, en route to Germany.[8]

ATR-4 proceeded from Holland to Bremerhaven via an old German coastal route that ran parallel to the coast about five miles offshore. The route was somewhat perilous at night because nearly all of the conical spar buoys, intended as aids to navigation, were unlighted and not in their charted positions. The tug also encountered strong currents off the mouth of the Weser River, but once inside, had only a short, sheltered passage upriver to reach Bremerhaven. *ATR-4* moored at the Kaiserhafen ("Emperor's Harbour") No. 1 Dock, in the early afternoon on 21 June, and her commanding officer, Lt. Thomas H. Rayburn, USN, reported to commander Task Force 126 for duty.[9]

Photo 15-1

Kaiserhafen dock in Bremerhaven.
http://www.usarmygermany.com/Sont.h tm?http&&&www.usarmygermany.com/ Units/Occupation/USAREUR_17thMaj orPort.htm

ATR-4 was assigned rescue tug duties for the remainder of the month and first eight days in July. As a part of the Navy's efforts to dispose of war materials, on 9 July she proceeded with barges loaded with German ammunition, into the Weser River en route to a dumping area off the coast. Three German landing craft also loaded with ammunition accompanied her. At the completion of this task, she returned in darkness to Bremerhaven early the following morning.[10]

The Disarmament Section of CTF-126 investigated and wrote reports on the status of German naval and merchant vessels, gun emplacements, and shore establishments. These included warehouses; petroleum, oil, and lubricant storage plants; and ammunition dumps. Recovered items were stored in central warehouses and categorized as "to be retained under the jurisdiction of the Navy," or as "common user" for turnover to the U.S. Army. War materials with no utility to either the Army or Navy, including German ammunition incompatible with American guns, were disposed of. Additional dumping missions were carried out, mid- to late-July, to "deep six" the last of the ammunition at Bremerhaven.[11]

From 27-31 July, *ATR-4* was assigned to river traffic control duty off Columbus Quay, to help ensure the safety of merchant vessels at anchor. A strong cross-current in the Bremerhaven Roadstead—created by sharp turns in the river—caused ships to ride at anchor, on ebb tides, with chain tending to port, and the slightest drag (movement of an anchor in river silt) would result in grounding on the west bank of the Weser. This type of misfortune required the service of a tug.[12]

The salvage ship *Diver* remained moored at Kaiserhafen No. 1 in standby duty status until 2 July, when she relieved *PC-565* as the guard (sentry) ship in the Nord Reede area of the Weser. She was released from this duty by the *Brant* on 6 July, and remained in port until it was her turn to relieve *PC-1176* as the Weser River Patrol ready ship. On 10 July *Diver* escorted five American merchant ships—*Atenas, Cape Horn, Cornelius Ford, Grace Abbott,* and *John McDonagh*—down the Weser River to sea. At completion of this duty, she berthed at Columbus Quay in Bremerhaven.[13]

Brant's duty, through late July, was similar to that of *Diver*; she escorted S.S. *Andrew Stevenson*, S.S. *Black Warrior*, a net tender, and a tug with tow downriver, and was assigned in rotation, standby status in port, ready ship, or guard ship duty on the Weser. These mundane duties ended on 25 July, when she moored at Columbus Quay for fuel and to load submarine equipment from Naval Technical Mission, Europe. By late afternoon, 404 pieces were aboard. Upon completion of loading the following morning, *Brant* got under way at 1101, in convoy for Londonderry, Ireland. Her duty, there, would be to escort war prizes greatly coveted by the U.S. Navy—German submarines *U-2513*, and *U-3008*—to America.[14]

After *Brant* departed, *Diver* was the only remaining salvage ship at Bremerhaven. She, like *Brant*, had been occupied by standby, guard, and ready ship duties. This changed on 27-28 July, with tasking to salvage a German minesweeper that had been damaged by an underwater explosion near Farge, approximately twenty-five miles upriver from Bremerhaven. The following month a second minesweeper struck a mine in the Weser above Brake, a sub-port of Bremen, and *Diver*'s salvors conducted rescue operations from 18-21 August. After three days of work to make the ship sufficiently seaworthy, the salvors were able to move her into a dry dock for repairs. The damage to both minesweepers was from river-emplaced ordnance, supposedly deactivated by German engineers prior to the commencement of sweep operations.[15]

The German mines in harbor areas and in the Weser River itself, varied in size from 600 to 2,200 pounds and were of four types; one of which was a new model that could not be swept. As a result, it was necessary for divers to locate the mines—a long and tedious operation—and either disarm or destroy them. Even with very skilled British and Dutch mine disposal parties engaged in this work, the ports and river were not officially declared cleared until 25 September. The mines in the river were neutralized through the use of cables which created electrical fields to drain the batteries inside the "ship killers."[16]

On 27 September *Diver* arrived at Uberseehafen, Bremen's principal harbor, to embark forty Navy men and one officer from the U.S. Naval Ship Salvage Group, for transport back to the United States. She proceeded downriver to Bremerhaven the following morning, and spent the next few days preparing for the Atlantic crossing. *Diver* left the port city on 4 October, in company with patrol craft *PC-565*, *568*, *619*, and *1176*. The group's first stop was a brief one—five hours in Jenny Cliff Bay, at Plymouth. Leaving England, the ships next touched land at Ponta Delgada in the Azores on 10 October, for fuel and water. The group departed São Miguel Island the morning of the 12th, and following an uneventful passage, entered Port Royal, Bermuda—site of the Royal Navy's principal base in the Western Atlantic—and moored at the Tender Pier. Standing out of the Great Sound the following day, there remained only two days of their voyage to Naval Operating Base, Norfolk, Virginia.[17]

Photo 15-2

German ocean liner S.S. *Europa*, before her conversion to the troop transport *Europa*.
Courtesy of Robert Bauer

Diver and the patrol craft were the last, of the seven vessels dispatched from Le Havre in June for duty at Bremerhaven, to leave that port. *ATR-4* had departed a little earlier on 28 September, but would be the very last to make her way home to America. From 7-11 September, she was assigned as the standby fire or emergency assistance ship for the transport *Europa* (AP-177), while the ex-German ocean liner fueled and prepared for sea alongside Columbus Quay. Built in 1929, the 50,000-ton ship had a cruising speed of 27.5 knots, enabling it to cross the Atlantic in a mere five days. Captured as a war prize, she was ideal for use as a troop transport ship. *ATR-4* escorted *Europa* to sea on the afternoon of 11 September. The large and fast vessel was bound for Southhampton, England, where she would load 4,500 American troops for passage to New York on her maiden voyage as a member of the Naval Transportation Service.[18]

Following this duty, *ATR-4* returned to Bremerhaven to undergo routine dry-docking and repairs. On 28 September it was finally her turn to depart Germany. She proceeded downriver and made passage to Sunderland on England's northeast coast. For the remainder of the year, the steam-propelled, wooden-hulled rescue tug—one of the eighty such U.S. Navy ships hurriedly built for war duty—performed towing assignments and odd chores such as dumping ammunition. The dawn of 1946 found her at Le Havre, France.[19]

Today, the former *ATR-4* is beached on Ile-aux-Grues (the island of cranes) near Quebec, Canada. Sporting a red hull and white superstructure, and named Le Bateau Ivre—the Drunken Boat, after the 19th century French poem—it is now a restaurant offering regional cuisine and a venue for get-togethers. It is a fitting ending to the veteran of the Normandy invasion that had sailed from New York Harbor for Europe on 25 March 1944.[20]

Photo 15-3

Ex *ATR-4* beached on l'Isle-aux-Grues (the island of cranes) near Quebec, Canada. Courtesy of Trip USA Canada (http://www.trip-usa-canada.com/wp-content/uploads/2014/05/MG_3440.jpg

Postscript

The EDENSHAW *has provided a fine example of resourcefulness and able handling in getting herself off the beach in good condition after being beached for over a month. During this time she underwent numerous strafing, bombing and shelling attacks. Recommendations for awards are the subject of separate correspondence.*

—Endorsement by Rear Adm. Frank J. Lowry, commander Task Force 81, on a report by commanding officer USS *Edenshaw* (YTB-459) on Operation SHINGLE, during which a strong storm set the harbor tug hard onto an Anzio assault beach.[1]

The unsung tugs and salvage ships that served in the African, European, and Mediterranean Theaters saved many vessels and cargos for future service, as well as the lives of men trapped aboard those aflame or sinking. Fleet, rescue, auxiliary, and harbor tugs supporting assault forces during landings also pulled off beaches scores of landing craft damaged by enemy aircraft attack, artillery, or coastal battery fire.

During violent gales, large ships operating near shore could normally hold their own, although some 441-foot Liberty ships were blown aground during the Invasion of Southern France. Smaller ships and craft with less powerful engines were more at the mercy of wind and wave. The diminutive harbor tug *Edenshaw* (YTB-459)—which, spanning a mere 102 feet, was smaller than the tank landing craft she routinely assisted—was washed by storm surge at Anzio over offshore sand bars onto the shore where, once the unusually large waves subsided, she was left high and dry.

METTLE OF TUG SAILORS

But for the valor of her commanding officer and crew, *Edenshaw* would have joined the list of tug and salvage ship casualties, presented following this account. Following her arrival at Anzio on 23 January 1944, *Edenshaw* commenced combat salvage operations; towing two tank landing craft off beaches, assisting in salvaging a third LCT, and towing the British fighter-direction ship HMS *Palomares* to Naples, Italy, for repair of damage caused by a mine strike. On 4 February, a heavy storm washed *Edenshaw*—then engaged in towing a section of a pontoon causeway—over a sand bar off Green beach. Efforts by her captain, R. L. Self, to back the tug clear were unsuccessful; so too were salvage efforts mounted by other ships, because of the severe weather. With no immediate hopes of salvation and his immobile ship as an obvious target, Self ordered most of the crew ashore, retaining only himself, the engineer, and two other men on board.[2]

Photo Postscript

Resolute (later renamed *Evea*), a sistership of *Edenshaw*, under way on 5 April 1942. Photo from the files of Gulfport Boiler and Welding Works; courtesy of Jim Swank and NavSource.

For the next thirty-two days 4 February to 7 March, *Edenshaw* remained beached and was subjected to aircraft attacks and heavy artillery fire. Despite strafing that caused structural damage to the tug, the skeleton crew kept the engines operative awaiting an opportunity to use them in refloating the ship. On 7 March the British rescue tug HMS *Prosperous* (W96) was able to run a wire to her—despite enemy fire then being directed at the smaller American tug and herself—and pulled *Edenshaw* clear to good water. *Edenshaw* assisted through the use of her propeller to scour sand away from the ship's hull.³

TUG AND SALVAGE SHIP LOSSES

Despite much time off hostile beaches and in other areas subject to attack, only one U.S. Navy salvage ship and three tugs were lost to enemy mine, torpedo, or aircraft ordnance in the African, Mediterranean, and European Theaters during the war. These losses coincided with the progression of Allied operations from North Africa across the narrow Sea of Sicily to the same named island, thence to Salerno and up the Italian boot, and finally at Normandy on the north coast of France. There were no American tug or salvage ship losses during the subsequent invasion of southern France.

Type Ship	Ship	Commanding Officer	Date Lost	Cause
salvage vessel	*Redwing* (ARS-4)	Lt. (jg) Martin C. Sibitsky, USN	27 Jun 1943	Sunk by mine off Bizerte, Tunisia
ocean tug	*Nauset* (AT-89)	Lt. Joseph Orleck, USN	9 Sep 1943	Sunk by German aircraft in the Gulf of Salerno, Italy
harbor tug	*YT-198*		18 Feb 1944	Sunk by a mine off Anzio, Italy; six crewmen were injured
old ocean tug	*Partridge* (ATO-138)	Lt. Adnah N. Caldin, USN	11 Jun 1944	Sunk after being torpedoed by German motor torpedo boats off Normandy, France

A fifth ship, *ATR-15*, incorrectly cited in some summaries of U.S. Navy ship losses as lost due to grounding off Normandy, France, on 19 June 1944, was actually repaired in England and returned to the United States.⁴

TRANSFER OF HARBOR TUGS TO THE FRENCH

In the final months of the war in Europe, as Allied forces continued to open French ports, the Eighth Fleet divested itself of the sister tugs *Evea* and *Edenshaw* as well as nineteen smaller harbor tugs (YTLs) via transfer to the French. In a representative handover, the French Navy took possession of *Edenshaw* and *Evea* under Lend-Lease at Toulon on 17 October and 10 November 1944, respectively. As 1945 broke, the French tugs *Evea* and *YTL-165* were attached to Port de Bouc, while other ex-U.S. Navy harbor tugs were already working in ports elsewhere in France and in North Africa.[5]

Date Transferred	Harbor Tugs
20 Mar 1944	*YTL-208, YTL-212*
12 Oct 1944	*YTL-186*
17 Oct 1944	*Edenshaw* (YTB-459)
19 Oct 1944	*YTL-161*
21 Oct 1944	*YTL-196*
27 Oct 1944	*YTL-210*
10 Nov 1944	*Evea* (YTB-458), *YTL-158, YTL-184*
14 Nov 1944	*YTL-197, YTL-207*
16 Nov 1944	*YTL-154, YTL-160*
29 Nov 1944	*YTL-165*
5 Jan 1945	*YTL-132, YTL-143, YTL-157, YTL-185*
1 Feb 1945	*YTL-209*
12 Feb 1945	*YTL-163*[6]

Admiral Hewitt had recommended that the salvage ship *Tackle* (ARS-37) be part of the transfer to the French along with *Evea* and *Edenshaw*. Subsequently the U.S. Navy chose instead to retain *Tackle* in service—at least until after she returned to America. Following the repair of her most grievous mine-inflicted damage, she was redesignated a salvage craft tender (ARST-4), and subsequently a miscellaneous unclassified ship (IX-217). Her new duty was short lived. With many more capable ships in excess following the war, there was no need for her service. The old work horse, which had been built in 1912, was decommissioned on 13 September 1945, and was struck from the Naval Vessel Register the following month.[7]

The Navy was also then disposing of old vessels that had served admirably in the American Theater. Disposal of *Allegheny* (ATO-19), commissioned in 1918, was representative of the others. She was a part of the Atlantic Fleet, serving out of Cape May, New Jersey, on anti-submarine patrol. After the war, she had an unceremonious end as recounted by former crewmember Thomas Runk:

> The ship went into a North Philadelphia dry dock for repairs. When an inspector was filling out his forms, he leaned against the outside hull for support. To his chagrin and our laughter, he fell though the rusted hull plates into the bilge. The ship was decommissioned 10 July 1945 and our reserve crewmembers were sent to Bainbridge for discharge.

As the old expression goes "She had given her all."[8]

Nearly all of the salvage ships, and fleet, rescue, and auxiliary tugs still plying African, Mediterranean, or European waters at the time of Germany's surrender returned to America. A few were sent to the Pacific Theater to join the large numbers of tugs and salvage ships preparing for the final push toward the Japanese home islands.

CONTINUED POST-WAR DOWNSIZING

Following the surrender of Japan in August 1945, the United States government accelerated the process of downsizing overseas military activities and services, and the Navy continued to downsize the Fleet. The transfer of some ships and craft to Allied nations overseas continued, but the majority of ships returned to the United States. The Navy laid up in Reserve Fleets the ones not required for active service, or disposed of them via transfer or lease to Allies, or by sale to private individuals.[9]

As previously noted, the Navy transferred all of its harbor tugs serving in the European Theater to the French Navy, except for *YT-198* and *YTM-392*. The *YT-198* had been sunk by a mine off Anzio, and *YTM-392* (later *Mecosta*) was retained for post-war service, and later sold. The larger 165-foot wooden rescue tugs and 143-foot steel auxiliary tugs returned to America. Most were disposed of. The powerful *Cherokee*-class 205-foot fleet tugs that returned from Europe were retained in service. Ten of these—*Abnaki*, *Algorma*, *Arapaho*, *Arikara*, *Bannock*, *Carib*, *Cocopa*, *Narragansett*, and *Pinto*—as well as the rescue tug *ATR-13* and salvage ship *Extricate*, sailed to join the Pacific war with Japan. *Arapaho*, *Arikara*, *Bannock*, and *Extricate* each earned a battle star at Okinawa, and *Pinto* one at Brunei Bay, Borneo. A summary of the service medals and unit awards that the tugs and salvage ships that served in the African, European, and Mediterranean Theaters received during World War II is provided in Appendix G.

Six fleet tugs: *Abnaki*, *Alsea*, *Arikara*, *Bannock*, *Cocopa*, and *Kiowa* continued to serve well beyond World War II. The last to leave naval service were *Abnaki* (ATF-96) and *Cocopa* (ATF-101), which were decommissioned on 30 September 1978 and struck from the Naval Register that same day.

Appendix A: Fleet Tugs

In the below table, the number of battle stars earned by a ship during World War II and/or the Korean War is indicated by a numeral, followed by a hyphen and BS for "battle star(s)." The acronyms for other unit awards listed follow:

CR:	Combat Action Ribbon
PUC:	Presidential Unit Citation
NUC:	Navy Unit Commendation
CGUC:	Coast Guard Unit Commendation
MUC:	Meritorious Unit Commendation
NE:	Navy Expeditionary Medal
KS:	Korean Service Medal
AE:	Armed Forces Expeditionary Medal
VS:	Vietnam Service Medal
PPUC:	Philippine Presidential Unit Citation
KPUC:	Korea Presidential Unit Citation
RVG:	Republic of Vietnam Gallantry Cross Unit Citation
RVM:	Republic of Vietnam Meritorious Unit Citation

Ship	Unit Awards	Commissioned	Commanding Officer	Disposition
Bethlehem Steel, Richmond, New York				
Navajo (ATF-64)	2-BS 1-CR	26 Jan 40	Lt. Comdr. M. E. Thomas	Exploded off Pago Pago and lost on 12 Sep 1943
Seminole (ATF-65)	1-BS 1-CR 1-NE 6-KS 2-AE 7-VS 8-RVM	8 Mar 40	Lt. Comdr. William G. Fewel	Sunk by gunfire off Tulagi, Solomon Islands, and lost on 25 Oct 1942
Cherokee (ATF-66)	1-BS	26 Apr 40	Lt. Comdr. P. L. F. Weaver	To Coast Guard 1946 as WATF-166
Charleston Shipbuilding, Charleston, South Carolina				
Apache (ATF-67)	7-BS 1-CR 2-NUC 1-MUC 2-KS 1-AE 1-VS	12 Dec 42	Lt. (jg) Clyde S. Horner	To Taiwan 1974 as *Ta Wan* (ATF-551), active
Arapaho (ATF-68)	4-BS	20 Jan 43	Lt. E. H. Wootan	To Argentina 1961 as *Comandante General Zapiola* (A-2), wrecked 1971

Name	Awards	Commissioned	Commanding Officer(s)	Disposition
Chippewa (ATF-69)		14 Feb 43	Lt. (jg) Anthony V. Swarthout	Decommissioned 1947, disposition unknown
Choctaw (ATF-70)		21 Apr 43	Lt. J. D. Garland	To Colombia 1961 as *Pedro de Heredia* (RM-72), active
Hopi (ATF-71)	4-BS	31 Mar 43	Lt. Oscar W. Huff	Struck 1963
Kiowa (ATF-72)	1-BS 1-NUC 1-NE 3-AE	7 Jun 43	Lt. William O. Kuykendall	Scrapped 1994
United Engineering Co., Alameda, California				
Menominee (ATF-73)	5-BS	25 Sep 42	Lt. Comdr. Emil C. Generaux Jr., USNR	To Indonesia 1961 as *Rakata* (A-922), active
Pawnee (ATF-74)	4-BS 1-PPUC	7 Nov 42	Lt. (jg) Frank C. Dilworth, USN	Struck 1962
Sioux (ATF-75)	5-BS 1-CR 1-KS 1-AE 5-VS	12 Jun 42	Lt. (jg) L. M. Jahnsen	To Turkey 1972 as *Gazal* (A-587), active
Ute (ATF-76)	5-BS 1-MUC 2-KS 9-VS	13 Dec 42	Lt. William F. Lewis	Sunk as target 1991
Hull numbers 77–80 used for old tugs later reclassified *ATF-77, 78, 79, 80*				
Bannock (ATF-81)	2-BS	28 Jun 43	Lt. Sam P. Morgan, Lt. John M. Goertner, USNR, Lt. Wesley C. Dreman	To Italy 1979 as CP-451, discarded
Carib (ATF-82)		24 Jul 43	Lt. Aubrey Hazel Gunn, USN	To Colombia 1979 as *Sebastian de Bedelcazar* (RM-73), active
Chickasaw (ATF-83)	8-BS 1-NUC 2-KS 1-PPUC	4 Feb 43	Lt. (jg) J. F. King	To Taiwan 1991 as *Ta Tung* (ATF-548), struck 1999
Cree (ATF-84)	6-BS 4-KS 1-AE	28 Mar 43	Lt. P. Bond	Sunk as target 1978
Lipan (ATF-85)	7-BS 2-NUC 4-KS 2-AE 3-VS 2-RVG	29 Apr 43	Lt. N. R. Terpening, Lt. Fred N. Beyer, Lt. Francis A. Butler, Lt. Comdr. Howard K. Smith, Lt. R. M. Hughson, Lt. Comdr. Donald L. Fitzgerald, Lt. Curtis O. Anderson, Lt. Comdr. Alex J. Viessmann, Lt. Comdr. David F. Chandler, Lt. Comdr. Joseph DeMarke, Lt. R. Genet	Sunk as target 1990
Mataco (ATF-86)	9-BS 4-KS 2-AE 7-VS	29 May 43	Lt. William G. Baker, Lt. Comdr. Downey M. Ware, Lt. Comdr. Robert A. Clair	Scrapped 1979

Fleet Tugs 275

Name	Awards	Commissioned	Commanding Officer(s)	Disposition
Cramp Shipbuilding Co., Philadelphia, Pennsylvania				
Moreno (ATF-87)	3-BS	30 Nov 42	Lt. (jg) Victor H. Kyllberg, USN	Struck 1961
Narragansett (ATF-88)	3-BS 1-CR	15 Jan 43	Lt. (jg) C. J. Wichmann	To Taiwan 1991, used for spare parts
Nauset (ATF-89)	2-BS	2 Mar 43	H. K. Wombacher, Lt. J. Orleck	Sunk by aircraft attack off Salerno 9 Sep 1943
Pinto (ATF-90)	2-BS 1-CR 1-NUC	1 Apr 43	Lt. Ralph Brown, USN	To Peru 1960 as *Guardian Rios* (ARA-123), active
Seneca (ATF-91)	4-NE 1-AE	30 Apr 43	Lt. Herman B. Conrad, Lt. Comdr. William C. Connell Jr., Lt. Comdr. James W. Hodges Jr., Lt. Comdr. Arcenio Alves Jr., Lt. Comdr. Stanley C. Orr, Lt. Dwight M. Agnew Jr., Lt. Comdr. Albert L. Henry Jr., Lt. Comdr. Allen M. Bissell, Lt. R. R. Lustman	Sunk as target 2003
Commercial Iron Works, Portland, Oregon				
Tawasa (ATF-92)	5-BS 2-MUC 2-KS 1-AE 7-VS 1-KPUC	17 Jul 43	Lt. Fred C. Clark	Struck 1976
Tekesta (ATF-93)	4-BS 1-CR	16 Aug 43	Lt. John O. Strickland, Lt. Comdr. Fred J. Fleiner	To Chile 1992 as *Yelcho* (AGS-64), discarded
Yuma (ATF-94)	4-BS 2-KS	31 Aug 43	Lt. W. R. J. Hayes	To Pakistan 1959 as *Madadgar* (A-42), struck 1995
Zuni (ATF-95)	4-BS	9 Oct 43	Lt. Ray E. Chance	To Coast Guard as *Tamaroa* (WATF-166), memorial in Richmond VA
Charleston Shipbuilding, Charleston, South Carolina				
Abnaki (ATF-96)	3-BS 2-NUC 3-KS 2-AE 6-VS	15 Nov 43	Lt. Dewey Walley	To Mexico 1978 as *Ehactl* (A-53), active
Alsea (ATF-97)		13 Dec 43	Lt. Cecil Cuthbert	Struck 1962
Arikara (ATF-98)	8-BS 1-CR 1-NUC 5-KS 4-VS	5 Jan 44	Lt. John Aitken	To Chile 1971 as *Sergento Aldea* (A-63), active
Chowanoc (ATF-100)	5-BS 1-NUC 1-KS 2-AE 7-VS	21 Feb 44	Lt. R. F. Snipes	To Ecuador 1960 as *Chimborazo* (RA-70), active

276   Appendix A

Name	Awards	Commissioned	Commanding Officers	Disposition
Cocopa (ATF-101)	1-BS 1-KS 4-AE 5-VS	25 Mar 44	Lt. Justin Cooper Hutchison, USNR	To Mexico 1978 as *Seri* (A-19), later *Tonatiuh* (R-54) 1993, *Seri* (ARE-03) 2001, active
Hidatsa (ATF-102)	2-BS 1-NUC 1-PPUC	25 Apr 44	Lt. Carroll F. Johnson	To Colombia 1979 as *Rodrigo de Bastedas* (RM-74), active
Hitchiti (ATF-103)	5-BS 2-MUC 3-KS 7-AE 3-VS	27 May 44	Lt. H. A. Guthrie, Lt. George W. DuCharme, Lt. Comdr. Edward M. Kline Jr., Lt. Gary S. Nelson	To Mexico 1978 as *Chac* (A-55), active
Jicarilla (ATF-104)	2-BS	26 Jun 44	Lt. Comdr. W. B. Coats	To Colombia 1979 as *Bahia Solano* (RM-75), struck 1987
Moctobi (ATF-105)	4-BS 2-KS 7-AE 2-VS 1-CGUC	25 Jul 44	Lt. Troy Braesher, Lt. John M. Geortner, Lt. John C. Uehlinger, Lt. Comdr. Richard O. Godden, Lt. Comdr. Peter A. C. Long	Sold 1997
United Engineering Co., Alameda, California				
Molala (ATF-106)	8-BS 3-KS 1-AE 4-VS 1RVG	29 Sep 43	Lt. Rudolph L. Ward	To Mexico 1978 as *Kukulkan* (A-52), active
Munsee (ATF-107)	3-BS 1-CR 1-KS 1-AE 4-VS	30 Oct 43	Lt. John F. Pingley, Lt. Charles H. Silvia Jr., Lt. Comdr. John Buday, Lt. Carl E. Kemmerer, Lt. Comdr. Miles R. Finley Jr., Lt. Comdr. Frank Dievendorff, Lt. Comdr. Arthur J. Ashurst, Lt. Comdr. Warren H. Fischer, Lt. Comdr. Robert L. Goodwin Jr.	Struck 1969
Pakana (ATF-108)	1-BS 1-CR	17 Dec 43	Lt. William E. White	Sunk as target 1975
Potowatomi (ATF-109)	2-BS 1-NUC 1-PPUC	12 Feb 44	Lt. Charles. H. Steadman, USNR	To Chile 1963, sunk 1965
Quapaw (ATF-110)	9-BS 1-NUC 1-MUC 5-KS 2-AE 7-VS	6 May 44	Lt. Comdr. N. H. Castle	Struck 1992
Sarsi (ATF-111)	2-BS 2-KS	24 Jun 44	Lt. Herbert J. Perry Jr., Lt. Jack C. Blakeney, Lt. John S. Malayter, Lt. John Buday, Lt. John A. Sprowl, Lt. Francis J. Leonard, Lt. William M. Howard	Mined off Korea and lost 1952

Fleet Tugs 277

Serrano (ATF-112)	1-BS 1-CR 1-MUC 2-AE 4-VS	22 Sep 44	Lt. Comdr. George E. Cook	Reclassified AGS-24 1960
Takelma (ATF-113)	2-BS 1-MUC 2-KS 2-VS	3 Aug 44	Lt. Charles Traub III, Lt. Comdr. Gerald G. Stangl, Lt. John D. O'Kane, Lt. Comdr. William J. Steward	To Argentina 1993 as *Suboficial Castillo* (A-11), active
Tawakoni (ATF-114)	5-BS 1-CR 1-NUC 3-KS 4-AE 4-VS	15 Sep 44	Lt. Comdr. Clarence L. Foushee	To Taiwan 1978 as *Ta Mo* (ATF-553), active
Tenino (ATF-115)	1-BS	18 Nov 44	Lt. Forrest L. Van Camp	Struck 1961
Tolowa (ATF-116)	1-BS	26 Dec 44	Lt. Eugene G. Sheasby, USNR	Struck 1970
Wateree (ATF-117)		17 Feb 45	Lt. Gilbert E. Perry	Sunk 1945
Wenatchee (ATF-118)	1-BS	24 Mar 45		To Taiwan 1991 as *Ta Feng* (ATF-555), active
Charleston Shipbuilding, Charleston, South Carolina				
Achomawi (ATF-148)		11 Nov 44	Lt. R. H. Teter	To Taiwan 1991 as *Ta Tu* (ATF-554), active
Atakapa (ATF-149)	3-NE 1-AE	1 Dec 44	Lt. George I. Nelson, Lt. Edmund S. Doty, Lt. Comdr. Donald Carpenter, Lt. E. A. McCammond, USCG, Lt. William C. Hall, Lt. Comdr. Edwardean Tucker, Lt. Thomas B. H. Askin Jr., Lt. Comdr. James C. Rowland, Lt. C. R. Anderson, Lt. Comdr. William B. Gott, Lt. Daniel J. Curtiss, Lt. Comdr. John O. Cullipher, Lt. Fred D. Sears, Lt. Comdr. Michael J. McGrath	Sunk as target 2000
Avoyel (ATF-150)	1-BS	8 Jan 45	Lt. Comdr. William R. Brown	To Coast Guard as WATF-150, sold 1970
Chawasha (ATF-151)	1-BS	6 Feb 45	Lt. H. K. Smith	Decommissioned 1946
Cahuilla (ATF-152)		10 Mar 45	Lt. A. C. Schoelpple	To Argentina 1961 as *Comandante General Irigoyen* (A-1), active
Chilula (ATF-153)		5 Apr 45	Lt. O. L. Guinn	To Coast Guard as WATF-153, sunk as target 1997
Chimariko (ATF-154)		28 Apr 45	Lt. W. R. Wurzler, Lt. Carl E. Kemmerer	Decommissioned 1946, used as a training hulk

Appendix A

Ship	Awards	Commissioned	Commanders	Disposition
Cusabo (ATF-155)		19 May 45	Lt. W. Hunnewell Jr.	To Ecuador 1960 as *Cayambe* (RA-71), active
Luiseno (ATF-156)	1-NUC 1-NE 1-AE	16 Jun 45	Lt. William O. Talley	To Argentina 1975 as *Francisco de Gurruchaga* (A-3), active
Nipmuc (ATF-157)	3-NE 3-AE	8 Jul 45	Lt. Robert G. Hoffman, Lt. Comdr. Dendall J. Chapman, Lt. Comdr. Charles C. Denman Jr., Lt. George M. Elliott, Lt. Comdr. Stephen P. Duermeyer, Lt. Dennis R. Moss, Lt. Comdr. Roy R. Twaddle, Lt. Mark Barbero, Lt. Roger L. Owens	To Venezuela 1978 as *Antonio Picardi* (RA-22), lost 1982
Mosopelia (ATF-158)	6-NE 1-AE	28 Jul 45	Lt. Comdr. Allen H. Jensen, Lt. Paul D. Butcher, Lt. Donald A. Dyer, Lt. Comdr. James G. Tallant, Lt. Comdr. Cecil Sherer, Lt. Richard W. Moore	Sunk as target 1999
Paiute (ATF-159)	1-MUC 2-NE 2-AE	27 Aug 45	Lt. Stanley John Lewandowski, USN	To NDRF (National Defense Reserve Fleet) 1997
Papago (ATF-160)	1-MUC 3-NE 2-AE	3 Oct 45	Lt. W. S. Hall	To NDRF 1997
Salinan (ATF-161)	4-MUC 1-AE	9 Nov 45	Lt. Comdr. Robert M. Whelpley, Lt. Comdr. John F. Rule, Lt. Richard M. Husty, Lt. Robert S. Swan, Lt. Peveril Blundell, Lt. Morton W. Kenyon, Lt. Robert J. Shade, Lt. Joe D. Wilbanks, Lt. Harland R. Bankert Jr., Lt. Mark Barbero, Lt. William L. Boyd	To Venezuela 1978 as *Contralmirante Miguel Rodriguez* (RA-23), active
Shakori (ATF-162)	1-NUC 1-MUC 5-NE 2-AE 1-VS	20 Dec 45	Lt. William L. Sloan, Lt. Robert B. Ramsey, Lt. Jerry R. McDonald	To Taiwan 1991 as *Ta Tai* (ATF-563), active
Utina (ATF-163)	2-NE 1-AE		Lt. A. J. Vetro	To Venezuela 1978 as *Felix Larrazabel* (RA-21) struck 1990
Yurok (ATF-164)		28 May 46	Lt. Comdr. Paul R. Hodgson	Reclassified, *Bluebird* (ASR-19)
Yustaga (ATF-165)	1-MUC	1 Mar 51	Lt. Comdr. Romolo Cousins	Reclassified, *Skylark* (ASR-20)

Appendix B: Rescue Tugs and Auxiliary Tugs

Note: See acronym key in Appendix A

Ship	Unit Awards	Commis-sioning	Commanding Officer or Name of Foreign Ship	Disposition
Wheeler Ship Building Corp., Whitestone, New York (165-foot, 1,312 ton ships)				
ATR-1	2-BS	24 Oct 43	Lt. (jg) H. L. MacGill, USN, Lt. (jg) M. S. Rygg, USNR, H. G. Labo	Struck 1946
ATR-2	1-BS 1-NUC	22 Nov 43	Lt. (jg) G. Ulrich, USN	Disposed of 1946
ATR-3	1-BS	27 Dec 43	Lt. (jg) Stanley John Lewandowski, USN	Disposed of 1946
ATR-4	1-BS	27 Jan 44	Lt. (jg) John S. Blank III, USNR	Disposed of 1946
ATR-5		28 Feb 44	Lt. M. J. Verville, USNR	Disposed of 1946
ATR-6		25 Mar 44	Lt. (jg) J. C. Parsons	Disposed of 1946
Frank L. Sample, Boothbay Harbor, Maine (165-foot, 1,312 ton ships)				
ATR-7		10 Feb 44	Lt. S. D. Frey, USN	Disposed of 1946
ATR-8		25 May 44	Lt. S. C. Conser	Disposed of 1946
ATR-9	1-BS	3 Aug 44	Lt. L. H. Reybine	Disposed of 1946
ATR-10	1-BS	4 Oct 44	Lt. R. P. Griffing Jr., Lt. P. E. Piellusch	Disposed of 1946
ATR-11		13 Dec 44	Lt. S. M. Meyer, USNR	Disposed of 1946
ATR-12		24 Feb 45	Lt. (jg) B. F. Gerttula, USNR	Disposed of 1946
Delaware Bay Shipbuilding, Leesburg, New Jersey (165-foot, 1,312 ton ships)				
ATR-13	1-BS	23 Dec 43	Lt. (jg) G. N. Hammond, USN	Disposed of 1946
ATR-14		29 Apr 44	Lt. W. K. Gillett, USNR	disposed of 1946
Jakobson Shipyard, Oyster Bay, New York (165-foot, 1,312 ton ships)				
ATR-15	1-BS	9 Feb 44	Lt. (jg) John Anto, USN	Decommissioned 28 May 1945
ATR-16		1 Jul 44	Lt. D. R. Luckham	Disposed of 1948
Camden Shipbuilding, Camden, Maine (165-foot, 1,312 ton ships)				
ATR-17		28 Dec 43	HMS *Director* (W137)	To Britain, returned 1946, sold 1948
ATR-18		2 Feb 44	HMS *Emulous* (W138)	To Britain, returned 1946, sold 1948
ATR-19		20 Mar 44	HMS *Freedom* (W139)	To Britain, returned 1946, sold 1948
ATR-20		24 Apr 44	HMS *Justice* (W140)	To Britain, returned 1946, sold to Argentina 1948 as *St. Christopher*, laid up 1954 in Ushuaia, later beached and abandoned
ATR-21		25 May 44	Lt. L. T. Switzer Jr., USNR	12 Jun 46
ATR-22		10 Jul 44	Lt. H. D. Howes, USNR	17 Jun 46

Appendix C

\multicolumn{6}{c}{**Fulton Shipyard, Antioch, California (165-foot, 1,312 ton ships)**}
ATR-23		3 Dec 43	Lt. (jg) J. A. Hein, USN	Disposed of 1946
ATR-24		9 Feb 44	Lt. (jg) W. S. Perry, USN	1 Jul 46
ATR-25		11 Apr 44	Lt. (jg) R. L. Hernlen, USN	8 May 46
ATR-26		9 Jun 44	Lt. (jg) J. H. Kelly, USN	27 Mar 46
ATR-27		1 Aug 44	Lt. Carl E. Kemmerer, USN	10 May 46
ATR-28		25 Sep 44	Lt. W. Swanson, USN	1 Jul 46
\multicolumn{6}{c}{**Wheeler Ship Building Corp., Whitestone, New York (165-foot, 1,312 ton ships)**}
ATR-29		20 Apr 44	Lt. (jg) E. McKenzie	5 Dec 45
ATR-30		11 May 44	Lt. N. P. Hendrick, USNR	31 Mar 46
\multicolumn{6}{c}{**Northwestern Shipbuilding, South Bellingham, Washington (165-foot, 1,312 ton ships)**}
ATR-31	2-BS 1-NUC	30 Oct 43	Lt. M. A. Heath, USN	Disposed of 1946
ATR-32		19 Jan 44	Lt. (jg) Clem R. Olivier, USN	1 Jul 46
ATR-33		28 Mar 44	Lt. (jg) E. R. Weaver, USN	1 May 46
ATR-34		31 May 44	Lt. (jg) Anthony Zito, USN	1 May 46
\multicolumn{6}{c}{**Lynch Shipbuilding, San Diego, California (165-foot, 1,312 ton ships)**}
ATR-35	1-BS	5 May 44	Lt. (jg) L. C. Gunn, USNR	30 Apr 46
ATR-36		27 Jul 44	Lt. R. A. Raikes, USN	1 Apr 46
ATR-37		20 Sep 44	Lt. F. W. Grove	1 May 46
ATR-38	1-BS	15 Nov 44	Lt. P.W. Dodson	Disposed of 1946
ATR-39		10 Jan 45	Lt. Comdr. A. W. Wilde	Disposed of 1946
ATR-40		30 Apr 45	Lt. (jg) P. A. Tyndall	Disposed of 1946
\multicolumn{6}{c}{**Levingston Shipbuilding, Orange, Texas (143-foot, 835 ton ships)**}
ATR-41		19 Apr 43	HMS *Advantage* (W133)	To Britain 1943, returned 1946, sold private 1948 as *Ming*
ATR-42		3 May 43	HMS *Aspirant* (W134)	To Britain 1943, returned 1946, sold private 1948 as *Vivi*
ATR-43	1-KS	29 May 43	Lt. (jg) A. C. Schoelpple	Reclassified *Sotoyomo* (ATA-121), to Mexico 1968
ATR-44	1-BS	Jun 43	Lt. M. L. Wright	Reclassified ATA-122, to Chile 1947 as *Lautaro* (PP-62), to Uruguay 1991 as ROU *San Jose*
ATR-45		30 Jun 43	Lt. (jg) J. L. Hostinsky	Reclassified ATA-123, later *Iuka*, to NDRF 1962, sold foreign 1976 as *Deka Exi*
ATR-46	1-BS	Jul 43	Lt. R. K. Thurman	Reclassified ATA-124, to Argentina 1947 as *Diaguita* (A5)
ATR-47	1-BS	12 Aug 43	Lt. (jg) Harry L. Lane, J. C. Griffin	Reclassified ATA-125, decommissioned 31 Mar 46, sold private 1947, to France 1964 as *Hippopotame*

Old Fleet Tugs and Yard Tugs   281

ATR-48		31 Aug 43	HMS *Mindful* (W135)	Reclassified ATA-126, sold private in 1948 as *Gay Moran*, later *Sea Lion*, *Harry J. Mosser*, and *Margaret Walsh*
ATR-49		2 Oct 43	HMS *Vagrant* (W136)	Reclassified ATA-127, sold private in 1948 as *Marion Moran*
Colberg Boat Works, Stockton, California (165-foot, 1,312 ton ships)				
ATR-50		5 May 44	Lt. August Billig	Disposed of 1946
ATR-51	2-BS	22 Jun 44	Lt. (jg) A. L. Larson	Disposed of 1946
ATR-52	1-BS	31 Jul 44	Lt. Charles A Miller	Disposed of 1946
ATR-53	1-BS	11 Sep 44	Lt. B. M. Stevenson	Disposed of 1946
Dachel-Carter Shipbuilding, Benton Harbor, Michigan (165-foot, 1,312 ton ships)				
ATR-54	1-BS	13 Nov 43	Lt. (jg) C. G. Sherwood, USN	Disposed of 1946
ATR-55		26 Apr 44	Lt. Comdr. Selwyn Eddy, USNR	Disposed of 1946
ATR-56	1-BS	28 Jun 44	Lt. Elwood C. McCoy, USNR	Disposed of 1946
ATR-57		17 Aug 44	Lt. Albert W. Vittek	Disposed of 1946
ATR-58		11 Aug 44	Lt. G. B. Barry	Disposed of 1946
ATR-59		7 Dec 44	Lt. F. H. Matthews	Disposed of 1946
Wheeler Shipbuilding Corp., Whitestone, New York (165-foot, 1,312 ton ships)				
ATR-60		31 May 44	Lt. Comdr. L. Riggs, III, USNR	Disposed of 1946
ATR-61	3-BS	24 Jun 44	Lt. W. M. Heywood Jr., USNR	Disposed of 1946
ATR-62	1-BS	14 Jul 44	Lt. J. M. Brown Jr.	Disposed of 1946
ATR-63		16 Aug 44	Lt. R. W. Coffey	Disposed of 1946
ATR-64		25 Sep 44	Lt. Edward R. Greeff, USNR	Sold 1950 as *Mogul*, later *Island Monarch*, *Seaspan Chinook* and *La Lumiere*
ATR-65		24 Oct 44	Lt. H. A. Preston	Disposed of 1946
Jakobson Shipyard, Oyster Bay, New York (165-foot, 1,312 ton ships)				
ATR-66		22 Jan 45	Lt. (jg) B. J. Begue	Disposed of 1946
ATR-67		14 Aug 45	Lt. Lawrence B. Elsbernd	Disposed of 1946
Bellingham Marine Railway, Bellingham, Washington (165-foot, 1,312 ton ships)				
ATR-68		15 May 44	Lt. E. A. McVey Jr.	Disposed of 1946
ATR-69		8 Jul 44	Lt. W. F. Reinkin	Disposed of 1946
ATR-70		28 Aug 44	Lt. W. L. Sloan	Disposed of 1946
ATR-71		12 Oct 44	Lt. (jg) J. B.Walker	Disposed of 1946
ATR-72		25 Nov 44	Lt. (jg) C. B. Hiner	Disposed of 1946
ATR-73		1 Jan 45	Lt. (jg) E. L. Givins	Disposed of 1946
Camden Shipbuilding, Camden, Maine (165-foot, 1,312 ton ships)				
ATR-74		14 Aug 44	Lt. W. W. Simpson, USN	Disposed of 1946
ATR-75		11 Sep 44	Lt. E. A. McCammond	Disposed of 1946
ATR-76		10 Oct 44	Lt. D. J. Myers	Disposed of 1946
ATR-77	1-BS	3 Nov 44	Lt. W. A. Jewett	Disposed of 1946
ATR-78		6 Jan 45	Lt. (jg) J. A. MacDonald	Disposed of 1946
ATR-79		9 Dec 44	Lt. D. J. McMillan	Disposed of 1946
Kruse & Banks, North Bend, Oregon (165-foot, 1,312 ton ships)				
ATR-80	2-BS	21 Feb 44	Lt. J. P. Dubrule	Disposed of 1946
ATR-81	1-BS	29 Apr 44	Lt. M. P. Smith	Disposed of 1946

Appendix C

Island Dock, Kingston, New York (165-foot, 1,312 ton ships)

Ship		Date	Commander	Fate
ATR-82		27 Jun 44	Lt. E. M. Stevenson, USNR	Disposed of 1946
ATR-83		19 Aug 44	Lt. M. T. Dalby	Disposed of 1946
ATR-84		15 Nov 44	Lt. R. R. Williams	Disposed of 1946
ATR-85		5 Feb 45	Lt. L. F. Danz, USNR	Disposed of 1946

Kruse & Banks, North Bend, Oregon (165-foot, 1,312 ton ships)

Ship		Date	Commander	Fate
ATR-86		22 Aug 44	Lt. (jg) Thomas V. Walter	Disposed of 1946
ATR-87	1-BS	31 Oct 44	Lt. Leo P. Le Bron, USNR	Disposed of 1946

Burger Boat, Manitowoc, Wisconsin (165-foot, 1,312 ton ships)

Ship		Date	Commander	Fate
ATR-88		8 Aug 44	Lt. B. F. Sass, USNR	Disposed of 1946
ATR-89		12 Oct 44	Lt. M. W. Thomas	Disposed of 1946

Gulfport Boiler & Welding Works, Port Arthur, Texas (143-foot, 835 ton ships)

Ship		Date	Commander	Fate
ATR-90		20 Jan 43	Lt. Comdr. Myron E. McFarland	Reclassified *Maricopa* ATA-146, to Argentina 1972 as *Yamona* (A6)

Levingston Shipbuilding, Orange, Texas (143-foot, 835 ton ships)

Ship	Date	Name	Fate
ATR-91	22 Oct 43	HMS *Patroclus* (W118)	Returned 1946, sold private 1947 as *Kevin Moran*, later *Mohawk*
ATR-92	13 Nov 43	HMS *Athlete* (W150)	Mined and lost off Livorno, Italy, 1945
ATR-93	7 Dec 43	HMS *Flare* (W151)	Returned 1946, sold private 1948 as *Ming 301*
ATR-94	21 Dec 43	HMS *Flaunt* (W152)	Returned 1946, sold private 1948 as *Ming 302*
ATR-95	18 Jan 44	HMS *Cheerly* (W153)	Returned 1946, sold private 1948
ATR-96	27 Jan 44	HMS *Emphatic* (W154)	Returned 1946, sold private 1948 as *Ifigua*

Gulfport Boiler & Welding Works, Port Arthur, Texas (143-foot, 835 ton ships)

Ship		Date	Commander	Fate
ATR-97	2-BS	7 Dec 43	Lt. W. C. Beatie Jr., USNR	Reclassified ATA-170, struck 1946
ATR-98		18 Jan 44	Lt. (jg) V. M. Meaden, USN	lost off the Azores in a collision with USS *Abnaki* (ATF-96) 12 April 1944
ATR-99	2-BS	23 Feb 44	Lt. (jg) Robert G. Hoffman, USN	Reclassified ATA-172, struck 1946
ATR-100		12 Apr 44	Lt. (jg) W. H. Moore	Reclassified ATA-173, decommissioned 1 June 1946

Levingston Shipbuilding, Orange, Texas (143-foot, 835 ton ships)

Ship	Date	Commander	Fate
ATR-101	20 Jul 44	Lt. A. J. Vetro	Reclassified *Wateree* ATA-174, to Peru 1961 as *Urunue* (AMB160)
ATR-102	3 Aug 44	Lt. H. R. Henkens, USN	Reclassified *Sonoma* ATA-175, sold foreign 1976 as *Deka Epta*

Old Fleet Tugs and Yard Tugs   283

ATR-103		19 Aug 44	Lt. (jg) Ralph T. Crane, Lt. (jg) Franklin J. Conrad	Reclassified *Tonkawa* ATA-176, to Taiwan 1962 as ROCS *Ta Sueh* (ATA547)
ATR-104		2 Sep 44	Lt. W. J. Little, USNR	Reclassified ATA-177, to Chile 1947 as *Lientur* (PP3)
ATR-105		15 Sep 44	Lt. J. L. Robinson	Reclassified *Tunica* ATA-178, decommissioned 23 Sep 47, struck 1 Sep 62
ATR-106	1-BS 1-PPUC	22 Sep 44	Lt. (jg) Thomas C. McLaren	Reclassified *Alleghenny* ATA-179, decommissioned, and struck 14 Dec 68
ATR-107		30 Sep 44	Lt. (jg) Robert S. Esdaile	Reclassified ATA-180, to Scripps Institute 1948 as RV *Horizon*
ATR-108	1-BS	7 Oct 44	Lt. C. M. Lacour, Lt. Comdr. Davis D. Leslie	Reclassified *Accokeek* ATA-181, decommissioned, 29 Jun 72, struck 31 Mar 86
ATR-109	2-BS 2-KS 1-KPUC	16 Oct 44	Lt. WM J. Bates, USNR	Reclassified *Unadilla* ATA-182, sold foreign 1976 as *Deka Okto*
ATR-110		26 Oct 44	Lt. Richard S. Lowry	Reclassified *Nottoway* ATA-183, decom 22 Oct 46, struck 1 Sep 62
ATR-111		6 Nov 44	Lt. (jg) William E. Hummel	Reclassified *Kalmia* ATA-184, decom 1 Jul 71, struck 31 Oct 77, to Colombia 1971 as ARC *Bahia Utria*
ATR-112	1-BS	16 Nov 44	Lt. (jg) Woodrow Sullivan	Reclassified *Koka* ATA-185, decommissioned, struck and sold in 1971
ATR-113		24 Nov 44	Lt. John T. Dillon, USNR	Reclassified *Cahokia* ATA-186, to Taiwan 1976 as ROCS *Ta Teng* (ATA367)
ATR-114	1-BS 1-MUC	7 Dec 44	Lt. Thomas G. Lewis	Reclassified *Salish* ATA-187, struck 1 Feb 75, transferred to Argentina as ARA *Alferez Sobral* (A9)

Appendix C

ATR-115	1-BS	12 Dec 44	Lt. F. C. Thompson, USN	Reclassified *Penobscot* ATA-188, sold private 1975
ATR-116		20 Dec 44	Lt. R. P. Moser, USNR	Reclassified *Reindeer* ATA-189, to NDRF 1961
ATR-117	1-BS	1 Jan 45	Lt. (jg) E. D. Twiehaus, USNR	Reclassified *Samoset* ATA-190, to Haiti 1978 as *Henri Christophe* (MH20)
ATR-118		12 Jan 45	Lt. (jg) R. T. Benedict, USNR	Reclassified ATA-191, sunk at Okinawa 1945
ATR-119	1-BS	23 Jan 45	Lt. (jg) W. C. Heck, USN	Reclassified *Tillamook* ATA-192, to Korea 1971
ATR-120	1-BS	1 Feb 45	Lt. A. Oliver, USN	Reclassified *Stallion* ATA-193, to Dominican Republic 1980 as *Enriquillo* (RM22)
ATR-121		14 Feb 45	Lt. (jg) W. J. Bryan, USN	Reclassified *Bagaduce* ATA-194, to USCG 1959 as *Modoc* (WMEC-194), now floating Bed-and-Breakfast *Modoc Pearl*, in Gig Harbor, Washington
ATR-122		26 Feb 45	Lt. (jg) G. E. Joyal, USN	Reclassified *Tatnuk* ATA-195
ATR-123		6 Mar 45	Lt. (jg) L. Phipps, USN	Reclassified *Mahopac* ATA-196, to Taiwan 1976 as ROCS *Ta Peng* (ATA395)
ATR-124		14 Mar 45	Lt. W. A. Rye, USNR	Reclassified *Sunnadin* ATA-197, sold private 1971
ATR-125	3-BS	19 Mar 45	Lt. J. L. Bean, USN	Reclassified *Keosanqua* ATA-198, to Korea 1962 as ROK *Yong Mun* (ATA2)
Gulfport Boiler & Welding Works, Port Arthur, Texas (143-foot, 835 ton ships)				
ATR-126		20 Oct 44	Lt. G. S. Flanigan, USNR	Reclassified *Undaunted* ATA-199, to USMMA 1963 as *Kings Pointer*, sold private 1998
ATR-127	1-BS	31 Oct 44	Lt. (jg) Robert W. Scott, USNR	Reclassified ATA-200, struck 1946
ATR-128		22 Nov 44	Lt. Max B. Parker	Reclassified *Challenge* ATA-201, now *Marine Commander*

Old Fleet Tugs and Yard Tugs

Ship	Unit Awards	Built or Commissioned	Commanding Officer	
ATR-129	1-BS	8 Dec 44	Lt. R. M. Kurz, USNR	Reclassified *Wampanoag* ATA-202, to USCG 1969 as *Comanche* (WMEC-202),
ATR-130	2-BS	1 Jan 45	Lt. J. E. Fuld Jr., USNR	Reclassified *Navigator* ATA-203
ATR-131		18 Jan 45	Lt. (jg) V. L. Ryan, USN	Reclassified *Wandank* ATA-204
ATR-132		30 Jan 45	Lt. Russell C. Schulke, USNR	Reclassified *Sciota* ATA-205
ATR-133		10 Feb 45	Lt. N. G. Neault, USNR	Reclassified *Pinola* ATA-206, to Korea 1962 as *Do Bang* (ATA3)
ATR-134		1 Mar 45	Lt. J. K. Hawkins, USN	Reclassified *Geronimo* ATA-207, to U.S. Dept. of Interior 1962, to Taiwan 1968
ATR-135		19 Mar 45	Lt. (jg) S. D. Northrop, USN	Reclassified *Sagamore* ATA-208, to Dominican Republic 1980 as *Caonabo* (RM18)
ATR-136		2 Apr 45	Lt. P. L. Courtney, USNR	Reclassified *Umpqua* ATA-209, to Colombia 1979
ATR-137		18 Apr 45	Lt. (jg) R. W. Standart, USNR	Reclassified *Catawba* ATA-210, to Argentina 1972 as *Comodoro Somellera* (A10)
ATR-138		3 May 45	Lt. (jg) J. G. McKnight, USN, Lt. P. W. Dodson, USN	Reclassified *Navajo* ATA-211, sold 1964, sold foreign 2005 as *Mr. Dylan*
ATR-139		21 May 45	Lt. (jg) Broadus S. Compere, USN	Reclassified *Algorma* ATA-212
ATR-140		1 Jun 45	Lt. V. A. Galterio, USNR	Reclassified *Keywadin* ATA-213

ATAs Reclassified From Other Type Vessels

Ship	Unit Awards	Length (ft.) Displ. (tons)	Built or Commissioned	Commanding Officer
Chetco (ATA-166)	2-BS	150/437	1919	Lt. (jg) Ronald E. Gill
Chatot (ATA-167)		142/144	1919	
ATA-214		194/1,515	25 Sep 44	Lt. (jg) Robert B. Leonnig, USN
ATA-215		194/1,515	23 Dec 44	Lt. Ernest J. Clark Jr., USNR
ATA-216		194/1,515	30 Oct 44	Lt. F. P. Mulligan, USNR
ATA-217		194/1,515	16 Jan 45	Lt. H. A. V. Post, USNR
ATA-218		194/1,515	10 Mar 45	Lt. Harry L. Lane

Appendix C: Old Fleet Tugs and Yard Tugs

In the below table, the number of battle stars earned by a ship during World War II is indicated by a numeral, followed by a hyphen and BS for "battle star(s)." The acronyms for other unit awards follow:

CR: Combat Action Ribbon (retroactive)
NUC: Navy Unit Commendation
PPUC: Philippine Presidential Unit Citation

Ship	Unit Awards	Built	Commanding Officer	Decommissioned/ Disposition
175-foot, 1,120 ton ships				
Sonoma (ATO-12)	5-BS 2-CR 1-NUC 1-PPUC	1912	Lt. Comdr. Joseph A. Ouellet, Lt. (jg) George I. Nelson	Lost to enemy action at Leyte, Philippines, 24 Oct 44
Ontario (ATO-13)	1-BS 1-CR	1912	Lt. Eldon C. Mayer, Lt. Theodore Wolcott, Lt. Eugene G.Sheasby, Lt. R. C. Schulke, Lt. H. F. Gordon, Lt. H. H. Branyon	3 Jun 46, struck 19 Jun 46
156-foot, 1,000 ton ships				
Allegheny (ATO-19)		18 May 18	Lt. R. F. Purcell, USN	10 Jul 46, struck 25 Sep 46
Sagamore (ATO-20)		8 Jun 18	Lt. C. L. Foushee, USN	31 Aug 46, struck 28 Jan 47
Bagaduce (ATO-21)		18 Sep 19	Lt. (jg) H. A. Brown, USNR	22 Jun 46, struck 31 Jul 46
Kewaydin (ATO-24)	1-BS	4 Nov 19	Lt. (jg) W. E. Loebmann, USNR	10 Dec 45, struck 3 Jan 46
Umpqua (ATO-25)		6 Dec 19	Lt. James J. Jenkins, USNR	24 May 46, struck 3 Jul 46
Wandank (ATO-26)		23 Mar 20	Lt. J. H. Trimble, USN	Sep 46, sold 47
157-foot, 1,000 ton ships				
Tatnuck (ATO-27)		26 Jul 19	Lt. (jg) F. Anderson, USN	12 Sep 46, struck 29 Oct 46
Sunnadin (ATO-28)	1-BS 1-CR	20 Oct 19	Lt. J. A. Smith, USN	4 Apr 46, struck 8 May 46
Mahopac (ATO-29)		20 Oct 19	Lt. (jg) H. G. Labo, USN	12 Sep 46, struck Nov 46
Sciota (ATO-30)		13 Nov 19	Lt. Comdr. W. R. Brown, USN	Struck 8 May 46
Napa (AT-32)	1-BS	5 Dec 19	Lt. Minter Dial, Ens. Perroneau B. Wingo	Scuttled by crew off Corregidor,

Name		Commissioned	Commanders	Fate
				Philippine Islands, 9 April 42
Pinola (ATO-33)		7 Feb 20	Lt. Z. T. Helm, USNR	31 Jan 46, struck 26 Feb 46
Algorma (ATO-34)	1-BS	15 May 20	Lt. Robert Marshall Whelpley, USN	18 Jun 46, struck 31 July 46
Iuka (ATO-37)		29 Oct 20	Lt. F. R. Christianson, USNR	15 Aug 46, placed out of service 15 Apr 47
Keosanqua (ATO-38)	1-BS 1-CR	9 Dec 20	Lt. (jg) F. J. Donovan, USNR	6 May 46, struck 7 Feb 47
Montcalm (ATO-39)		19 Jan 21	Lt. N. V. Sanborn, USN	24 May 46, struck 13 Jun 46
170-foot, 1,000 ton ship				
Genesee (AT-55) ex-*Monocacy*	1-BS	1905	Chief Boatswain E. L. Boyd, USN	Scuttled on 5 May 42 at Corregidor to avoid capture
152-foot, 860 ton ship				
Acushnet (ATO-63)		1908	Lt. (jg) R. C. Edwards, USN	14 Dec 45, struck 8 Jan 46
188-foot, 950 ton ships				
Bobolink (ATO-131)		28 Jan 19	Lt. James L. Foley, Ens. F. G. Reed, Lt. H. L. Sigleer, Lt. Elmar L. A. Rau, Lt. (jg) E. L. Givins	22 Feb 46, sold 5 Oct 46
Brant (AT-132)		6 Sep 18		Later ARS-32, sold 46
Cormorant (ATO-133)	1-BS	15 May 19		29 Mar 46, sold 8 Jan 47
Grebe (AT-134)	1-BS	1 May 19		Grounded at Vuanta Vatoa, Fiji, 6 Dec 42, wrecked by hurricane, 1-2 January 43
Kingfisher (ATO-135)	1-BS	28 May 19	Lt. R. L. Ward, Ens. August B. Billig, Lt. (jg) Jack T. Moritz, Lt. (jg) W. W. Collins	6 Feb 46, sold 3 Jun 47
Oriole (ATO-136)		5 Nov 18	Lt. Albert J. Wheaton, Lt. Comdr. Mellish M. Lindsay Jr.	6 Feb 46, struck 12 Mar 46
Owl (ATO-137)	1-BS	11 Jul 18	Lt. Comdr. Charles G. Rucker, Lt. Frederick G. Coffin, Lt. Adnah N. Caldin, Lt. (jg) Samuel D. Tuttle, Lt. James C. W. White, Lt. John H. Thomas	26 Jul 46, struck 46, sold for scrap 27 June 47
Patridge (ATO-138)	1-BS	17 Jun 19	Lt. Comdr. Samuel E. Kenney	Lost to enemy action 11 Jun 44, torpedoed by German E-Boat
Rail (ATO-139)	4-BS	5 Jun 18	Lt. Comdr. F. W. Beard, Lt. (jg) L. C. Oaks, Lt. (jg) Herbert K. Smith, Lt. (jg) Thomas P. Pierce, Lt. (jg) E. D. White, Lt. D. F. Allen	29 Apr 46, struck that same day

Name		Date	Officers	Disposition
Robin (ATO-140)		29 Aug 18	Lt. David G. Greenlee Jr., Lt. John J. Branson, Lt. (jg) Ellsworth C. Avery, Lt. Comdr. Anie Jerome Roy	9 Nov 45, struck 28 Nov 45
Seagull (ATO-141)		6 Mar 19	Lt. Comdr. Daniel B. Candler Jr.	5 Sep 46, struck 15 Oct 46
Tern (ATO-142)		17 May 19	Lt. Walton B. Pendleton, Lt. (jg) Herbert J. Perry Jr., Lt. (jg) G. F. Carey, Lt. (jg) W. E. Hummel	23 Nov 45, struck 5 Dec 45
Turkey (ATO-143)		13 Dec 18	Lt. Comdr. Thompson F. Fowler, Lt. Samuel B. Neff, Lt. Robert J. Melchor, Lt. (jg) Robert A. Botsford, Lt. J. M. C. Tighe	6 Nov 45, struck 28 Nov 45
Vireo (ATO-144)	6-BS	16 Oct 19	Lt. Comdr. Frederick J. Ilsemann, Lt. James C. Legg, Lt. (jg) Charles H. Stedman, Lt. (jg) Robert W. Ekberg, Lt. (jg) Stewart D. Northrop, Lt. (jg) Melvin E. Seymour, Lt. Broughton J. Barber	18 Apr 46, struck 8 May 46
Woodcock (ATO-145)		19 Feb 19	Lt. Comdr. Paul E. Howard, Lt. Jerence W. Greene, Lt. Benjamin P. Clark, USCG	30 Sep 46, struck 23 Apr 47
Lark (ATO-168)		12 Apr 19	Lt. Comdr. Hugh P. Thompson, Lt. Comdr. Rowe, Lt. Comdr. Paul Lindlay, Lt. Hugo	7 Feb 46, to Maritime Commission for disposal 15 Jan 47
Whippoorwill (ATO-169)		1 Apr 19	Lt. Comdr. Charles A. Ferriter	17 April 46, struck 10 Jun 46, scrapped 47
92-foot, 192 ton ship				
Iwana (YTM-2) ex AT-2/ YT-2		1891		Transferred to the War Shipping Administration, 20 March 46
110-foot, 335 ton ship				
Unadilla (YTM-4) ex AT-4/ YT-4		1895		Struck May 47
92-foot, 230 ton ships				
Samoset (YTM-5) ex AT-5/ YT-5		1897		To Maritime Commission 9 Jan 47
Penacook (YTM-6) ex AT-6/ YT-6		1898		Placed out of service September 45, sold 12 Aug 47
Pawtucket (YTM-7) ex AT-7/ YT-7		1898		Placed out of service 13 Dec 46, scrapped 47

Sotoyomo (YTM-9) ex AT-9/ YT-9	1-BS 1-CR	1903		Struck 15 Feb 46, destroyed, 15 Feb 46
		122-foot, 575 ton ships		
Tillamook (YTM-122) ex AT-16/ YT-122		2 Dec 14		Placed out of service, 28 Apr 47, sold 47
Wando (YTB-123) ex AT-17/ YT-123		3 Apr 17		3 Jul 46, struck 30 Dec 46, sold 28 Apr 47
		143-foot, 450 ton ship		
Undaunted (ATO-58) ex AT-58/ YT-125		1917		1 Jul 46, struck 25 Sep 46
		129-foot, 515 ton ship		
Challenge (YTM-126) ex *Defiance*/ AT-59/YT-126		1889		Struck 21 Jan 46
		150-foot, 510 ton ships		
Bay Spring (YNG-19) ex AT-60		1921		To Maritime Commission 47
Cahokia (YTB-135) ex USCG/ YT-135/ AT-61		1920		To Maritime Commission 8 Aug 47
		161-foot, 705 ton ship		
Tamaroa (YTB-136) ex USCG/ YT-136/ AT-62		1919	Lt. (jg) V. Major, USN (Ret.)	Sunk by collision with USS *Jupiter* (AVS-8), 27 January 46

Appendix D: Anzio Naval Order of Battle

Asterisks denote ships and craft lost as a result of Operation SHINGLE.

Task Force 81: Rear Adm. Frank J. Lowry, USN

Task Group	Function	Ships/Craft Assigned
CTG 81.1	Force Flagship	*Biscayne* (AVP-11): Rear Admiral Lowry, USN
CTG 81.2	Ranger Group: Capt. Errol C. L. Turner, RN	LCI(L)-76, LCI(L)-229, LCI(L)-231 Control Unit: SC-522, SC-530, SC-1029 British: HMS *Royal Ulsterman* (F76), HMS *Princess Beatrix* (4.44), M.V. *Winchester Castle*, LSI(M)s
CTG 81.3	Red Beach Group: Comdr. William O. Floyd, USN	Headquarters Unit: Flagship LCI(L)-233, LCI(L)-48 Landing Craft Unit: LSTs *4, 197, *348, 349, 352, 358, 359, 360, 378, 379* Pontoon carry LSTs: *383, 384* LCI(L)s *2, 3, 4, 5, 8, 11, 12, 13, *32, 33, 36, 37, 47, 188, 189, 190, 191, 192, 193, 194, 195, 211, 212, 213, 214, 215, 216, 217, 218* LCT(5)s *32, 33, 34, *35, *36, 203, 204, 212, 333* Control Unit: PCs *551, 626, 1226, 1227*; SCs *497, 506, 525, 534, 639, 692* British LCT(Mk 4)s *548, 550, 552, 554, 559, 563, 581, 589, 601, 607, 615, 633* British Support Craft: *LCG-4, LCF-4, LCT(R)-140*
CTG 81.4	Green Beach Group: Comdr. O. F. Gregor, USN (Commander Mine Squadron Six)	Flagship: *LCI(L)-196* LSTs *377, 385* LCI(L)s *9, 14, 15, 16, 17, 40, 41, 42, 46, 48, 75, 220, 234, 235, 236, 238* LCT(5)s *155, 216, 221, 223, 237, 268* Control Unit: PC-543, SC-649, SC-676 British LSIs *Ascania, Circasia* British *LCT (Mk 3)-386*, and LCT (Mk 4)s *536, 579, 587, 617* British Support Craft: *LCG-8, LCF-10, LCT(R)-136*
CTG 81.5	First Follow-up Group: Capt. J. P. Clay, USN (CDS-7)	Flagship *Plunkett* (DD-431), *Gleaves* (DD-423), *Niblack* (DD-424), *Trippe* (DD-403) Minesweepers *Steady* (AM-118), *Sustain* (AM-119) Rescue tug *ATR-1* Liberty ships S.S. *Bret Harte*, S.S. *Hillary Herbert*, S.S. *John Banvard*, S.S. *Lawton B. Evans* Tank landing ship *LST-16* Large infantry landing craft: LCI(L)s **20, 38, 39, 43, 44, 45, 221* British LSTs *9, 11, 62, 64, 159, 160, 162, 163, 164, 165, 198, 199, 200, 214, 237, 301, 302, *305, 319, 321, 322, 364, 366,*

		367, 406, 408, 412, 415, 418, 419, 420, 423, 427, 428 British LCI(L)s 260, 272, 274, 281, 292 British: Destroyer HMS *Croome* (L62) Tank landing ship HMS *Thruster* (F131) Tug HMS *Prosperous* (W96) Boom defense vessels HMS *Barndale* (Z92), HMS *Barmond* (Z232) Greek: HHMS *Themistocles* (L51)
	Other Follow-on ships	LST-385, *HMS *LST-422*, *HM *LSI(L)-273*
CTG 81.6	Escort Group: Capt. J. P. Clay, USN, in *Plunkett*; Capt. Harry Sanders, USN (CDS-13), after *Plunkett* was damaged	Flagship: *Plunkett* (DD-431), *Fredrick C. Davis* (DE-136), *Gleaves* (DD-423), *Herbert C. Jones* (DE-137), *Niblack* (DD-424), *Steady* (AM-118), *Sustain* (AM-119) British: HMS *Croome* (L62), HMS *Ulster Queen* Greek: HHMS *Themistocles* (L51)
CTG 81.7	Sweeper Group: Comdr. Alfred H. Richards, USN	Flagship: *Pilot* (AM-104), *Dextrous* (AM-341), *Pioneer* (AM-105), *Strive* (AM-117), *Sway* (AM-120), *Symbol* (AM-123), **Portent* (AM-106), *Prevail* (AM-107); YMSs 3, 29, *30, 34, 36, 43, 58, 62, 69, 82, 83, 207, 208, 226; SC-770
CTG 81.8	Gunfire Support Group: Capt. Robert W. Cary Jr., USN (CO, *Brooklyn*)	Flagship: *Brooklyn* (CL-40), *Edison* (DD-439), *Ludlow* (DD-438), *Mayo* (DD-422), *Trippe* (DD-403), *Woolsey* (DD-437), flagship of Capt. Harry Sanders, USN; CDS-13) British: *HMS *Penelope* (97), HMS *Loyal* (G15), LCG(4), LCG(8)
CTG 81.9	Beach Identification Group: Commanding Officer, HHMS *Kriti*	PC-556, PC-559, PC-627, SC-693, SC-697 British: HMS *Uproar* (P31) Greek: HHMS *Kriti* (L84), former HMS *Hursely* (L84)
CTG 81.10	Beach Company Group: Lt. Comdr. J. V. Eubank Jr., USNR, CO, 1st Beach Battalion	1st Navy Beach Battalion
CTG 81.11	Salvage Group: Lt. Comdr. Gordon Raymond, USNR, 8th Amphibious Force Salvage Officer	Headquarters ship *LCI(L)-10* LCI(L)s 219, 232 LCT(5)s 212, 221, 288 ATR-1, *Edenshaw* (YTB-459), *Hopi* (AT-71), *Restorer* (ARS-17), *Weight* (ARS-35) British: *Weasel* (W120); LCI(L)s 15, 16, 209; LCT(5)-189
CTG 81.12	Air Navigation Group	PT-201, PT-216

Task Force Peter:
Rear Adm. Thomas Hope Troubridge, RN

Force flagship HMS *Bulolo* (F82): Rear Admiral Troubridge, RN
Troop ships: LSI(L) S.S. *Derbyshire*, Infantry landing ship HMS *Glengyle* (4.196), Polish liner M.S. *Sobieski*
Anti-aircraft and fighter-director ships: HMS *Palomares*, HMS *Ulster Queen*
Light cruisers: HMS *Dido* (37), HMS *Mauritius* (80), HMS *Orion* (85), *HMS *Spartan* (95)
Destroyers: HMS *Beaufort* (L14), HMS *Brecon* (L76), HMS *Faulknor* (H 62), *HMS *Inglefield* (D02), *HMS *Janus* (F53), HMS *Jervis* (F00), HMS *Kempenfelt* (R03), *HMS *Laforey* (G99), HMS *Loyal* (G15), HMS *Tenacious* (R45), HMS *Tetcott* (L99), HMS *Urchin* (R99), HMS *Wilton* (L128), French FR *Le Fantasque*
Dutch sloops: HMNS *Flores* (F76), HMNS *Soemba* (T199)
Minesweepers: HMS *Bude* (J116), HMS *Cadmus* (J230), HMS *Fly* (J306), HMS *Rinaldo* (J225), HMS

Anzio Naval Order of Battle 293

Rothesay (J19), HMS *Waterwitch* (J304)
Tank landing ships: HMS *Boxer* (F121), HMS *Bruiser* (F127), HMS *Thruster* (F131)

Patrol craft - Trawlers: HMS *Hornpipe* (T120), HMS *Sheppey* (T292), HMS *St. Kilda* (T209), HMS *Two Step* (T142), USS *PC-550*, USS *PC-621*, USS *PC-624*, USS *SC-508*, USS *SC-638* (The PCs and SC comprised the Reference Vessel Group which, with submarine HMS *Ultor*, helped guide landing craft to beaches, and later served as patrol craft.)

British Tank landing ships: LSTs *62, 63, 160, 198, 200, 214, 303, 304, 322, 366, 410, 412, 415, *418, 419, 420, 421, 427, 428*
British Large infantry landing craft: LCI(L)s *6, 97*
U.S. LSTs *197*, 327, **348, 352, 358, 359, 377, 379, 384*
U.S. LCI(L)s *2, 3, 4, 8, 9, 11, 12, 14, 212, 213, 215, 216, 218, 219*
British *LCT(Mk 2)-315*
U.S. Tank landing craft: LCT(5)s *16, 24, 26, 31, 125, 136, 137, 140, 148, 152, 210, 217, 219, *220, 224, 237, 277, 340*

Oiler: S.S *British Chancellor*

Boom defense vessel: HMS *Barndale* (Z92)

Tug: USS *Edenshaw* (YT-459), towed causeways to Peter beach and returned to X-Ray beaches
British hospital ships: HMHS *Leinster*, HMHS *St. Andrew*, HMHS *St. David*, HMHS *St. Julien*
Beacon submarine: HMS *Ultor* (P53)

Appendix E: U.S. Tugs at Normandy

The meaning of the acronym SNO used in the table is Senior Naval Officer; Dungeness, Portsmouth, and Selsey are port cities in England. SNO Selsey, for example, was the title for the senior officer (Royal Navy) at Selsey.

U.S. Navy Tugs

Navy Tug	Assigned to	Assignment
Algorma (AT-34)	SNO Dungeness	Tow two B1 Mulberry units
Arikara (AT-98)	SNO Selsey	Tow Phoenix and Whale units
Bannock (AT-81)	SNO Selsey	Tow Phoenix and Whale units
Cormorant (AT-133)	SNO Selsey	Tow Phoenix and Whale units
Kewaydin (AT-24)	SNO Dungeness	Tow two B-1 Mulberry units
Kiowa (AT-72)	SNO Selsey	Tow Phoenix and Whale units
Owl (AT-137)	SNO Selsey	Tow Phoenix and Whale units
Partridge (AT-138)	SNO Selsey	Tow Phoenix and Whale units
Pinto (AT-90)	SNO Selsey	Tow Phoenix and Whale units
ATA-125	SNO Selsey	Tow Phoenix and Whale units
ATA-170	SNO Selsey	Tow Phoenix and Whale units
ATA-172		
ATR-2		
ATR-13	SNO Selsey	Tow Phoenix and Whale units
ATR-15		
ATR-47		
ATR-54	SNO Selsey	Tow Phoenix and Whale units
ATR-97		
ATR-99	SNO Selsey	Tow Phoenix and Whale units

WSA Tugs (Managed by Moran Towing)

WSA Tug	Assigned to	Assignment
Black Rock		Tow Phoenix units
Bodie Island		Tow Phoenix units
Farallon		Tow Phoenix units
Gay Head		Tow Phoenix units
Great Isaac		Tow Phoenix units
Hillsboro Inlet		Tow Phoenix units
Moose Peak		Tow Phoenix units
Sankaty Head		Tow Phoenix units
Trinidad Head		Tow Phoenix units

U.S. Army Tugs

Army Tug	Assigned to	Assignment
Large tug *LT-2*	SNO Portsmouth	Tow two barges from Exmouth
Large tug *LT-4*	SNO Portsmouth	Tow two barges from Exmouth
Large tug *LT-5*	SNO Portsmouth	Tow two barges from Exmouth
Large tug *LT-22*	SNO Portsmouth	Tow two barges from Exmouth

Appendix E

Large tug *LT-23*	SNO Portsmouth	Tow two barges from Exmouth
Large tug *LT-62*		
Large tug *LT-118*		
Large tug *LT-119*		
Large tug *LT-130*	SNO Portsmouth	Tow two barges from Exmouth
Large tug *LT-136*		
Large tug *LT-152*		Tow crane from Belfast to Plymouth
Large tug *LT-155*		
Large tug *LT-156*		Tow barges to Omaha beach
Large tug *LT-159*		
Large tug *LT-194*		
Large tug *LT-214*		
Large tug *LT-374*		
Large tug *LT-389*		Arrived in Plymouth on 17 Aug 1944
Large tug *LT-456*		
Large tug *LT-532*		Tow crane from Glasgow to Falmouth
Large tug *LT-533*		
Large tug *LT-534*		
Large tug *LT-638*		
Large tug *LT-639*		
Large tug *LT-653*		
Large tug *LT-719*		
Large tug *LT-785*		
Large tug *LT-786*		
Large tug *LT-787*		
Large tug *LT-788*		
Small tug *ST-16*		
Small tug *ST-247*		Position Mulberries and Gooseberries
Small tug *ST-248*		Position Mulberries and Gooseberries
Small tug *ST-253*		Position Mulberries and Gooseberries
Small tug *ST-335*		
Small tug *ST-338*		Position Mulberries and Gooseberries
Small tug *ST-344*		Position Mulberries and Gooseberries
Small tug *ST-698*		
Small tug *ST-705*		Position Mulberries and Gooseberries
Small tug *ST-758*		Position Mulberries and Gooseberries
Small tug *ST-759*		Position Mulberries and Gooseberries
Small tug *ST-760*		Position Mulberries and Gooseberries
Small tug *ST-761*		Position Mulberries and Gooseberries
Small tug *ST-762*		Position Mulberries and Gooseberries
Small tug *ST-763*		Position Mulberries and Gooseberries
Small tug *ST-766*		Position Mulberries and Gooseberries
Small tug *ST-767*		Position Mulberries and Gooseberries
Small tug *ST-768*		Position blockships for sinking
Small tug *ST-769*		Position Mulberries and Gooseberries
Small tug *ST-770*		Position Mulberries and Gooseberries
Small tug *ST-771*		Position Mulberries and Gooseberries
Small tug *ST-772*		Position Mulberries and Gooseberries
Small tug *ST-773*		Position Mulberries and Gooseberries
Small tug *ST-774*		
Small tug *ST-775*		

Small tug *ST-776*	
Small tug *ST-778*	Position Mulberries and Gooseberries
Small tug *ST-780*	
Small tug *ST-781*	Position Mulberries and Gooseberries
Small tug *ST-794*	Position Mulberries and Gooseberries
Small tug *ST-795*	Position Mulberries and Gooseberries

Appendix F: Terms of Surrender for German Forces

29 August 1944

Commanding Officer, U.S.S. *PHILADELPHIA*, Captain Walter Ansel, United States Navy, is authorized to accept the surrender of German Forces on the Islands of Pomegues, Ratonneux and Fortress D'If in the terms below set forth for Commander Support Forces, Allied Western Naval Task Force.

L. A. Davidson,
Rear Admiral, U.S. Navy,
Commanding Support Forces (86),
Allied Western Naval Task Force

I agree to the surrender of the officers and garrison of the defenses of the Islands of Pomegues, Ratonneux and Fortress D'If in the harbor of Marseilles, along with their defense installations, on this 29th day of August 1944, to the forces of the United States Navy, represented by Rear Admiral L. A. Davidson, Commander Task Force Eighty-Six, Commanding Support Forces, Allied Naval Forces, Mediterranean.

Terms of surrender include:

1. The surrender is unconditional. No promises or engagements are made as to the eventual disposition of the prisoners, except that treatment accorded will be as specified in the Geneva Conventions.

2. (a) All officers and men shall be assembled and shall lay down their arms. Each individual must produce an arm to lay down appropriate to his position.
   (b) A master list of the officers and troops in these garrisons shall be rendered.
   (c) Officers and men may retain their insignia of rank; officers may retain their sword.

3. Any spare supply of arms and all ammunition for all arms shall be assembled and turned over.

4. No arms, guns, or defense installations shall be disturbed or injured. They shall be left intact as now exists.

5. Prisoners of war shall be fed on German supplies until removed from the island.

6. The German command undertakes to clear all land mines and remove demolition charges and to deliver charts and information showing the sea and harbor defenses including mines and fire control equipment. This includes radar installations.

7. While on the Island, the German military organization shall remain intact and the officers and petty officers thereof shall be responsible for the conduct and discipline of the troops under their command. The prisoners of war will be guarded by

detachments of United States Marines from the U.S.S. *AUGUSTA* and U.S.S. *PHILADELPHIA*. The prisoners are required to obey the orders and commands of the Commanding Officers and the guards regularly stationed from these detachments.

/s/ Kapitan Leutenant FULLGRABE

Accepted for Commander Support Forces, Allied Western Naval Task Force.

The signature of Kapitan Leutenant FULLGRABE above was affixed at 1816, G.C.T. on the 29th day of August 1944.

/s/ WALTER ANSEL,
Captain, United States Navy,
Commanding Officer, U.S.S. *PHILADELPHIA*

Appendix G: Tug and Salvage Ship Unit Awards

The below listed ships served in the African, European, or Mediterranean Theaters of war, and received the American Campaign Medal and the World War II Victory Medal, as well as other service medals identified in the table. Three of the fleet tugs earned American Defense Service Medals as well; *Algorma* and *Kewaydin* (with fleet clasp) for duty between 8 September 1939 and 7 December 1941, and *Cherokee* (with bronze "A" clasp) for duty in actual or potential belligerent contact with Axis Powers in the Atlantic Ocean between June 22 and 7 December 1941. Additionally, the fleet tugs *Arikara* and *Pinto*, and rescue tug *ATR-2* earned the Navy Unit Commendation for the period 7-12 June 1944.

Fleet Tugs (AT) were reclassified in 1944 as ATF (Fleet Tug) or ATO (Old Fleet Tug)

Ship	Europe-Africa-Middle East Campaign Medal	Occupation Service Medal (with Europe Clasp)	Asiatic-Pacific Campaign Medal	Occupation Service Medal (with Asia clasp)
Abnaki (AT-96/ATF-96)			X	X
Algorma (AT-34/ATO-34)	1 battle star		X	
Alsea (AT-97/ATF-97)				
Arapaho (AT-68/ATF-68)			4 battle stars	X
Arikara (AT-98/ATF-98)	2 battle stars		1 battle star	X
Bannock (AT-81/ATF-81)	1 battle star		1 battle star	X
Carib (AT-82/ATF-82)			X	X
Cherokee (AT-66/ATF-66)	1 battle star			
Chippewa (AT-69/ATF-69)				
Choctaw (AT-70/ATF-70)				
Cocopa (AT-101/ATF-101)			X	X
Hopi (AT-71/ATF-71)	4 battle stars			

Appendix G

Ship				
Kewaydin (AT-24/ATO-24)	1 battle star			
Kiowa (AT-72/ATF-72)	1 battle star			
Moreno (AT-87/ATF-87)	3 battle stars			
Narragansett (AT-88/ATF-88)	3 battle stars		X	
Nauset (AT-89/ATF-89)	2 battle stars			
Pinto (AT-90/ATF-90)	2 battle stars		1 battle star	

Rescue Tugs (ATR)/Auxiliary Tugs (ATA)

Ship	Europe-Africa-Middle East Campaign Medal	Occupation Service Medal (with Europe Clasp)	Asiatic-Pacific Campaign Medal	Occupation Service Medal (with Asia clasp)
ATR-1	2 battle stars			
ATR-2	1 battle star			
ATR-3	1 battle star			
ATR-4	1 battle star	X		
ATR-5				
ATR-6				
ATR-13	1 battle star		X	X
ATR-15	1 battle star			
ATR-47/ATA-125	2 battle stars			
ATR-97/ATA-170	2 battle stars			
ATR-98/ATA-171				
ATR-99/ATA-172	2 battle stars			

Salvage Ships (ARS)

Ship	Europe-Africa-Middle East Campaign Medal	Navy Occupation Service Medal (with Europe Clasp)	Asiatic-Pacific Campaign Medal	Navy Occupation Service Medal (with Asia clasp)
Diver (ARS-5)	1 battle star	X		
Extricate (ARS-16)	1 battle star		1 battle star	X
Restorer (ARS-17)	2 battle stars			
Weight (ARS-35)	2 battle stars			
Swivel (ARS-36)	1 battle star			
Tackle (ARS-37)	2 battle stars			

Yard/Harbor Tugs (YT/YTB/YTM/YTL)

Ship	Europe-Africa-Middle East Campaign Medal	Ship Disposition (all but two of the below listed ships, YT-198 and Mecosta, were transferred to the French)
Evea (YT-458/YTB-458)	3 battle stars	As FNS Malabar
Edenshaw (YT-459/YTB-459)	4 battle stars	As FNS Coolie (A684)

Tug and Salvage Ship Unit Awards 303

Mecosta (YT-392/YTB-392/YTM-392)		Struck, date unknown, sold for commercial service 1 Jul 81, fate unknown
YT-132/YTL-132		In North Africa, named *Mouette*
YT-143/YTL-143		In North Africa, named *Pinson*
YT-154/YTL-154		In North Africa, named *Pont du Fahs*
YT-157/YTL-157		In North Africa, named *Mésange*
YT-158/YTL-158		In North Africa, named *Santa Cruz*
YT-160/YTL-160	1 battle star	In North Africa, named *Pluvier*
YT-161/YTL-161	2 battle stars	In 1944, named *Hirondelle*
YT-163/YTL-163		In North Africa, named *Caille*
YT-165/YTL-165		In North Africa, named *Chardonneret*
YT-184/YTL-184		In North Africa, named *Santon*
YT-185/YTL-185		In North Africa, named *Rouge-Gorge*
YT-186/YTL-186		In North Africa, named *Cormoran*
YT-196/YTL-196		In North Africa, named *Rossignol*
YT-197/YTL-197		In 1944 and named *Kasserine* (Y660)
YT-198	1 battle star	Sunk after hitting a mine, 18 Feb 44 off Anzio
YT-207/YTL-207		In North Africa, named *Medgez el Bab*
YT-208/YTL-208		In North Africa, named *Anfa*
YT-209/YTL-209		In North Africa, named *Canastel*
YT-210/YTL-210		In North Africa, named *Courlis*
YT-212/YTL-212		In North Africa, named *Mamora*

Bibliography

Administrative History of U.S. Naval Forces in Europe, 1940-1946, Vol. 5. London, 1946.

Annussek, Greg. *Hitler's Raid to Save Mussolini: The Most Infamous Commando Operation of World War II.* Cambridge, MA: Da Capo Press, 2005.

Anzio Beachhead 22 January - 25 May 1944. Washington, DC: U.S. Army Center of Military History, 1990.

Barbey, Daniel E. *MacArthur's Amphibious Navy.* Annapolis: U.S. Naval Institute, 1969.

Bartholomew, Charles A. and William I. Milwee Jr. *Mud, Muscle, and Miracles: Marine Salvage in the United States Navy.* Washington, D.C.: Naval History & Heritage Command and Naval Sea Systems Command, 2009.

HMSO. *Battle Summary No. 39 "Operation Neptune" Landings in Normandy June 1944.* London: Her Majesty's Stationery Office, 1994.

Bruhn, David D. *Wooden Ships and Iron Men: The U.S. Navy's Coastal and Motor Minesweepers, 1941-1953.* Westminster, MD: Heritage Books, 2009.

Conway's All the World's Fighting Ships, 1922-1946. Annapolis: U.S. Naval Institute, 2006.

Cressman, Robert. *The Official Chronology of the U.S. Navy in World War II.* Annapolis: U.S. Naval Institute, 2000.

Dockery, Kevin. *Navy SEALs: A History of the Early Years.* New York: Berkeley Publishing, 2001.

Elliot, Peter. *Allied Minesweeping in World War 2.* Annapolis: U.S. Naval Institute, 1979.

Garland, Albert N. and Howard McGaw Smyth. *United States Army in World War II Mediterranean Theater of Operations: Sicily and the Surrender of Italy.* Washington, D.C.: Center of Military History, U.S. Army, 1993.

Grosvenor, J. and L. M. Bates *Open The Ports - The Story of the Human Minesweepers.* London: William Kimber, 1956.

Howe, George F. *United States Army in World War II Mediterranean Theater of Operations Northwest Africa: Seizing the Initiative In the West.* Washington, D.C.: Dept. of the Army, 1957.

Lott, Arnold. *Most Dangerous Sea.* Annapolis: U.S. Naval Institute, 1959.

Mather, Carol. *When the Grass Stops Growing.* Barnsley, South Yorkshire: Pen & Sword Military, 2006.

Morison, Samuel Eliot. *History of United States Naval Operations in World War II, Operations in North African Waters, October 1942-June 1943.* Boston: Little, Brown, 1962.

—*History of United States Naval Operations in World War II, Sicily-Salerno-Anzio January 1943-June 1944.* Boston: Little, Brown, 1984.

—*History of United States Naval Operations in World War II, The Battle of the Atlantic, 1939-1943.* Boston: Little, Brown, 1984.

—*The Two-Ocean War.* Boston: Little, Brown, 1963.

Roskill, S. W. *History of the Second World War – The War at Sea*. London: HMSO, 1961.

Tomblin, Barbara. *With Utmost Spirit: Allied Naval Operations in the Mediterranean, 1942-1945*. Lexington. KY: University of Kentucky Press, 2004.

United States Naval Administration in World War II, *The Invasion of Normandy: Operation NEPTUNE, Commander, U.S. Naval Forces in Europe: Volume V*. 1948

United States Naval Administration in World War II, *History of the Naval Armed Guard Afloat World War II*. Washington, D.C.: Office of Naval Operations, 1949.

Ziemke, Earl F. *The U.S. Army in the Occupation of Germany 1944-1946*. Washington, D.C.: Center of Military History, U.S. Army, 1990.

NOTES

ACRONYMS USED IN CHAPTER NOTES

CINCLANT	Commander-in-Chief, Atlantic Fleet
CO	Commanding Officer
ComDesDiv	Commander Destroyer Division
ComEighthFlt	Commander U.S. Eighth Fleet
ComMinRon	Commander Mine Squadron
ComDesRon	Commander Destroyer Squadron
ComEastSeaFron	Commander Eastern Sea Frontier
ComNavEur	Commander U.S. Naval Forces in Europe
ComNogr EastSeaFron	Commander Northern Group Eastern Sea Frontier
ComSerForLant	Commander Service Force Atlantic
CTF	Commander Task Force
CTG	Commander Task Group
CTU	Commander Task Unit
CWNTF:	Commander Western Naval Task Force
NOB	Naval Operating Base
ONI	Office of Naval Intelligence
OPLAN	Operation Plan
WNTF	Western Naval Task Force

SHIP WAR DIARIES

ATR-1, ATR-3, ATR-4, ATR-47, ATR-13, Bannock, Barnett, Benson, Brant, Cherokee, Cole, Dallas, Diver, Harry Lee, Hopi, Ingham, Marsh, McLanahan, Monrovia, Moreno, Narragansett, Nauset, Leary, LST-313, LST-326, LST-988, PC-619, SC-697, SC-1029, Schenck, Swivel, YMS-20, YMS-83

OPERATIONAL/ADMINISTRATIVE COMMANDS

CincLant; ComDesDiv 26; ComDesRon 13; ComEastSeaFron; ComEighthFlt; ComMinRon 6; ComNogr EastSeaFron; Commander Landing Craft and Bases, Amphibious Force, Eighth Fleet; Commander Landing Craft and Bases, Amphibious Force, Northwest African Waters; Com LST Group One; ComNavEur; Commandant NOB Palermo; Commander U.S. Naval Forces, Northwest African Waters; Commander U.S. Navy Salvage Base Dellys, Algeria; Commander U.S. Ports and Bases, France; ComSerForLant; CTF 81; CTF-84; CTF-126; NOB Iceland; Norfolk Navy Yard; U.S. Naval Advanced Base Bremen, Commander Naval Advanced Bases, U.S. Eighth Fleet Germany; U.S. Naval Detachment Port de Bouc, France; U.S. Naval Forces Navy 815; U.S. Naval Operating Base, Bermuda; U.S. Navy Port Office, Port de Bouc, France

PREFACE NOTES
[1] Comdr. Edward H. Lundquist, "Fleet Tugs in World War II" (http://navy.memorieshop.com/Tug-Boats/ATR-7/WWII.html: accessed 2 October 2013).

CHAPTER 1 NOTES
[1] ONI Combat Narratives, The Landings in North Africa, p. 1.
[2] ONI Combat Narratives, The Landings in North Africa, p. 2; Samuel Eliot Morison, *History of United States Naval Operations in World War II, Operations in North African Waters, October 1942-June 1943* (Boston: Little, Brown, 1962) p. 12-13.
[3] ONI Combat Narratives, The Landings in North Africa, p. 2, 6.
[4] ONI Combat Narratives, The Landings in North Africa, p. 6-7; Morison, *History of United States Naval Operations in World War II, Operations in North African Waters, October 1942-June 1943*, p. 41-42.
[5] "Operation Torch: Sub-Task Force Goalpost Capture Port Lyautey," *Historynet.com* (http://www.historynet.com/operation-torch-sub-task-force-goalpost-capture-port-lyautey.htm: accessed 21 September 2013).
[6] Kevin Dockery, *Navy SEALs: A History of the Early Years* (New York: Berkeley Publishing, 2001), p. 34; Charles A. Bartholomew and William I. Milwee Jr., *Mud, Muscle, and Miracles: Marine Salvage in the United States Navy* (Washington, D.C.: Naval History & Heritage Command and Naval Sea Systems Command, 2009), p. 101.
[7] "*Cherokee* (ATF-66)," NavSource (http://www.navsource.org/archives/09/39/39066.htm: accessed 22 September 2013).
[8] *Cherokee* War Diary, October 1942.
[9] CTF 34, Torch Operation, preliminary report of, 28 November 1942; *Cherokee* War Diary, October 1942; Morison, *History of United States Naval Operations in World War II, Operations in North African Waters, October 1942-June 1943*, p. 8.
[10] *Cole* and *Dallas* War Diary, October 1942.
[11] *Dallas* War Diary, October 1942.
[12] *Dallas* War Diary, November 1942.
[13] George F. Howe, *United States Army in World War II Mediterranean Theater of Operations Northwest Africa: Seizing the Initiative In the West* (Washington, D.C.: Dept. of the Army, 1957), p. 147; "Operation Torch: Sub-Task Force Goalpost Capture Port Lyautey," *Historynet.com*.
[14] CO, USS *George Clymer*, After Battle Report – Port Lyautey (Mehedia), French Morocco, Africa, period November 7-11, 1942, Inclusive, 20 November 1942; *Brant* War Diary, October 1942.
[15] CO, USS *George Clymer*, After Battle Report – Port Lyautey (Mehedia), French Morocco, Africa, period November 7-11, 1942, Inclusive, 20 November 1942.
[16] Ibid.

[17] CTF 34, TORCH Operation, preliminary report of, 28 November 1942; Morison, *History of United States Naval Operations in World War II, Operations in North African Waters, October 1942-June 1943*, p. 31, 115, 116, 118, 123; Patrick Masell "The Curtiss P-40 Warhawk" (http://www.chuckhawks.com/p40.htm: accessed 30 September 2013).
[18] CTF 34, TORCH Operation, preliminary report of, 28 November 1942; Morison, *History of United States Naval Operations in World War II, Operations in North African Waters, October 1942-June 1943*, p. 125.
[19] CO, USS *George Clymer*, After Battle Report – Port Lyautey (Mehedia), French Morocco, Africa, period November 7-11, 1942, Inclusive, 20 November 1942; Morison, *History of United States Naval Operations in World War II, Operations in North African Waters, October 1942-June 1943*, p. 125.
[20] CO, USS *George Clymer*, After Battle Report – Port Lyautey (Mehedia), French Morocco, Africa, period November 7-11, 1942, Inclusive, 20 November 1942.
[21] CO, USS *Dallas* (DD-199), Report of action against enemy between November 7 and 11, 1942, 19 November 1942; Morison, *History of United States Naval Operations in World War II, Operations in North African Waters, October 1942-June 1943*, p. 129.
[22] CO, USS *Dallas* (DD-199), Report of action against enemy between November 7 and 11, 1942, 19 November 1942.
[23] Ibid.
[24] Ibid.
[25] CO, USS *Dallas* (DD-199), Report of action against enemy between November 7 and 11, 1942, 19 November 1942; *Dallas* War Diary, November 1942; Morison, *History of United States Naval Operations in World War II, Operations in North African Waters, October 1942-June 1943*, p. 131.
[26] General Orders: Commander in Chief, Atlantic: Serial 0335 10 February 1943.
[27] George F. Howe, *United States Army in World War II Mediterranean Theater of Operations Northwest Africa: Seizing the Initiative In the West*, p. 147-148.
[28] General Orders: Bureau of Naval Personnel Information Bulletin No. 317 of August 1943.
[29] *Cherokee* War Diary, November 1942; Morison, *History of United States Naval Operations in World War II, Operations in North African Waters, October 1942-June 1943*, p. 139.
[30] Morison, *History of United States Naval Operations in World War II, Operations in North African Waters, October 1942-June 1943*, p. 143-146.
[31] *Cherokee* War Diary, November 1942; Morison, *History of United States Naval Operations in World War II, Operations in North African Waters, October 1942-June 1943*, p. 147-148.
[32] *Cherokee* War Diary, November 1942.
[33] *Cherokee* War Diary, November 1942; USS *Joseph Hewes* (AP 50), Uboat.net (http://uboat.net/allies/merchants/ships/2407.html: accessed 26 September 2013); *Joseph Hewes*, DANFS.
[34] *Cherokee* War Diary, November 1942.

[35] Morison, *History of United States Naval Operations in World War II, Operations in North African Waters, October 1942-June 1943*, p. 177.
[36] *Cherokee, DANFS*.

CHAPTER 2 NOTES
[1] Lundquist, "Fleet Tugs in World War II".
[2] Lundquist, "Fleet Tugs in World War II"; *U.S. Navy Salvage Manual*, Appendix G.
[3] Lundquist, "Fleet Tugs in World War II"; Bartholomew and Milwee Jr., *Mud, Muscle, and Miracles*, p. 54.
[4] Lundquist, "Fleet Tugs in World War II".
[5] Stephen S. Roberts, "U. S. Navy Auxiliary Vessel Ship Types, 1920-1945" (http://www.shipscribe.com/usnaux/ATR/ATR01.html: 17 October 2013).
[6] Commodore Sullivan, Naval Salvage Service, 9 December 1943.
[7] Roberts, "U. S. Navy Auxiliary Vessel Ship Types, 1920-1945".
[8] Ibid.
[9] Ibid.
[10] Lundquist, "Fleet Tugs in World War II".
[11] Roberts, "U. S. Navy Auxiliary Vessel Ship Types, 1920-1945".
[12] Ibid.
[13] Ibid.
[14] Lundquist, "Fleet Tugs in World War II"; *Navy Seagoing Tugs and Related Craft, General Characteristics and Considerations Governing Use of*; Roberts, "U. S. Navy Auxiliary Vessel Ship Types, 1920-1945"; "Auxiliary Fleet Tug (ATA) Index," NavSource.
[15] *Navy Seagoing Tugs and Related Craft, General Characteristics and Considerations Governing Use of*.
[16] Ibid.
[17] Tim Colton, "Ocean Tugs (AT, ATA, ATF, ATO, ATR)" (http://www.shipbuildinghistory.com/history/smallships/auxoceantugs.htm: accessed 23 October 2013); Hans van der Ster, "Directory of Tugs of the Auxiliary Fleet Tugs- ATA" (http://www.towingline.com/wp-content/uploads/2009/08/ATA-Auxiliary-Fleet-Tugs.pdf: accessed 28 August 2013); Auxiliary Fleet Tug – ATA Index, NavSource (http://www.navsource.org/archives/09/38/38idx.htm: accessed 28 August 2013).
[18] Lundquist, "Fleet Tugs in World War II".
[19] District Harbor Tug (YT) Index, NavSource (http://www.navsource.org/archives/14/08idx.htm: accessed 13 October 2013).
[20] *YTM-2*, NavSource (http://www.navsource.org/archives/14/08002.htm: accessed 13 October 2013); *Iwana, DANFS*.
[21] "Rescue Ocean Tug (ATR) Index," NavSource (http://www.navsource.org/archives/09/40/40idx.htm); "Auxiliary Fleet Tug (ATA) Index," NavSource

(http://www.navsource.org/archives/09/38/38idx.htm: accessed 24 October 2013); Tim Colton, "Ocean Tugs (AT, ATA, ATF, ATO, ATR)".
[22] Royal Australian Navy Ship/Unit Approved Battle Honours, March 2010 (http://web.archive.org/web/20110614064156/http://www.navy.gov.au/w/images/Units_entitlement_list.pdf: accessed 2 May 2013).
[23] "Rescue Ocean Tug (ATR) Index," NavSource; "Ships of the Royal Navy," U-boat.net (http://www.uboat.net/allies/warships/navy/HMS.html: accessed 23 October 2013).
[24] "HM Rescue Tug *Eminent*," World Naval Ships Forum (http://www.worldnavalships.com/forums/showthread.php?t=11557: accessed 23 October 2013); Allied Warships Rescue Tugs *Favourite* class (http://uboat.net/allies/warships/class/358.html: 23 October 2013).
[25] "Auxiliary Fleet Tug (ATA) Index," NavSource.
[26] Stephen S. Roberts, "Salvage Vessels (ARS)" (http://www.Shipscribe.com/usnaux/ARS/ARStype.html: accessed 1 December 2014).
[27] *Weight*, NavSource (http://www.navsource.org/archives/09/37/3735.htm: accessed 15 December 2014).

CHAPTER 3 NOTES
[1] ComNogr, EastSeaFron War Diary, 1 June-31 August 1942; *Pessacus* (YT-192), *DANFS*; *Uncas* (YTB-242), NavSource (http://www.navsource.org/archives/14/08242.htm: accessed 15 September 2013)
[2] Bartholomew and Milwee Jr., *Mud, Muscle, and Miracles*, p. 56.
[3] Arnold Hague Convoy Database (http://www.convoyweb.org.uk/sc/index.html: accessed 12 September 2013); Tom Linclau *"SC-107,"* Uboat.net (http://uboat.net/ops/convoys/convoys.php?convoy=SC-107: accessed 14 September 2013); CO, USS *Pleiades* (AK-46), Report on Submarine Attacks on Convoy SC 107, 1 March 1945.
[4] Hague Convoy Database; Linclau *"SC-107,"* Uboat.net; CO, USS *Pleiades* (AK-46), Report on Submarine Attacks on Convoy SC 107.
[5] Roger Sarty, "The Royal Canadian Navy and the Battle of the Atlantic, 1939-1945" (http://www.warmuseum.ca/education/online-educational-resources/dispatches/the-royal-canadian-navy-and-the-battle-of-the-atlantic-1939-1945/: accessed 21 December 2014).
[6] Linclau, *"SC-107,"* Uboat.net; *"U-520"* (http://www.uboat.net/boats/u520.htm) and *"U-658"* (http://www.uboat.net/boats/u658.htm: all accessed 14 September 2013).
[7] Linclau, *"SC-107,"* Uboat.net.
[8] Linclau, *"SC-107,"* Uboat.net; *"U-132,"* Uboat.net (http://www.uboat.net/boats/u132.htm: accessed 14 September 2013).
[9] CO, USS *Pleiades* (AK-46), Report on Submarine Attacks on Convoy SC 107.

[10] Steve Johnson, "Rockets, More Rockets, Hale and Boxer Rockets – Flares and Signals Too!" (http://www.cyber-heritage.co.uk/rocketrocket/rockets.htm: accessed 15 September 2013).
[11] CO, USS *Pleiades* (AK-46), Report on Submarine Attacks on Convoy SC 107.
[12] "*SC-107*," Uboat.net (http://uboat.net/ops/convoys/convoys.php?convoy=SC-107: accessed 14 September 2013).
[13] *Ingham* War Diary, November 1942
[14] *SC-107*," Uboat.net (http://uboat.net/ops/convoys/convoys.php?convoy=SC-107: accessed 14 September 2013).
[15] General Orders: Bureau of Naval Personnel Information Bulletin No. 319 (October 1943).
[16] Linclau, "*SC-107*," Uboat.net; "*U-132*," Uboat.net; Samuel Eliot Morison, *History of United States Naval Operations in World War II, The Battle of the Atlantic, 1939-1943* (Boston: Little, Brown, 1984), p. 320.
[17] *Ingham, Leary*, and *Schenck* War Diary, November 1942.
[18] *Ingham* War Diary, November 1942; NOB Iceland War Diary, 1 Apr 1942-28 February 1943; Roger Sarty, "The Royal Canadian Navy and the Battle of the Atlantic, 1939-1945."

CHAPTER 4 NOTES
[1] Cominch Opnav Joint Serial 344, 28 February 1942.
[2] ComEastSeaFron War Diary, December 1943.
[3] Commodore Sullivan, Naval Salvage Service, 9 December 1943; Bartholomew and Milwee Jr., *Mud, Muscle, and Miracles*, p. 49, 70; *Osprey, DANFS*; "Class: *VIKING* (ARS-1)" Shipscribe (http://www.shipscribe.com/usnaux/ARS/ARS01.html: accessed 29 November 2013).
[4] "Merritt-Chapman and Scott: They made Marine Salvage a Major Enterprise" (https://docs.google.com/file/d/0B2KS6sfqM0fOel9Kc2lFY1V2SDg/edit?pli=1: accessed 24 November 2013); Bartholomew and Milwee Jr., *Mud, Muscle, and Miracles*, p. 6.
[5] "Merritt-Chapman and Scott: They made Marine Salvage a Major Enterprise."
[6] Commodore Sullivan, Naval Salvage Service, 9 December 1943; Bartholomew and Milwee Jr., *Mud, Muscle, and Miracles*, p. 70.
[7] Commodore Sullivan, Naval Salvage Service, 9 December 1943; "Rescue and Salvage Ship (ARS) Index," NavSource (http://www.navsource.org/archives/09/37/37idx.htm: accessed 22 November 2013); "Class: *VIKING* (ARS-1)," Shipscribe; *Killerig, Relief*, and *Resolute, DANFS*.
[8] Bartholomew and Milwee Jr., *Mud, Muscle, and Miracles*, p. 71, 197, 526; *Osprey, DANFS*; "Class: *VIKING* (ARS-1)," Shipscribe.

[9] Commodore Sullivan, Naval Salvage Service, 9 December 1943.
[10] Ibid.
[11] ComEastSeaFron War Diary, December 1943; Tim Colton, "Ocean Tugs (AT, ATA, ATF, ATO, ATR)"; "Fleet Tug (AT) Index," NavSource (http://www.navsource.org/archives/09/47/47idx.htm: accessed 20 November 2013).
[12] ComEastSeaFron War Diary, December 1943.
[13] Bob Umbdenstock, "Salvage Contracts: Why Terms Matter - Apr 2002," Marcon International Inc. (http://www.marcon.com/marcon2c.cfm?SectionListsID=85&PageID=279: accessed 27 November 2013).
[14] Commodore Sullivan, Naval Salvage Service, 9 December 1943.
[15] Commodore Sullivan, Naval Salvage Service, 9 December 1943; Bartholomew and Milwee Jr., *Mud, Muscle, and Miracles*, p. 90-91.
[16] Bartholomew and Milwee Jr., *Mud, Muscle, and Miracles*, p. 85.
[17] "Merritt-Chapman and Scott: They made Marine Salvage a Major Enterprise;" *Lafayette, DANFS*.
[18] Commodore Sullivan, Naval Salvage Service, 9 December 1943.
[19] Commodore Sullivan, Naval Salvage Service, 9 December 1943; Bartholomew and Milwee Jr., *Mud, Muscle, and Miracles*, p. 88, 100.
[20] Commodore Sullivan, Naval Salvage Service, 9 December 1943.
[21] Ibid.

CHAPTER 5 NOTES

[1] CWNTF, Action Report – The Sicilian Campaign Operation "Husky" July-August, 1943 (http://www.history.navy.mil/library/online/siciliancampaign_admhistory148c.htm: accessed 6 October 2013).
[2] Greg Annussek, *Hitler's Raid to Save Mussolini: The Most Infamous Commando Operation of World War II* (Da Capo Press, 2005).
[3] Ibid.
[4] CWNTF, Action Report – The Sicilian Campaign Operation "Husky" July-August, 1943; Samuel Eliot Morison, *The Two-Ocean War* (Boston: Little, Brown, 1963), p. 246.
[5] Commander U.S Naval Forces, Northwest African Waters, War Diary; forwarding of, 6 April 1944.
[6] Commander Landing Craft and Bases, Amphibious Force, Eighth Fleet War Diary, April and June 1943.
[7] Commander U.S. Navy Salvage Base Dellys, Algeria War Diary, June-December 1943; "William A. Sullivan Rear Admiral, United States Navy," Arlington National Cemetery website (http://www.arlingtoncemetery.net/wasullivan.htm: accessed 12 November 2013).
[8] Commander U.S. Navy Salvage Base Dellys, Algeria War Diary, June-December 1943.
[9] Ibid.

[10] Commander U.S. Navy Salvage Base Dellys, Algeria War Diary, June-December 1943; Lt. Harvey M. Andersen Navy Cross Citation (http://projects.militarytimes.com/citations-medals-awards/recipient.php?recipientid=21197: accessed 13 November 2013); Bartholomew and Milwee Jr., *Mud, Muscle, and Miracles*, p. 122.
[11] Commander U.S. Navy Salvage Base Dellys, Algeria War Diary, June-December 1943; Bartholomew and Milwee Jr., *Mud, Muscle, and Miracles*, p. 122.
[12] Bartholomew and Milwee Jr., *Mud, Muscle, and Miracles*, p. 120-121; William H. Stoneman, "War Supplies Salvage on Beached Ship Husky American Experts Taking $16,000,000 Cargo From Vessel's Holds," *Syracuse Herald-Journal*, 1943 (http://fultonhistory.com/Newspaper%2015/Syracuse%20NY%20Journal/Syracuse%20NY%20Journal%201943/Syracuse%20NY%20Journal%201943%20-%200976.pdf: accessed 13 November 2012)
[13] Bartholomew and Milwee Jr., *Mud, Muscle, and Miracles*, p. 120-121; Stoneman, "War Supplies Salvage on Beached Ship Husky American Experts Taking $16,000,000 Cargo From Vessel's Holds," *Syracuse Herald-Journal*, 1943.
[14] Ibid.
[15] CWNTF, Action Report – The Sicilian Campaign Operation "Husky" July-August, 1943; Morison, *The Two-Ocean War*, p. 247-248.
[16] CWNTF, Action Report – The Sicilian Campaign Operation "Husky" July-August, 1943; Morison, *The Two-Ocean War*, p. 248, 252.
[17] CWNTF, Action Report – The Sicilian Campaign Operation "Husky" July-August, 1943.
[18] CO, USS *Redwing*, Action Report, 12 July 1943.
[19] Ibid.
[20] "Gulfport Shipbuilding, Port Arthur TX" (http://www.shipbuildinghistory.com/history/shipyards/2large/inactive/gulfport.htm: accessed 27 October 2013); *Busy*, *DANFS*; "Yard Tugs (YT, YTB, YTM, YTL) Built or Acquired During WWII" (http://www.shipbuildinghistory.com/history/smallships/yt2.htm: accessed 27 October 2013); "District Harbor Tug (YT) Index," NavSource; CTF 81 War Diary, June 1943; Bartholomew and Milwee Jr., *Mud, Muscle, and Miracles*, p. 119.
[21] Commander U.S Naval Forces, Northwest African Waters, War Diary; forwarding of, 6 April 1944.
[22] Commander CENT Attack Force, Operation "HUSKY" – Report upon, 21 July 1943.
[23] CTF 81 War Diary, July 1943; CTF 81, Action Report – Operation "HUSKY," Serial 00179.
[24] CTF 81 War Diary, July 1943.
[25] CTF 81, Action Report – Operation "HUSKY"; Morison, *The Two-Ocean War*, p. 253-254.
[26] Commander CENT Attack Force, Operation "HUSKY" – Report upon, 21 July 1943.

[27] CTF 81, Action Report – Operation "HUSKY".
[28] Ibid.
[29] Ibid.
[30] Com LST Group One War Diary, July 1943.
[31] *Hopi* War Diary, July 1943.
[32] Ibid.
[33] *Hopi* War Diary, July 1943; CTF 81, Action Report – Operation "HUSKY"; Com LST Group One War Diary, July 1943; Action Report of the USS *LST 313*, 19 July 1943, and War Diary from 8-10 July 1943.
[34] CO, USS *LST 313*, Action Report of the USS *LST 313*, 19 July 1943, and War Diary from 8-10 July 1943.
[35] Ibid.
[36] *Hopi* War Diary, July 1943; CO, USS *LST 312*, Report; Action, 22 July 1943.
[37] *Hopi* and *Barnett* War Diary, July 1943; CTF 81, Action Report – Operation "HUSKY".
[38] CWNTF, Action Report – The Sicilian Campaign Operation "Husky" July-August, 1943; *Hopi* War Diary, July 1943; CTF 81, Action Report – Operation "HUSKY".
[39] *Hopi* and *McLanahan* War Diary, July 1943; CTF 81, Action Report – Operation "HUSKY".
[40] *Hopi* War Diary, July 1943; *Hopi* "Anti-Aircraft Action by Surface Ships" report of 11 July 1943;
[41] *Hopi* War Diary, July 1943.
[42] CTF 81, Action Report – Operation "HUSKY".
[43] Lt. Comdr. Harvey M. Andersen Legion of Merit Medal Citation (http://projects.militarytimes.com/citations-medals-awards/recipient.php?recipientid=21197: accessed 13 November 2013).
[44] Commander CENT Attack Force, Operation "HUSKY" – Report upon, 21 July 1943; Morison, *The Two-Ocean War*, p. 258-259; CWNTF, Action Report – The Sicilian Campaign Operation "Husky" July-August, 1943.
[45] Commander CENT Attack Force, Operation "HUSKY" – Report upon, 21 July 1943.
[46] *Narragansett* and *Nauset* War Diary, July 1943; Commander CENT Attack Force, Operation "HUSKY" – Report upon, 21 July 1943.
[47] *Narragansett* and *Nauset* War Diary, July 1943.
[48] Ibid.
[49] *Narragansett* War Diary, July 1943.
[50] *Narragansett* and *Nauset* War Diary, July 1943; Commander CENT Attack Force (ComPhibLant), Operation "HUSKY" – Report upon, 21 July 1943.
[51] Commander Landing Craft and Bases, Amphibious Force, Northwest African Waters War Diary, July 1943.
[52] Ibid.
[53] Ibid.

[54] Commander Landing Craft and Bases, Amphibious Force, Northwest African Waters War Diary, July 1943; CWNTF, Action Report – The Sicilian Campaign Operation "Husky" July-August, 1943.
[55] CTF 81, Action Report – Operation "HUSKY"; The Executive Officer, USS *MADDOX* (DD 622), USS *MADDOX* (DD 622) – Report of battle and the loss of, 15 July 1943.
[56] CTF 81, Action Report – Operation "HUSKY"; Morison, *The Two-Ocean War*, p. 254.
[57] The Executive Officer, USS *MADDOX* (DD 622), USS *MADDOX* (DD 622) – Report of battle and the loss of; CTF 81, Action Report – Operation "HUSKY"; *Harry Lee* War Diary, July 1943.
[58] *Moreno* War Diary, July 1943; Commander Landing Craft and Bases, Amphibious Force, Northwest African Waters War Diary, July 1943; CWNTF, Action Report – The Sicilian Campaign Operation "Husky" July-August, 1943.
[59] Ibid.
[60] *Moreno* War Diary, July 1943; CWNTF, Action Report – The Sicilian Campaign Operation "Husky" July-August, 1943.
[61] Ibid.
[62] CTF 81, Action Report – Operation "HUSKY".
[63] *Moreno* War Diary, July 1943;
[64] *Moreno* War Diary, July 1943; Commander Landing Craft and Bases, Amphibious Force, Northwest African Waters War Diary, July 1943.
[65] *Moreno* War Diary, July 1943; Arnold Lott, *Most Dangerous Sea* (Annapolis: U.S. Naval Institute, 1959), p. 119.
[66] Ibid.
[67] *Moreno* War Diary, July 1943; *Staff*, *DANFS*.
[68] Ibid.
[69] Ibid.
[70] *Benson* War Diary, August 1943.
[71] Ibid.
[72] *Brant*, *DANFS*.
[73] Ibid.
[74] General Orders: Bureau of Naval Personnel Information Bulletin No. 325 (April 1944); "USS *Knight* DD633" (http://www.oocities.org/pentagon/base/1250/knight.html: accessed 7 September 2014).
[75] CWNTF, Action Report – The Sicilian Campaign Operation "Husky" July-August, 1943.
[76] *Monrovia* War Diary, July 1943; Morison, *The Two-Ocean War*, p. 261-262; CO, USS *Philadelphia*, Operations from 27 July to 8 August 1943, 19 August 1943.
[77] "Patton's Career A Brilliant One," obituary in the *New York Times*, 22 December 1945 (http://www.nytimes.com/learning/general/onthisday/bday/1111.html: accessed 2 November 2013).

[78] Bartholomew and Milwee Jr., *Mud, Muscle, and Miracles*, p. 125-126.
[79] Ibid.
[80] Ibid.
[81] Ibid.
[82] "Gulfport Shipbuilding, Port Arthur TX"; *Busy*, *DANFS*; "Yard Tugs (YT, YTB, YTM, YTL) Built or Acquired During WWII"; "District Harbor Tug (YT) Index," NavSource; CTF 81 War Diary, June 1943; Bartholomew and Milwee Jr., *Mud, Muscle, and Miracles*, p. 56-57, 127.

CHAPTER 6 NOTES
[1] ComEighthFlt (CWNTF), The Italian Campaign, 11 January 1945.
[2] ComEighthFlt (CWNTF), The Italian Campaign; Morison, *The Two-Ocean War*, p. 350.
[3] ComEighthFlt (CWNTF), The Italian Campaign.
[4] "Invasion of Southern Italy" (http://olive-drab.com/od_history_ww2_ops_battles_1943soitaly.php); C. Peter Chen, "Operation Avalanche" (http://ww2db.com/battle_spec.php?battle_id=307: both accessed 31 December 2014)
[5] Ibid.
[6] ComEighthFlt (CWNTF), The Italian Campaign; C. Peter Chen, "Operation Avalanche."
[7] Morison, *The Two-Ocean War*, p. 350; Robert M. Citino, "Avalanche: How Both Sides Lost at Salerno" (http://www.historynet.com/avalanche-how-both-sides-lost-at-salerno.htm: accessed 9 December 2013).
[8] Morison, *The Two-Ocean War*, p. 353.
[9] "RN Beach Commandos and Operation Avalanche The Salerno Landings September 9th 1943" (http://www.relaysystem.co.uk/RNBC_1943Salerno.pdf: accessed 23 December 2013); J. D. Lock, "World War II – North Africa/Europe" (http://www.armyranger.com/index.php/history/modern-era: accessed 25 December 2013).
[10] "Patton's Career A Brilliant One," obituary in the New York Times, 22 December 1945; Citino, "Avalanche: How Both Sides Lost at Salerno".
[11] ComEighthFlt (CWNTF), The Italian Campaign; Bartholomew and Milwee Jr., *Mud, Muscle, and Miracles*, p. 92-93.
[12] Bartholomew and Milwee Jr., *Mud, Muscle, and Miracles*, p. 92-93.
[13] Ibid.
[14] ComEighthFlt (CWNTF), The Italian Campaign; Bartholomew and Milwee Jr., *Mud, Muscle, and Miracles*, p. 127-128, 131, 133.
[15] ComEighthFlt (CWNTF), The Italian Campaign.
[16] Senior Surviving Officer, USS *Nauset* (AT89), USS *Nauset* (AT89) – Loss of, 16 September 1943.
[17] Ibid.
[18] Commander U.S. Naval Forces, Northwest African Waters, War Diary; forwarding of, 6 April 1944.
[19] Ibid.

[20] Ibid.
[21] Senior Surviving Officer, USS *Nauset* (AT89), USS *Nauset* (AT89) – Loss of, 16 September 1943.
[22] Ibid.
[23] Ibid.
[24] Ibid.
[25] Ibid.
[26] Ibid.
[27] Senior Surviving Officer, USS *Nauset* (AT89), USS *Nauset* (AT89) – Loss of, 16 September 1943; CO, USS *LST 351*, Action Report [word redacted] Avalanche Operation, November 10, 1943.
[28] Senior Surviving Officer, USS *Nauset* (AT89), USS *Nauset* (AT89) – Loss of, 16 September 1943.
[29] ComEighthFlt (CWNTF), The Italian Campaign.
[30] ComEighthFlt (CWNTF), The Italian Campaign; ComEighthFlt, Action Reports for the Salerno Operation, 7 March 1945.
[31] ComEighthFlt (CWNTF), The Italian Campaign.
[32] Ibid.
[33] CTU 85.1.7, Report of Salvage Operation on "UNCLE" Beaches during Avalanche Operation, 17 September 1943; CTG 85.1, Operation AVALANCHE - Additional Report of, 21 November 1943.
[34] CTU 85.1.7, Report of Salvage Operation on "UNCLE" Beaches during Avalanche Operation.
[35] Ibid.
[36] Ibid.
[37] Ibid.
[38] CTF 81 (Commander, Eighth Amphibious Force), Report on Operation "AVALANCHE," 17 October 1943.
[39] Ibid.
[40] CTF 81 (Commander, Eighth Amphibious Force), Report on Operation "AVALANCHE"; Lott, *Most Dangerous Sea*, p. 122-123.
[41] CTF 81 (Commander, Eighth Amphibious Force), Report on Operation "AVALANCHE".
[42] CTF 81 (Commander, Eighth Amphibious Force), Report on Operation "AVALANCHE"; "E-boat German Schnellboot (S-Boot)" (http://ww2-weapons.com/Warships/German/E-Boats/S-boat.htm: accessed 29 December 2013).
[43] *Rowan*, *DANFS*; CO, USS *Bristol* (DD453), Action between Allied Forces and U.S.S. *BRISTOL* on 8-11 September, 1943 – report on, 12 September 1943.
[44] *Moreno* War Diary, September 1943; "HMS *ABERCROMBIE* - Roberts-class 15in gun Monitor" (http://www.naval-history.net/xGM-Chrono-03Mon-Abercrombie.htm: accessed 5 January 2014); HMS *Abercrombie* (F 109) (http://www.uboat.net/allies/warships/ship/5463.html: accessed 31 December 2014).
[45] *Moreno* War Diary, September 1943.

[46] Ibid.
[47] *Moreno* War Diary, September 1943; "*Flores* History," (http://netherlandsnavy.nl/Flores_his.htm: accessed 29 December 2013).
[48] *Savannnah, DANFS*.
[49] Ibid.
[50] *Moreno* War Diary, September 1943.
[51] *Moreno* War Diary, September 1943; Robert Cressman, *The Official Chronology of the U.S. Navy in World War II* (Annapolis: U.S. Naval Institute, 2000), p. 180.
[52] CTG 85.1, Operation AVALANCHE - Additional Report of.
[53] *Moreno* War Diary, September 1943; Andrew Carroll, "An Army Nurse Describes a Deadly Attack on a Hospital Ship," History.net (http://www.historynet.com/an-army-nurse-describes-a-deadly-attack-on-a-hospital-ship.htm: accessed 4October 2014).
[54] *Moreno* War Diary, September 1943.
[55] Ibid.
[56] *Moreno* War Diary, September 1943; Bartholomew and Milwee Jr., *Mud, Muscle, and Miracles*, p. 130.
[57] *Moreno* War Diary, September 1943.
[58] *Moreno* War Diary, September 1943; "Historical RFA" (http://historicalrfa.org/: accessed 1 January 2014).
[59] "Force Five at Salerno" (http://www.lancaster.ac.uk/staff/ecagrs/salerno.htm: accessed 9 December 2013).
[60] "Force Five at Salerno"; "HMS *Warspite* 03," Uboat.net (http://www.uboat.net/allies/warships/ship/4057.html: accessed 15 December 2013).
[61] "Force Five at Salerno"; "PC 1400 FX "Fritz X" Guided Bomb," Luftwaffe Resource Center: A Warbirds Resource Group Site (http://www.warbirdsresourcegroup.org/LRG/fritz.html: accessed 15 December 2013).
[62] "Force Five at Salerno".
[63] Ibid.
[64] *Hopi* War Diary, September 1943; Bartholomew and Milwee Jr., *Mud, Muscle, and Miracles: Marine Salvage in the United States Navy*, p. 131-132.
[65] *Hopi* War Diary, September 1943.
[66] CO, USS *Hopi*, Action Report, 26[or 28] September 1943.
[67] *Moreno* and *Narragansett* War Diary, September 1943; Bartholomew and Milwee Jr., *Mud, Muscle, and Miracles*, p. 132.
[68] *Narragansett* War Diary, September 1943; Bartholomew and Milwee Jr., *Mud, Muscle, and Miracles*, p. 132.
[69] *Narragansett* War Diary, September 1943.
[70] Ibid.
[71] ComEighthFlt (CWNTF), The Italian Campaign.
[72] Ibid.
[73] Ibid.

[74] ComEighthFlt (CWNTF), The Italian Campaign; Bartholomew and Milwee Jr., *Mud, Muscle, and Miracles*, p. 129, 133.
[75] ComEighthFlt (CWNTF), The Italian Campaign.
[76] Albert N. Garland and Howard McGaw Smyth, *United States Army in World War II Mediterranean Theater of Operations: Sicily and the Surrender of Italy* (Washington, D.C.: Center of Military History, U.S. Army, 1993), p. 552.
[77] Garland and Smyth, *United States Army in World War II Mediterranean Theater of Operations: Sicily and the Surrender of Italy*, p. 552; Citino, "Avalanche: How Both Sides Lost at Salerno."

CHAPTER 7 NOTES

[1] Samuel Eliot Morison, *History of United States Naval Operations in World War II, Sicily-Salerno-Anzio, January 1943-June 1944* (Boston: Little, Brown, 1984), p. 325.
[2] Admiralty War Diaries, 22 January 1944; Clayton D. Laurie, *Anzio 1944* (Washington D.C.: U.S. Army Center of Military History), p. 3-5; Morison, *History of United States Naval Operations in World War II, Sicily-Salerno-Anzio, January 1943-June 1944*, p. 336-340.
[3] Admiralty War Diaries, 22 January 1944; Clayton D. Laurie "Anzio 1944."
[4] Morison, *History of United States Naval Operations in World War II: Sicily-Salerno-Anzio, January 1943-June 1944*, p. 336-340.
[5] Admiralty War Diaries, 22 January 1944; Laurie, *Anzio 1944*, p. 3; Morison, *History of United States Naval Operations in World War II, Sicily-Salerno-Anzio, January 1943-June 1944*, p. 341-342.
[6] Admiralty War Diaries, 22 January 1944; Eric Alley, "The Landings at Anzio - A View from the Sea" (http://www.bbc.co.uk/history/ww2peopleswar/stories/43/a4015243.shtml: accessed 30 July 2014).
[7] Admiralty War Diaries, 22 January 1944; CO, USS *Biscayne*, Action Report Covering Operation "Shingle" from 21 January 1944 through 1 February 1944 – forwarding of, 21 March 1944; CO, USS *LCI(L) 20*, Report of Loss of USS *LCI(L) 20*; Submission of, 11 February 1944; Commander LCT(5) Group Twenty-Eight, Flotilla Ten, Operation Shingle, Peter Section—Action Report, 9 March 1944; ComDesRon 13 War Diary, January 1944.
[8] Morison, *History of United States Naval Operations in World War II, Sicily-Salerno-Anzio, January 1943-June 1944*, p. 354-355.
[9] *Anzio Beachhead 22 January - 25 May 1944* (Washington, DC: U.S. Army Center of Military History, 1990), p. 1-18 (http://www.history.army.mil/books/wwii/anziobeach/anzio-landing.htm: accessed 23 July 2014); Admiralty War Diaries, 22 January 1944.
[10] Admiralty War Diaries, 22 January 1944.
[11] Lott, *Most Dangerous Sea*, p. 125; CTG 81.7, Action Report of Sweeper Group Operation Shingle, 8 February 1944; CO, *LCI(L)-76*, Operation Shingle, Report of, 25 January 1944; ComMinRon 6 War Diary, 28 December 1943-4 February 1944; Office of Naval-Officer-in-Charge, Anzio, Operation "Shingle" Report of the Ranger Landing and Development of Port Anzio,

31st January,1944; CTG 81.14 CTG 81.11, Action Report Operation Shingle; CTG 81.5, Report of Task Group 81.5 During Operation Shingle, 28 January 1944; Morison, *History of United States Naval Operations in World War II, Sicily – Salerno-Anzio, January 1943-June 1944*, p. 395-396; Commander LCT(5) Group Twenty-Eight, Flotilla Ten, Operation Shingle, Peter Section—Action Report.

[12] "Royal Navy Vessels Lost at Sea, 1939-45 – by Theater" (http://www.naval-history.net/WW2BritishLossesbyArea08.htm: accessed 26 July 2014).

[13] "Casualties: U.S. Navy and Coast Guard Vessels, Sunk or Damaged Beyond Repair during World War II, 7 December 1941-1 October 1945" (http://www.history.navy.mil/faqs/faq82-1.htm: accessed 26 July 2014); "USS *LST-348*," Uboat.net (http://www.uboat.net/allies/merchants/ships/3194.html: accessed 26 July 2014); Officer-in-Charge, U.S. *LCT(5) #35*, Loss of Ship – Report of, 10 March 1944.

[14] CO, USS *LCI(L) 10*, Report of operations during landings near Cape D'Anzio, Italy, participated in by this ship, 13 February 1944; CTG 81. 14 CTG 81.11, Action Report Operation Shingle, Serial No. 006-44; CTG 81.4, Report of Amphibious Operations during landings near Cape D'Anzio, Italy, participated in by Task Group 81.4, 20 February 1944.

[15] Bartholomew and Milwee Jr., *Mud, Muscle, and Miracles*, p. 135-136

[16] Lott, *Most Dangerous Sea*, p. 125; CTG 81.7, Action Report of Sweeper Group Operation Shingle, 8 February 1944; CO, *LCI(L)-76*, Operation Shingle, Report of, 25 January 1944; ComMinRon 6 War Diary, 28 December 1943-4 February 1944; Office of Naval-Officer-in-Charge, Anzio, Operation "Shingle" Report of the Ranger Landing and Development of Port Anzio, 31st January,1944; CTG 81.14 CTG 81.11, Action Report Operation Shingle; CTG 81.5, Report of Task Group 81.5 During Operation Shingle, 28 January 1944; Morison, *History of United States Naval Operations in World War II, Sicily – Salerno-Anzio, January 1943-June 1944*, p. 395-396; Commander LCT(5) Group Twenty-Eight, Flotilla Ten, Operation Shingle, Peter Section—Action Report.

[17] *Navy Seagoing Tugs and Related Craft, General Characteristics and Considerations Governing Use of.*

[18] *ATR-1* War Diary, September-November 1943.

[19] *ATR-1* War Diary, September-November 1943; "USS *ATR-1*," NavSource (http://www.navsource.org/archives/09/40/40001.htm: accessed 1 September 2013).

[20] *ATR-1* War Diary, November 1943.

[21] Hague Convoy Database; ComDesDiv 26 War Diary, November 1943.

[22] ComDesDiv 26 War Diary, November 1943.

[23] ComDesDiv 26 War Diary, November 1943; *ATR-1* War Diary, December 1943.

[24] *ATR-1* War Diary, December 1943.

[25] "Ships Hit by U-boats, *John S. Copley*," Uboat.net (http://uboat.net/allies/merchants/3151.html: accessed 2 September 2013); *ATR-1* and *ATR-47* War Diary, December 1943.

[26] *ATR-1* War Diary, December 1943, January 1944.
[27] *ATR-1* War Diary, January 1944.
[28] Ibid.
[29] Ibid.
[33] *ATR-1* War Diary, January 1944.
[34] *ATR-1* War Diary, January 1944; Morison, *History of United States Naval Operations in World War II, Sicily-Salerno-Anzio, January 1943-June 1944*, p. 344; "HMS *Janus* (F 53)," Uboat.net (http://uboat.net/allies/warships/ship/4450.html; "HMS *Jervis* (F 00)," Uboat.net (http://uboat.net/allies/warships/ship/4448.html: both accessed 9 September 2013).
[35] Morison, *History of United States Naval Operations in World War II, Sicily-Salerno-Anzio, January 1943-June 1944*, p. 355; David D. Bruhn, *Wooden Ships and Iron Men: The U.S. Navy's Coastal and Motor Minesweepers, 1941-1953* (Westminster, MD: Heritage Books, 2009), p. 63.
[36] *ATR-1* War Diary, January 1944; Morison, *History of United States Naval Operations in World War II, Sicily-Salerno-Anzio, January 1943-June 1944*, p. 345-346; "The Angels of Anzio, The Nurse Corps: Sicily to Anzio" (http://darbysrangers.tripod.com/id76.htm: accessed 10 September 2013).
[37] *ATR-1* War Diary, January 1944; CO, USS *Frederick C. Davis* (DE-136), Report of Service, 22 January-11 June, 1944, (Operation Shingle), 5 August 1944.
[38] *ATR-1* War Diary, January 1944; Morison, *History of United States Naval Operations in World War II, Sicily-Salerno-Anzio, January 1943-June 1944*, p. 348.
[39] *ATR-1* War Diary, January 1944; "The Sinking of the *LST-422*," 83rd Chemical Mortar Battalion (http://www.dvrbs.com/history-mil/LST-422.htm: accessed 10 September 2013).
[40] *ATR-1* War Diary, January 1944.
[41] *ATR-1* War Diary, January 1944; "The Sinking of the *LST-422*," 83rd Chemical Mortar Battalion.
[42] *ATR-1* War Diary, January 1944.
[43] *ATR-1* War Diary, January 1944; Morison, *History of United States Naval Operations in World War II, Sicily-Salerno-Anzio, January 1943-June 1944*, p. 349.
[44] *ATR-1* War Diary, January 1944; Morison, *History of United States Naval Operations in World War II, Sicily-Salerno-Anzio, January 1943-June 1944*, p. 351.
[45] *LST-326* War Diary, January 1944; "HMS *Sparta*n '*Dido*' Class Cruiser 1939" (http://myweb.tiscali.co.uk/hmsspartan/dido.htm: accessed 25 July 2014).
[46] *ATR-1* and *LST-326* War Diary, January 1944; CTG 81.4, Report of Amphibious Operations during landings near Cape D'Anzio, Italy, participated in by Task Group 81.4.
[47] *ATR-1* War Diary, January 1944; Senior Officer Smoke Patrol, Smoke Patrol – Operation Shingle – January 22, 1944 to February 5, 1944, 17 February 1944.
[48] Ibid.
[49] Senior Officer Smoke Patrol.

[50] *ATR-1* War Diary, January 1944.
[51] *ATR-1* War Diary, January 1944; CO, USS *Strive* (AM-117), Additional comments to join action report submitted by CTG 81.7.2 and CO; "HMS *Spartan*, A Voyage" (http://home.aut.ac.nz/staff/dhughes/mairangi.html: accessed 25 July 2014).
[52] USS *Strive* (AM 117), 18 February 1944.
[53] *ATR-1* War Diary, January 1944; David Hughes, "HMS *Spartan*, A Voyage";DNC 6/R.322, Report by the Admiralty Department of Naval Construction, based on evidence given at, and the findings of, The Board of Enquiry, held on 9 February 1944 at Naples, transcribed/edited: David Hughes - September 2000
(http://home.aut.ac.nz/staff/dhughes/sinking_1.html: accessed 3 September 2013).
[54] CO, USS *LCI(L)-219*, Report of Amphibious Operations during Landings near Cape D'Anzio, Italy participated in by this ship, 15 February 1944; CO, USS *LCI(L)-4*, Report of Amphibious Operations during Landings near Cape D'Anzio, Italy, participated in by this ship, 1 March 1944; *SC-697* and *SC-1029* War Diary, January 1944.
[55] "The Loss of HMS *Spartan* 29th January, 1944" (http://www.world-war.co.uk/spartan_loss.php3: accessed 21 January 2014).
[56] *ATR-1* War Diary, January 1944; Morison, *History of United States Naval Operations in World War II, Sicily-Salerno-Anzio, January 1943-June 1944*, p. 355; CTF 81, Action Report - Operation Shingle, 22 February 1944.
[57] David Hughes, 13 August 2014.
[58] *ATR-1* War Diary, January 1944.
[59] Ibid.
[60] Ibid.
[61] ComTaskFor 81, Action Report – Operation Shingle, 22 February 1944.
[62] *ATR-1* War Diary, January 1944; CTG 81.4, Report of Amphibious Operations during landings near Cape D'Anzio, Italy, participated in by Task Group 81.4.
[63] *ATR-1* War Diary, January 1944; CTG 81.4, Report of Amphibious Operations during landings near Cape D'Anzio, Italy, participated in by Task Group 81.4; CO, USS *LCI(L) #4*, Report of Amphibious Operations during Landings near Cape D'Anzio, Italy, participated in by this ship, 1 March 1944.
[64] *ATR-1* War Diary, January 1944; George W. Butenschoen, "The Sailors Log" (http://ww2lct.org/history/stories/the_sailors_log.htm: accessed 4 September 2013).
[65] *ATR-1* War Diary, January 1944.
[66] Ibid.
[67] "Army and Navy Medals Awarded to Mariners During World War II" (http://www.usmm.org/medalsmilitary.html: accessed 4 August 2014).
[68] *History of the Naval Armed Guard Afloat* (Washington, DC: Office of Naval Operations, 1949), p. 171.
[69] CO, USS *Frederick C. Davis* (DE-136), Report of Service, 22 January-11 June, 1944, (Operation Shingle).

[70] "HMS *Spartan* 'Dido' Class Cruiser 1939."
[71] CO, USS *Frederick C. Davis* (DE-136), Report of Service, 22 January-11 June, 1944, (Operation Shingle).
[72] Ibid.
[73] Ibid.
[74] "Operation Single," Anzio Beachhead Veterans of World War II (http://anziobeachheadveterans.com/anzio-1944/operation-shingle: accessed 5 August 2014).
[75] Zane Orr, "WWII Veteran Zane Orr: My Service in the U.S. Navy," As told to Maureen Carden, posted 28 September 2014 " (http://memoircenter.com/wwii-veteran-zane-orr-my-service-in-the-u-s-navy/: accessed 1 October 2014).
[76] Ibid.
[77] Ibid.
[78] "Medal of Honor," Anzio Beachhead Veterans of World War II (http://anziobeachheadveterans.com/anzio-heritage/medal-of-honor: accessed 3 January 2015).
[79] "The Battle of Anzio" (http://www.public.navy.mil/surflant/cg68/Pages/Battle.aspx: accessed 11 August 2014).

CHAPTER 8 NOTES

[1] "D-Day and the Battle of Normandy" (http://www.ddaymuseum co.uk/d-day/d-day-and-the-battle-of-normandy-your-questions-answered#troops: accessed January 4, 2015); "Juno Beach" (http://www.junobeach.info/juno-4-20.htm: accessed 11 January 2015).
[2] Ibid.
[3] *United States Naval Administration in World War II. United States Naval Forces, Europe. Histories Vol. 5* (http://www.history.navy.mil/library/online/comnaveu/comnaveu-contents.htm: accessed 4 January 2015)
[4] Naval Commander, Western Task Force (CTF 122), Operation OVERLORD Report of Naval Commander Western Task Force (C.T.F. 122), 15 July 1944.
[5] Ibid.
[6] "Numbered Fleets," Federation of American Scientists Military Analysis Network (http://www.fas.org/man/dod-101/navy/unit/fleet_n.htm: accessed 24 January 2014).
[7] *Marsh* War Diary, April 1944; CincLant War Diary, March 1944.
[8] van der Ster, "Directory of the Ocean Going Tugs type V4".
[9] ComSerForLant War Diary, June 1944.
[10] *ATR-4* War Diary, January-June 1944.
[11] Ibid.
[12] Ibid.
[13] Ibid.

[14] Ibid.
[15] "Mulberry" (http://www.skylighters.org/encyclopedia/mulberry.html: accessed 13 January 2014).
[16] Ibid.
[17] Ibid.
[18] *Building the Navy's Bases in World War II History of the Bureau of Yards and Docks and the Civil Engineer Corps 1940-1946 Vol. II* (Washington, DC: U.S. Government Printing Office, 1947), p. 108.
[19] "Mulberry Harbour and COTUG," Thames Tugs, (http://thamestugs.co.uk/MULBERRY-HARBOUR--and--COTUG.php: accessed 14 January 2015).
[20] *The Master, Mate and Pilot*, February 1945; "Operation Mulberry (D-Day 1944)," U.S. Army Transportation Museum (http://www.transchool.lee.army.mil/museum/transportation%20museum/mulberry.htm: accessed 3 January 2015).
[21] "Army and Navy Medals Awarded to Mariners During World War II," American Merchant Marine at War (http://www.usmm.org/medalsmilitary.html: accessed 3 January 2015).
[22] *The Master, Mate and Pilot*, February 1945.
[23] Narrative by Lieutenant James C. W. White, USNR, USS *Partridge* Normandy Invasion, Naval Records and Library, CNO Personal Interviews; *Queens Cross* log, Thames Tugs (http://thamestugs.co.uk/QUEENS-CROSS%3B-ROODE-ZEE%3B-SESAME%3B-STOKE.php: accessed 14 January 2015).
[24] Narrative by Lieutenant James C. W. White, USNR; Commanding Officer USS *Partridge* (ATO-138), Action Report: USS *Partridge* – loss of, 29 July 1944; CTF 128 War Diary, June 1944; "Royal Navy (RN) Officers 1939-1945" (http://www.unithistories.com/officers/RN_officersK3.html: accessed 14 January 2015).
[25] CTF 128 War Diary, June 1944; Bartholomew and Milwee Jr., *Mud, Muscle, and Miracles*, p. 138-139.
[26] *Queens Cross* log.
[27] Narrative by Lieutenant James C. W. White, USNR, USS *Partridge* Normandy Invasion.
[28] Narrative by Lieutenant James C. W. White, USNR, USS *Partridge* Normandy Invasion; Commanding Officer USS *Partridge* (ATO-138), Action Report: USS Partridge – loss of, 29 July 1944.
[29] Ibid.
[30] Ibid.
[31] Report by N.C.O. in Charge of Passage Crew on Whale Unit No. *S.513* when HMT *Sesame* was lost (http://thamestugs.co.uk/QUEENS-CROSS%3B-ROODE-ZEE%3B-SESAME%3B-STOKE.php: accessed 14 January 2015).
[32] Report by N.C.O. in Charge of Passage Crew on Whale Unit No. *S.513* when HMT *Sesame* was lost; "Mulberry Tugs," Thames Tugs

(http://thamestugs.co.uk/MULBERRY-TUGS-%5B3%5D.php: accessed 14 January 2015)

[33] Report by N.C.O. in Charge of Passage Crew on Whale Unit No. *S.513* when HMT *Sesame* was lost.

[34] *The Master, Mate and Pilot*, February 1945.

[35] "Mulberry"; Steve Karoly, "The 25th NCR at Normandy" (http://www.seabeecook.com/history/25th_ncr/the_25th_ncr_at_normandy.htm: accessed 24 January 2014).

[36] "Mulberry"; Steve Karoly, "The 25th NCR at Normandy"; "US Navy Construction Battalions (Seabees) In France and Germany During World War Two" (http://www.history.navy.mil/library/online/constructfrancegermanyww2.htm: accessed 24 January 2014); *Building the Navy's Bases in World War II History of the Bureau of Yards and Docks and the Civil Engineer Corps 1940-1946 Vol. II*, p. 104.

[37] Byron S. Huie Jr., "Salvage ships Operations in Normandy Invasion" (http://www.ibiblio.org/hyperwar/USN/rep/Normandy/Salvage-Huie.html: accessed 2 March 2014).

[38] Commander Eleventh Amphibious Force, Operations of Combat Salvage and Firefighting Unit (*Pinto, Arikara, ATR-2*) attached to Force "O" during Assault Phase – Report on, 13 July 1944.

[39] Byron S. Huie Jr., "Salvage ships Operations in Normandy Invasion;" Commanding Officer, USS *Quincy*, Action Report – 25 June 1944, 29 June 1944.

[40] Byron S. Huie Jr., "Salvage ships Operations in Normandy Invasion;" Bartholomew and Milwee Jr., *Mud, Muscle, and Miracles*, p. 137-138.

[41] Bartholomew and Milwee Jr., *Mud, Muscle, and Miracles*, p. 138.

[42] Byron S. Huie Jr., "Salvage ships Operations in Normandy Invasion".

[43] Ibid.

[44] Ibid.

[45] Ibid.

[46] Commander Eleventh Amphibious Force, Operations of Combat Salvage and Firefighting Unit (*Pinto, Arikara, ATR-2*) attached to Force "O" during Assault Phase – Report on.

[47] Byron S. Huie Jr., "Salvage ships Operations in Normandy Invasion;" *Susan B. Anthony, DANFS*.

[48] Byron S. Huie Jr., "Salvage ships Operations in Normandy Invasion;" CO, USS *Pinto*, U.S.S. *Pinto* participation in the U.S.S. *Susan B. Anthony* Disaster, - report of, 11 June 1944.

[49] Byron S. Huie Jr., "Salvage ships Operations in Normandy Invasion;" Lott, *Most Dangerous Sea*, p. 189; CO, USS *Pinto*, U.S.S. *Pinto* participation in the U.S.S. *Susan B. Anthony* Disaster, - report of.

[50] CO, USS *Pinto*, U.S.S. *Pinto* participation in the U.S.S. *Susan B. Anthony* Disaster, - report of.

[51] Byron S. Huie Jr., "Salvage ships Operations in Normandy Invasion."

[52] Ibid.

[53] Morison, *The Two-Ocean War*, p. 408-409; Byron S. Huie Jr., "Salvage ships Operations in Normandy Invasion".
[54] Morison, *The Two-Ocean War*, p. 408-409; Byron S. Huie Jr., "Salvage ships Operations in Normandy Invasion;" "Thames Tugs" (http://www.thamestugs.co.uk/MULBERRY-TUGS-%5B2%5D.php: accessed 17 March 2014).
[55] Morison, *The Two-Ocean War*, p. 408-409; Byron S. Huie Jr., "Salvage ships Operations in Normandy Invasion".
[56] Byron S. Huie Jr., "Salvage ships Operations in Normandy Invasion;" "Naval Trawlers" (http://www.battleships-cruisers.co.uk/naval_trawlers.htm: accessed 4 March 2014).
[57] *ATR-4* War Diary, January-June 1944.
[58] Ibid.
[59] "HMS *Halsted* (K 556)" (http://uboat.net/allies/warships/ship/5662.html: accessed 23 January 2014); *ATR-4* War Diary, January-June 1944.
[60] *ATR-4* War Diary, January-June 1944.
[61] Ibid.
[62] Ibid.
[63] Ibid.
[64] Ibid.
[65] Ibid.
[66] Ibid.
[67] Ibid.
[68] Naval Commander Western Task Force (CTF122), Operation Normandy Invasion – Report of Naval Commander Western Task Force (CTF122), 25 July 1944

CHAPTER 9 NOTES

[1] Commander Task Force Eighty Six, Reports of Preliminary Interrogation of Six German POWs after Human Torpedo Attacks in Ventinifia Area 10 Sept. 1944, 12 September 1944.
[2] USN Motor Torpedo Boat Activity in the English Channel Area, unofficial report prepared by A. H. Harris, Commander PT Squadron, 11th Amphibious Force, R.S. No. 11095; Michael Whitby, "Masters of the Channel Night: The 10th Destroyer Flotilla's Victory off Ile De Batz, 9 June 1944," HMS *Tatar* Association (http://www.hmstartar.co.uk: accessed 7 January 2015).
[3] "Casualties: U.S. Navy and Coast Guard Vessels Sunk or Damaged Beyond Repair during World War II" (http://www.history.navy.mil/faqs/faq82-2.htm: accessed 5 January 2015).
[4] "Royal Navy Vessels Lost at Sea, 1939-45" (http://www.naval-history.net/WW2BritishLossesbyArea06.htm: accessed 5 January 2015); Mark Stille, *Axis Midget Submarines: 1939-45* (Osprey, 2014), p. 20-21.

[5] Graham Pickles, "The K-Verband" (http://www.thelincolnshireregiment.org/waal1945/KVerband.pdf: accessed 7 January 2015).
[6] Ibid.
[7] Roy Conyers Nesbit, Ultra Versus U-Boats: Enigma Decrypts in the National Archives (Great Britain, Sword & Sword Military, 2008), p. 186.
[8] "Human Torpedoes," German U-Boat (http://www.uboataces.com/weapon-human-torpedo.shtml: accessed 5 January 2015); Roy Conyers Nesbit, *Ultra Versus U-Boats: Enigma Decrypts in the National Archives* (Great Britain, Pen & Sword, 2008), p. 186.
[9] Memorials & Monuments in Portsmouth, Portsmouth Cathedral - HMS Isis – (http://www.memorials.inportsmouth.co.uk/churches/cathedral/isis.htm: accessed 11 January 2015).
[10] "Human Torpedoes," German U-Boat (http://www.uboataces.com/weapon-human-torpedo.shtml: accessed 8 January 2015).
[11] Stille, *Axis Midget Submarines: 1939-45*, p. 21.
[12] Admiralty War Diaries, 1 August-30 September 1944.
[13] *PC-522* War Diary, August 1944
[14] Ibid.
[15] Ibid.
[16] Alfons Steck, "Sinking the Quorn," Report of Ferdinand Hoffmann (http://www.uboat.net/allies/warships/ship/4628.html: accessed 21 April 2014).
[17] Ibid.
[18] Ibid.
[19] Ibid.
[20] "Greatest World War II Weapons: Human Torpedo." *Defencyclopedia* (http://defencyclopedia.com/2014/06/14/world-war-weapons-part-1-human-torpedo/: accessed 7 September 2014).

CHAPTER 10 NOTES

[1] Monograph, Official Study of Port of Cherbourg, 1944-1945.
[2] Byron S. Huie Jr., "Salvage ships Operations in Normandy Invasion;" Bartholomew and Milwee Jr., *Mud, Muscle, and Miracles*, p. 145.
[3] Bartholomew and Milwee Jr., *Mud, Muscle, and Miracles*, p. 138-139.
[4] Huie Jr., "Salvage ships Operations in Normandy Invasion;" "Cherbourg Port Reconstruction," Office of the Chief Engineer – European Theater of Operations (http://www.fold3.com/image/287479515/: accessed 5 March 2014); J. Grosvenor and Lt. Cdr. L. M. Bates, RNVR, *Open The Ports - The Story of the Human Minesweepers* (London, William Kimber, 1956); S. W. Roskill, *History of the Second World War – The War at Sea* (London: Her Majesty's Stationery Office, 1961), p. 70.
[5] Huie, "Salvage ships Operations in Normandy Invasion;" "Cherbourg Port Reconstruction," Office of the Chief Engineer – European Theater of

Operations; Grosvenor and Bates, *Open The Ports - The Story of the Human Minesweepers*; Roskill, *History of the Second World War – The War at Sea*, p. 70.
[6] Ibid.
[7] WNTF OpPlan No. 7-44, 22 June 1944; Rob Hoole, 6 March and 2 April, 2014.
[8] *Brant* and *Diver* War Diary, June 1944.
[9] Grosvenor and Bates, *Open The Ports - The Story of the Human Minesweepers*.
[10] Ibid.
[11] Grosvenor and Bates, *Open The Ports - The Story of the Human Minesweepers*; Tamara Stevens, "Henry Redder, Navy salvage diver during WWII: I was so lucky" (http://www.emmetcounty.org/henry-redder,-wwii-646: accessed 26 March 2014).
[12] Grosvenor and Bates, *Open The Ports - The Story of the Human Minesweepers*.
[13] Ibid.
[14] Huie, "Salvage ships Operations in Normandy Invasion;" "Cherbourg Port Reconstruction," Office of the Chief Engineer – European Theater of Operations; *Brant* War Diary, July 1944; Rob Hoole, 2 April 2014.
[15] *Diver* War Diary, July 1944; *Diver*, *DANFS*; *Swivel* War Diary, July-October 1944; *Swivel*, *DANFS*.
[16] Peter Elliot, *Allied Minesweeping in World War 2* (Annapolis: U.S. Naval Institute, 1979), p. 129.
[17] Elliot, *Allied Minesweeping in World War 2*, p. 129-131.
[18] Ibid.
[19] Ibid.
[20] Lott, *Most Dangerous Sea*, p. 194-195; Monograph, Official Study of Port of Cherbourg, 1944-1945; "Cherbourg Port Reconstruction," Office of the Chief Engineer – European Theater of Operations; Tom Butterworth's diary; Commander U.S. Ports and Bases, France, War Diary, August 1944; "Royal Navy Vessels Lost at Sea, 1939-45 – By Date" (http://www.naval-history.net/WW2BritishLossesbyDate3.htm: accessed 30 March 2014).
[21] WNTF OPLAN No. 7-44; Commander "Y" Squadrons, Special Action Report, Submission of, 20 July 1944; CO, USS *Chimo*, Action Report – 6 June to 20 June 1944 – Allied Expeditionary Force, Western Naval Task Force, Bai de Seine, France, 4 September 1944; Commander U.S. Ports and Bases, France, War Diary, August 1944; *Battle Summary No. 39 "Operation Neptune" Landings in Normandy June 1944* (London: HMSO, 1994), p. 149, Appendix A(1).
[22] Rob Hoole, "WWII Awards for RN Minesweeping" (http://www.mcdoa.org.uk/ww_ii_awards_for_rn_minesweeping_A.htm: accessed 28 March 2014).
[23] *London Gazette*, 16 January 1945; Rob Hoole, 3 April 2014.
[24] Commander Mine Squadron Seven, Action Report of CTU 125.9.3 Operations with CTF 129 on 25 June 1944, 9 July 1944; Lott, *Most Dangerous Sea*, p. 194; General Orders: Bureau of Naval Personnel Information Bulletin No. 337 (April 1945);

[25] *The Invasion of Normandy: Operation NEPTUNE, United States Naval Administration in World War II, Commander, U.S. Naval Forces in Europe: Volume* V, 1948, p. 446 (http://www.history.navy.mil/library/online/comnaveu/comnaveu_Index.htm: accessed 30 March 30, 2014)
[26] Grosvenor and Bates, *Open The Ports - The Story of the Human Minesweepers*; "Cherbourg Port Reconstruction," Office of the Chief Engineer – European Theater of Operations".
[27] Grosvenor and Bates, *Open The Ports - The Story of the Human Minesweepers*; Rob Hoole, 2 April 2014.
[28] Grosvenor and Bates, *Open The Ports - The Story of the Human Minesweepers*; "Cherbourg Port Reconstruction," Office of the Chief Engineer – European Theater of Operations".
[29] "Cherbourg Port Reconstruction," Office of the Chief Engineer – European Theater of Operations; Grosvenor and Bates, *Open The Ports - The Story of the Human Minesweepers*; Elliot, *Allied Minesweeping in World War 2*, p. 131.
[30] Monograph, Official Study of Port of Cherbourg, 1944-1945; Lott, *Most Dangerous Sea*, p. 195-196; "Administrative History of U.S. Naval Forces in Europe, 1940-1946." Vol. 5. (London, 1946), p. 301-337; Commander "Y" Squadrons, Special Action Report, Submission of; Western Naval Task Force Operation Order No. BB-44.
[31] "Cherbourg Port Reconstruction," Office of the Chief Engineer – European Theater of Operations.
[32] *ATR*-3 War Diary, July 1944; *ATR-13* War Diary, July and August 1944.
[33] *ATR*-3 War Diary, July 1944.
[34] Commander, U.S. Ports and Bases, France, War Diary, July 1944; Morison, *The Two-Ocean War*, p. 411; Elliot, *Allied Minesweeping in World War 2*, p. 131.
[35] Commander, U.S. Ports and Bases, France, War Diary, July 1944.
[36] Commander, U.S. Ports and Bases, France, War Diary, November 1944.

CHAPTER 11 NOTES

[1] Alwyn Thomas, "HMS *Bruiser*'s Mediterranean Commission 1943 – 1945," WWII People's War (http://www.bbc.co.uk/history/ww2peopleswar/stories/07/a3322207.shtml: accessed 19 August 2014)
[2] "Britain's Navy Fighting Ships - Operations – History" (http://www.britainsnavy.co.uk/Battle%20Honours/South%20France%201944.htm: accessed 23 August 1944).
[3] Interview of Adm. Henry K. Hewitt at the Navy Department in Washington, DC on 26 June 1945. Narrative by Admiral Henry K. Hewitt, USN, Mediterranean Area Campaign – North Africa Landing to Southern France; recording by Hewitt on 26 June 1945 describing "the operations in which I was involved in the landings in Africa and the Mediterranean."

[4] Naval Commander, Western Task Force, Preliminary Report on the Amphibious Invasion of Southern France, 1 October 1944.
[5] Ibid.
[6] Ibid.
[7] WNTF OPLAN No. 4-44; Morison, *The Two-Ocean War*, p. 414.
[8] Ibid.
[9] WNTF OPLAN No. 4-44; Morison, *The Two-Ocean War*, p. 414.
[10] Commander Support Force (CTF 86), Operations and action of the Support Force Eighth Fleet during Invasion of Southern France, 15 August 1944 and attack on Defenses of Toulon and Marseilles in support of the Allied Armies, and support of the Right Flank, 18 August to 25 September, 1944; report on, 21 October 1944.
[11] "History of the First Special Service Force" (http://www.firstspecialserviceforce.net/History.html: accessed 18 August 2014).
[12] ComEighthFlt, Invasion of Southern France, 29 November 1944; Commander Support Force (CTF 86), Operations and action of the Support Force Eighth Fleet during Invasion of Southern France.
[13] Commander Support Force (CTF 86), Operations and action of the Support Force Eighth Fleet during Invasion of Southern France.
[14] Ibid.
[15] Ibid.
[16] ComEighthFlt, Invasion of Southern France, 29 November 1944; Barbara Tomblin, *With Utmost Spirit: Allied Naval Operations in the Mediterranean, 1942-1945* (Lexington, KY: University of Kentucky Press, 2004), p. 393.
[17] Commander Support Force (CTF 86), Operations and action of the Support Force Eighth Fleet during Invasion of Southern France.
[18] Ibid.
[19] Ibid.
[20] "German Naval History" (http://www.german-navy.de/information/index.html: accessed 2 September 2014).
[21] ComEighthFlt, Invasion of Southern France, 29 November 1944.
[22] Commander Support Force (CTF 86), Operations and action of the Support Force Eighth Fleet during Invasion of Southern France.
[23] ComEighthFlt, Invasion of Southern France, 29 November 1944.
[24] Adm. Henry K. Hewitt interview on 26 June 1945; ComEighthFlt, Invasion of Southern France, 29 November 1944.
[25] CTF 84 (ComPhibs8thFleet), Action Report of Amphibious Operations from 9 August 1944 to 25 August 1944 of Salvage Ships in Task Group 84.9, 18 October 1944.
[26] ComEighthFlt, Invasion of Southern France, 29 November 1944.
[27] ComEighthFlt, Invasion of Southern France, 29 November 1944; Bartholomew and Milwee Jr., *Mud, Muscle, and Miracles*, p. 143.
[28] CTG 84.9, Action Report on Amphibious Operations from 9 August to 25 August 1944 of Salvage Ships in Task Group 84.9, 10 September 1944; WNTF OPLAN Plan No 4-44.

[29] Senior Fire Fighting Officer, CTG 84.9, "Action Report," 4 September 1944; WNTF OPLAN No 4-44; CO, *LCI(L) 37*, Action Report 12 to 25 August 1944, 1 September 1944.
[30] Senior Fire Fighting Officer, CTG 84.9, "Action Report," 4 September 1944; WNTF OPLAN No 4-44; *Moreno* War Diary, August 1944.
[31] *LST-988* War Diary, August 1944; The Commander Salvage Force, Northwest African Waters, Action Report of Amphibious Operations from 9 to 25 August 1944, of Salvage Ships in the Western Naval Task Force, 1 October 1944; Commander Task Force Eight Seven, Action Report – Assault on the beaches of Southern France, 7 September 1944.
[32] The Commander Salvage Force, Northwest African Waters, Action Report of Amphibious Operations from 9 to 25 August 1944; Commander Task Force Eight Seven, Action Report – Assault on the beaches of Southern France, 7 September 1944.
[33] Commander Task Force Eight Seven, Action Report – Assault on the beaches of Southern France, 7 September 1944; Lott, *Most Dangerous Sea*, p. 202; General Orders: *All Hands* magazine(July 1957).
[34] Bartholomew and Milwee Jr., *Mud, Muscle, and Miracles*, p. 142.
[35] "Britain's Navy Fighting Ships - Operations – History" (http://www.britainsnavy.co.uk/start.htm: accessed 28 August 2014).
[36] ComEighthFlt War Diary, August 1944.

CHAPTER 12 NOTES

[1] CTG 80.4, Operation Dragoon; Report on, 4 September 1944.
[2] CO, USS *Endicott*, Report of Action with Enemy Surface Vessels on 17 August 1944, 23 August 1944; "US Navy Beach Jumpers" (http://www.vietnamwar50th.com/US_Navy_Beach__Jumpers/: accessed 17 January 2015).
[3] CTG 80.4, Operation Dragoon; Report on, 4 September 1944.
[4] CTG 80.4, Operation Dragoon; Report on, 4 September 1944; Jon Guttman, "Specialist in Diversion," interview of Douglas Fairbanks Jr. (http://www.military.com/Content/MoreContent?file=PRdoug: accessed 19 August 2014).
[5] CTG 80.4, Operation Dragoon; Report on, 4 September 1944; Guttman, "Specialist in Diversion," interview of Douglas Fairbanks Jr.; Carol Mather, *When the Grass Stops Growing* (Barnsley, South Yorkshire: Pen & Sword Military, 2006); Rob Burn, 26 August 2014.
[6] CTG 80.4, Operation Dragoon; Report on, 4 September 1944; Guttman, "Specialist in Diversion," interview of Douglas Fairbanks Jr.
[7] Ibid.
[8] Ibid.
[9] Ibid.
[10] CO, USS *Endicott*, Report of Action with Enemy Surface Vessels on 17 August 1944, 23 August 1944.
[11] Ibid.
[12] Ibid.

[13] Ibid.
[14] Ibid.

CHAPTER 13 NOTES
[1] ComEighthFlt, Invasion of Southern France, 29 November 1944.
[2] Narrative by Admiral Henry K. Hewitt, USN, Mediterranean Area Campaign – North Africa Landing to Southern France; recording by Hewitt on 26 June 1945 describing "the operations in which I was involved in the landings in Africa and the Mediterranean."
[3] Ibid
[4] Ibid.
[5] Narrative by Admiral Henry K. Hewitt, USN, Mediterranean Area Campaign – North Africa Landing to Southern France; *Nevada*, *DANFS*.
[6] Narrative by Admiral Henry K. Hewitt, USN, Mediterranean Area Campaign – North Africa Landing to Southern France.
[7] ComEighthFlt, Invasion of Southern France, 29 November 1944; Commander Support Force (CTF 86), Operations and action of the Support Force Eighth Fleet during Invasion of Southern France; CTG 80.10, Report of Action – Operation DRAGOON – for period 0503B 17 August 1944 to 2230A 24 September 1944, 2 October 1944; Narrative by Admiral Henry K. Hewitt, USN, Mediterranean Area Campaign – North Africa Landing to Southern France.
[8] Sweepers Unit, H.M.S. "ROTHESAY," 1st September 1944, Reference Number 0.2810/64.
[9] CTG 80.10, Report of Action – Operation DRAGOON.
[10] Ibid.
[11] Sweepers Unit, H.M.S. "ROTHESAY," 1st September 1944; Commander Section Two of Task Unit 84.8.2, Action Report Covering [redacted] Operation – Submission of, 2 September 1944.
[12] Ibid.
[13] Report from The CO *H.M.M.L. 575* (Senior Officer Present 3rd M.L. Flotilla) to The Senior Officer, 13th Minesweeping Flotilla of 1 September 1944.
[14] Sweepers Unit, H.M.S. "ROTHESAY," 1st September 1944.
[15] Sweepers Unit, H.M.S. "ROTHESAY," 1st September 1944; Lott, *Most Dangerous Sea*, p. 203.
[16] ComEighthFlt, Invasion of Southern France, 29 November 1944; Commander Support Force (CTF 86), Operations and actions of the Support Force Eighth Fleet during the Invasion of Southern France, 15 August 1944 and attack on Defenses of Toulon and Marseilles in support of the Allied Armies, and support of the Right Flank, 18 August to 25 August, 1944; report on, 21 October 1944; Lott, *Most Dangerous Sea*, p. 203; CTG 80.10, Report of Action – Operation DRAGOON.
[17] CO, USS *Philadelphia*, Report of Operations and Action, Period 18 to 31 August 1944.
[18] Sweepers Unit, H.M.S. "ROTHESAY," 1st September 1944.

[19] Ibid.
[20] USS *Philadelphia*, Battle Records of various U.S. Naval units released by Navy Department for Morning Newspapers of Friday, 27 November 1944; CO, USS *Philadelphia*, Report of Operations and Action, Period 18 to 31 August 1944.
[21] ComEighthFlt, Invasion of Southern France, 29 November 1944; CTG 80.10, Report of Action – Operation DRAGOON.
[22] CTU 84.8.2 correspondence to The Commander in Chief, United States Fleet of 3 September 1944, First Endorsement on OC, BMS Section 2 Action Report.
[23] USS *Philadelphia*, Report of Operations and Action, Period 18 to 31 August 1944; *Hopi* War Diary, August 1944.
[24] ComEighthFlt, Invasion of Southern France, 29 November 1944; U.S. Naval Detachment Port de Bouc, France War Diary, 26-31 August 1944.
[25] Ibid.
[26] Ibid.
[27] Ibid.
[28] ComEighthFlt, Invasion of Southern France, 29 November 1944; U.S. Naval Detachment Port de Bouc, France War Diary, 26-31 August 1944; *ATR-1* War Diary, August 1944.
[29] Ibid.
[30] U.S. Naval Detachment Port de Bouc, France War Diary, 26-31 August 1944; "Maréchal Pétain/La Marseillaise/
Arosa Sky/Bianca C 1949 – 1961"
(http://www.thegreatoceanliners.com/lamarseillaise.html: accessed 18 April 2014); USS *Philadelphia*, Report of Operations and Action, Period 18 to 31 August 1944.
[31] ComEighthFlt, Invasion of Southern France, 29 November 1944.
[32] CO, USS *Tackle* (ARS-37), War Damage, report of, 16 September 1944; U.S. Naval Detachment Port de Bouc, France War Diary, September 1944; *YMS-20* War Diary, September 1944; CTG 80.10, Report of Action – Operation DRAGOON; Sweepers Unit, H.M.S. "ROTHESAY," 1st September 1944.
[33] U.S. Naval Detachment Port de Bouc, France War Diary, September 1944.
[34] *YMS-83* War Diary, August 1944.
[35] ComEighthFlt, Invasion of Southern France, 29 November 1944; CTG 80.10, Report of Action – Operation DRAGOON; Bartholomew and Milwee Jr., *Mud, Muscle, and Miracles*, p. 144.
[36] CTG 80.10, Report of Action – Operation DRAGOON.
[37] "Royal Naval Reserve (RNR) Officers 1939-1945"
(http://www.unithistories.com/officers/RNR_officersM.html: 18 October 2014).
[38] Sweepers Unit, H.M.S. "ROTHESAY," 1st September 1944.

[39] ComEighthFlt, Invasion of Southern France, 29 November 1944; Narrative by Admiral Henry K. Hewitt, USN, Mediterranean Area Campaign – North Africa Landing to Southern France.

CHAPTER 14 NOTES
[1] Ernest J. King, United States at War, Final Official Report to the Secretary of the Navy, covering the Period March 1, 1945, to October 1, 1945.
[2] Ibid.
[3] Ibid.
[4] Ibid.
[5] ComNavEur War Diary, July 1945; Chip Marshall, "EASY BOATS Schnellboote in the US Navy," PrinzEugen.com Schnellboot Archive (http://www.prinzeugen.com/USNSchnell.htm: accessed 19 July 2014).
[6] B. G. Marshall, British Motor Powerboat Team (http://www.bmpt.co.uk/e-boat-machinery_topic13.html: accessed 19 July 2014).
[7] ComNavEur War Diary, July 1945; "*Eagle*, 1946 ex-*Horst Wessel*, WIX-327" (http://www.uscg.mil/history/webcutters/eagle_1946.asp: accessed 18 July 2014).
[8] ComNavEur War Diary, July 1945; *T-35* (DD-935), NavSource (http://www.navsource.org/archives/05/935.htm: accessed 19 July 2014); *Conway's All the World's Fighting Ships, 1922-1946* (Annapolis: U.S. Naval Institute, 2006), p. 234, 238; CincLant War Diary, August 1945.
[9] *Brant* War Diary 1945; Derek Waller, "The U-Boats that Surrendered - U-Boats at Lisahally in Lough Foyle, near Londonderry, N. Ireland 1945 to 1949," Uboat.net (http://www.uboat.net/articles/95.html: accessed July 13, 2014).
[10] Waller, "The U-Boats that Surrendered".
[11] Ibid.
[12] Ibid.
[13] *Brant* War Diary and *Brant* Navy Muster Rolls 1945; Waller, "The U-Boats that Surrendered.

CHAPTER 15 NOTES
[1] Daniel E. Barbey, *MacArthur's Amphibious Navy* (Annapolis: U.S. Naval Institute, 1969), p. 323.
[2] Earl F. Ziemke, The U.S. Army in the Occupation of Germany 1944-1946 (Washington, D.C.: Center of Military History, U.S. Army, 1990), p. v, 320.
[3] ComNavEur War Diary, August 1945; CTF 126 War Diary, September 1945.
[4] Bartholomew and Milwee Jr., *Mud, Muscle, and Miracles*, p. 175-176.
[5] CTF 126 War Diary, June 1945.
[6] Ibid.
[7] CTF 126 War Diary, June and September 1945.
[8] *Brant* War Diary, June 1945.

[9] *ATR-4* War Diary, June 1945.
[10] *ATR-4* War Diary, June and July 1945; CTF-126 War Diary, September 1945.
[11] CTF-126 War Diary, June 1945.
[12] *ATR-4* War Diary, July 1945.
[13] *Diver* War Diary, June and July 1945.
[14] *Brant* War Diary, July 1945.
[15] *Diver* War Diary, July and August 1945; U.S. Naval Advanced Base Bremen, Germany War Diary, July-September 1945.
[16] U.S. Naval Advanced Base Bremen, Germany War Diary, July-September 1945.
[17] U.S. Naval Operating Base, Bermuda, Norfolk Navy Yard, and U.S. Naval Forces Navy 815, *PC-619* War Diary, October 1945.
[18] *ATR-4* and CTF-126 War Diary, September 1945.
[19] *ATR-4* War Diary, September-November 1945.
[20] *ATR-4*, NavSource (http://www.navsource.org/archives/09/40/40004.htm; Calvin Woodward, "Splendid isolation in the St. Lawrence River," 5 September 2013 (http://bigstory.ap.org/article/splendid-isolation-st-lawrence-river: both accessed 7 November 2014).

POSTSCRIPT NOTES

[1] Eighth Amphibious Force Memorandum No. 9-44, Salvage of U.S.S. *Edenshaw*, 16 March 1944.
[2] Eighth Amphibious Force Memorandum No. 9-44, Salvage of U.S.S. *Edenshaw*, 16 March 1944; CO, USS *Edenshaw* (YT-459), Operation Shingle – report on, 11 March 1944.
[3] Ibid.
[4] "Casualties: U.S. Navy and Coast Guard Vessels, Sunk or Damaged Beyond Repair during World War II, 7 December 1941-1 October 1945"; *Bannock* War Diary, April 1944; Commandant NOB Palermo War Diary, February 1944.
[5] ComEighthFlt War Diary, 1 January-30 November 1944.
[6] NAVSHIPS 250-012 – Ship's Data U.S. Naval Vessels, Volume III – Auxiliary, District Craft and Unclassified Vessels (15 April 1945).
[7] ComEighthFlt War Diary, 1 January-30 November 1944; Commander Naval Advanced Bases, U.S. Eighth Fleet War Diary, October 1944; U.S. Navy Port Office, Port de Bouc, France War Diary, January 1945.
[8] Thomas Runk, "*Allegheny* Airedale," *Towline*, National Association of Fleet Tug Sailors.
[9] ComNavEur War Diary, August 1945.

Index

Abbas II, Hilmi Bey, 229
Aitken, John, 155, 223, 275
Alden, John G., 22
Alexander, Harold, 54, 87
Alexander, Samuel H., 66
Andersen, Harvey M., 8, 32, 55-58, 68, 222
Andrews, Adolphus, 47
Ansel, Walter, 181, 243, 299-300
Antolak, Sylvester, 147
Arsenault, Fredrick L., 15
Ashcraft, John, T., 104-105
Attlee, Clement, 256
Badoglio, Pietro, 53, 86
Barbey, Daniel E., xxvi, 259, 305
Barfoot, Van T., 147
Bataille (Capitaine de Frégate), 241-242
Battle of
   Berlin, 252
   Jutland, 108
   the Atlantic, 42
   the Java Sea, Makassar Strait, 57
Beatie Jr., W. C., 155, 222, 282
Belknap (Lt.), 249
Blank III, John S., 155, 279
Bourgeois, Alonzo J., 83
Boyce, Howard, 241
Boyd, C. M., 32, 140, 223
Bretz, George, 24
Brigen, J. F., 217
British
   Army,
      First Infantry Division, 116
      Second Army, 151
      Eighth Army, xxii, xxiii, 59, 82, 86, 105, 119
      Royal Fusiliers Company Z, 146
      X Corps, 87, 97
   Royal Navy
      10th Destroyer Flotilla, 181
      Dockyard,
         Grassy Bay, Bermuda, 6
         Portsmouth, 178, 207
         South Hampton, 157
         Valletta, Malta, 104
      Fleet Auxiliary, 107

            Force H, 107
            Hedgerow bombs, 91, 93
            HMS Hannibal barracks, 136
            HMS Vernon, 204-205
            Minesweeping Flotilla/Group
                9th, 192, 197
                13th, 239-241, 248-249
                15th, 102nd, 131st, 139th, 165th, 167th, 169th, 200
                19th, 240
                157th, 168th, 170th, 200-202
                159th, 192, 197
                163rd, 200, 261
                206th, 197-198, 201
                Port Clearance Parties/Divers, xvii, xix, xxiv, 183, 194-196, 203-206, 261
        Royal Air Force, 40, 59, 181
        Royal Marine Commandos, 87-88, 116
    Brodie Jr., Robert J., 12-13
    Brooks, L. J., 222
    Brown, L. R., 223-224
    Brown, Ralph, 155, 172, 222, 275
    Bulkeley, John D., xxv-xxvi, 214, 227-235
    Burke, John J., 83
    Bush, Frances W., 104
    Caldin, Adnah N., 155, 269, 288
    Canada/Canadian
        1st Infantry Division, xxii, 54, 86
        3rd Infantry Division, 175
        Air Force Digby and Hudson aircraft, 36
        Halifax, Nova Scotia, 35
        Joint Canadian-American 1st Special Service Force, 214-216
        Navy, 42, 183
            31st Minesweeping Flotillas, 197, 200
            Western Local Escort Force, Escort Group C4, Royal Air Force, 35-36
        Ottawa, 42
    Chandler, Theodore E., 214
    Chapman, W. F., 222
    Christian, Herbert F., 147
    Christianson, F. R., 155
    Churchill, Winston, xxii-xxiv, 81, 113, 115, 158, 197, 208, 211-212, 226, 256
    Clark, Mark W., 87, 116, 145
    Clifton, Edward Ernest, 235
    Coleman, Robert L., 66
    Conolly, Richard L., 59, 72, 87, 109
    Conrad, Herman B., 155, 275
    Corsi, Albert J., 140

Crawford, Grover W., 140
Cunningham, Andrew B., 54, 87, 92, 106
Cuthbert, Cecil, 155, 275
Dahlquist, John E., 214
Darroch, James W., 9, 14
Davidson, Lyal A., 81, 213, 242, 245, 299
de Lattre, Jean, 213
Dervishian, Ernest H., 147
Donitz, Karl, 35, 252, 256
Doust, W. Alec, 90
Dowling, Roy B., 14
Drisler Jr., W. A., 140
Duffy (Lt.), 249
Dutcher, Lloyd E., 140
Dutko, John W., 147
Eagles, William W., 214
Edmundson (Lt.), 245
Egypt, 1-2
   Alexandria, 2, 85, 92
   Port Said, 125
   Suez Canal, 2
Eisenhower, Dwight D., 2, 54, 87, 89, 179, 211
Emmanuel III, Victor, 53
English (Capt.), 244
Evanisko, Stephen, 9, 80-81
Fairbanks Jr., Douglas E., xxv-xxvi, 214, 217, 227-234
Forrestal, James, 226, 229
Fowler, Thomas W., 147
France/French
   Algeria, xx, xxi, 2, 15, 17, 59
      Algiers, Oran, xx, xxi, 2, 17
      Arzew, 55
   Army B, 213, 215, 245
   Cannes, 211, 219, 227
   Cavalaire, 212, 214-215, 238, 240, 244
   Cherbourg, xvii, xxiv, xxv, 159, 169, 175, 183, 191-210, 212, 239, 251
   Ciotat, 214, 219, 227, 234
   Corsica (Ajaccio and Calvi), 212, 218-219, 221, 223, 230
   First Groupe Commandos/Groupe Navale d'Assaut, 214-216
   Foreign Legion, 9, 16
   Marseilles, 207, 212, 215, 217, 219-221, 227, 230, 237-252, 299
   Morocco,
      1st and 7th Regiments Moroccan Tirailleurs, 9
      Casablanca, 2-4, 8, 15, 17-18, 57, 158, 252
      Fedala, Mehdia/Port Lyautey, Safi, xx, 2-17
   Toulon, 212, 215, 219-221, 227, 230, 238-239, 241, 245-251, 269

340   Index

Vichy, xx, 4, 9, 215
Fraser, Charles Robertson, 249
Freeman, William, R., 14
Frey, S. D., 155, 279
Gamon (Reverend), 176
Garland, J. D., 155, 274
Gault, William W., 147
Gentile, Ernest J., 14
Georges-Régis (Lt. Col.), 214-215
Geortner, J. M., 155
Geppert, R. D., 222
German/Germany
   Air Force (Luftwaffe), xx, xxiii, xxv, 62, 73, 105, 109, 128-129, 134, 197, 212
      Glider-bomb, xix, xxii, xxiii, 102-109, 120-121, 132-144, 197, 223
   Army
      Tenth and Fourteenth Armies, 119
      21st Panzer Division, 243rd, 709th, and 716th Limited Employment Divisions, 352nd Field Infantry Division, 151
      Tiger tanks, 85, 146
   Bremen-Bremerhaven Enclave/Weser River, xxvi, 259-266
   Italian Social Republic (German puppet state), 53
   military aircraft
      Dornier Do-217, 103, 129, 133
      Focke-Wulf Fw-190 fighter-bomber, 107, 118, 128, 131, 176
      Focke-Wulf Fw-200 bomber, 67, 223
      Heinkel He-111 twin-engine bomber, 67
      Junkers Ju-87 "Stuka" dive-bomber, 73
      Junkers Ju-88 fighter-bomber, 67-69, 73,176
      Messerschmitt Me-109 fast fighter-bomber, 65, 69, 71, 75, 128, 133
   Navy (Kriegsmarine), 100, 182, 184, 218, 220, 237, 252-253, 255-256
      Explosive boats and "human torpedoes"/"Solo Fighers, xxiv, 181-190
      K-Flotillas 361 and 362, 186
      Katy mines, xxiv, 198-199, 203-204
      U-boat Wolf Pack, 28, 33-42
   Paratroopers/DFS 230 gliders, 53
Ghormley, Robert L., 252-253, 260
Gibson, Eric G., 147
Gillespie, J. M., 32, 111
Gillett, W. K., 155, 279
Godt, Eberhard, 261
Goodrich, Earl W., 83
Gould, Elwood, 23
Gray, Thomas L., 171
Greely, Joseph, 14
Green (Lt. Comdr.), 222

Greene, T. H., 244, 249
Guja, Arthur T., 33, 40
Gunn, Aubrey Hazel, 155
Hall, George J., 147
Hall Jr., John L., 52, 59, 87, 99, 151, 158
Hammond, G. N., 155, 207, 279
Hanney (Army Lt. Col.), 8-10
Harrison, Drayton, 33
Hauffman, Percy H., 140-141
Hawkesworth, Edward Albert, 235
Hawks, Lloyd C., 147
Helen, Robert R., 82-83
Henderson, Charles F., 222
Hewitt, Henry, Kent, xxi, xxii, xxvi, 3, 17, 53-55, 59, 81, 85, 87, 90, 92, 96, 106, 111, 213-214, 219-220, 225-226, 228-229, 237-238, 244-246, 251, 259-260, 270
Heye, Helmuth, 184
Higgins, Andrew, 64
Hinch, Marvin O., 83
Hitler, Adolf, 53, 91, 118, 144, 190-192, 252
Hoffman, Robert G., 155, 223, 278, 282
Hoffmann, Ferdinand, 188-189
Holcomb, H. R., 260
Hollyer, Daniel D., 155
House, Andrew J., 14
Huff, Owen W., 68, 84, 109, 111, 140, 155, 222, 274
Huff, Paul B., 147
Huie Jr., Byron S., 167-169
Hutchison, Justin Cooper, 155, 276
Iceland
    Hafnarfjörður, 38
    Reykjavik, 34, 39-41
Imlay, Miles H., 98-99
Italy/Italian,
    Anzio, xix, xxiii, 115-148
    Catania, xxii, 59
    Civitavecchia, 118
    Grand Council of Fascism, 53
    Gustav Line (Minturno to Ortona), 115, 117-119
    Littoria (renamed Latina), 128
    Messina, xxii, 59, 82, 85-86, 109-110, 113
    Naples, 86, 88, 90, 111-113, 116, 127-128, 130, 136, 139, 141, 252, 267
    Nettuno, 115, 117-118
    Palermo, xxii, 59, 81-83, 90, 99, 112, 252
    Rome, 86, 113-119, 129, 144, 146, 212
    Salerno, 85-114, 129, 269, 275

Sicily, 53-87, 89-90, 92, 99, 110, 112, 115, 191, 269
Syracuse, xxii, 54, 57, 59
Jeffs, C. R., 260
Jenkins (Lt.), 249
Jodl, Alfred, 252, 256
Johnson, Elden H., 147
Johnson, Henry C., 214, 230, 233
Johnson, Louis Gerald, 155
Johnson, Raymond E., 14
Johnson, William H., 147
Joyce, Richard W., 14
Keitel, Wilhelm, 252
Kelly, Monroe, 7
Kesselring, Albert, 86-87, 119, 145
Kessler, Patrick L., 147
King, Ernest, 152
Kirk, Alan G., 59, 62, 151-152, 178, 226
Knappenberger, Alton W., 147
Koch, William H., 77
Kuykendall, William O., 155, 274
Kyllberg, Victor H., 84, 111, 155, 223, 275
Laessle, Frank W., 102
Lane, Harry L., 126, 155, 222, 280, 285
Lawson, Jacob F., 5
Leake, Kenneth E., 140
Leamond, Frederick J., 32, 112, 140, 223
Le Houllier, Raymond S., 83
Lewandowski, Stanley J., 155, 278-279
Loebmann, W. E., 155, 287
Lowry, Frank J., 115-116, 127, 214, 220, 222, 267, 283, 291
Lucas, John P., 115, 117, 145,
MacArthur, Douglas, xxv, xxvi, 214, 259-260,
MacClung, Marshall L., 168
MacDonald, John A., 83
MacGill, H. L., 141, 123, 127-128, 131-132, 135, 137-138, 140, 155, 222, 279
Malavergne, Rene, 11-12
Malta, 79-80, 83, 90, 92, 102, 104, 107, 109-110, 136-137
Martin, Alister Angus, 239, 241-244, 248-249
Merrill, Leslie C., 224
Merrill, Richard, 167
Merritt, Israel J., 44
Messmer, W. L., 243
Miller, Murray M., 83
Mills, James H., 147
Montgomery, Bernard, xxii, 59, 82-83, 86
Montgomery, Jack C., 147

Moon, Don P., 151
Moore, W. H., 155, 282
Moran, Edwin, 47, 162
Morgan, Sam Patterson, 155, 274
Morley (Lt.), 249
Morley, Norman Eyre, 249
Morrison, M. J., 140
Mullen, A. B., 222
Murphy, L. J., 260
Music Jr., William A., 14
Mussolini, Benito, xxii, 53
Newman, Beryl R., 147
Norr, O. W., 84, 222
O'Daniel, John W., 214
Oliver, Geoffrey N., 87, 90
Olson, Truman O., 147
Operation
    AVALANCHE (Salerno), xv, xxii-xxiii, 85-114
    BAYTOWN AND SLAPSTICK (support of AVALANCHE), 86-87
    DRAGOON (ROMEO and SITKA) (southern France), xv, 211-236
    HUSKY (Sicily), xv, xxi, xxii, 53-84
    MINCEMEAT (southern Spain), 63
    OVERLORD (Normandy), xv, xvii, xxii-xxiv, 149-190
    SHINGLE (Anzio), xv, xxiii, 115-148
    TORCH (BLACKSTONE, BRUSHWOOD, and GOALPOST) (North Africa), xv, 1-18
Orleck, Joseph, 84, 94-96, 111, 269, 275
Packer, Herbert A., 108
Patch, Alexander M., 214, 237
Patton, George S., xxii, xxv, 3, 17, 52, 59, 81-83, 88-89, 107, 211
Payne, E. J. T., 260
Payne, R. V., 131-132
Penney, Ronald, 116
Perry, Lucas J., 15
Piers, Desmond W., 36
Plander, Henry, 203
Pollenz, Hermann, 230
Price, W. C., 155
Ramsay, Bertram, 54, 151, 179
Randolph, H. V., 155
Rayburn, Thomas H., 262
Raymond, Gordon, 122, 292
Reel, Edwin L., 93-94
Reep, Fred, 62, 111
Robbins Jr., Reginals Chancy, 142-143
Robinson, Arthur G., 253, 260-261

Rockbridge, Chester H., 84
Rodgers, Bertram J., 214, 222
Rogers, Maurice, 147
Rommel, Erwin, 2
Rooklidge, Chester H., 111, 223
Roosevelt, Franklin D., 1, 31, 83, 211
Runyon, Paul M., 112
Sarsfield, Eugene, S., 74
Schauer, Henry, 147
Schneider, George F., 222
Schoelpple, A. C., 155, 277, 280
Self, R. L., 84, 140, 223, 258
Seriot, R. (Capitaine de Frégate), 214-215, 217
Sharp, George A., 255-257
Shelley, Richard G., 15
Sherwood, C. G., 155, 281
Ships and Craft
    Australian
        Reserve, Sprightly, Tancred, 28-29
    British
        Abercrombie, 102
        Admiral Sir John Lawford, Maria, Tehana, 175, 193
        Advantage, Aimwell, Bold, Destiny, Eminent, Favourite, Flare, Flaunt, Integrity, Lariat, Masterful, Patroclus, 28-29
        Agincour, 229
        Antares, Arcturus, Brave, Calm, Rosario, Satsa, Spanker, 240
        Aphis, Scarab, 214, 219, 227-235
        Ardrossan, Bangor, Blackpool, Bootle, Boston, Bridlington, Bridport, Bryher, BYMS-2032, BYMS-2034, BYMS-2035, BYMS-2038, BYMS-2039, BYMS-2041, BYMS-2047, BYMS-2050, BYMS-2051, BYMS-2052, BYMS-2055, BYMS-2058, BYMS-2061, BYMS-2069, BYMS-2070, BYMS-2071, BYMS-2076, BYMS-2078, BYMS-2079, BYMS-2141, BYMS-2154, BYMS-2155, BYMS-2156, BYMS-2157, BYMS-2167, BYMS-2173, BYMS-2182, BYMS-2188, BYMS-2202, BYMS-2205, BYMS-2206, BYMS-2210, BYMS-2211, BYMS-2213, BYMS-2214, BYMS-2221, BYMS-2230, BYMS-2233, BYMS-2234, BYMS-2252, BYMS-2255, BYMS-2256, Conway Castle, Courtier, Dalmatia, Dorothy Lambert, Dunbar, Eastbourne, Fort York, Fraserburgh, Georgette, Ijuin, James Lay, Llandudno, Lyme Regis, MMS-15, MMS-19, MMS- 40, MMS-44, MMS-45, MMS-56, MMS-59, MMS-71, MMS-78, MMS-110, MMS-113, MMS-115, MMS-181, MMS-1002, MMS-1004, MMS-1019, MMS-1020, MMS-1047, MMS-1048, MMS-1077, Niblick, Northcoates, Perdrant, Probe, Proctor, Prowless, Sidmouth, Sigma, Sir Agravaine, Sir Gareth, Sir Geraint, Sir Kay, Sir Lamorak, Sir Tristram, Tenby, Worthing, 200-201
        Aries, 239, 249

Archer, 47
Aspirant, Athlete, 28, 222, 280-282
ASRC-14, ASRC-21, ASRC-24, ASRC-37, 228-231
Aurora, 136-136
Bardolf, Barholm, 223, 225, 245
Barford, 222, 225
Barmond, 135, 223, 225, 292
Borealis, Brixham, Nebb, Polruan, Stornoway, 239-240
Bruiser, 211, 293
Bude, 239, 292
Bulolo, 292
Cato, 183-184
Celandine, 36, 40
Charon, 222
Cheerly, 28, 153, 157, 282
Dalcroy, Daleby, 36, 41
Delhi, 108, 136
Derwentdale, 107
Dido, 118, 292
Director, Emulous, Freedom, Justice, 22, 29, 279
Emphatic, 28, 153, 282
Empire Ann, Empire Spitfire, 222, 246,
Empire Antelope, Empire Sunrise, 36, 41
Empire Bascobeal, Empire John, 174
Empire Broadsword, Fratton, Fury, Lawford, Lord Austin, Lord Wakefield, Minster, MGB-17, MGB-313, MGB-326, MMS-55, MMS-229, MTB-430, MTB-434, Sesame, Swift, Trollope, Wrestler, 183
Empire Leopard, 36, 41
Empire Lynx, 38-40
Euryalus, 109
Fort Lac La Ronge, LCG(L)-764, Samlong, 187
Furious, 102
Gairsay, 183-184, 187
Grenville, 187
Halstead, 176
Hartington, 36
Hatimura, Jeypore, 38-39, 41
Hengist, Valiant, 107
Hilary, 90
Inglefield, 118, 121, 292
Isis, 183, 185
Jacinta, 178
Janus, 121, 129, 292
Jervis, 129, 292
Kempenfelt, 118, 292
Kimberley, 226

Laforey, 129, 292
LCA-323, 394, 428, 697, 121
LCI(L)-273, 121, 292
LCM-9, LCM-11, 170
LCM-204, 623, 910, 930, 1022, 1064, 1173, 121
LCP(L)-66, 356, 373, 121
LCP(L)-267, 199
LCS(M)-46, 121
LCT-2423, 175
LCT(A)-2037, 170
LCT-2441, LSE-2, 177
Leinster, 130, 293
LST-162, 130, 291
LST-305, 121, 291
LST-366, 132, 291, 293
LST-368, 98
LST-383, 132, 221, 233
LST-409, 139
LST-418, 121, 292-293
LST-422, 121, 130-132, 292
LST-428, 129, 292-293
Lyminge, xxiii, 104-105
Magic, 183-184
Maritima, 36, 41
Mauritius, 292
Mendip, 172
Mindful, 29, 223, 245, 280
ML-121, ML-134, 246
ML-139, ML-142, ML-257, ML-275, 203
ML-338, ML-462, ML-554, ML-565, ML-569, ML-575, 241, 246
ML-563, 224
MMS-8, 183, 200
Newfoundland, xxiii, 105-107
Nimble, 110
Norbo, 172
Oriana, 29, 110
Palomares, 267, 292
Penelope, 121, 292
Princess Beatrix, Royal Ulsterman, 291
Product, 110
Prosperous, 122, 135, 142, 268, 292
Pylades, 183-184
Quorn, 183, 187-188,
Ramillies, 216, 238
Reserve, Sprightly, Tancred, 28-29
Restive, 127

Rinaldo, Waterwitch, 240, 292-293
Rothesay, 239, 241-242, 293
Safari, 72-73
Salventure, 90, 221, 223
Spartan, xix, 121-122, 132-137, 142-144, 292
St. Andrew, 130, 293
St. David, 121, 130, 293
Stockport, 39-40
Teakwood, 157
Uganda, 110
Ulster Queen, 129, 292
Vagrant, 29, 223, 281
Vanessa, 347
Walker, Wanderer, 35
Warspite, xxiii, 107-110
Weasel, 29, 122, 292
Winchester Castle, 136, 291

Canadian
   Algoma, 36, 38
   Amherst, 36
   Arvida, 35-36, 40
   Bayfield, Blairmore, Caraquet, Fort William, Green Howard, Gunner, Malpeque, Milltown, Minas, ML-345, ML-454, ML-465, ML-473, Mulgrave, Wasaga, 200
   Buxton, Kamsack, Trois Rivieres, Columbia, Elk, Fennel, Grandmere, Regina, 35
   Cowichan, 35, 200
   Moose Jaw, Restigouche, 36
   MTB-460, MTB-463, 183
   Prince Henry, 214
   Thunder, 203

Dutch
   Flores, 102, 292
   Hobbema, 38-39, 41
   Indrapoera, 127

French
   Champollion, 136
   Le Dauphine, Le Langangere, Marechal Petain (later *La Marseillaise*), 246
   Le Fantasque, 118, 292
   Lorraine, 238
   Provencal, 246-248

German
   Eichberg, Veservehr, 261
   Horst Wessel, xxvi, 253
   S-116, S-218, S-225, S-706, 253
   S-boot (*Schnellboot* or E-boat), xxiii, xxvi, 100-101, 162-163, 165, 176,

        181-183, 186, 253, 288
    SG-21 (ex-French sloop *Amiral Sénès*), *UJ-6081* (ex-Italian corvette *Comocio*), 217-218
    T-35, *Z-39*, xxvi, 254-255
    U-71, *U-84*, *U-89*, *U-132*, *U-381*, *U-402*, *U-437*, *U-438*, *U-442*, *U-454*, *U-520*, *U-521*, *U-522*, *U-571*, *U-658*, *U-704*, 35
    U-73, 125
    U-173, 17
    U-410, 121
    U-2513, *U-3008*, xxvi, 255-257, 263
    UJ-6073 (ex-yacht *Nimet Allah*), *UJ-6083* (ex-Italian corvette *Capriolo*), 229, 231
  Greek
    Kriti, *Themistocles*, 292
    Mount Pelion, *Parthenon*, 36, 41
    Rinos, 36
  Icelandic, *Bruarfoss*, 41
  Norwegian, *Svenner*, 183
  Polish, *Dragon*, 183-184
  U.S. Army
    Cayhead, 174
    LT-2, *LT-4*, *LT-5*, *LT-22*, *LT-62*, *LT-118*, *LT-119*, *LT-130*, *LT-136*, *LT-152*, *LT-155*, *LT-156*, *LT-159*, *LT-194*, *LT-214*, *LT-374*, *LT-389*, *LT-456*, *LT-532*, *LT-533*, *LT-534*, *LT-638*, *LT-639*, *LT-653*, *LT-719*, *LT-785*, *LT-786*, *LT-787*, *LT-788*, 285-296
    LT-23, 153-154, 296
    ST-247, *ST-248*, *ST-335*, *ST-338*, *ST-698*, *ST-705*, *ST-758*, *ST-759*, *ST-760*, *ST-761*, *ST-762*, *ST-763*, *ST-766*, *ST-767*, *ST-768*, *ST-769*, *ST-770*, *ST-771*, *ST-772*, *ST-773*, *ST-774*, *ST-775*, *ST-776*, *ST-778*, *ST-780*, *ST-781*, *ST-794*, *ST-795*, 296
    ST-253, 199, 296
    ST-344, 199, 207, 296
  U.S. Coast Guard
    Eagle (ex-German sail training ship *Horst Wessel*), xxvi, 254
    Ingham, 38
  U.S. Merchant Marine or Civilian
    Andrew Stevenson, *Atenas*, *Black Warrior*, *Cape Horn*, *Cornelius Ford*, *Grace Abbott*, *John McDonagh*, 263
    Ann Skakel, 41-42
    Bodie Island, *Black Rock*, *Farallon*, *Gay Head*, *Great Isaac*, *Hillsboro Inlet*, *Moose Peak*, *Sabine Pass*, *Sankaty Head*, 153, 161, 295
    Brazos, *Cumco*, *Dry Tortugas*, *Edward L. Doheny*, *Henry W. Card*, *P. F. Marin*, *Rescue*, *Samson*, *Wellfleet*, *Yaquina Head*, 47-48
    Elihu Yale, 121
    Fred W. Weller, *L. V. Stanford*, *Olney*, *Tidewater*, 42
    Hahira, 38, 42

Hillary A. Herbert, 140-144, 291
James W. Marshall, xxiii, 106-107
John Banvard, 131, 291
John S. Copley, 125-126
Lancaster, 57
Robert Rowan, 67-71
Samuel Huntington, 121, 137-139
Thomas E. Moran, 25, 47-48
Trinidad Head, 48, 153, 161, 295
W. R. Chamberlain Jr. (later *Tackle* ARS-37), 32, 56, 247

U.S. Navy
  amphibious/transport
    Achernar, 224
    Ancon, 90, 169
    Barnett, 67, 69
    Bayfield, 200, 214, 223-224
    Biscayne, 71-73, 93, 104-105, 214, 291
    Catoctin, 229
    Dickman, 69
    Duane, 214
    Europa, 254-265
    George Clymer, 4-14
    Harry Lee, 74
    James O'Hara, 70-71
    Joseph Hewes, 17
    Lafayette (ex-*Normandie*), xvii, 49-51
    Lakehurst, 6, 16
    LCI(L)-1, 75-76
    LCI(L)-4, 135
    LCI(L)-10, 75-76, 122, 140
    LCI(L)-15, *LCI(L)-16*, 122, 140
    LCI(L)-17, *LCI(L)-188*, *LCI(L)-220*, 69
    LCI(L)-20, 76, 118, 121, 128
    LCI(L)-32, LCI(L)-273, LCI(L)-48, 121-122
    LCI(L)-37, *LCI(L)-41*, *LCI(L)-42*, *LCI(L)-43*, *LCI(L)-234*,
        LCI(L)-235, 222, 225
    LCI(L)-74, 88
    LCI(L)-76, 223-225
    LCI(L)-87, 76, 89
    LCI(L)-88, 76
    LCI(L)-100, 223
    LCI(L)-196, 138
    LCI(L)-209, 140
    LCI(L)-219, 122, 135, 140
    LCI(L)-232, 122, 140
    LCI(L)-236, 135

LCI(L)-319, *LCI(L)-324*, 89, 98
LCI(L)-349, 89, 97-98
LCT-16, 222, 225, 246
LCT-19, 75, 106
LCT-20, *LCT-27*, *LCT-197*, *LCT-200*, *LCT-294*, *LCT-541*, *LCT-590*, *LCT-612*, 170
LCT-31, 220-222, 225
LCT-35, 121
LCT-36, 69
LCT-146, 89
LCT-164, *LCT-169*, 90
LCT-198, 122, 135, 140
LCT-209, 122
LCT-210, 76, 170
LCT-217, 118
LCT-220, 76, 121
LCT-221, 122, 139-140
LCT-243, 76
LCT-288, 140
LCT-415, 89
LCT-624, *LCT-625*, 172
LCVP ("Higgins boats"), 17, 64, 70, 72, 78, 169, 220, 244, 249
Leonard Wood, 171
LST-16, *LST-268*, 246
LST-134, 170, 245
LST-157, *LST-351*, *LST-372*, 95
LST-158, *LST-385*, 76
LST-282, 223-224
LST-291, 193-194
LST-310, 97
LST-311, 66
LST-312, *LST-313*, 65-66, 69
LST-314, 98, 182
LST-318, 74
LST-326, 132-133
LST-331, 70
LST-337, 107
LST-338, 65
LST-348, 121
LST-366, 132
LST-368, 98
LST-375, 98, 170
LST-376, *LST-496*, *LST-499*, *LST-523*, 182
LST-383, 132, 221
LST-391, 199
LST-409, 139

LST-422, 130-132
Monrovia, 81
Susan B. Anthony, 11, 167, 171-172, 182
Titania, 16
auxiliary/service
  Abnaki, 153, 155, 271, 275, 282, 301
  Acushnet, 48, 288
  Algorma, 155, 174, 271, 285, 288, 295, 301
  Allegheny, 48, 270, 283, 287
  Alsea, 153, 155, 271, 275, 301
  Apache, Chickasaw, Chowanoc, Hidatsa, Quapaw, 167, 273-276
  Arapaho, 271, 273, 301
  Arikara, 153, 155, 167-172, 223, 225, 271, 275, 295, 301
  ATA-121 (ex-*ATR-43*), 155, 280
  ATA-125 (ex-*ATR-47*), 155, 174, 222, 280, 295, 302
  ATA-146 (ex-*ATR-90*), 155, 282
  ATA-166, ATA-167, 25, 285
  ATA-170 (ex-*ATR-97*), 24, 155, 222, 282, 295, 302
  ATA-172 (ex-*ATR-99*), 155, 223, 282, 295, 302
  ATA-173 (ex-*ATR-100*), 155, 282
  ATA-214, ATA-215, ATA-216, ATA-217, ATA-218, 25, 285
  ATR-1, xix, 23, 122-140, 142, 155-156, 222, 225, 245-246
  ATR-2, 155, 167-170, 172
  ATR-3, 155, 168, 175, 206-207
  ATR-4, 153, 155-157, 175-178, 262-265
  ATR-6, 167
  ATR-7, 23, 155
  ATR-13, 153, 155, 174, 207, 271
  ATR-15, 22, 153, 155-156, 177-178, 269
  ATR-31, 23, 25, 167
  ATR-36, 24
  ATR-47 (later *ATA-125*), 125, 222
  ATR-54, 155
  ATR-90, 28
  ATR-97 (later *ATA-170*), 24, 153
  ATR-98, 153
  ATR-99 (later *ATA-172*), 153, 223
  Bannock, 153, 155, 168, 175, 271, 274, 295, 301
  Brant, xx, xxii, xxvii, 4, 6, 8, 14, 30, 32, 46, 52, 57, 59-60, 62, 77-80, 84, 90, 111-112, 154-155, 168-169, 192-194, 196, 255-257, 262-263, 288
  Carib, 155, 271, 274, 301
  Cherokee, xx, 4-6, 8, 14-18, 20, 52, 155, 271, 273, 301
  Chetco, Chatot, 25, 285
  Chippewa, Choctaw, 155, 274, 301
  Cocopa, 155, 271, 276, 301

Cormorant, 155, 174, 288, 295
Crusader (ex AM-29), *Discoverer* (ex AM-38), *Viking* (ex AM-32), *Warbler* (ex AM-53), *Willet* (ex AM-54), 30, 45-46
Diver, 30, 32, 154-155, 168-169, 192-194, 196, 262-264, 302
Edenshaw (ex-*Intent*), 61, 84, 111, 122, 140, 223, 225, 245-247, 267-270, 292-293, 302
Evea (ex-*Resolute*), 61, 84, 111, 222, 225, 268, 270, 302
Extricate, 30, 32, 112, 221, 223, 225, 271, 302
Gauger, *Gemini*, 34, 40, 42
Hopi, xxii, 55, 59, 61-62, 65-68, 70-71, 78, 84, 89, 99, 104, 109-112, 140, 155, 222, 225, 244, 274, 292, 301
Housatonic, 6
Intent (renamed *Edenshaw*), 59; 61-62, 71-74, 84, 89, 92, 94-95, 111, 135
Iuka, 155, 280, 288
Iwana, *Pawtucket*, *Penacook*, *Samoset*, *Unadilla*, 27, 283-289
Kalmia, 155, 283
Kewaydin, 155, 287, 295, 301
Killerig, 45
Kiowa, 153, 155, 168, 207, 271, 274, 295, 302
Maumee, 153
Moreno, 55, 59, 70, 72-77, 84, 89, 99, 101-111, 155, 223-225, 275, 302
Narragansett, 55, 62, 70-71, 84-89, 91, 95, 98, 110-111, 155, 222, 225, 271, 275, 302
Nauset, xxii, 55, 59, 61-62, 70-71, 79-80, 84, 89, 91-97, 111, 269, 275, 302
Owl, 155, 176, 208, 288, 295
Paiute, *Papago*, *Takelma*, 18, 277-278
Partridge, 155, 162-165, 182, 269, 295
Pessacus, *Uncas*, xxi, 28-42
Pinto, 153, 155, 167-172, 222, 225, 271, 275, 295, 301-302
Pleiades, 33-34, 37, 41-42
Redwing (ex AM-48), xxii, 5, 30-32, 46, 52, 60-61, 269
Relief, 45
Resolute (renamed *Evea*), 45, 57, 60-61, 72, 76, 81, 84, 89, 98, 111, 268
Restorer, 30, 32, 122, 140, 144, 221, 223, 225, 292, 302
Sagamore, *Sciota*, *Umpqua*, *Wandank*, 48, 285, 287
Seneca, 155, 275
Swivel, 30, 32, 154-155, 168-169, 193, 196, 302
Tackle, 30-32, 56-57, 90, 111-112, 139, 225, 245-248, 270, 302
Tawakoni, 19, 277
Weight, 30-32, 112, 122, 140, 221, 223, 225, 292, 302
Winooski, 17
YT-2/YTM-2, *YT-4/YTM-4*, *YT-5/YTM-5*, *YT-6/YTM-6*, *YT-7/YTM-7*, 27

YTL-132, YTL-143, YTL-158, YTL-163, YTL-184, YTL-185, YTL-207, YTL-208, YTL-209, YTL-212, 270
YT-154/ YTL-154, 60, 111, 270
YTL-157, 111, 270
YTL-160, 225, 270
YT-161/YTL-161, 60-62, 67-68, 84, 225, 270
YT-165/YTL-165, 60-62, 84, 89, 97-99, 222, 225, 269-270
YT-186/YTL-186, 60-62, 67, 84, 89, 97, 99, 222, 225, 270
YTL-196, 222, 225, 270
YT-197/YTL-197, 60-62, 84, 89, 98-99, 111, 270
YT-198, 269, 271
YT-210/YTL-210, 89, 99, 223-225, 270
YTM-392, 271

combatants
  aircraft carriers
    Chenango, xx, 4, 9, 13
    Ranger, Santee, Suwannee, xxvii-xxviii, 6
    Sangamon, 6, 9
  battleships
    Arkansas, 170
    Maine, 44
    Nevada, 238
    Texas, 7
  cruisers
    Augusta, 226, 238, 242-243, 300
    Boise, 64, 67, 107
    Brooklyn, 128, 292
    Cleveland, 6
    Marblehead, 56-57
    Philadelphia, 69, 81-82, 107, 242-243, 299-300
    Quincy, 242
    Savannah, xxiii, 13, 64, 81, 102-104
  destroyers
    Benson, 78-80
    Bernadou, 6-7, 16
    Bristol, 63, 72, 101
    Butler, Cowie, Herndon, 81
    Cole, 6, 16
    Corry, Meredith, Rich, 182
    Dallas, xx, 4-16
    DD-935, DD-939, 255
    Endicott, 219, 227-234
    Frederick C. Davis, 129-130, 142-144, 292
    Glennon, 81, 182
    Hambleton, 17
    Herbert C. Jones, 120, 129, 143, 292

Jeffers, 64, 67
Knight, 81
Leary, Schenck, 38, 41
Maddox, 69, 71, 73-74
Marsh, Moffett, Runels, 153
McLanahan, 67
Plunkett, 106, 129, 291-292
Rodman, 241
Rowan, xxiii, 100-101
Shubrick, 64, 79-81
Somers, 217-218, 241
Tatum, 153, 157
Trippe, 128, 291-292

small boat/patrol craft/motor torpedo boats, sub-chasers
C-105180 (ex-German E-boat *S-218*), 253
PC-543, 73, 291
PC-552, 187-188
PC-564, PC-567, PC-617, PC-618, PC-1232, PC-1233, PC-1252, PC-1262, PC-1263, 153
PC-565, 261, 263-264
PC-568, 261, 264
PC-619, PC-1176, 261, 263-264
PC-1261, 182
PC-1263, 157
PT-202, PT-218, 224
PT-555, 241-242
SC-497, SC-506, SC-532, SC-533, SC-692, 133
SC-522, SC-697, SC-1029, 135
SC-649, 69
SC-978, 244

mine warfare
Auk, Broadbill, Chickadee, Nuthatch, Pheasant, Threat, 203
Barricade, 243-244
Dextrous, Pioneer, 240, 292
Incredible, Mainstay, Seer, 240
Osprey, Tide, 182
Portent, 118, 121, 292
Prevail, 129, 240-241, 292
Sentinel, 73
Skill, 77
Staff, 77-78, 153
Strive, 99, 134, 292
Swift, 153, 203
YMS-13, 133, 247
YMS-20, 247
YMS-21, 246

Index 355

    YMS-24, 224
    YMS-27, *YMS-199*, *YMS-251*, 244, 247-248
    YMS-30, 121
    YMS-36, *YMS-78*, 133
    YMS-37, *YMS-55*, *YMS-62*, *YMS-64*, *YMS-69*, *YMS-207*,
        YMS-208, *YMS-227*, 99
    YMS-82, 77, 99, 133, 292
    YMS-83, 243, 247
    YMS-84, 77
    YMS-226, 71, 99, 292
    YMS-231, *YMS-247*, *YMS-305*, *YMS-346*, *YMS-348*, *YMS-349*,
        YMS-351, *YMS-352*, *YMS-356*, *YMS-358*, *YMS-375*, *YMS-377*, *YMS-379*, *YMS-380*, *YMS-381*, *YMS-382*, *YMS-406*, 200
    YMS-304, *YMS-350*, *YMS-378*, 182, 199-200
    YMS-347, 199-200
Shorts, Calhoun, 140
Sibitsky, Martin C., 32, 60-61, 155, 168, 193, 269
Sidney, William, 147
Skorzeny, Otto, 53
Smith, Abigail, 191
Smith, Charles W., 33, 40
Smith, Edward, 217
Smith, Furman L., 147
Smith, Raymond Harold, 206
Sperry, Edwin, 14
Squires, John C., 147
Stalin, Joseph, 256
Stanley, Howard J., 140
Stark, Harold R., 152, 161, 251, 253, 259
Starkweather, Mark W., 8-9, 14-15
Steck, Alfons, 188
Stumpff, Hans-Jürgen, 252
Sullivan, William A., xv, xx, xxv, 21, 49-52, 55, 57, 90, 106-107, 168, 191-193,
    196, 206-207, 260
Swarthout, Avery Vernon, 155, 274
Tedder, Arthur W., 87, 252
Thomas, Alwyn, 211
Thompson, Roger George, 202
Thompson, Rodger W. D., 203
Torkelson, T. O., 222
Tornberg, John N., 111, 155
Troubridge, Thomas Hope, 116, 292
Truman, Harry S., xxvi, 251, 256, 259
Truscott Jr., Lucian K., 4, 8, 145, 214, 226
Tunisia, xx, xxii, 2, 55, 59, 70, 72
    Bizerte, xxii, 55, 60-62, 70, 72, 78, 80, 90, 99, 109, 112, 252, 269

Tunis, 55
Ulrich, G., 155, 279
United States
    Army
        First Army, 151, 192
        1st Infantry Division, 53, 59
        Third Army, xxv, 211
        3rd Infantry Division, 59, 72-73, 82, 116-117, 213-214
        Fifth Army, xxiii, 85-87, 116-119, 145
        VI Corps, 87, 99, 116-117, 145, 214-215, 226
        Seventh Army, xxii, 59, 81-82, 213-214, 237
        9th Infantry Division, 8
        36th Infantry Division, 99, 213-214
        45th Infantry Division, 59, 70, 116, 147, 213-214
        46th Infantry Division, 97
        79th Infantry Division, xxiv, 192
        82nd Airborne Division, 112, 116-117
        83rd Chemical Battalion, Motorized, 130
        141st and 142nd Assault Regiments, 100
        Fort Bowie and Fort Devens, 190
        Joint Canadian-American 1st Special Service Force, 215
        Rangers, 87, 117
    Coast and Geodetic Survey, 45
    Intelligence organizations, OSS (Office of Strategic Services)/CIA, 11
    military aircraft
        P-38 Lightning fighter aircraft, 103
        P-40 Curtiss Warhawk figher and land attack aircraft, 9, 13, 133
    Navy/Naval
        Bases/Stations
            Amphibious Training Base, Little Creek, 4
            Landing Craft and Bases, 55, 61, 71, 152, 157
            Naval Advanced Base(s)
                Bizerte, 55, 252
                Bremen, Bremerhaven, 260
                Cherbourg, 207
            Naval Operating Base
                Bermuda, 7
                Casa Blanca, 52
                Iceland, xxi, 34, 41-42
                Norfolk, 5, 264
                Oran, 55, 78, 85, 99-100, 125-127, 171, 252
            Navy Salvage Base, Dellys (Algeria), 55-57, 245
        Beach jumpers, 234
        Construction Battalion ("SeaBees"), 74, 160, 164, 166, 175, 237
            CBMU 636, 260
            1040th, 245-246

District
   First Naval, 255
   Third Naval, 156, 253
   Fifteenth Naval, 46
Division
   Destroyer Division 26, 125
   Mine Division 16, 250
Fleet
   Tenth, 125
   Twelfth, xxvi, 152, 251, 259-260
Force(s)
   Amphibious
      Eighth, 99, 127
      Eleventh, 152, 157
      Northwest African Waters, 55, 61, 63, 71
   Naval Forces, France, 226
   Naval Forces, Germany, 252, 260
   Naval Forces in Europe, 152, 161, 251, 253
   Naval Forces, Northwest African Waters, xxi, xxii, 55, 251
Ports and Bases
   France, 200, 209
   Germany, 253, 260
Rescue Tug Service, xx, xxi, 21, 43-49, 162
Salvage
   Service, xx, 21, 43-52
   Group, 90, 99, 122, 206, 225, 244, 260, 264, 292
Sea Frontier
   Eastern, 47
   Moroccan, 52, 55, 125, 252
Squadron
   Destroyer Squadron Eight, 81
   Mine Squadron Six, 291
   Mine Squadron Seven, 203
   Motor Torpedo Boat Squadron Fifteen, 81
   Service Squadron One, 34, 154-155
   Y1 Squadron, 200
   Y2 Squadron, 197, 200
Transportation Service, 265

Vian, Philip, 151, 175
von Friedeburg, Hans-Georg, 252
Wagner, Arthur, 14
Walker (Lt.), 242
Walker (Lt. Comdr.), 77
Walker, Edwin A., 214-215
Walker, William M., 223
Walley, Dewey, 155, 275

Waters, Eric Fletcher, and Waters, Roger (father and son),
Watson, Bertram Chalmers, 39
Watson, William W., 140
Way, William F., 260
Webb, Roland H., xxiii, 149
Whelpley, Robert Marshall, 155, 278, 288
White, James C. W., 155, 162-164
Wichmann, Charles J., 84, 110-111, 155, 222, 275
Wisniewski, Edward L., 14
Wright, W. D., 65
Zhukov, Georgi, 252
Zymroz, Czeslaw, 14

About the Author

Commander David D. Bruhn, U.S. Navy (Retired) served twenty-two years on active duty and two in the Naval Reserve, as both an enlisted man and as an officer, between 1977 and 2001.

Following completion of basic training, he served as a sonar technician aboard USS *Miller* (FF 1091) and USS *Leftwich* (DD 984). He was commissioned in 1983 following graduation from California State University at Chico. His initial assignment was to USS *Excel* (MSO 439), serving as supply officer, damage control assistant, and chief engineer. He then served in USS *Thach* (FFG 43) as chief engineer and Destroyer Squadron Thirteen as material officer.

After graduation from the Naval Postgraduate School, Commander Bruhn was assigned to Secretary of the Navy and Chief of Naval Operation staffs as a budget analyst and resources planner before attending the Naval War College in 1996, following which he commanded the mine countermeasures ships USS *Gladiator* (MCM 11) and USS *Dextrous* (MCM 13) in the Persian Gulf.

Commander Bruhn's final assignment was executive assistant to a senior (SES 4) government service executive at the Ballistic Missile Defense Organization in Washington, D.C.

Following military service, he was a high school teacher and track coach for ten years, and is now a USA Track & Field official. He lives in northern California with his wife Nancy and has two sons, David and Michael.

www.ingramcontent.com/pod-product-compliance
Lightning Source LLC
Chambersburg PA
CBHW051626230426
43669CB00013B/2192